PASHAS

Pashas

TRADERS AND TRAVELLERS IN THE ISLAMIC WORLD

❖

JAMES MATHER

YALE UNIVERSITY PRESS | NEW HAVEN AND LONDON

For information about this and other Yale University Press publications, please contact:
U.S. Office: sales.press@yale.edu   www.yalebooks.com
Europe Office: sales@yaleup.co.uk   www.yalebooks.co.uk

Set in Adobe Caslon by IDSUK (DataConnection) Ltd.
Printed in Great Britain by TJ International Ltd, Padstow, Cornwall

Library of Congress Control Number: 2009937501

ISBN 978-0-300-12639-6

A catalogue record for this book is available from the British Library.

10 9 8 7 6 5 4 3 2 1

Contents

Illustrations

———— ❖ ————

1. *Views from Arabia, Judea, Chaldea, Syria, Jerusalem, Antiochia, Aleppo, Mecca etc. / Gesicht in Jerusalem* (1672) © Trustees of the British Museum.
2. Detail from Herman Moll, *A new & correct map of the whole World* (1719). Author's collection.
3. Prospect of Aleppo from Cornelis Le Bruyn, *Voyage to the Levant* (1702). Wellcome Library, London.
4. View of Scanderoon from Cornelis Le Bruyn, *Voyage to the Levant* (1702). Wellcome Library, London.
5. Prospect of Aleppo from Henry Maundrell, *Journey from Aleppo to Jerusalem* (1703). Author's collection.
6. John Seller, *A chart of the Levant or easternmost part of the Mediterranean Sea* (1675) © National Maritime Museum, Greenwich, London.
7. Gold beaker bearing the arms of the Levant Company © Trustees of the British Museum.
8. William Sherwin, *South-west prospect of the Royal Exchange* (1674) © Trustees of the British Museum.
9. Sir Godfrey Kneller, *The Harvey Family* (1721) © Tate, London 2009.
10. Willem van de Velde the Elder, *The Plymouth* (c.1675) © National Maritime Museum, Greenwich, London.
11. Willem van de Velde, *An English merchant ship in a Mediterranean Harbour* (1694) © National Maritime Museum, Greenwich, London.
12. Khan al-Gumruk, Aleppo. Author's collection.

13. Andrea Soldi, *Portrait of Henry Lannoy Hunter in Oriental Dress* (c.1733–6) © Tate, London 2009.

14. Interior of Turks' houses, from Alexander Russell, *The Natural History of Aleppo* (1756). Wellcome Library, London.

15. *Views from Arabia, Judea, Chaldea, Syria, Jerusalem, Antiochia, Aleppo, Mecca etc. / Mecha in Arabia* (1672) © Trustees of the British Museum.

16. Galata bridge, Istanbul. Author's collection.

17. Prospect of Constantinople, from Cornelis Le Bruyn, *Voyage to the Levant* (1702). Wellcome Library, London.

18. Jan Pieter van Bredael, *Cavalry Engagement against the Turks, with a Distant View of a Town* (c.1710) © Victoria and Albert Museum, London.

19. *Sir Dudley North* (unknown artist), c.1680 © National Portrait Gallery.

20. Jean-Etienne Liotard, *Monsieur Levett and Mademoiselle Helene Glavany in Turkish Costumes* (c.1740) © Bridgeman Art Library.

21. Francis Smith (attributed to), *The Audience of the Grand Signior* (c.1755–1765) © National Portrait Gallery.

22. Jean Baptiste Vanmour, *Gezicht op Constantinopel en het Serail vanuit de Hollandse ambassade* © Rijksmuseum Amsterdam.

23. *A briefe relation of the Turckes, their kings, Emperors, or Grandsigneurs, their conquests, religion, customes, habbits, etc / Mahzar* © Trustees of the British Museum.

24. *Gezicht op de Turkse stad Smyrna met op de voorgrond een voorstelling van de ontvangst van de Nederlandse consul* (1687) © Rijksmuseum Amsterdam.

25. A Leopard Addressing the Army, from MS. Pococke 400, fol.75b. The Bodleian Library, University of Oxford.

26. The Seraglio, from Cornelis Le Bruyn, *Voyage to the Levant* (1702). Wellcome Library, London.

27. *The Viceroy of Egypt in conversation with British officials, with attendants looking on, Alexandria, Egypt.* Coloured lithograph by Louis Haghe after David Roberts, 1849. Wellcome Library, London

28. Alexandria, from Cornelis Le Bruyn's *Voyage to the Levant* (1702) Wellcome Library, London.

29. Willem van de Velde, the younger, *An English Ship in Action with Barbary Vessels* (1678) © National Maritime Museum, Greenwich, London.

30. Smyrna, from Cornelis Le Bruyn, *Voyage to the Levant* (1702) Wellcome Library, London.

31. *An encampment outside Alexandria in four plates* (c.1798–1808) © Trustees of the British Museum.

32. *Sir Paul Rycaut*, after Sir Peter Lely (c.1680) © National Portrait Gallery.

33. *Going to cut up a turkey; or, continental epicures!!* (1802) © Trustees of the British Museum.

$\mathcal{P}$reface

———— ❖ ————

My journey towards this book began in northern Syria, amidst the hum of Aleppo's *souk*. In midsummer, scents hang thick in antique mists: vegetables and drying meat, spices and soap. The press of human traffic in the byways carries you forward half-willingly, past carpets and jewellery, on past garish plastics and tracksuits, past butcheries and pastry shops, as the train of bodies twists and loses itself in the thrill of unfamiliarity. But there comes a point when, suddenly and inexplicably, trepidation takes over and visitors reach for sketch-maps promising a way out of the morass. By the time that Aleppo's great citadel finally appears, a hulk of stone rising sharply from dull alleyways to catch the day's brightness, it brings relief. It seems to beckon out of the commotion into open air; and the temptation is to follow, making a beeline for one of the pavement cafés hugging the moat.

So it was only by chance that I stumbled on the *Khan al-Gumruk*. There are no plaques to identify the spot and in the guidebooks it merits only the barest of mentions, unlike the colonial-style hotel a mile or so up the road where Agatha Christie and Lawrence of Arabia once rested their heads. It is an enchanting and, at first glance, unremarkable sight for this part of the world: an expansive courtyard enclosed by a line of buildings, dotted with cloth shops and decorated by fine Islamic colonnades. I had seen many khans like this one, the motels and business parks of their day. Perhaps there was another reason, though, why the place seemed so familiar. For it inevitably conjures up the 'timeless' Middle East of brochures and Disney cartoons, painted in prose by Richard Burton's translation of the *Arabian Nights* and T.E. Lawrence's *Seven Pillars of Wisdom*, or in oils by John Frederick Lewis: an exotic land of fountains and sherbet forever alien to our own.

Even today, this Victorian and patronising vision dominates our representations of both the Middle East and the Islamic World. Its contours owe not a little to Britain's encounter with the region in modern times. Since the nineteenth century, that encounter has largely involved trampling it underfoot: figuratively, by demeaning and romanticising it in books, paintings and films; and in fact, by drawing it into economic dependence or casting it as strategic threat, then marching finally onto its streets. Some variation on that theme has taken occupying British armies into Cairo in the later nineteenth century, Jerusalem and Damascus in the early twentieth, and Basra at the beginning of the twenty-first.

This was a history all too familiar to me, so when I heard mention of the Britons who had resided here in an earlier era, I wanted to know more. For as long as a quarter of a millennium, I soon learned, an English community had lived, worked, prayed and died in this khan. Hidden like the history played out in its midst, the story of these 'pashas' – the word coined by contemporaries for the merchants who traded in the parts of the world now known as the Middle East – slowly illuminated a British encounter with the region at odds with the notorious ones of later times.[1]

The Levant Company, whose activities brought them here, is a name heard less frequently than it ought to be.[2] The only comprehensive account of its history in print dates back to 1935.[3] The contrast with its illustrious child, the East India Company, whose every aspect has received detailed scrutiny from historians, could hardly be greater. In one sense that is hardly surprising. The East India Company's trade quite quickly outstripped that of its Levantine counterpart. Moreover, whilst the former paved the way for centuries of territorial empire on the Indian subcontinent, the latter was scuttled a half-century before Britain's imperial moment in the Middle East. Its commerce in no sense led to colonisation.

Not least for that reason, though, its story speaks powerfully to our post-imperial times. Through the work of Linda Colley and others, interest has recently been growing in Britons' intensifying web of connections with the wider world from Elizabethan times – a story that cannot be reduced to the rise of a monolithic 'British Empire', but a richer one that in many ways mirrors the more recent processes we call 'globalisation'.[4] The pashas' experiences resonate all the more today, moreover, because the world into which they were absorbed was an Islamic one. The distinctiveness of early modern attitudes to Islam has been forcefully demonstrated in the work of Nabil Matar, Gerald Maclean and others, whose insights are an important influence on the interpretations advanced here.[5] Yet this book's story also spans the decisive shift in the global balance of power during the later eighteenth century, when the relationship between Islam and Britain (like the West generally) decisively 'went wrong', to echo the resonant title of Bernard Lewis's polemic on the subject, and its modern shape was born.[6]

Exploring such themes calls for a different approach from traditional studies touching on the Levantine trade. These have usually deployed its records, well represented in the British National Archives, to write the history of an institution. The letter books among them, though, also offer rich material from which to reconstruct experiences at the level of individuals. A good smattering of other personal and business correspondence survives elsewhere. Large numbers of traders, Company officials and travellers also set down their impressions for publication. Not all made it into print, but they offer a deep well of insights into these Britons' mentalities and the minutiae of their lives.

This book's sources, then, are English voices. It nonetheless sets out to locate them firmly within an Ottoman, Islamic world. The possibilities for doing so have grown with the flourishing of Ottoman history in recent decades. The work of Amnon Cohen, Edhem Eldem, Suraiya Faroqhi, Daniel Goffman, Abraham Marcus, Bruce Masters and others has transformed our understanding of everyday existence within the sultans' realms and this book, for one, is indebted to them.

Acknowledgements

———— ❖ ————

Over the course of writing this book I have incurred many other debts. My fascination with past lives owes much to the teaching of Keith Perry at St Paul's School and the formidable history regime of Neil McKendrick at Gonville and Caius College. Whilst at Cambridge I was lucky to benefit from the teaching of Chris Bayly and John Iliffe, who first instilled in me a passion for Asian and North African history. Thereafter, my time at Harvard University offered, alongside the constant provocation of Samuel Huntington's seminars, a wonderfully stimulating environment in which to develop a number of the ideas expressed in these pages.

I am particularly grateful to James Barr, Colin Heywood and Gerald Maclean, each of whom offered detailed and expert feedback on parts of the text at various stages of its evolution. I am similarly grateful to my anonymous reader at Yale University Press, who provided invaluable comments on the whole manuscript. Among others who have helped me, whether with suggestions and advice, as travelling companions to the Middle East, or in helping to sustain my enthusiasm when it threatened to wane, are Tabitha Barber, Hussein el-Mudarris, Luke Franklin, Michael Hunter, Maya Jasanoff, Tristan Jones, Simon Lambe, Sam Morgan, Miles Ogborn, John Riley, Samson Spanier, Ben Wilson, David Yates and Tom Young. I also owe a debt of gratitude to the staff of the various libraries where I carried out research, principally the National

Archives at Kew, the Institute of Historical Research, the British Library, the Wellcome Library, the School of Oriental and African Studies and the Widener Library at Harvard University.

I am especially grateful to my agent, Peter Robinson and, at Yale University Press, Robert Baldock, whose enthusiasm for the project has been an indispensable ingredient in its coming to fruition. The entire team at Yale has proved a delight to work with and my sincere thanks go to Elizabeth Bourgoin, Candida Brazil, Loulou Brown, Sarah Harrison and Rachael Lonsdale.

Last but by no means least, this book could not have been completed without Helen McCarthy's immense powers of critical engagement and emotional endurance. I dedicate it to her with all my heart.

Dramatis Personae

❖

George Baldwin (1744–1826): born in London, he began his career trading in Cyprus and Acre. He thereafter moved to Egypt, pursuing his vision of a direct trade with India through the Red Sea. In 1786, he was appointed consul-general to Egypt and, fifteen years later, witnessed the British landings at Abu Qir.

Robert Bargrave (1628–1661): the second surviving son of the dean of Canterbury, Bargrave first travelled to the Ottoman Empire in 1647 in the entourage of Sir Thomas Bendish, ambassador to Constantinople. A successful merchant in Smyrna (Izmir), on his return to England he became personal secretary to Sir Heneage Finch, third earl of Winchilsea. When Winchilsea was appointed ambassador to Constantinople, he decided to return to the Levant, but died of a fever en route.

James Caulfield, first earl of Charlemont (1728–1799): born into considerable means in County Tyrone, in 1746 Caulfield embarked together with his tutor on an ambitious grand tour taking in not just western Europe, but Egypt, Greece and Turkey. An admirer of William Pitt, on his return he pursued a successful political career, but maintained his interest in travel and antiquities through membership of the Society of Dilettanti and, in later life, the Royal Irish Academy.

Sir Heneage Finch, third earl of Winchilsea (1621–1682): a staunch royalist of Kentish extraction, Winchilsea was Charles II's first appointment as ambassador to Constantinople, embarking with his wife for the Ottoman Empire in 1660. He remained in the post for nine years, successfully strengthening the hand of the Company abroad, before returning to England to resume his position as a local grandee.

Sir John Finch (1626–1682): after training as a physician in Cambridge and Padua, in 1665 Finch was appointed the English resident at Florence. In 1672, he was chosen to go as ambassador to Constantinople, accompanied there by his lifelong companion, Sir Thomas Baines. Remaining until 1681, he secured the 'capitulations' which were to form the basis of the Levant Company's trade for the remainder of its existence.

William Harborne (c.1542–1617): born in Norfolk, Harborne established himself as a successful merchant in a number of Mediterranean trades, before departing for Constantinople in July 1578. The outcome of this mission was the first set of capitulations, paving the way for both Anglo-Ottoman diplomatic relations and the Levant Company's trade. After the foundation of the Company, Harborne returned to Constantinople as Elizabeth I's representative there.

Sir William Hedges (1632–1701): made his fortune as a merchant in Smyrna and Constantinople and upon his return to London attained senior positions first in the Levant Company and later the East India Company. In 1681, the latter despatched him to administer its factories in Bengal and conduct negotiations with the Mughal emperor. Outflanked by the resident nabobs, his mission was not a success, but he continued to flourish in city politics on his return.

Henry Maundrell (c.1665–1701): a fellow of Exeter College, Oxford and curate, in 1695 he was appointed chaplain to Aleppo. He intended the post to be a springboard to greater things, but in the event did not outlive his tenure. In 1697 he made a pilgrimage to Jerusalem, his successful account of which was published posthumously. Forever blighted by ill-health in the Middle East, in 1701 he died of a fever.

Lady Mary Wortley Montagu (c.1667–1726): born into aristocracy, in 1712 she eloped with her future husband, Edward, who four years later was despatched as ambassador to Constantinople. Lady Mary accompanied him, recording her experiences there over the next years in the justly celebrated *Embassy Letters*. Her time in the Ottoman Empire was cut short when her husband fell out of political favour and was abruptly replaced.

Sir Dudley North (1641–1691): introduced to a life of trade at an early age, like Hedges he began his Levantine in career in Smyrna, before moving to a leading trading house in Constantinople, where he made a sizeable fortune and was appointed to the prestigious post of treasurer to the factory there. On his return, North widened his trading interests, entered politics and penned influential works of economic theory.

Edward Pococke (1604–1691): quickly making a name as an oriental scholar at Oxford, he was appointed chaplain to the Aleppo factory in 1630. He used his time in the role to improve his oriental languages and collect oriental manuscripts with powerful financial backing. Later he was appointed professor of Arabic at Oxford University, where his collection of manuscripts remains in the Bodleian Library.

Sir James Porter (1710–1776): served as a diplomat in western Europe, before being appointed in 1746 as ambassador to Constantinople. He remained in the post for over fifteen years, marrying the daughter of the Dutch ambassador whilst there. In spite of his efforts, his tenure coincided with a time of decline in the British trade in the Levant and growing French influence.

Sir Paul Rycaut (1629–1700): the son of a wealthy merchant, in 1660 he departed for Constantinople as secretary to the earl of Winchilsea. In the course of a long career there, he was also appointed consul to Smyrna, before returning to England in 1678. Rycaut became well-known in his lifetime for his encyclopaedic works on the Ottoman Empire, which were widely influential.

John Sanderson (1560–1627): apprenticed somewhat unwillingly to a 'Turkey merchant', he sailed for the Levant in 1584, serving as William

Harborne's steward in Constantinople. He rose through the ranks and later deputised for the ambassador during his absences (though his fiery temper blocked his path to even greater preferment), as well as participating in early attempts to open direct trade with both Egypt and India.

John Verney (1640–1717): born into the gentry, he was apprenticed to a Levant Company merchant and, after a spell in the city of London, departed for Aleppo in 1662, where he traded for the next six years. He made enough in these years to launch a successful career as a London merchant, in time amassing a sizeable fortune. The unexpected deaths of his elder brothers, making him his father's heir, then prompted his entry into politics.

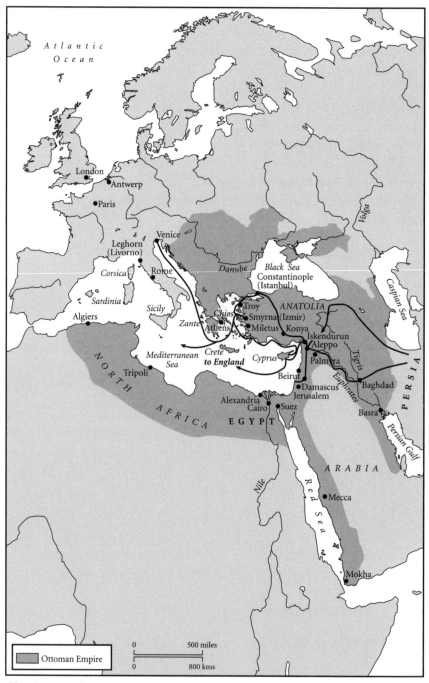

The Ottoman Empire and its main routes of trade to England

Jerusalem

❖

On 11 December 1917, four centuries of Ottoman dominion over the most famous city in the world came to an end. The guns had fallen silent days earlier, but with an eye to an opportunity, the British government decided that General Allenby would make a ceremonial entrance before the world's newsreel cameras. Fifty soldiers, plucked from battle weeks beforehand and preened for the occasion, stood assembled at the Jaffa Gate. Journalists jostled about them for position, offsetting the stiff geometry of the parade, and onlookers packed into the walkway atop the gatehouse. Just before noon, Allenby's Rolls-Royce pulled up. The hush of anticipation gave way to a thud of boots on blanched earth and a chorus of cheers as he marched forward, flanked by dignitaries and an entourage of officials. Two days after Hanukah and, just as the prime minister had demanded, in time for Christmas, the British commander passed through the ancient wall, still emblazoned with the crescent of the Ottoman flag plastered onto its stonework. Inside, he paused to proclaim a brief message of reconciliation, then declared martial law and dispatched British Muslim troops to guard the *Haram al-Sharif*, Islam's third-holiest shrine.[1]

The capture of the city that had, as the popular press trumpeted, 'for centuries baffled the efforts of Christendom', marked the pinnacle of Britain's military and political domination over the Islamic world.[2] Precisely because the British Empire now held sway over more than half the earth's Muslims, though, Allenby was under strict instructions to avoid any hint of triumphalism. So it was that, unlike the German kaiser, who before the war rode a white horse through a hole in the wall made purposely for the occasion, the British general entered meekly on foot. 'How could it be otherwise,' he is supposed to have said, 'where One has walked before?'[3]

Yet Britons, too, had walked there before, in centuries when it could hardly be imagined that the Muslim map would one day be painted in shades of British imperial pink. Take John Sanderson, the curmudgeonly son of a London haberdasher, who had strolled through this same wall on 30 June 1601. Whether by mistake or defiant design, he wore about him a sword, so disobeying an Ottoman stricture on Christians bearing arms in the city. Promptly arrested and hauled before the deputy governor, his obduracy in the face of questioning would have landed him in gaol, had he not been able to produce a letter of recommendation from the sultan himself. Even then, it took the intercessions of his Ottoman-Jewish travelling companions and hefty bribes to secure his release.[4] It was no use proclaiming the rights of the true-born Englishman in this era. For when another Elizabethan tried that as a means of escaping his own captivity in the city, he found that 'the Turks flatly denied . . . they had ever heard either of [his] Queen or country'.[5]

1 An early modern view of Jerusalem, in the midst of its centuries under Ottoman sovereignty.

Sanderson was one of the very first Britons to make a career in the Levant trade. He criss-crossed the Mediterranean several times over, made his home at various times in Egypt, Syria and Turkey, and died a wealthy London magnate. Along the way, he was shipwrecked and twice nearly drowned, struck down with fever that consigned him for months to a diet of barley water and chicken broth, and in one fit of pique hit a steward of the English embassy at Constantinople so hard with the brass butt of his pistol that it split in his hand. His story was in many ways representative of an earlier generation of English globetrotters, drawn to the Middle East by the impulse less of conquest than of peaceable commerce. For a quarter of a millennium, the Levant Company's trade encouraged Britons to come to the region in unprecedented numbers and, just as central to this book's concerns, spawned their first sustained contacts with the world of Islam. Together, their stories cast new light on the relationship between Britain and the Middle East. By extension, they illuminate a pivotal chapter in the historical encounter between 'Islam and the West'.

For the milieu into which these Britons stepped had little in common with later, better-known, British visitations on the region (or, for that matter, the sparser ones of even earlier times). Nor did it much resemble the one encountered, at roughly the same time, by the East India Company. In India, from an early stage, traders built forts, planted flags, fired rifles and laid claim to patches of earth.[6] In the Middle East, by contrast, Britons came as guests into a world of open trade that was not at all of their own making, governed by an Islamic polity which, as some of them freely admitted, outshone their own. This was a context that might have allowed room to make their presence felt in local politics, but not simply to stamp their will. Instead of planting the seeds of colonisation, they found themselves absorbed into someone else's empire, the mighty Ottoman dominion which still held sway over large chunks of Asia and Europe. Not until the later eighteenth century, when a fully fledged territorial British Empire appeared, was this older pattern of Middle Eastern trade to melt away, together with the mode of accommodation between Britain and the Islamic world which it had nurtured.

Unlike the 'nabobs' who gathered their fortunes in Bengal, these Britons fitted awkwardly into the traditional narrative of their nation's domineering expansion across the globe in past times. But to contemporaries they seemed, for a time, no less visible. They called them the 'pashas'; and this book aims to reclaim their place at the forefront of Britain's modern encounter both with Islam and the wider world.

Company Men

What follows is the story of a group of Britons who, from the reign of Elizabeth I until well into the nineteenth century, could be found hustling in the marts of the Ottoman Empire stretching right across the Middle East. The thread linking their lives is the Levant Company itself. Tracing its origins to a charter that Queen Elizabeth I granted to London's pioneering 'Turkey merchants' in 1581, this was the indispensable motor of the whole enterprise, a well-nigh permanent presence in the pashas' lives. Its creators championed the negotiations which first wrought permission for Britons to trade within the Ottomans' empire. Two centuries later, their company would still be offering the stamp of authority required to conduct business there. Lesser-known nowadays than its East India counterpart, the latter began life as no more than its humble offshoot. In its prime, the Levant Company represented indisputably one of the most flourishing commercial bodies on the London scene: 'grown to that height', it could be said by 1638, 'that (without comparison) it is the most flourishing and beneficial company to the commonwealth of any in England'.[7] Rather like the East India Company in a slightly later period, it became famous for making names and launching dynasties, for propelling men into states of political influence, social clout and gout-ridden personal girth.

Whilst its *raison d'être* was at root mercenary, the Company's business fortunes were closely tied both to domestic and international politics. From the outset, it was deeply engaged in most aspects of several trading worlds. Set against the power of the Company presence in the Middle East, the influence of the English state paled into insignificance for much of the period covered by this book. Into the eighteenth century, the English ambassador at Constantinople would receive two separate sets of instructions – one from the Company and one from the King (not surprisingly, he often found these two sides of his mandate wholly at odds). Outside the Ottoman capital, in places like Smyrna (Izmir) and Aleppo, the work of 'English' consuls was focused almost wholly on Company affairs, their appointment strictly in Company hands.

The Levant Company was in that sense a player in its own right on the table of diplomacy, aggressively pushing forward the interests of its company men. No Briton voyaging to the Middle East could avoid being drawn into its orbit. Even the emerging breed of travellers, without commercial ties, might find themselves put up in the house of one of its merchants, perhaps even in the ambassadorial palace at Constantinople. Others still might join one of its caravans inbound from the Mediterranean coast, or engage in some impromptu negotiation on its behalf. So the net is cast wide enough in what follows to incorporate a larger constellation of characters beyond traders themselves. There were diplomats and secretaries, pilgrims and chaplains, families and entourages, aristocratic tourists and roving antiquarians: all of them formed part of the pashas' wider milieu. This book is concerned, in part, with their personal stories, for these were the individual encounters which collectively made for a meeting of civilisations.

An individual focus, indeed, is one which the Company's own way of operating dictates. Unlike some of the overseas trading companies of the period, it did not for long remain a joint-stock enterprise pooling its capital, sharing its risks and ossifying into a smart, city-based bureaucracy. Instead, it evolved a hands-off approach, which relied for its corporate prosperity – and founded its corporate personality – on gutsy individuals and small-scale partnerships, men willing to chance their money and their lives on the weather and the market. Success in the Middle East, as should become clear, actively required them to leave their desks and mingle with the Jews, Muslims and Orthodox Christians who peopled the Ottoman world. As we shall also see, this business was nothing if not risky. That they were prepared to take such risks to some extent marked out the pashas from the ordinary run of people: these were men with 'learning enough . . . but not phlegm enough for any sedentary profession'.[8]

There was much else about being a Briton in the Middle East during this era that tended to universalise the experience. They were, for instance, an intensely cultured and literary lot, who liked to while away spare hours not only in hunting and feasting, but in playing musical instruments, acting out dramas or reading books of poetry posted from home. Thankfully for us, they would spend them in writing, too. On the one hand, writing was an essential part of their business, for they had to keep their contacts, whether in London, around the eastern Mediterranean, or further afield, closely apprised of factory affairs, politics and prices, and their regular intelligence digests survive in droves. But on the other hand, their business left them plenty of time to write for pleasure, so that posterity has been well supplied with diaries, travelogues and personal letters, which throw shards of light on the darker corners of their daily lives.

Together they help to answer a question which goes to the heart of this book's concerns. What was it like to be transported hundreds of miles in the claustrophobia of a boat, tossed on the waves seemingly for an eternity, then dumped unceremoniously onto shores in every sense distant from home? It is a question which might equally be addressed to the experiences of any number of Britons who ventured, voluntarily or not, to far-flung parts of the globe in the two centuries after 1550 – whether to the Americas or Africa, to the Indian subcontinent or the Far East. Yet those who went to the Middle East in our period inevitably offer up a rather special answer, and one which provides a key to unlocking the pashas' collective experience.

An image first published in 1719 can begin to reveal why. It is the frontispiece to a new map of the world prepared by the celebrated cartographer Herman Moll, and in it the four continents have metamorphosed into human form.[9] If what we expect to find here is some unadulterated display of western chauvinism, a first glance appears not to disappoint. Europe grabs us before all else, shining bright and bathed in the full light of the sun, whose sacred connotations are suggested by its Hebrew caption. He is apparelled in elaborate armour and strikes a chivalric pose. Already in this, the second decade of the eighteenth century, he stands out for possessing the fruits of technology: a mark of superiority that his rifle plainly shows. Contrast that with the Native American standing behind him, or with Africa on the far right of the image. Dark-skinned and scantily clad, armed only with bows and arrows, these pagans are cast to the world's margins and excluded from God's light. Here, then, is the predictable contrast between the noble European and the barbarian 'other'.

But look at the embodiment of Asia. He, like Europe, is finely clad and fully covered. His turban and the crescent on his flag boldly proclaim his religious affiliation. By itself that brings him closer to Europe than the godless African or American; and, indeed, that is precisely where the image places him within its frame. True, he cannot boast gunpowder, but the standard that he carries implies an urbane statehood. It may not be Christian faith that he professes but is he too not catching the beams of God's revelatory light?

2 Detail from Herman Moll's *A new & correct map of the whole World* (1719).

If much of the globe could, by now, be imaginatively divided into Europe and the inferior rest, it had to be admitted that the Muslims stood apart. Not that the suggestions of an image like this are by any means all kindly ones. The warlike face which Asia presents to Christendom was Islam's most deeply rooted caricature in Britain, not much younger than Islam itself. It underscores how the Ottoman challenge to Christian Europe, both military and spiritual, to some degree persisted throughout most of the period covered by this book. In response, the time-worn clichés of an 'Islamic' threat, once propounded by the crusaders, were rolled out time and again. This was a hostile vocabulary in which all the pashas would have been well schooled. It painted a version of global politics in which Christian Europe and Islamic Asia were cast as eternal enemies: religion and civilisation conspired to pull them apart, and where they met there could only be conflict. There continued to be enough actual military fracas throughout most of the period covered by this book to give such an idea continued purchase.

Much less remembered today, on the other hand, is the extent to which trade brought these imagined continents together. It was trade, 'the grand interest that hath engaged England to a Communication and Correspondence with these remote Parts', which helped to prepare the ground for a different outlook on Islam.[10] By the beginnings of a British presence in the Ottoman Empire, its lands stood squarely between Europe and the lucrative spices and drugs originating further east, albeit that Christian ships were already bypassing these territories by sea. The eastern Mediterranean shore appeared much like an island standing in the midst of two great, inhospitable realms: to the east the desert and the riches of Anatolia, Persia and the Indies; to the west, the Mediterranean sea itself and beyond that the Atlantic, home to the new wealth of northern Europe. Living at the meeting point of these two vast regions, a place that seemed fated to emerge as a bulging, bustling entrepôt, Britons experienced a Middle Eastern world which was alluring, dynamic and diverse. Where their own society seemed stultifying in its homogeneity, the Ottoman Empire was striking for its tolerance and cosmopolitanism – a reality which lived ill with the blood-curdling claims of propaganda about the Islamic threat to Christians.

It is almost tempting to cast the society these Britons encountered as presaging the global marketplace of our own times, not least in the seeming power of 'mutuell commerce' to burst through the bonds of religious and sectional differences. That would be going too far: as we shall see, there were clear limits to the Ottoman culture of tolerance. But even so, if one was determined to trace a pre-history of the 'global values' of trade, now most closely associated with the United States of America, for the seventeenth century one might plausibly turn to the Ottoman Empire as their most flourishing realm.[11] The business of trading inside it inevitably revealed to Britons the sophistication of its civilisation. However grudgingly, it required the bitter religious rhetoric about 'infidels' to be modified. 'I was of opinion', as one of the better-known travellers of the early seventeenth century wrote, 'that he who would behold these times in their greatest glory, coulde not finde a better *scene* than *Turky*'; for the '*Turkish* way', he continued, may not be 'absolutely barbarous, as we are given to understand', but rather 'an other kinde of civilitie, different from ours, but no lesse pretending'.[12] It is, one of the more radical seventeenth-century voices on the world of Islam went so far as to opine, 'more the Interest of the Princes & Nobles, then of the People, which at present keeps all Europe from submitting to the Turks'.[13]

8

So it is the clash between two very different outlooks on the Middle East which explains the ambivalence of Herman Moll's image. Islamic Asia confronts Europe as at once more frightening, and altogether more accomplished, than anything which the rest of the extra-European world could muster. That this latter, more positive, strand registers at all in this sort of image is testimony to how profound was the pashas' legacy before the later hardening of attitudes, first under the Georgians and again under the Victorians. When Dr Johnson quipped that there were 'two objects of curiosity, the Christian world and the Mahumetan' since 'all the rest . . . may be considered as barbarous', he spoke for an attitude of mind which for a time was commonplace on the streets of London.[14] And it was first forged in the souks and byways of the Middle East.

Pashas

This book is motivated by an attempt to discover both how that encounter was born and why its survival was all too brief in the modern age. The first-hand contacts that took place between Britons and Islam in the early-modern period were for a long time paid less attention than those of a later era.[15] The Levant traders accounted for by far the greater part of them. The trading milieu which they inhabited represented the most numerically significant of Britons' encounters with any Islamic civilisation until their large-scale establishment on Mughal territories in the Indian subcontinent. The numbers of traders involved were, compared to later imperial ventures, fairly small, but cumulatively they amounted to something very much worth remembering. In Aleppo, they reached a peak of perhaps eighty by the later seventeenth century; in the port of Smyrna, as many as one hundred.[16] A substantial English community also existed further north in Constantinople, while others were scattered across manifold smaller locations throughout the Levant. All in all, it seems likely that there were, in the seventeenth to earlier eighteenth centuries, at least two hundred Englishmen (and they were nearly all men) living in the Middle East at any one time; and, in all probability, there were as many as twice that number. The foundation of the Company ushered in a pattern of settlement that, by the time it was disbanded in the early nineteenth century, would bring many thousands of Britons to live and work in the Middle East.

A migration of Britons on this scale is, by itself, a striking phenomenon which demands our historical scrutiny. But it is all the more worth noting for its bearing on how we regard England's early-modern encounter with the Islamic world. For the counterpoint to the amnesia which has surrounded these Britons (those, that is, who actually lived in the Middle East before the mid-eighteenth century) has been a disproportionate emphasis on the poisoned rhetoric of clerics and other religious polemicists (who, for the most part, did not). The only other early-modern Britons in the Middle East to attract much attention from historians have been those who fell captive to Barbary corsairs and found themselves enslaved in the Islamic world. Both groups, to be sure, exerted in their different ways a powerful influence; and both were inclined, not surprisingly, to paint a picture of their Islamic enemy that was profoundly hostile.

Through the Levant trade, on the other hand, Britons simultaneously became engaged in a sustained and constructive relationship with the Muslim world over several centuries, bringing them into unprecedented contact not just with its Muslim masters, but with its Jews, Armenians and Greeks. East–west trade had to some degree punctured the iron wall of political conflict between Christendom and the *dār al-harb* ever since medieval times. It had dispersed goods and ideas from the one to the other, a pattern which dramatically increased in scope and scale during the Renaissance. The English role in that exchange was, however, for a long time a distant and indirect one. Only with the emergence of substantial settlements of Company traders in the Ottoman Empire by the seventeenth century did it spawn an extensive presence of Britons in Islamic lands. For reasons that will unfold in what follows, but which are at least in part self-evident, the circumstances of that encounter lent themselves to a perspective on the society they found there quite different from that of the priests or the prisoners, and generally less hostile.

To that extent, this book may be seen as seeking to add to the growing chorus which calls, if not for the abandonment of the controversial scholar Edward Said's 'orientalism' thesis, at least for its careful qualification and confinement largely to the contexts of the later eighteenth and nineteenth centuries.[17] Even so, we must be fully alert at the outset to how ambivalent the pashas' outlook remained. It is difficult, in the cosmopolitan, multicultural Britain of the twenty-first century, to conceive of how disorientating individual and collective experiences of this region must have been. If one force more than any other came to shape how these Britons tried to make sense of these encounters in the two centuries after 1550, it was the rise of modern empiricism. The pashas, like Britons generally, increasingly prided themselves on telling fact from fiction, truth from falsehood. Yet that might only exacerbate their confusion – for these were equally men who had been taught at least in some degree that good Christians must fear and despise what they encountered in the abode of Islam.

Said was not wrong, therefore, to suggest that a consistent strand of anti-Islamic thought had been detectable in the 'West' almost as long as the religion had existed. Nor did first-hand experience ineluctably conquer prejudice. The most that can be said is that the more sympathetic strand of ideas dissected in these pages uneasily co-existed with the hostile polemic of old, and their inter-relationship was contingent on the pattern of politics, as well as wider currents of social and economic change. But if attitudes never stood still, that is why there is a history to tell.

The story of how the clash of ideas was played out transports the narrative to the manifold locations across the Middle East where Britons made their temporary homes during these centuries. It leads it, too, on plenty of journeys: both overland, on the pilgrimage route that led through Damascus, into Palestine and on to Jerusalem, or along the great silk route that wound eastwards along the Euphrates into modern-day Iraq and Iran; and also by sea, making detours into the Barbary Coast, or

3 A caravan of horses and camels approaches Aleppo from the Mediterranean coast in the late seventeenth century.

shuttling between major centres of the British trade, like Alexandretta, Izmir and Cyprus. That geography is more than incidental to the story itself. For contemporaries, each of these diverse locations became infused with peculiar resonances. There were places that might evoke reverence; those which instilled fear; some towns were notorious for inflicting disease; others known for instilling delight. This book aims to recover this multitude of meanings, to see these locations refracted through the prism of the pashas' collective experiences. In this way travel is intended to take us through the changing contours, not just of physical realms, but of mental worlds in the quarter-millennium of the narrative's span.

The book travels widely, but three cities nonetheless root the narrative, each embodying different periods of time and distinct aspects of the encounter. To the first we have already made a brief visit: Aleppo, together with the English 'factory' in the midst of its souk, offers as fine a base as any from which to discover the nuts and bolts of the Levant trade in its central period. From there we briefly step backwards in time to trace the origins of the trade into the Middle East. But the main concern is to reconstruct the everyday existence of Britons living there, the commerce in which they became engaged and their interactions with the wider society that they found. In doing so, the broader contours emerge of their relationship with the Ottoman world.

The second part of the book takes us to Constantinople, a markedly different universe. The narrative shifts between the Italianate enclave of Galata and 'Stamboul' proper on the other side of the Golden Horn, home both to the sultan's palace and the most celebrated Islamic architecture of the Ottoman capital. Where Aleppo was the ultimate traders' town, Constantinople was as much a place for politics and, in time, *bon ton* travel, activities each casting its imperial masters in different hues. Yet the distinctive mentalities of the Enlightenment informed all these perceptions of this Ottoman world. For a fleeting moment, they seemed to illuminate the path to an accommodation quite absent from both earlier and later times.

In its third part, the book shifts to Alexandria, whose links with the Red Sea traffic to the Far East had, from an early date, made it a prime target of English trading ambitions. In that era, those ambitions were confounded, and Britons failed to establish a foothold. But by the nineteenth century, that earlier mark of British impotence lasting into Hanoverian times had come to change. Now, Britons would find themselves entrenched in Egypt – though not as traders in the old manner.

Their presence was a more ominous one, which reflected the Middle East's metamorphosis into a theatre of strategic importance for their Indian empire. And now, too, the strand in thought towards 'the Orient' which emphasised its supposed vice and intrinsic inferiority to Europe came to prominence: a foretaste of the outright racism that held sway by the later nineteenth century.

As the focus of our scrutiny shifts between these cities, just about everything else changes along the way. The heyday of the Company's trade, in the latter part of the seventeenth century and early part of the eighteenth, coincided with Britain's first transformation from underdeveloped Atlantic outcrop to leading emporium and prime mover of international trade. Throughout that time, the ties of the English to the islands from whence they came remained but faint. True, they talked of their 'nation', referring to the community of English traders in the Ottoman Empire. Yet they also identified themselves with fellow 'franks' – the Venetian, Dutch and French merchants who similarly sought fortunes in the Middle East – or even non-Muslim subjects of the sultan. All such loyalties, moreover, were fickle. Commercial competition with other Europeans was keenly felt, but there was none of the jingoism which would mark imperial rivalries of late Georgian and Victorian times. The pashas' contacts cut blithely across national, religious and social lines. Sectarian divides were effortlessly trumped by the appeal of Mammon.

Britain's rise to global prominence meanwhile reflected a wider shift in the global balance of power, by which the Christian 'West' ultimately attained the military, technological and economic ascendancy over the Ottoman Empire – and Islamic world generally – which were to be marks of modern times. From the mid-nineteenth century, it is broadly true to say, the manufactories of Europe were able to foist goods on Middle Eastern markets, whilst gradually forcing their economies to the periphery of global trade as suppliers of cheap raw materials and perennial debtors of the world's industrial producers. Just as the science of the Enlightenment lent Europe a decisive industrial advantage, its men of letters would now launch a concerted assault on the Orient in the cultural realm, turning their new-found knowledge of this corner of the wider world to the ends of asserting political dominance over it. Well before British troops ever set foot in the countries of the Middle East, the ground had been softened by this combined economic and cultural barrage. Britons' belief in their own superiority, moreover, had by then become enshrined in a rigid national identity.

Still, if all that was to come, the story of the Company's trade contradicts any idea that Britain's modern forays into the Islamic world possessed from the first the colonial character which they would later acquire. The appearance of English traders in the Levant from the later sixteenth century, alongside their French and Dutch counterparts, might be seen as signalling the decisive arrival onto the eastern Mediterranean scene of Atlantic capitalism. In the latter's expansion lay the genesis of a modern world-system, in which the Islamic world was fated to play the role of a subordinate. Yet it would be wrong to think of Britain's commercial empire, or the wider Atlantic economy, as having absorbed the trading world of the Ottoman Empire into a western-centred global economy in this earlier era. London and Amsterdam might already have grown into mighty commercial hubs, whose networks stretched out many thousands of miles to span oceans and continents, but into the eighteenth century, precisely the same remained true of Constantinople, Cairo and Aleppo. For a tantalising time, the economic colossi of the Atlantic and Middle Eastern worlds were able to coexist.

It was the wholesale shift in the balance of global politics during the later eighteenth century which would quite abruptly change that relationship, built on terms of something approaching cultural and economic equality, and bring the curtain down on this book's peculiar story. If Elizabethan Englanders found that the Turks had heard neither of their nation nor their queen, it spoke of an era when the mighty Ottoman Empire was famed around the world and the British Empire not yet born. By the period in which the Company's history ended, the skies were darkening for the Middle East, prefiguring a time when the British would arrive here not as guests but as colonisers. Yet this tale of a time before the British Empire underlines that it was not always thus. And it need hardly be added that, with a continued British military presence in the Middle East, the pashas' story of a constructive engagement with Islam seems to hold out some grounds for hope. For if one thing should come out of what follows, it is that there was (and is) nothing quintessential, ineluctable or necessary about conflict and misunderstanding between Crescent and Cross, East and West, Muslim and Christian.

PART ONE

❖

ALEPPO

1

Peace and Trade

———— ❖ ————

Caravans

For English merchants approaching from the westward Mediterranean coast in the seventeenth and eighteenth centuries, Aleppo's citadel was both compass and consolation. The heights outside the city's perimeter ensured that, on the usual route through Antioch, its cupolas and minarets were quite obscured until one was two or three miles away. Only the citadel, rising over the hills as it does above the souk, might be discerned from any distance. Its appearance on the horizon presaged the end of a deeply hazardous journey. Even at its kindest, the volatile sea churned stomachs and strained nerves. Just as often, it pounded and overturned ships, inflicted its 'long diseases and mortall, as the Calenture, Scorbut or Scurvie, Fevers, Fluxes [and] Aches', or unleashed corsairs.[1] Landfall itself could not eliminate this final hazard in the early years. A visitor in the 1620s found Scanderoon, Aleppo's main seaport, 'full of the carcases of houses . . . it having been sackt by Turkish pyrats'; and a decade earlier, such raids had been the pretext for the authorities closing it down altogether as a 'veritable temptation to pirates'.[2] There were, too, hostile Spanish or Dutch ships to contend with and, later, the French navy, whose attacks on the open sea slowly superseded those of pirates and privateers. In 1693, a Levant-bound merchant fleet was destroyed utterly, its cargo lost. Thomas Macaulay wrote that London merchants, on hearing the news, 'went away from the royal exchange as pale as if they had received sentence of death'; and in Aleppo itself, the shockwaves were still being felt over a decade later.[3]

Scanderoon seemed, to one trader, 'the hottest, and most unwholesome place in the Straights'; to another, 'the unwholesomest place in the world'.[4] There were the 'grosse fogges that both discend from the mountains, and ascend from the moorish [marshy] valleys'.[5] Then there was the annual infestation of frogs, whose croaking rivalled, for its eeriness, the howling of the 'multitude of jack-calls' which was perennially audible from the plains.[6] When the marshes dried up the amphibians would expire en masse, infecting the air with a fetid stench and, foreigners believed, emitting the diseases for which Scanderoon became notorious. 'There is a certain indisposition which attends the *European* factors', one visitor wrote, 'which makes them as it were Paralitick, and besides that, they are of a very yellow, and a bad complexion, and almost continually Feverish.'[7]

The climate did nothing to help. It was 'intolerably hot' for six months of the year; in winter it could be bitterly cold, the roads impassable for snow.[8] Then, as now, it was prone to earthquakes, sometimes so severe that they 'made men fall as they walked on the ground, tossed our dishes on our tables, made the tops of tall Cypress trees from a faire distance almost kisse each other, made the Shipps daunse on the Seae, & our

4 Merchant ships from northern Europe lying in harbour at Scanderoon, the warehouses of which can be seen hugging the shore.

houses over our heads'.[9] In 1705 the Company's trading house on the shoreline 'suffered very much' at the hands of one such tremor, 'one of the Main Beams being broken, and several of the Travis shook out of their places, so that the Tirrass was in great danger of falling, which would undoubtedly have brought down a great part of the house with it'.[10] 'I pray God protect us from these terrible judgements,' proclaimed a terrified Aleppo trader in the wake of another.[11] Many Englishmen never made it out, falling victim to illness or the excess of drink in which they sought solace, and space had to be made in the Greek churchyard to bury them.[12] At times, the death rate reached such proportions that people could hardly be found to work on the shipping.[13]

Even to embark on the final leg to Aleppo, another ninety or so miles to the east, was not to leave danger behind. It took experienced messengers up to four days to complete the route; heavily laden caravans might need eight.[14] The featurelessness of the plains along the way was matched only by the treacherousness of the passes, which became progressively more steep and culminated in 'the most horrible precipice that can be imagined', made all the more terrifying by the path's exposure to gunfire from looting Bedouin on the opposite mountain.[15] True, there might have been 'watchmen, as they said, patrolling for the security of the roads'; but these men did more to harass than to reassure. They 'never failed to ask a *baksheesh*' and, this wise traveller added, 'I never failed to comply with their request; because it would be very idle to wrangle for a trifle with those who, if they please, can take the whole.'[16] The guards were, anyway, too few to ward off 'those lawless freebooters', the nomadic Bedouin tribesmen prevalent in these parts, of whom at times could be seen 'thousands . . . armed on the summit of the steep mountain' above Antioch, threatening even the town itself.[17]

All told this was, as another wrote, 'such travelling as I could not have believed had I not seen it'.[18] Camels and horses set an agonisingly slow pace, weighed down with cloth, more rarely tin, the unwieldy baggage that accompanied a 'factor' – as the traders were known – freshly arrived from London, and the beds and provisions for the journey, 'to which the Europeans, who love good cheer, add wine'.[19] Even inebriation, though, could do little to mollify the 'piercing rays of the sun' by day and 'the dangerous night-dews, which fall in great quantity' after dark.[20] So when Aleppo's citadel eventually appeared, it invariably brought relief. Eulogies to its 'magnificent appearance', atop a hill 'almost as high as that upon which Edinburgh Castle stands', are a stock-in-trade of the accounts of their travels that English visitors penned in the seventeenth and eighteenth centuries.[21] All those who made the journey would have gazed on this spectre for hours at a stretch – old-timers awaiting the moment its features took on familiar form to signal their destination near at hand, newcomers consumed in pondering the profits that would sanction return passage.

When Henry Maundrell headed this way in 1696, though, his thoughts were turned to a task at once less lucrative and more daunting. For he was charged with a matter 'tending to the glory of God', no less than 'the reputation of the Company and the benefit of the English Nation there resident'.[22] This man had been dispatched to safeguard Christian souls in a heathen land.

Maundrell was a clever, well-connected churchman from Bromley, appointed chaplain to Aleppo's English factory in December 1695 after delivering a rousing sermon to the Company's court in London. He was finally spurred to Syria not so much by missionary zeal, though, as a domestic entanglement.[23] A sickly and somewhat donnish thirty-year-old, in some regards he embodied the impulse so beloved of the culture of the early Enlightenment to enquire, discover and explore. This was a milieu with which Maundrell was entirely at home. After a spell in an Oxford fellowship, his uncle, a prominent East India merchant who had also done time in the Levant, gave him entry to the circle surrounding Thomas Sprat, Bishop of Rochester. Sprat was a staunch Baconian, renowned for his devotion to sweeping away the 'rubbish of the ages' (his *History of the Royal Society* was still featured in Dr Johnson's shortlist of essential reads a century later).[24] Exploration of the world and intellectual renaissance were, it seemed to him, merely two sides of the same coin, for England's historic destiny was to be not only 'mistress of the Ocean', as he put it, but also 'the most proper seat for the advancement of knowledge'.[25]

Maundrell apparently subscribed to much of this dogma, and it cannot have been lost on him that his new appointment embodied just such a nexus between intellectual curiosity and trade. It was certainly not lost on Sprat himself, a man who had eulogised the '*noble* and *inquisitive Genius*' of the English merchant-voyager and regarded him as the international trailblazer of the new science. Through the young clergyman's uncle, he repeatedly enquired after him during the long absence.[26] Maundrell did not disappoint his patron, composing a description of the journey that he undertook to Jerusalem, whose tone of detachment accorded perfectly with Sprat's empiricist ideals. Albeit that it was clothed in the medium of a pilgrimage, perhaps regarded as rather old-fashioned now that modern travel-writing was emerging as a distinctly secular affair, Robert Curzon still felt able to rely on this account as his vade mecum in the 1840s.[27]

If in the eyes of some city big-wigs one object of exporting men of the cloth to the region was to marry Protestant providentialism with the Levant Company's aggressive commercialism, no place seemed better suited for such a project than Aleppo. Other great Ottoman cities, admittedly, made a more immediate impression on English sensibilities. Even Maundrell, a staunchly prosaic observer of his surroundings, was moved to raptures when, several months later, he first set eyes on Damascus: a city whose spiritual, esoteric overtones were already powerfully embedded within English culture.[28] 'Certainly no place in the world', he wrote, 'can promise the beholder ... greater voluptuousness.'[29] Cairo, likewise, seemed to many contemporary observers a place of almost unearthly delight, dotted with 'courts *spacious*, set with faire trees for *shade* . . . delicious *Gardens* watered with *fountains*, and *rivulets*; beside the infinite

5 The prospect of Aleppo and its imposing citadel, possibly after a sketch by Henry Maundrell.

21

varietie of strange *Plants* ... trees of *Cassia, Oranges, Lemons, Figs of Pharoe, Tamarinds, Palmes*'.[30] Then, of course, there was Constantinople: 'Pregnant with fine gilded spires, and stately domes', less utopian in appearance, perhaps, but no less awe-inspiring for that.[31]

The prospect of Aleppo from the hills outside promised something similar. From here, it was generally agreed, 'the cytty shews most beautiful'.[32] It could not have been framed more perfectly. The landscape alone saw to that, for it was bounded 'to the north by mount Taurus, to the west by mount Amanus, and to the east by the Euphrates, stretching away to the south beyond the valley of salt, as far as the large barren deserts of Palmyra'.[33] But marks of civilisation, too, conspired to add to the delight. On the expansive plain lying to the front of the city could be seen 'the *Turks* and *Arabians* ... exercising themselves on Horseback with their Lances'.[34] Next to it, at the entrance of the flourishing suburbs, there were gardens and small 'houses of recreation', enclosed within a wall of stone hewn long ago by the Mamelukes.[35] These gardens, watered by a river, were adorned with fruit and flowers – 'apples, peares, plums, apricocks, peaches, cereys, figgs, pistachoes' – and even graced by the odd peacock; in summer, parties of well-to-do locals who had paid a fee to spend their afternoon there could be seen lounging in them.[36] Behind stood the 'high walls and towers' guarding the city itself.[37] And beyond them, gracing its skyline, stood Aleppo's 'very fine minarets or steeples ... from the gallery of which the hours of prayer are proclaimed by the Mollahs with a loud voice', so that even a first glimpse of the 'very magnificent' mosques of its interior might be preceded by the sounds of the *muezzin* wafting over the hills.[38]

After the excitement of the approach, though, closer inspection usually brought deflation and disappointment. At ground level, the high stone walls lining the streets made them appear gloomy and narrower than they really were. 'Some even containing the best private houses', one visitor wrote half a century later, 'seem little better than alleys winding among the melancholy walls of nunneries; for a few high windows guarded with lattices are only visible, and silence and solitude reign over all.'[39] The buildings, another complained, are 'not high in proportion to the size, and the domes are raised so little above them, that they appear low and flat, though built with great expense'.[40] For all the richness of the trade, the shops were most conspicuous for their 'mean appearance'; the baths and fountains were strangely unadorned; and even the mosques and the palaces, 'striking the eye transiently through the court gates', added 'little, on a cursory view, to the embellishment of the city'.[41] All in all, concluded the most sceptical of contemporaries, 'there is nothing curious or agreeable to be seen about the place'.[42] At best, it could on a close view be described as functional and well placed, rather than a place of much aesthetic merit, 'a pretty large and well-built city; and though remote from the sea . . . second to few others, except Damascus, for the beauty and advantage of its situation'.[43]

And yet, to complain that Aleppo lacked picturesque flourish was rather to miss the point, for this city was first and foremost an economic powerhouse. The gathering place for opulent goods from Baghdad, Mosul, Diarbekr and the eastern Turkish and Persian cities and, most crucially for the English market, for silk from Persia, western Turkey and the regions of Syria itself, the souk's trade was at least as eclectic then as now. There were 'boot and slipper makers; box-makers; copper-smiths; cotton-wool workers; gold and silver smiths . . . vendors of second-hand cloaths, guns, pistols, and horse furniture; fruiterers; saddle and bridle makers; clothiers, mercers and vendors of all kinds of silks, cottons, muslins and embroidery; druggists; workers in embroidery . . . cooks' shops, coffee houses, and apothecaries'.[44] Aleppo enticed, in short, because for tradespeople its streets were very nearly paved with gold.

The richness of Aleppo's trade reflected the fertile conditions for commerce bred both by the Islamic world system at large and the Ottoman Empire in particular.[45] The polity over which the Ottoman dynasty held sway consisted at the beginning of the fourteenth century of no more than forty thousand tents of Turcoman nomads, just one of many such groupings squeezed between the worlds of Byzantium and of Islam.[46] Over two centuries later, Suleyman the Magnificent could introduce himself to the King of France (however immodestly) as 'the sultan of sultans, Sovereign of Sovereigns, Distributor of Crowns to Monarchs over the whole Surface of the Globe, God's Shadow on Earth, sultan and Padishah of the White Sea and the Black Sea, of Rumelia and Anatolia, of Karaman and the countries of Rum, Zulcadir, Diyarbekir, Kurdistan, Azerbaijan, Persia, Damascus, Aleppo, Cairo, Mecca, Medina, Jerusalem and all Arabia, Yemen and many other lands that my noble forbears and illustrious ancestors . . . conquered by the force of their arms and that my August Majesty has also conquered with my blazing sword and victorious sabre . . .'[47]

If by then the Ottomans had attained infamy in Christendom, it was primarily for their breakout from the Anatolian heartlands into the Balkans and the seizure in 1453 of Constantinople, city of the Caesars. Their subsequent advance into Hungary, led by Suleyman himself, would further inflame Christian souls. But as Fernand Braudel has long since pointed out, however dramatic the toppling of the Byzantine capital in the mid-fifteenth century, the major event in the rise of the Ottoman Empire was not so much this as the successful conquests of the earlier sixteenth century. Through this second great phase of expansion, led not by Mehmed the Conqueror but by the lesser-remembered Selim I, and played out on the stage of historical Mamluk rather than Byzantine advance, the Ottomans acquired Syria in 1516. In the year afterwards, their armies traversed the Sinai and conquered Egypt.[48] It was in the reign of Selim I, too, that more westerly parts of the North African littoral first came decisively under Ottoman influence. These thrusts south were, perhaps, less instantly daunting to the Christian states of Europe than the Ottomans' westward ones both before and since. Yet so far as those states' economic and strategic interests were concerned, they would prove no less portentous.

Their most basic consequence was that, well before the time Maundrell caught his first glimpse of Aleppo, the Ottoman Empire had attained pre-eminence throughout the terrains that nowadays we would refer to as the Middle East, encompassing not just the eastern Mediterranean (including, in addition to Syria, the modern-day regions of Israel–Palestine, Jordan and Lebanon) but large parts of the Maghreb and the Arabian peninsula. That in turn elevated the Ottomans to undisputed primacy in the Islamic world, as possessors of the three Holy Cities of Mecca, Medina and Jerusalem. It was not until centuries later that Ottoman sultans pushed their claim to the title of caliph of the *dār al-Islām* and the prerogatives that went with it, but their pre-eminence among the globe's Islamic potentates was sufficiently acknowledged when, on 17 July 1517, the Sherif of Mecca sent to Selim's palace in Constantinople the key to the *Kaaba*.[49]

A consequence of the sixteenth-century conquests perhaps all the more profound than this sacred one, however, was that in the sphere of trade. The enlarged Empire stood squarely between, on the one side, the states of northern and western Europe and, on the other, the spices and other eastern luxuries which they so prized. The warlike face of this empire has long been its best known, yet it was no less remarkable in its guise as economic superpower than as warrior state.[50] Through the conquest of Egypt, the Ottomans gained mastery of one historic spice route linking the Indian Ocean, both through and alongside the Red Sea, up to the Mediterranean at Alexandria. (It is testament to the Empire's ambition that, more than three centuries before the opening of the Suez Canal by European colonists, the Ottomans made serious strides towards constructing a waterway linking these two seas.)[51] Suleyman's capture of Baghdad less than two decades after the invasion of Egypt paved the way for capture of another such route: through the subsequent extension of Ottoman power into southern Iraq, marked by the full incorporation of Basra into the Empire by the later 1540s, they attained an outlet into the Persian Gulf. It was this latter development, indeed, which did much to propel Aleppo to its renown as an international emporium by the later sixteenth century. Indian products, whether spices, indigo or cotton cloth, could now travel in some security up the Euphrates route, causing Aleppo to eclipse the trade of the more southerly Damascus.[52] The westward trade routes along which Persian silk principally flowed – and this, as we shall see, was a matter of even greater significance for the Levant Company's trade – would now be largely under Ottoman sovereignty until they reached well into the Mediterranean sea.[53]

This traffic in oriental luxuries has long been infused with a romance in western narratives of Ottoman trade. It should not be forgotten, though, quite what a richly productive patch of earth the Empire itself encompassed (its deserts excepted). The staple of economic exchange in places like Aleppo, Smyrna and Constantinople was the rich agricultural produce of Anatolia rather than anything of more exotic extraction. Silk of Anatolian as well as Persian origin could be found on sale in Aleppo, increasingly so in the eighteenth century. The rise even of a town like Smyrna, renowned in time for the internationalism of its trade, was owed primarily to the growing marketability of specifically regional produce – cotton, tobacco, beeswax, grain – to the merchants of northern Europe.[54] And as to the allure of such home-grown products to English palates, the richness of Ottoman markets' offering was enhanced considerably by yet another arena of the Empire's expansion: the Mediterranean itself.

In the sixteenth and seventeenth centuries, the Mediterranean was (at least so far as its land masses were concerned) transformed into an increasingly Ottoman sea. We have already charted the Ottoman advance around the entirety of its eastern shoreline and, even further west, along its southern boundary, such that this stretch of water came to furnish an 'internal lake that linked the European, Anatolian and Arab provinces of the empire'.[55] The setbacks suffered in the Mediterranean arena by the Ottoman Empire at its height – the lifting of the Suleymanic siege of Malta in 1565 and the Holy League's victory over the Ottoman fleet off Lepanto in 1571 – caused the joyful ringing of church bells in Christendom. In the course of the seventeenth century, indeed, the Mediterranean sea was unique in representing a sphere of Ottoman power in which the English were able to assert a military presence.[56] Yet in spite of all this, its islands were a site of continued Ottoman expansion well beyond the era of classical greatness. Rhodes might have fallen to Suleyman a few years after the annexation of Syria and Egypt, Chios and Cyprus following suit respectively in 1566 and 1571. The conquest of Crete, on the other hand, which had remained a Christian island in an essentially Islamic sea for a century thereafter, would not be complete until 1669.[57] These islands supplemented the tally of Ottoman products entering international markets in important ways, adding such temptations as the currants of Zante and Cephalonia, and the sweet wines of Cyprus and Crete. But the Mediterranean's significance for Levantine commerce also went much further, in constituting a major outlet from the Ottoman Empire onto the trade of Christian Europe.

Ashore, Ottoman rule was vital in safeguarding the richly laden caravans pressing eastwards or heading back towards the coast, warding off banditry through bribery or brute force.[58] Along the principal routes, which throughout the central period of the Levant Company's trade were under the fairly close control of the Ottoman state, these caravans might be several thousand camels strong, their progress painfully slow (an advance of twenty-five miles in a day was considered good going).[59] But though hardly high-speed, these highways of the pre-modern Islamic world furnished a comprehensive transport network linking the Empire's major hubs of trade; and the caravans themselves were agents of an unfailing relay of economic exchange between those hubs.[60] Thus Istanbul was linked to Aleppo and Damascus via the pilgrimage route through Konya, ultimately winding its way to Mecca, while another eastward route ran to Erzurum and onwards into Iran. West of the capital, yet another major route ran to Edirne, from where onward roads could be taken to Salonica, to Belgrade or to Sarajevo and beyond. As for

Aleppo, it not only stood on the route connecting Istanbul with Mecca, but was linked both eastward to the Euphrates and Baghdad, and westward to the Mediterranean coast.[61] From Scanderoon, craft also plied the route to coastal towns like Beirut and Tripoli, as well as further afield.

Like their Islamic predecessors, the Ottomans were energetic at putting up caravanserais along the major routes to house their travelling salesmen. An eighteenth-century English traveller described one such place, lying at *Ma'arrat al-Nu'man*, between Aleppo and Damascus: 'It is large strong and built of free-stone, not unlike the Leaden Hall or rather the Exchange in London . . . It is of that sort of inns which are endowed by their founders, where a traveller may have bread, pilaw and mutton gratis; adjoin the khan is a bagnio and a street containing a coffee-house and five or six shops on each side . . .'[62] Later, they acquired a reputation for seediness and their provisioning was basic: one could 'expect nothing here but bare walls', one Englishman complained, and 'as for the other accommodations of meat, drink, bread, fire, provender, with these it must be everyone's care to furnish himself'.[63] True, the Ottoman constructions were more workaday than the magnificent Seljuk examples still standing east of Konya and stretching into Iran. Yet their most foremost virtue was sheer abundance, for on the principal highways they were spaced no more than a day's march apart. Hardly less important than modest comfort was the security they offered, those lying on the road usually being protected by garrisons to ward off attack. In the early eighteenth century a concerted effort was made to strengthen further the lines of communication linking Constantinople to central Anatolia and Syria, new khans being put up along the route and old ones repaired.[64]

Aleppo illustrates the energy with which the commercial institutions of cities themselves were also built under the Ottomans, paid for mostly by pious charitable foundations.[65] The size of Aleppo's commercial core more than doubled in the first half-century of Ottoman rule, to include fifty-six separate markets and fifty-three caravanserais.[66] Building of commercial institutions remained very active throughout the seventeenth and into the eighteenth centuries. It furnished the city not just with the framework of the souk and *bedestan*, but a whole gamut of supporting institutions: mosques, courthouses, schools, bathhouses and hospitals.[67] The city's burgeoning trade in turn threw up the wealth to pay for the handsome houses lining its suburbs, where (for all the sniping of English observers) the streets were spacious and well paved with flagstones.[68]

If all this was intended to draw in the wandering merchants of the world, Aleppo illustrates the strategy's emphatic success. The 'Trafficke in this place is exceeding great', Fynes Moryson had declared as early as 1596, since 'the goods of all Asia and the Easterne Ilands are brought hither'.[69] The encyclopaedic *Merchants Map of Commerce*, which an ambitious Levant Company official named Lewes Roberts published early in the following century, made much the same point: 'The *commodities* which are found in this Citie, are commonly all the commodities of *Asia* and *Africa*, as *spices* of all sorts, *drugs* of all sorts, *silkes* of *Persia, jems* of *India, spices* of *Arabia*, and the common *commodities* proper to the Countrey, as *Grograms, grograme yarne, galles, Cottons*, and *cotton yarne, silke* of *Tripoli, Bacai, Bedovine*, and *Damasco*, and other sorts in great quantitie.'[70] And like the goods they brought with them, the merchants who assembled here stemmed from far and wide. Aleppo was, one visitor wrote, the 'greatest place of traffique for a dry towne that is in all those parts: for thither resort Jewes, Tartarians, Persians, Armenians, Egyptians, Indians, and many sorts of Christians'.[71] Venetians established a firm presence during the sixteenth century. 'Aleppo . . . is now the most famous Citie in all the *grand* Signiors Dominions,' Roberts wrote during the next, 'for the wonderfull confluence of *Merchants* of all Nations and Countries that come hither to traffique . . . There are of all *Easterne, Southerne*, and *Westerne* Nations *Merchants* found therein.'[72]

As for the English, the merchant Anthony Jenkinson had been in the city as early as 1553, managing to obtain from Suleyman the Magnificent a safe-conduct which permitted him to trade in Turkish ports. And by the time Maundrell arrived, they had been prominent amongst Aleppo's wandering traders for a century or more.

In the Lands of the Sultan

'Who ever saw before this regiment,' swelled the early prophet of empire Richard Hakluyt in the 'Epistle Dedicatorie' of the 1589 edition of his celebrated *Principal Navigations*, 'an English Ligier in the stately porch of the Grand Signior at Constantinople? who ever found English Consuls & Agents at Tripolis in Syria, at Aleppo, at Babylon [Baghdad], at Balsara [Basra] . . . ?' True, the appearance in these parts of 'ambassadors' and 'consuls' was a novelty of the Elizabethan age. The story of England's diplomatic involvement with the Ottoman Empire began in the year

1580. That is when a set of 'capitulations', or formal trading concessions allowing the English to reside in his sovereign lands, was granted by the Ottoman sultan to their queen. But even earlier than that, the English had traded in places like Aleppo in small but significant numbers. Inside the Ottoman domains, they were able to assume the diplomatic protection of the French, whose own capitulations predated the English ones by at least a decade.[73] Hakluyt speaks of 'divers tall ships of London' visiting Mediterranean ports as far east as those of Crete and the Lebanese coast from the second decade of the sixteenth century.[74]

In that sense, one wonders why the Levant Company's own story should only really have begun with the exploits of William Harborne, a veteran merchant-traveller from the east country. This was the man who, armed with a mandate from the court of Queen Elizabeth I, sailed from London in July 1578 to conduct England's first formal negotiations with the Ottomans. Travelling for the most part overland through central Europe, he attached himself to a Turkish caravan returning to Constantinople from Poland, disguised in native costume to hide news of his mission from rival European states who might try to stand in his way. He arrived in Constantinople on 28 October and, having secured contact with the Grand Vizier, rapidly won his approval. Thereafter the negotiations were nothing if not convoluted, but their final success was marked by the arrival on 9 June 1584 of an English merchant ship at Constantinople, which sailed openly for the first time under its own flag rather than the French one. By then, Harborne himself had been appointed the Queen's 'orator, messenger, deputie and agent' to Constantinople – in all but name, the first English ambassador to grace the city. One of his actions in the post was to entrench and extend the English presence in the region with the appointment of consuls in Cairo, Alexandria, Aleppo, Damascus, Algiers, Tunis, Tripoli in Barbary and Tripoli in Syria.[75] Even by 1590, nearly twenty ships were going every year to Turkey, Venice and the Greek islands.[76]

Why had all this not happened long before? By 1580, it had been open knowledge for decades already that seaborne trade into the Middle East was both possible and profitable. Beginning with Hakluyt, historians have usually noted a hiatus in the progress of English traffic with the eastern Mediterranean. A decades-long lull divided the promising voyages of the earlier part of the sixteenth century from the belated renewal of interest, epitomised by Harborne's mission, towards its end. Hakluyt himself

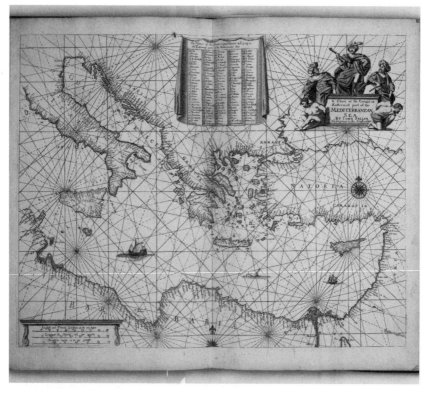

6 An English map of the Levant dating from 1675.

explained this in terms of the trajectory of Ottoman naval strength, whose pinnacle was reached with their capture of the islands of Chios and Cyprus in 1566 and 1571 respectively. This, he suggested, had frightened English shipping out of an increasingly Islamic sea. 'The Turke is growen mighty,' as a former trader to Chios declared in this period, 'whereby our ships doe not trade as they were woont.'[77] It took the Battle of Lepanto, in 1571, to restore the sea's Christian hue and license the return of the English in the final decades of the century.

There is at least the ring of truth to this claim. Security on the seas was a fundamental consideration for international traders throughout the sixteenth and seventeenth centuries. Captain Roger Bodenham's voyage to Chios in 1551, the last full-scale trading expedition to be mounted for more than two decades, illustrates why. Refused a safe-conduct by the Ottomans, he was continually harassed by 'Turkes gallies' and lucky to elude capture or annihilation – something achieved only by means of subterfuge, since any attempt to match their force of arms would surely have failed. The subsequent chronology fits Hakluyt's argument rather well, for English ships were thereafter absent from the Levant until Ottoman sea power was eclipsed by that of Christendom in 1571.[78] The Ottoman–Venetian war which raged over Cyprus between 1570 and 1573 also weakened the hold of Venetian shipping and to some degree provided the immediate occasion for English penetration.[79] The era of English maritime puissance in the Mediterranean would fairly soon begin, albeit that corsairs flying the crescent (and, not necessarily less troublesome, the cross) often dented it in the decades ahead.

Even so, the emphasis on a mid-century 'lull', which supposedly afflicted a pattern of English trade to the Levant first established in the early decades of the sixteenth century, is apt to mislead. For that trade was neither as significant in its early decades, nor as wholly absent after mid-century, as this schema implied.[80] And what in fact emerged in its final decades was a trade wholly unprecedented in volume and sophistication – unrecognisable, that is, from the rather insubstantial one existing at any earlier point in the sixteenth century. It is the timing of this new, post-1580 phenomenon, intimately bound up with the birth of the Levant Company itself, which we most need to explain.

The answer cannot be framed purely in terms of economics, since at least one major and long-running constraint on this sort of development was squarely political. As the French king jealously speculated at the time, 'not commerce, but some deeper design, was at the root of the Queen's action'.[81] For Christians, well versed in the bigotry about Islam which weekly issued from their pulpits, peculiar difficulties had necessarily accompanied dealings with an infidel power. The notion of a 'common corps of Christendom' somewhat united medieval Europe against the Islamic threat, if never entirely successfully, and it was by no means a dead letter in the Renaissance. Even *after* the flurry of diplomatic engagement which marked the final decades of the sixteenth century, King James I refused to receive an embassy from Constantinople on the grounds that it would be 'unbecoming to a Christian prince'.[82] Private traders might be ready enough to put profit before religion, and it is striking the extent to which the subjects of Christian states traded with the Ottomans even at the height of political animosity between them. Yet godly rulers were on the whole less mercenary.

That impediment abruptly lost its force in the later sixteenth century. True, it always proved easier for the northerly powers of Europe, removed from the full spectre of the Ottoman military threat (whose immense power to stir up Christian dread we shall encounter in a future chapter), to dispense with religious chauvinism, as the example of France suggests. Even further back than that, the city-states of Italy had surrendered to commercial realities in the Mediterranean and reached accommodation with the sultans over trade: Genoa's capitulations dated to 1352; those granted to Venice to the late 1380s.[83] The more immediate impetus for Elizabeth I to follow suit and countenance diplomatic contacts with the Turks, however, was her final expulsion from the Catholic Church in February 1570, by means of a papal bull which declared 'Elizabeth, pretended Queen of England, and her followers, heretics'. This event quite altered the strategic context, precipitating the outbreak of war with Catholic Spain, and in turn lending unprecedented appeal to the idea of engaging with the Ottomans. The Muslims were 'heretics', perhaps, but nowadays, so too were the English in the eyes of Rome. That in itself encouraged the two to become diplomatic bedfellows, and to view each other's place in global affairs more through the prism of the pragmatic (uniting them, not least, in shared enmity with Catholic Spain) and less through that of holy war.

Looking back on the progress of the burgeoning 'Turkey trade' a century or so after its commencement, there were those who found in all this clear signs of God's providential hand at work. Did not Britain's splendid isolation uniquely position her to build warm relations with the Ottomans – however much they might apparently be despised – based on shared commercial and diplomatic interests? For the Turks' unlucky neighbours in continental Europe, so this sort of argument went, 'the peril is unrelenting', but a northern maritime power such as England was protected by the oceans from 'the Red and Yoke of this great Oppressor'.[84] As another contemporary put it, between England and the 'cruell and horrible Pagans stands the Germaine nation as the Bullwark of Christendome'.[85]

Insofar as the Muslim threat was posed primarily to Catholic powers, all this seemed to illuminate the workings of a God who favoured Protestants. Thus 'all West-Christendom oweth her quiet sleep', it was pointed out, to the King of Spain's 'constant waking, who with his galleys muzzleth the mouth of Tunis and Algiers'. That was because 'God in his Providence hath ordered it, that the dominions of Catholic princes . . . are the case and corner of the east and south to keep and fence the

Protestant countries'.[86] As another early historian of the Turks put it much later, Britons, 'barrocado'd and fortified by the Seas', ought to bless God that they were . . .

> . . . born in so happy and so secure a Country [and] . . . have never felt any smart of the rod of this great oppressor of Christianity, and yet have tasted of the good and benefit which hath proceeded from a free and open Trade, and an amicable Correspondence and Friendship with this People.[87]

This sort of narrative could assist Britons in casting aside their qualms over supping at the table of the 'antichrist', as the clerics were stubbornly inclined to think of the Ottoman sultan and his Prophet alike. Associating with the Ottomans might always require excusing – Hakluyt devoted a good deal of space to an apologia for this prima facie Christian sin even as he eulogised Harborne's exploits – but plenty of Englishmen felt quite readily able to do so.[88]

Their narrative might even allow them to present such engagement as positively *advancing* the Protestant cause, a strain of self-justification apparent from the earliest dealings between the two powers. In her very first communication with the sultan in 1579, for instance, Elizabeth refers to herself as 'the most invincible and most mighty defender of the Christian faith against all kinds of idolatries, of all that live among the Christians, and falsely profess the Name of Christ' – a pointed reference to the waywardness of Latin Christianity.[89] Francis Bacon wrote an impassioned reply to an attack on English policy towards the Ottomans penned by the English Jesuit, Father Robert Parsons. If the sultan had seemed to favour the English ambassador, Bacon argued, that was due to none other than the Catholic King of Spain himself, 'for that honour [the English] have won upon [the King of Spain] by opposition hath given us reputation throughout the world'.[90] Alternatively, England might offer herself as a Trojan horse for Christianity inside a still-expanding Ottoman world. Hakluyt, a few years later, accordingly praised 'the great good and Christian offices which the sacred majestie by her extraordinary favour hath done for the king and kingdome of Poland, and other Christian Princes'.[91] Either way, these were narratives which preserved no role for a united Christendom in confronting the Ottoman threat. Even if Elizabeth I pointedly ignored an Ottoman suggestion that the two states enter into a 'league and most holy alliance', among the most important duties of the first ambassadors would be to urge the sultan to send a fleet against the Mediterranean coast of Spain during the threat of the Armada and after it.[92]

Thus it took the Reformation to render England's 'Turkey trade' conscionable. A second group of considerations to encourage its formalisation in the latter part of the sixteenth century, however, were indeed economic.[93] English ships might have entered the eastern Mediterranean on a small scale before 1580. But further back even than that, English products – primarily unfinished woollen cloth – had done so on a much grander scale; and correspondingly, goods of Turkish origin, alongside those from further east which had passed through Ottoman hands, found their way onto the English market in significant volumes. This exchange was conducted through the middlemen of Venice and, increasingly in the sixteenth century as the latter's decline deepened, Antwerp. By the latter decades of the century, though, both these European hubs were suffering from severe disruption that reflected both short-term wars and longer-term economic eclipse.

It is perhaps unsurprising that the tale of William Harborne, a charismatic Elizabethan adventurer extending the horizons of English influence across the globe, should have appealed deeply to Victorian historians of their supposedly 'imperial' forbears. In relating his tale, they tended to paint both Harborne and his fellow Elizabethans as thrusting imperialists after their own image: as men driven, above all, by the restless search for export markets that nineteenth-century Britons recognised as pushing outwards the boundaries of their own empire.[94] That focus on exports as a motivating factor is one which many subsequent historians have been prepared to endorse. It was the disruption of traditional cloth markets (especially Antwerp) on the European continent, so the argument goes, which pushed Elizabethan merchants towards seeking out new consumers beyond Germany and the Low Countries and embracing ever more distant shores.

The Ottomans certainly felt an urgent requirement for English imports in this era, and not just ones of cloth. The decimation of their navy at Lepanto, followed by equally destructive wars against Venice and Persia, created a pressing need for military raw materials. These were goods which England was naturally well placed to supply – particularly wool and tin for uniforms and weaponry. They were goods, too, which Catholic

Christendom was prohibited from offering to the infidel by dint of papal authority. Rejoicing in its heretical role, Protestant England would from now on cheerfully ship out metals ransacked from the monasteries to be melted down and forged into Ottoman artillery and munitions. As the French ambassador in Constantinople complained, even Harborne himself had 'brought in a large amount of steel and bits of broken images of brass and latten to cast ordnance, and promises to bring in a great deal more of it secretly in future, which is a form of contraband hateful and pernicious to all Christendom'.[95] This was, in fact, an aspect of the trade still going strong a century later, fed by an almost continual demand in the Ottoman Empire for military products. 'There appears little preparation for a war,' the English ambassador observed of the Ottoman camp in December 1689, 'and indeed it will be difficult to find materials, there being not much Tin to be had. For that, as well as cloth & all English commodities, are more wanting in this scale, than have been at any time (as I am inform'd) since our trade has first been settled in this countrie.'[96]

Politically, these military needs did much to shape the Ottomans' response to Harborne's overtures. In searching for the impulses driving the expanding horizons of Elizabethan trade, we ought to focus more heavily on merchants' quest to secure imports.[97] The collapse of well-worn routes for luxury imports through Venice or Antwerp, after all, was felt no less keenly than the loss of corresponding export channels through these same places. That in itself provided an impetus to raise the volume of trade conducted directly with the Ottoman Empire. Besides, there existed an intrinsic cost-cutting rationale for removing the intermediary in the quest for distant and exotic goods. At its most basic level, it was this rationale which impelled the whole eastward drift of English trade in these years into the Mediterranean (and eventually around the Cape of Good Hope and beyond).[98] It chimed, too, with the mercantilist economic dogma which was the orthodoxy of the time. 'You shall cent your owne Commodities with most proffitte which before did fall into strangers handes,' Walsingham had enthused of the prospect of the new trading link with Constantinople.[99]

So it was the thirst for imports, reflecting the burgeoning wants of English consumers, which before all else stoked the economic allure of eastern Mediterranean routes soon connecting London with the Levantine world.[100] This force would drive not only the first English forays to Constantinople, but the profitability of the Company's activities in the Middle East for centuries to come.

Foundations

In May 1580, Harborne had obtained from Murad III the charter of privileges which was to underpin the English trade in the region for the next three centuries. On 11 September 1581, from her throne in Westminster Hall, Elizabeth I presided over preparation of the letters patent which first breathed life into the 'Turkey Company'.[101] They gave to just four merchants, with power to nominate up to eight more, a monopoly over the whole trade with the Ottoman Empire for the next seven years.[102] In this company, there emerged the joint-stock investment mechanism that was, to begin with, assumed indispensable for financing the slow, capital-intensive and downright risky enterprise of maritime trade with these distant parts. If the sultan's granting of the capitulations marked the eastward foundation stone of the Levant trade, the Queen's chartering of the Turkey Company in the following year marked its westward one.

Protestant propagandists writing for the Elizabethan stage liked to imply that one effect of England's new-found pariah status, outside the Catholic fold, had been to beget a greater dynamism in her stance towards the wider world. Not by coincidence, they suggested, was this the moment when their trading horizons first ranged beyond western and northern Europe, when the 'fleets of the Protestant countries . . . felt themselves strong enough to force the Straits of Gibraltar'.[103] But if that was so, it was of necessity a cadre of self-starting merchants, rather than the sinews of the state, which gave practical effect to the new spirit of adventure. True, the calculations of the English court – particularly those of Elizabeth's long-serving secretary of state, Sir Francis Walsingham, who evinced a particular enthusiasm for the whole project – were never far from the surface in the turn of events that spawned England's early trade with the Ottomans. The Queen and a handful of contributors linked to her were responsible for contributing no less than £40,000 to the new company's capital, half its total.[104] The final initiative at every stage nonetheless lay with London's merchants.

It was two such merchants, Edward Osborne and Richard Staper, who had dispatched Harborne in the first place. They prepared the ground in 1575 by sending a pair of agents to secure a safe-conduct for the subsequent mission, and it was they who put up the finance for both journeys. The new company's monopoly was regarded as recompense for these efforts, a just reward for men who 'by their adventure & industry & to their great costes and charges, travelled & caused travel [to be] taken aswell by secret & good meanes as by dangerous waies and passagies to set upon' the trade.[105] Osborne, lauded in the 1581 patent as 'the principall setter foorth and doer in the opening, and putting in use' of the trade, was made governor of the new body. Draconian powers were granted to ward off anyone who thought to disregard the company's monopoly, whilst the monarch extracted in return a promise to pay £500 every year in customs duties.

If the flourishing home consumer market had greatly expanded the possibilities for English merchants profitably to tap far-flung supply routes, the coterie who capitalised on the avalanche of opportunities was tightly knit. Familiar faces lurked behind a whole range of ventures across the globe, conducted for the most part through chartered trading companies. Osborne and Staper between them had a hand in the Spanish, Muscovy and Barbary trades.[106] The backgrounds of the twelve merchants to be included in the original charter of the Turkey Company confirm this to be a well-marked pattern. Of them, nine were Muscovy Company investors, ten were Spanish Company members (whose trade had been heavily disrupted by war, so encouraging them towards fresh Mediterranean ventures) and eight were involved in both. Only one had no connection with either company.[107]

That a patchwork of monopolies, granted to an array of trading companies, encompassed essentially the whole of England's overseas commerce had the virtue of allowing gains made in one branch of trade to be funnelled into the breaking-open of another. It also prompted, for all their overlaps in personnel, a flurry of turf-wars. The Turkey Company was soon enmeshed in a particularly bitter wrangle, for the terms of its monopoly brought it into direct competition with the Venice Company, the company of English merchants which in 1583 had been granted a monopoly on trade with the Venetian islands and the Morea. Both vied to cater for Londoners' huge appetite for currants from the Mediterranean. When the Turkey Company's original charter came up for renewal in 1588, it sought to expand its own privileges to encompass trading rights in the Venice Company's territories, geographically convenient for its own ships. After strained negotiations, in which each cabal of merchants volleyed insults at the other, it was resolved to meld the two together.

It was thus by means of a merger, uniting the nascent Turkey and Venice companies as one, that the Levant Company proper came into being in 1592. The new body was to be more than the sum of its parts: the charter provided for a relatively large membership, of fifty-three merchants. Here was a combine that monopolised trade not only to 'Turkey' (encompassing the whole of the Ottoman Empire), but also to the sphere of Venice, including Zante, Cephalonia and Crete; and for good measure, it was also handed rights to the land routes to the East Indies 'lately discovered'.

It was not long after the demise of an independent Venice Company, however, that another company was born, whose trade would pose a longer-running threat to Levant merchants. This was the East India Company. The Ottoman Empire might have stood squarely between Europe and the land routes to the Indies; when the Portuguese rounded the Cape of Good Hope at the end of the fifteenth century, though, they had created the

7 A gold beaker bearing the Levant Company's arms, presented to Katherine, Lady Trumbull, in April 1687, on her departure for Constantinople as a diplomatic wife.

possibility of skirting around those routes altogether, sourcing luxury goods direct from the Far East and transporting them by sea. In the early sixteenth century, the Ottomans' own ambitions to tap the riches of the Indies drew them into direct confrontation with these Portuguese newcomers. The sultan's forces laid siege to Hormuz and the fort of Diu on the coast of Gujarat, as well as establishing themselves in Yemen.[108] Save for the last of these campaigns, they were not a great success, but the establishment of a province at Basra in mid-century enabled them to make their presence felt upon another route to the Indian Ocean. Whilst Portuguese sea power might occasionally have reached into the Gulf of Aden, moreover, the Red Sea remained firmly under Ottoman control.[109] By the middle part of the sixteenth century, the trade routes through the Middle East under Ottoman control had largely regained their former importance, in spite of the Portuguese intrusion. So it was that the earliest English imports from the Levant could still be dominated by the likes of Indian and Indonesian nutmegs, indigo, pepper and drugs.[110]

Even so, the price at which such goods were to be had naturally became the more exorbitant the further west they were bought. By the time they reached Aleppo, they might have passed through the hands of scores of middlemen and toll collectors, each of whom would take a cut. The impetus to purchase them as far east as possible was as a result felt keenly (this was the mere extension of the logic which had brought Englishmen to the Levant at all) and the first generation of traders was by no means content to halt at the eastern Mediterranean shore. The terms of the Company's first charter, as we have seen, categorically extended its monopoly to the land routes of trade with the East Indies, a nod to the globe-girdling voyages of a decade or so earlier. The scope of the Company's landward ambition in this direction is hinted at in Lord Burghley's notes on the towns and commodities of the Levant, thought to date from around 1582:

> . . . from Aleppo to Rasslea [possibly Ra'ssu 'l-'Ain, east of Biricek] upon Euphrates, *which* is .3. dayes Iorney by land than down by water to bagdett [Baghdad] . . . which is about xiii dayes sayling. From thence into yet Tygirs and so to balszara [Basra]. Here ye best baulm is made. From balsara to Ormus [Hormuz] in xv dayes sayling. From thence to Goa.[111]

In 1583, Osborne and Staper sponsored an ambitious reconnaissance east of Aleppo by John Newbery, Ralph Fitch (who would also serve as a consul in Aleppo) and a handful of other merchants probing this passage to India. They made their way through Baghdad and Basra to Hormuz, on the Persian Gulf, where they were promptly arrested by the Portuguese. Once released, they pressed on to Goa, from where Fitch 'journeyed by river to the Ganges Delta and Hooghly, saw much of Bengal, visited Malacca and returned by way of Ceylon, Cochin, Goa, Chaul and Hormuz'.[112] He then wended his way back through Persia and Aleppo to London. Newbery was less fortunate: last seen somewhere near Fatepur, his eventual fate is unknown.

The pashas' correspondence reveals that, fairly routinely, they ventured on business as far east as modern-day Iraq during the seventeenth century. The Aleppo consul would supply the ambassador in Constantinople with a steady stream of intelligence from Persia and India, and stock him with his tea.[113] Nonetheless, the political difficulty of trying to regularise their presence in such places was considerable. The early ambition to create a network of English trading posts spanning the land route between the Mediterranean and the Persian Gulf seems to have quickly faded. Even had the Company been successful in doing so, it could not have neutralised the danger that cheaper maritime transportation between England and the Far East would one day heavily undercut the Mediterranean spice trade.

If only for its unimpeachable economics, the attraction of opening such a sea route for themselves was always apparent to Levant traders.[114] In 1590, John Sanderson participated in the first English voyage that attempted to repeat the Portuguese feat of rounding the Cape. Even as the Company's charter was being granted, James Lancaster, who cut his teeth in command of a Levant trade vessel, was in the midst of the first of his pioneering voyages to these parts.[115] None of these early forays achieved much commercial success and, meanwhile, in the late 1580s the Dutch managed not only to reach the Indies, but to return in a convoy laden with sumptuous cargoes. With this development, the death knell of the older pattern of trade between Europe and the eastern Mediterranean really was sounded. The Middle Eastern spice trade to England soon became visibly diminished. An even more immediate effect, though, was to spark panic amongst English traders, both in the field and in London. 'This trading to the Indies [by the Dutch] have clean overthrown our dealings to Aleppo, as by experience ere long we shall see', John Sanderson's agent wrote to him in the capital.[116]

It was this panic among Levant merchants which provided the immediate impulse for the foundation in 1600 of the East India Company. In the first decades of its existence, the new company was little more than an outgrowth of the Levant Company, a sort of 'special purpose vehicle' for breaking open the East India trade. Its early voyages relied heavily on Levant Company ships. Long after that had ceased to be the case, it was heavily dominated by Levant Company men. As late as the 1630s, no less than twenty-eight of the forty-seven directors chosen for the East India Company court were Levant Company members.[117]

Indeed, the formation of a dedicated company to pursue the East India trade might not have been necessary at all had not the Levant Company by then ceased to trade on a joint-stock basis. The early East India Company voyages called for huge investments to be sunk: 'a trade so far remote cannot be managed but by a joint and united stock', as the promoters of the new company had put it in petitioning the Privy Council for a charter in 1599.[118] The Levant Company, as a mere regulated company, was just not up to this task. The use of a joint-stock vehicle, by contrast, was soon copied by the Dutch and paved the way for a highly successful trade to the Indian Ocean.

So far as the traffic in spices was concerned, the pashas' prophecies of doom in the trade through the Mediterranean were not far off the mark. Their more general pessimism about the Levant trade itself, though, proved unwarranted and its marts showed considerable resilience. For one thing, some small amounts of spices continued even now to reach England by this route for several decades more. More importantly, as early as 1614, pepper from East India Company voyages began to be re-exported to the eastern Mediterranean via English ports. Even after its long Atlantic diversion, it could be sold more cheaply in Levantine markets than goods carried there via the Gulf or Red Sea caravans. Cloth exports from England were slow to make their mark in the Levant, notwithstanding a policy of cut-throat price competition, but re-exported eastern and colonial products (at prices that could only strike their Ottoman buyers as bargains) did so immediately. They would have the added virtue of enabling the Levant trade to curry increasing favour with mercantilists, who were sounding the alarm at the heavy export of bullion which the activities of most overseas trading companies of the period required.

We shall see, though, that what would truly rescue the European– Middle Eastern trading nexus from an early demise in the wake of the spice route's diversion was the trade in silk. The international silk trade was big business within the Ottoman Empire: in the mid-seventeenth century, six to ten caravans of silk arrived each year in Constantinople from Iran, two from Basra as well as three to four from Aleppo.[119] Anatolia itself was also an important region of silk production. The beginnings of the Company's activities coincided with the growing taste for luxury consumer goods ushered in during the Renaissance that would be popularised even further by the long eighteenth century.[120] Silk therefore presented itself as the perfect surrogate for spice, ensuring almost single-handedly that, in spite of the burgeoning success of the East India Company, the Levantine world still exercised a powerful draw on ambitious Britons well into Hanoverian times.

From its earliest days, the Company's direct traffic with the Mediterranean had proved an instant success, 'very gainful' from the outset and yielding profits of up to 300 per cent that made all its risks seem worth taking.[121] As early as 1596, Fynes Moryson looked back to the past fifteen years as a period when 'the Turkey company in London' had established itself as 'the richest of all other, silently enjoying the safety and profit of [its] trafficke'.[122] Reviewing their trade at the beginning of that decade, the Company itself reckoned that it had employed nineteen ships during the time that it had held their charter, which had completed twenty-seven voyages and employed 787 men in them.[123] A 'Petition of the Turkey Company for sending an ambassador [to Constantinople]', dating probably from 1582, illuminates what a panoply of goods the trade consisted in during these early years. As for 'Commodities of this Realme servinge for the partes of Turkie', it stated, they were: 'Kersies and all sortes and cullers. Clothes the lyke dyed and dressed. Cottons. Tynn in barrs. Conyskyns. Pewter.' Those commodities 'to be returned from Turkie', on the other hand, were: 'Unwrought and wrought sylke. Spyces of all sortes. Gaules. Cotton woole and cotton yearne. Grograins. Chambletts watred and unwatred. Ryse and Wormseed. Sope. Oyles. All kinds of drugs for potycaries. Lynnen cloth made of cotton woole. Carpetts and quyltes of silke. Allam, corrante, damaske, reysons. Indigo for dyers. Gotes skynnes as also Buffes. Wax and woole. Dates and anyseeds. Hides and fells.'[124]

The sheer range of these imports reflected the diverse locations over which the Company had entrenched its trade in the early decades. An island like Cyprus, a natural stopping point en route to the eastern corner of the Mediterranean, was supplied with a consul nearly from the outset, Zante and Chios likewise in the early phase of the Company's life.[125] These latter were places that had initially been mainstays of the Venice Company's trade; and after the combined Levant Company came into being in 1592, currants imported from the islands were a staple of its traffic. In the decades that followed, the number of English traders based here, together with their entourage of chaplains, officials and servants, grew exponentially. For if Harborne's diplomatic triumph of 1580 presaged the institutionalisation of the Levant trade in the domestic arena, there can be no doubt that it was as much a necessary precursor to the establishment of semi-permanent settlements in the Middle East, which were to play such a central part in the English involvement with the region during the two centuries that followed.

The process of English settlement in places like Aleppo, accordingly, began almost immediately after 1580. The mechanics of long-distance trade created a powerful logic for establishing a year-round foothold in such market-centres as this. It allowed ships to offload domestic manufactures into warehouses and replace their holds with local purchases. The actual business of trading could then be done partly in their absence, somewhat freed from the time constraints that an imminent homeward voyage might impose. Aleppo's commercial importance for this traffic was quick to be recognised and there was, thanks to Harborne, an English vice-consul resident in the city within two years of the capitulations being obtained.[126] For the next quarter of a millennium, the souk's luxuries would flow into London's marts, ornamenting its well-to-do citizens and swelling the pockets of its 'Turkey merchants'.

2

Trading Places

❖

Compass of the World

Seventeenth-century Londoners imagined that the triangular patch of ground where the Royal Exchange stood, squeezed between Cornhill and Threadneedle Street, must be the most valuable on earth.[1] If you walk into the city today, the Gherkin seems to pull the city's commercial epicentre further east, the dome of St Paul's to root its soul further west. In Sir Christopher Wren's vision for resurrecting the city in the wake of the Great Fire, though, the Exchange was to be accorded a place right at 'the Nave or Center of the Town, from whence the 60 feet Streets as so many Rays should proceed'.[2] Quite apart from its actual topography, there was nowhere in the early-modern capital so apt to conjure the sense of being at the hub of things.[3] Rather like the skyscrapers now cutting jigsaws into the skyline, the Exchange, beating heart of England's burgeoning overseas commerce, was the most palpable outward symbol of the capital's early claims to world-city status. Should one be more impressed, a foreign visitor wondered at the end of the sixteenth century, by 'the stateliness of the building, the assemblage of different nations, or the quantities of merchandise'?[4] All three spoke, in their way, of London's first emergence as a global emporium, fattening visibly on the fruits of its commerce.[5]

'We are to consider that we are a very little spot in the map of the world', Sir George Savile, Marquis of Halifax, remarked in the 1680s,

8 The south-west prospect of the Royal Exchange, as rebuilt after the Great Fire of London.

'and make a great figure only by trade.'[6] Distant sea routes seemed to stretch out from the capital like great sinews, connecting it with marts across the earth. The merchants who daily gathered there trumpeted a eulogy to the place penned during the Restoration, 'bring Turkey and Spaine into London, and carry London thither'.[7] Almost single-handedly, Joseph Addison was driven to suggest early in the next century, the Exchange made 'this metropolis a kind of emporium for the whole earth'.[8] To visit the place, he added, was immediately to feel a 'citizen of the world', for its ground floor was arranged into little constellations of nations and trades. If you entered from Sweeting's alley, there would be Armenians clustering in the arcade; a little further and to the right, Italians flogged silks next to the moustachioed Dutch, while to the left, the Spain merchants rubbed shoulders with the Jews; past them, there were stockbrokers and moneymen oiling the whole enterprise. On the other side of the courtyard, next to the East India men, the Turkey merchants plied their trade – 'buying, selling, bearing news, and doing business generally', as a continental traveller reported at the turn of the seventeenth century.[9]

For all the augustness of its edifice, the actual floor of the Exchange was boisterous and businesslike. 'One would think all the World was converted into News-Mongers and Intellingencers, for that's the first Salutation among all Mankind that frequent that Place', a contemporary jibed. 'What News from *Scandaroon* and *Aleppo?* says the *Turkey* Merchant. What Price bears Currants at *Zant?* Apes at *Tunis?* Religion at *Rome?* Cutting a Throat at *Naples?* Whores at *Venice?* And the Cure of a Clap at *Padua?*'[10] Francis Bacon did not exaggerate when, in 1619, he told James I that 'your merchants [embrace] the whole compass of the world, east, west, north, and south'.[11] London was, John Dryden declared half a century later, a 'fam'd emporium' whose maritime empire extended from 'Guinny' to the 'Turkish Courts'.[12]

It was a few hundred feet from this spot, at a church on the opposite side of Threadneedle Street, that the youngest of Peter and Mary Rycaut's ten sons was baptised on 23 December 1629. No place could have been more apposite to mark his entry into the world, for Paul Rycaut was to live his life surrounded by new money. His father, a Protestant immigrant from Antwerp, had rapidly amassed wealth in the Mediterranean trade, multiplied it as one of the capital's leading financiers, then bought status by snapping up land in Kent.[13] As a younger son of a star-crossed family, Paul was destined to see none of this wealth. But his mercantile stock did give him ready entry into the swelling networks of overseas trade and it was here that his own fame and fortune would be made.

Dudley North and John Verney, too, were London-born, and they, too, were younger sons of families who had known riches and somehow lost them. The family misfortunes suffered by all three stemmed to some degree from the fractured times in which they lived. For as they grew up, England descended into civil war. Two days before John was born, in

November 1640, the Long Parliament had assembled (the fourth baron North, Dudley's father, amongst its members). In the weeks before Dudley himself came into the world, the capital's streets were resounding to the sound of mobs chanting for blood. On 12 May 1641, the Earl of Strafford, one of the early victims of the growing strife, went to the scaffold on Tower Hill; four days later and a few minutes' stroll to the southeast, Dudley was born at the family's Charterhouse mansion.

War tore into childhoods. In the fifth year of John's life, his parents fled with their elder son to France, leaving him to fend for himself for the next four years at the family's Buckinghamshire estate, cared for fleetingly by servants and aunts. (It is hardly surprising that when his mother returned to England, she found her son living a worryingly 'ill-ordered' life.)[14] For the Rycaut family – like the Verneys, ardent royalists – these years were no less calamitous. When Paul was in his early teens, his father and elder brother were thrown into the Tower of London and the family estate sequestrated. Both later regained their freedoms, but Sir Peter was left penniless and he died a broken man. In his formative years, much of Paul's energies would be devoted to attempting to restore his family's pre-war riches, by recovering a small fortune which his father had loaned to Spain. No trace of it was destined to be seen again.

Even amidst the political anarchy, though, business went on, if not quite as usual. In the Royal Exchange, Charles I's execution might have prompted the demolition of the statue of the monarch which had graced the floor (the words 'Exit tyrannorum ultimus' were scrawled up instead in a lazy declaration of political correctness), but the shopping was surprisingly little diminished.[15] For the three boys, there were careers to be considered.

It was in Paul's case that the path from London childhood to Levant Company officialdom could most readily have been predicted. Benjamin Disraeli's much-quoted line that the 'East is a career' was not penned until the nineteenth century, but it would have had a certain ring of truth even by the Civil War era. The Levant Company offered all its officials quite generous salaries in the field, even if it occasionally failed to pay them.[16] These were posts which threw up plenty of financial opportunities on the side, too: chaplains were allowed to supplement their income by trading on their own account, and whilst consuls might not, in practice the rule was fairly easily flouted. Even amongst the obedient, Paul was by no means unusual in successfully turning his hand to trade in

London soon after leaving his post, profiteering on his host of Levantine and city contacts. For an able and ambitious son of mercantile, *nouveau riche* stock, Company service would have been a natural choice by the later seventeenth century. 'You will have great applications to you to entertain the sons or relations of gentlemen in order to their preferment or to make their fortunes, and perhaps you will not be able to resist their importunities', as Paul would in later years forewarn an ambassador embarking to the Porte.[17]

Paul's socially uppish father ensured that even the youngest of his sons received his education at Trinity College, Cambridge, followed by the Inns of Court (the place in those days where 'almost all young gentlemen spend part of their time', as Archbishop Laud once observed).[18] When he failed to inherit money, Paul consoled himself with the reflection that this pedigree was all the legacy he could ever need. It was an added part of the Levant Company's allure to men like him that service within its ranks offered the glamour of travel and, with it, the chance to gain repute as a man of learning on the streets of Restoration London. That was Paul's ambition from the start. It was shared by a good number of Company men, amongst them not just Henry Maundrell but Dudley, who would make his name through his essays on the theory of trade, drawing heavily on his Middle Eastern experience. Paul, who recorded his experiences from the first journey out with publication explicitly in mind, would prove indisputably the most successful amongst this circle of Levantine literati, in time lauded with a knighthood and election to the Royal Society for his encyclopaedic works on the Ottoman Empire.[19]

It remained more difficult for bona fide children of the gentry, as John and Dudley both were, to countenance dirtying their hands in the marts of the Middle East. To an earlier generation, this path would largely have been off-limits, but attitudes were by now changing. Dudley's father wrote, in a book of advice aimed at gentry families of the period, that there was much to recommend the employment of younger sons 'in some Profession of the more noble way viz. Church, Law, Arms or Physic'; but, he added, 'neither is Merchandise to be contemned whereunto in forain Lands persons of the most Honourable condition do apply themselves'.[20] 'To become a merchant of Foreign commerce hath been allowed as no disparagement to a gentleman born,' another agreed, 'especially to a younger brother.' As the tone of these remarks implies, the merchant's stock generally ranked below that of the barrister, army officer or churchman. John's hope that his chosen line of work would, in his father's eyes, be 'noe less satisfactory then if I had beene an Inns of Court Gentleman' was probably sanguine. Even in the mid-seventeenth century, there were those who clung to the view that, by entering an apprenticeship, the young gentleman unavoidably surrendered his *noblesse*.[21] Yet that point of view was certainly becoming less widespread and by the early decades of the eighteenth century it seemed a common-place that 'now the greatest gentlemen affect to make their junior sons Turkey merchants'.[22]

Dudley's parents 'designed [him] . . . to be a merchant' from an early age. Partly that was because, when dispatched to a grammar school, he gave a 'sorry account . . . of his scholarship'; and he was eventually diverted to a writing school, where he could concentrate on commercial subjects and learn to keep accounts. Yet the child also showed a 'strange bent for traffic' and, in the eyes of his kin, considerable precocity as an entrepreneur. Once, he dispatched the family porter to negotiate a knock-down price for apples from a street seller. When the porter returned empty-handed, Dudley sent him off again, this time with a button which he was supposed to pass off as a farthing. The ruse failed, but the tale lodged in the North family mythology, and seemed to mark Dudley out for the cut and thrust of the market.

The Norths might have encouraged their child toward commerce, but John's father initially had other ideas for his son. As for Dudley, it was the boy's aptitudes (or, more accurately, those he lacked) which first and foremost pushed him in the direction of trade. He failed to shine at his French and Latin and, with his 'miserably crooked legs', was plainly not military material, but he took to 'areathmatique', writing and accounting. By his teenage years, moreover, John was determined to enter business. 'My youngest son was bent upon it, to be a Turkey Merchant', his father later recalled, and 'neither I nor any of his friends could persuade him from it though I ever intended him to the law . . . I thank God he loves his profession.'[23] 'I am not a little satisfied in this kind of life . . . which you have done me the honour . . . to let me choose,' John later wrote to his father.[24]

His father's misgivings were not without cause. The career of a merchant was notoriously hit-and-miss and, for all the Company's lucre, individuals' financial gains might in the event be quite modest. Real success tended to be concentrated in the hands of a relative few: often, as we shall see, those who would embrace the mighty risks involved in lending out money to Muslims, or who had a large trading capital to begin with, or who through sheer luck found themselves doing business amidst a boom. A trusted adviser of the Verneys did all he could to discourage John's going into it: some men might 'have the knack of it', he warned, but in truth 'not one in three of them thrives'.[25] More than the odd apprentice, brought to the Levant by filial piety and little more, proved a reluctant student and floundered. A flurry of letters amongst the papers of the Aleppo factory illuminates the disastrous efforts of Sir John Lethieullier, a prominent and powerful London merchant of Huguenot stock, to secure a career for his son in the trade. The boy's drinking, womanising and aversion to work quickly ruffled feathers amongst the factors and his master rejoiced when Sir John eventually gave him leave to return home.[26] This sort of scenario, where costly apprenticeships were abandoned midway and losses cut, was common enough: as many as a third to a half were not seen through in the period.[27]

There were also the risks to life and limb to be considered. If the Levant trade was considered particularly apt as a pursuit for the younger sons of gentry, in part that was because such sons were relatively dispensable. John's apprenticeship bond spelt out, as was usual, what was to become of the £1,000 surety advanced by his father should he succumb to one of the Levant's mortal dangers. Just as pressingly, though, it allowed him to return straight home should his elder brother die. Elevated to the status of heir-apparent, he would require surer safeguarding from an early grave than this career could ever allow. Even second sons were generally steered away from careers in the Levant on the ground of its dangers.

Professional success could be rendered far more likely by apprenticeship to a well-regarded master, but this was not easy to secure. In letters from London, the well connected would pester Aleppo factors to find plum positions for their sons. With the right man, those who survived the hazards of their first years might find themselves set up for life, and suitably painstaking negotiations would precede the finalising of arrangements. 'I recommended to you our Mr Denby, as a proper Person for a Master to your son,' one trader updated a London merchant, 'who being since dead, I know not how you can dispose of him better, than to Mr Nathaniel Harley of this place, who being a gentleman of a very good estate, and brother to the speaker [of the House of Commons, Sir Robert Harley], I presume designs not to stay long here . . . if you can prevail with

[him] . . . to take your son apprentice, I believe his fortune is made.'[28] Even for wealthy fathers, though, such eminent apprenticeships would represent very large outlays, for merchants made their price 'according to the plenty of their offers'.[29] John's father paid £400 to his master and granted a bond of £1,000; Dudley's father forked out £350. It was difficult to get away with any less than £300 in the period.[30] Even those sorts of sums would appear modest by the early decades of the eighteenth century, when £1,000 or more was regularly being paid.[31] These were vast amounts and a major discouragement. 'The Turky merchants ask so extravagantly that I cannot advise it,' one merchant advised at century's end, '& it is almost now become a state fit only for rich citizens sons.'[32]

For all its uncertainties, Paul, John and Dudley were entering the world of foreign trade from London at a time of remarkable dynamism in its history. Seventeenth-century England experienced a 'commercial revolution', which saw the value of its overseas traffic rise fivefold, transforming it into one of the great trading powers of Europe.[33] The total tonnage of the English merchant shipping fleet doubled in the half-century preceding the Restoration alone.[34] As well as increasing in scale, the geographical locus of foreign trade was reorientated decisively, away from its domination by woollen cloth exports to northern Europe and instead towards southern Europe and the Near and Far East.[35] Unlike in days gone by, the fruits of this trade would accrue almost entirely to merchants who were home-grown. The Venetians that had once controlled English cloth exports left London in 1533 and Southampton in 1587, whilst Hanseatic merchants were deprived of their privileges in 1552 and by the end of the century had been evicted altogether.[36] An Englishman entering the Levant trade at the dawn of the Restoration was well placed to prosper.

The pashas' mercenary motivations emerge powerfully from their correspondence. As John and Dudley both demonstrate, a career in the trade exerted an especial appeal for those whose families had fallen on hard times. Such men might hope, as one Aleppo factor wrote to his brother in London, 'in a few years to be able not only to pay my debts, but also to get the wherewithal to live comfortably in my own country'.[37] Yet this was a profession for the socially ambitious as well as the merely impecunious, beating a path which the nabobs of the East India Company would later follow with greater notoriety. 'You gentlemen will know', as another wrote, 'that the inducements to a man living abroad and more especially in a country like this, are the hopes and expectations

9 Fruits of the Levant trade: Sir Godfrey Kneller's 1721 portrait of the Harvey family, whose dynastic wealth was founded on commerce in the eastern Mediterranean.

he has of gaining in his earlier days wherewithal to return to his native country to spend the latter part of his life with some comfort.'[38] Building up such riches would, for many, be the crucial precondition of returning home with head held high. 'I think you are much in the Right in preferring the pleasures of old England, before those of Aleppo', wrote one envious trader from the *Khan al-Gumruk* to a retired colleague wallowing in the domestic comforts bought of his profits. As for his own part, he added, he could only live 'in hopes, that some kind turn of affairs, may call me home, to the enjoyment of my native country, and friends'.[39] These men tended to be driven by the ambition of founding a landed dynasty, acquiring deer parks and Van Dykes along the way. Not a few would succeed.

At home, the Turkey merchants' place in the city's pecking order steadily rose as the seventeenth century progressed. Their firmament was 'composed of the wealthiest and ablest merchants in the City', as one contemporary put it in mid-century.[40] The Company was 'for its height and eminency' now 'second to none other of this land', Lewes Roberts similarly declared in 1638. Robert Brenner has demonstrated that there was a wholesale shift which by the dawn of the Civil War had advanced the Levant and East India Company merchants (there was much overlap, for reasons that will emerge) into a pre-eminent position in the city's power structure. When, in 1640, the Crown sought a loan from 140 of the leading citizens of London, thirty-one of those to whom it turned were Levant traders.[41] In the same period, almost half of those elected to the elite court of aldermen of the City of London were Levant Company traders, East India Company directors or both.[42] The Company's growing eminence was also evident in the stature of its governors. Sir Thomas Lowe, nominated in the Charter of James I as the first of the reconstituted company, was also governor of the Company of Merchant Adventurers.[43] His successor was governor of the Muscovy Company and Lord Mayor of London, and so too was his own successor in the post.[44]

From this rise to prominence in the earlier decades of the seventeenth century, the Company's eminence would remain entrenched for decades to come. Governed by 'a Wise and Grave Company of Experienced Merchants', Paul himself observed when reflecting in later years on his career, 'our Commerce and Trade with the Turk hath been in its increase' ever since the first granting of the capitulations and 'brought an inestimable Treasure and advantage to the English Nation'.[45] Writing in 1771 of the period three decades beforehand, Sir James Porter, one-time ambassador to the Porte, could still write (though, by then, with an undoubted degree of exaggeration) that 'The Turkey merchants at that time formed the most opulent and respectable body of men in the City.'[46] 'Who is ignorant that in the early part of the century', an anonymous pamphleteer asked two decades later, 'a Turkey merchant was the most respectable character on the Exchange of London?'[47] The choice of appointments for ambassador to Constantinople was another straw in the wind. Always a prominent posting into the eighteenth century ('a post of more honour, and more profit, than Paris', one Stuart diplomat declared), their pedigree was of the highest.[48]

Of all branches of 'foreign commerce' which one might enter, it was accordingly the Levant trade which appeared the most promising to many discriminating judges of Stuart society. The more successful amongst the pashas could translate an early career in the Middle East into real stature in London. Partly that was because, as wealthy Londoners sent their own sons out to trade, these men would be guaranteed a leg-up upon return. This is what Sir John Lethieullier had planned for his wayward child; so too did the prominent merchant George Boddington, whose son narrowly escaped death in the Smyrna fleet disaster of 1693 and was destined for a glittering city career.[49] Yet the scope for factors to progress to the highest positions under their own steam was also growing. Domestic openings flourished, as the respective careers of John and Dudley would illustrate. On his return to London, John obtained the freedom of the Levant Company and continued to do a lucrative business. From this base he progressed to governorship of the Royal Africa Company and eventually a seat in Parliament. Similarly, Dudley combined prominence in the city, as an investor in the Levant, East India and Africa trades and governor of the Muscovy Company, with a stint as a corpulent Member of Parliament.

The secret to the new-found wealth and prestige of the merchants flocking to the floor of the Exchange was exposed in the shops lining its upper levels. For the dynamism of the English economy in this era sprung less from exports than from imports, whose value so much as tripled in the first four decades of the seventeenth century.[50] Captured in that stark statistic is an explosion of consumer demand, daily visible in the 'walks above [in the Royal Exchange] . . . Wherein great Ladies do frequent and love/ There to come, because of that Rich sort/of Wares therein, which by fam'd report/ There you may have'.[51] It was a running joke amongst merchants that their hard-won gains on the trading floor would be squandered by their fashion-conscious wives on the upper levels. 'The merchants should keep their wives from visiting the upper rooms too often,' a contemporary warned, 'lest they tire their purses by attiring themselves.'[52] It was here, if anywhere, that Adam Smith's nexus between graft and greed was on display. Trinkets and trifling vanities made the pashas' worlds go round.

The birth of consumerism in England, of a society which celebrated, shopped for and conspicuously devoured life's luxuries, is a phenomenon most conventionally associated with the eighteenth century.[53] As the historian Linda Levy Peck has recently argued, though, something deceptively similar was also going on in this earlier period.[54] The luxury trades boomed, 'feeding the appetites of the rich with silks, satins, linens and other fine cloths, with wines, sugars and spices, gold and silver ware, jewellery, perfumes and medicaments'.[55] Wines, silks – manufactured and raw – sugar, raisins, currants, pepper and tobacco alone accounted for 43 per cent of imports in the 1630s, twice their proportion early in Elizabeth's reign.[56] This emerging consumerism, moreover, 'embraced not only the nobility and gentry and the substantial English yeomen, but included humble peasants, labourers, and servants as well'.[57]

This is not to suggest that the 'consumer revolution' which some attribute to the later eighteenth century actually took place a century or more earlier. The seventeenth-century transformation was different to that of the later period. It was not so much that (as would happen in Georgian times) shops became flooded with home-made manufactures aping eastern wares, as British goods were foisted on new colonial markets and Britain itself converted into the 'workshop of the world'.[58] This earlier phase of consumer-led growth was underpinned, instead, by the allure of foreign products themselves. The genius of domestic manufacture played a smaller role. Straight re-export of colonial goods aside, the make-up of English exports changed little. It was the rapidly growing wants of English consumers which did much to bring about a decisive shift in England's participation in the world economy.

The Levant was feeding the retail frenzy with all manner of goods: carpets and cloves, opium and copper, elephant's teeth and squirrel skins.[59] Yet the trade thrived above all on two staples. The first was the currants of Zante, Crete and Cephalonia. In the first four decades of the seventeenth century, imports of Levantine currants increased fourfold, prompting the Company to appoint consuls to Zante and Cephalonia in 1638.[60] These were among the most commonplace of luxuries, so widely consumed that there was said to be a season when it was so dishonourable for a man not to be able to consume currants that he would hang himself in shame.[61] In the third decade of the century, they were 'much used in meats', and with good cause, for 'beside their pleasantness in taste, they excite the appetite, strengthen the stomack, comfort and refresh weak bodies, and are profitable for the melt [and] are verie good and wholsome for euerie season, age, and constitution'.[62] By the Restoration they cropped up in cookery books, and apothecaries cast them as the mainstay of a whole host of quack remedies. Come the final decade of the century, they had evolved from cure to disease: the overconsumption of raisins and currants, along with spices and sugar, with which people supplemented their daily bread was being blamed for 'put[ting] all into discord and confusion' and causing 'the Body [to be] precipitated into Fevers, Consumptions, or some other cruel Distemper, according to the Nature of each Mans Constitution'.[63]

The second staple on which trade thrived was silk, imports of which exhibited an even more spectacular increase. If currants underpinned much of the Levant Company's prosperity in the early decades, silk was its staple import throughout the central part of its existence, accounting for well over two-thirds of its goods shipped in from the Ottoman Empire by the end of the seventeenth century.[64] The Company heavily imported fine silk fabrics from Italy, too.[65] The changing volume of total raw-silk imports to England gives a good idea of the growing scale of the Company's business: totalling around 12,000 pounds in 1560, they had reached 120,000 by 1620 and thereafter doubled in the next half-century.[66] Imports by the Levant Company, rather than those from northern Europe or East India, made up a growing share of the whole and by the end of the seventeenth century overwhelmingly predominated.[67]

As Peck points out, silk became the most valuable of all raw material imports throughout the middle and later seventeenth century.[68] It fed a burgeoning silk-weaving industry, most famously of Spitalfields, selling silk first to Londoners and, after mid-century, across the country, and quickly outdoing French and Italian imports.[69] That industry was claimed to employ as many as forty thousand people in London in the 1690s, while it displayed a precocious appetite for new technology.[70] Silk stockings became a veritable obsession for socialites. 'What d'ye lack, Ladies? fine Mazarine Hoods, Fontanges, Girdles, Sable Tippets, choice of fine Gloves and Ribbands', Shadwell's retailers cry out in his Restoration comedy *Bury Fair*. 'Stockins, Silk Stockins; choice of Silk Stockins: very fine Silk Stockins.'[71] That the manufacturing processes required to produce these goods was done at home particularly recommended it as a product. As Defoe wrote in 1728:

> The Importation of Silk is an Article of home Consumption, grown up now to a prodigious Height, and is the more profitable to his Nation, in that it is all manufactur'd within our selves; and as it is grown up to such a Magnitude as was never known before, employs abundance of our Poor,

who, by Decay of other Branches of Commerce, began to be threaten'd with want of Employment.[72]

Key though its imports were, the success of the Company's exports should not be ignored. In the early decades, the cargoes of cloth shipped out in an attempt to pay for all the riches carried home came nowhere close to doing so and they had to be supplemented by large amounts of bullion. The 'new draperies' on which the English cloth industry pinned its hopes in European markets during the seventeenth century had little appeal in an eastern Mediterranean market already well supplied with cotton textiles, manufactured closer to home.[73] Instead, the pashas had to push the traditional, heavier woollen broadcloth, finished in a bewildering variety of colours ('when in doubt send red', one factor urged from Aleppo).[74] Initially, they made very little impression indeed. From the 1620s, though, cheap West Country cloth took off and by the middle of the next decade the Company was selling as many as six thousand long- and short-cloths at Aleppo alone, representing a substantial proportion of England's exports of 'old draperies'.[75] Throughout the first half of the century, exports to the Levant were worth only half as much as imports from it.[76] But even by then, in a sign of things to come, some of the imbalance in the trade was also being made up for by re-exports from the fledgling colonial trades: pepper, ginger and indigo; red and white lead, cochineal, sugar and brazil wood.[77]

For all the uncertainty that life in the Company entailed, it deserved its growing repute as a route to wealth. 'It has pleased God to put . . . you in a way', Dudley's father lectured his son soon after he embarked on his apprenticeship, 'wherein you are likely to prosper if you be not wanting to yourself.'[78] 'You are going to a place where I presume your gaines will not only keepe you, but if you behave yourselfe well, I hope you may lay up Money too,' John's father similarly wrote shortly before his son's departure, 'or else the greate charge I was at when I bound you (and since too) was but ill-bestowed.'[79]

Apprentices

So it was that, within a few months of each other, John and Dudley found themselves indentured as apprentices, Dudley to a 'Mr. Davis' and John to Sir Gabriel Roberts, a notable figure in the Company. They proffered the usual promises, not just to obey their masters but to avoid 'fornication . . . matrimony . . . cards, dice, tables . . . taverns [and] play-houses'. In return, they were to be instructed in the 'craft, mastery, and occupation' of the trade and provided with meat, drink, linen and shoes besides. In the three years that followed, the pair spent their days across the road from the Royal Exchange. Dudley found his boarding with a packer in Threadneedle Street, so that the hours not spent weighing and measuring silk in his master's busy warehouse would be occupied packing bales of cloth into parcels, for dispatch onto ships awaiting in the Thames.[80] Lived out a few doors down this same street, John's daily existence was much the same, though he seems to have been luckier than Dudley in his master. Sir Gabriel quickly took John under his wing, welcoming him onto the family table at dinner times (a mark of affection rarely accorded to boys of his humble station).

John and Dudley found themselves apprentices in an era when the practice was at its height. This was, by now, a routine stage on the path to full adulthood, not just for Levant traders, but for most sons of the husbandsmen, yeomen and lesser gentry of rural society, just as for sons of the tradesmen, merchants, professionals and artisans of towns.[81] Lawsuits from the period cast light on what sheer misery it might be, revealing 'a female apprentice who was stripped naked, strung up by her thumbs and given twenty-one lashes; a boy who was beaten so severely that he could not stand upright and who spat blood for a fortnight; another who was flogged, salted and then held naked to a fire; another who was beaten so severely with a boat-hook that his hip was broken'.[82] But it would be wrong to suggest that such sadism represented the norm. Much more commonplace was the complaint of sheer drudgery.[83] There was much tedious detail that success in the Levant business required the new recruit to pick up, whether about the mechanics of packing, weighing and making entries on ledger books, learning the wiles of bartering, or exploiting the ebb and flow of prices at the Exchange. Unglamorous but indispensable, these were the nuts and bolts of the trade.

Apprenticeship was the most laborious route into the trade, but not the only one. As the new charter that was granted to the Company in 1661 would prescribe, other than members of the Company, only sons of members, or apprentices or former apprentices, were permitted to operate as factors in the Levant. By the eighteenth century, this stricture was being ignored, wealthy fathers simply buying partnerships in firms for their offspring, but in Dudley and John's day, it was not readily circumvented.[84]

The Company might periodically declare its intention 'not to appropriate the trade to any limited number of merchants, nor to any one city, nor to suffer the same to be used in any degree of monopoly, but to lay open the same to all'.[85] In truth, though, entry was stifled and carefully manipulated for the sake of better lining its members' pockets. Financial barriers were only part of this story. In the first place, admission was restricted to 'mere merchants' – those who 'hath used only merchandising in foreign parts and no other profession for one whole year'.[86] After the Restoration, the further stipulation was added that, nobility aside, no one residing within twenty miles of London should be admitted unless he become a freeman of the city of London. The restrictive effect of these regulations was buttressed by the indispensability of kinship networks in forging commercial success. Dudley and Paul both had brothers out in the Levant at the same time as themselves; John's wish to trade in Aleppo was impelled by his already having relatives there. Henry Maundrell secured the appointment to the chaplaincy in the city largely through the offices of his uncle, who had preceded him to the region.[87] In fact, up to half of all active Levant Company traders had fathers, fathers-in-law or brothers already in the Company when they joined.[88] If anything, its circles of recruitment narrowed as time progressed.[89]

The really big gains won by the Levant trade were, as a result, siphoned off to only a handful of fat-cat dynasties. For those included within the fold, the Company was resolutely democratic. Though presided over by a governor and a small clique of officials, important decisions were always taken by a general court of members according to the principle of 'one man one vote' (a practice mirrored in the Middle Eastern factories).[90] Yet to those outside, it must have seemed frustratingly inaccessible. There was much force in one contemporary's excoriation of the pashas as men 'born rich and adding wealth to wealth by trading in a beaten road to wealth'.[91]

Not least because they resembled, to some degree, the elephantine corporations of more recent times, the early-modern trading companies which fashioned this selective enrichment have always provoked controversy. To their admirers, they were brave handmaidens of a global capitalism. By enabling risk to be spread many ways and casual investment to be split off from careful management, so the argument goes, they dramatically extended the horizons of entrepreneurial endeavour and spurred new ventures promising only distant and uncertain returns. To their detractors, they were vessels of brazen, state-sponsored monopoly that served only the interests of their cabals of over-bloated members in the metropolis. As Adam Smith himself would berate them (and with the Levant Company specifically in mind):

> The constant view of such companies is always to raise the rate of their own profit as high as they can; to keep the market, both for the goods which they export, and for those which they import, as much understocked as they can: which can be done only by restraining the competition, or by discouraging new adventurers from entering into the trade.[92]

The Levant Company would seem especially prone to criticism since, despite the Turkey Company having been a pioneer of the joint-stock basis of organisation, the Company proper traded on a joint stock for a few years at most after 1592.[93] For most of its history, rather, the Levant trade was organised on a 'regulated' basis: company members had a monopoly on the trade, but it was individual members themselves and not the company that actually conducted it, members who ultimately made their own investment decisions, profits and losses. That state of affairs was by no means unusual for trading companies of the time. The East India Company, famously a joint-stock affair, was something of an exception (if a prominent one), whilst companies such as the Spain, Baltic and Barbary Companies resembled their Levantine counterpart.

Still, it follows that the Levant 'Company' was no company at all in our modern sense. In abandoning the joint-stock basis of their endeavours, its merchants had apparently dispensed with the two overwhelming advantages of incorporation. No longer could the risks attached to individual members' capital investments be parcelled out.[94] No longer could the skilled merchant put to good use the easy money of the dilettante investor. Now, individual merchants or, more usually, partnerships were routinely exposed to catastrophic loss, and even when profits were destined to be made, it might be months or years before they could be realised.[95] In this trade, moreover, London merchant-investors had to be deeply involved in every aspect of their factors' business, as their frequent letters back and forth amply testify. The quality of their judgement might do as much as the actions of factors in the field to shape success or calamity. Each individual traded, as one contemporary put it, 'in his own way, and on his own bottom'.[96]

For all that, the Company's monopoly was not indefensible. In this era of strictly limited state means, the outsourcing of the collective aspects of far-flung enterprise was routine and to a large extent necessary. It tended to be individual merchants, the likes of Osborne and Staper, who first ventured the capital allowing distant and uncertain markets to be probed at all. The expectation of monopoly rights in return was regarded as the quid pro quo of their hazardous ventures: a rationale which Elizabeth I had been prepared to accept. It was the Company which would absorb (though not without a good deal of grumbling) the heavy cost of maintaining the Constantinople embassies and consular network. This had always been a Company responsibility, the Crown 'contributing nothing but credentials'.[97] More than that, a strong company organisation was made necessary by the manner in which the Levant trade enmeshed its protagonists, quite unavoidably, in political intrigue both at home and abroad. This required the collective flexing of muscle, not to mention regular showerings of cash. The pashas' skill in turning the resources of the state, as well as the state-like powers of their own combine, to keeping others' hands off the fruits of the trade was an indispensable ingredient in their commercial success.

If the pashas traded as individuals or in small partnerships, the commercial penetration of their 'nation' into Levantine markets operated in important ways as a co-operative endeavour. The 'weaker witted', Harborne warned in defence of a joint stock, risked being 'inveigled by the malicious Turk and crafty Moor and faithless Greek' and 'by selling at under prices not only bring those our commodities out of estimation, but also through their overhasty imprudence . . . raise the foreign commodities to excessive price'.[98] The pursuit of prosperity also required them to displace the Venetian traders who had long been selling cloth to Ottoman buyers. The promise of doing so, and thus creating an outlet for cloth 'in its full perfection, dyed and dressed' by English manufacturers, was of course a deeply attractive one to London's merchants and politicians alike.[99] English exporters naturally benefitted from their country's competitive labour costs, a by-product of the underdevelopment of their economy compared with those of the Italian city-states. Nonetheless, manufacturers, traders and King conspired in a policy of ruthless price warfare against the Venetians, taking to the Levant market low-quality cloth which aped the Venetian real article and pricing it so cheaply that rivals were quite quickly forced out.[100] That strategy, which proved a brilliant success, was premised both on a tight monopoly and a low-taxing monarch.

The dynamic between the individual quest for profits and the collective position of the Company in the Middle East would prove an important one in the pashas' daily lives. Domestically, there was never any doubt that the major role reserved to the Company consisted in lobbying for the upkeep of its members' privileges. Constant vigilance was called for to ward off the monarch's attempts to tap into their profits and the Company's *pas de deux* with the Crown to this end dominated its earlier domestic history.[101] It even appointed a special committee to watch over proceedings in Parliament and the Privy Council.[102] Successive spats in the long-running war over customs duties provide a yardstick of the prevailing balance of power between Company and Crown in the decades preceding the Civil War.

The Company's attempt, at the dawn of the seventeenth century, to extract a customs levy from non-members on imports of currants caused a furious Elizabeth I to revoke its charter altogether.[103] Fairly quickly, tempers cooled and a compromise was reached, whereby the customs were farmed out to the Company – collected by it, a healthy dollop creamed off, then a fixed sum handed over to the Queen – so setting the pattern for centuries of sharing the spoils of the trade between merchant capitalists and Crown. Yet the incident epitomised a tendency on both sides towards brinksmanship, which again became apparent during the early years of James I's reign. In this era, the Turkey merchants renounced their patent and dissolved the Company, in the hope of wriggling out of the money which they had promised to pay his predecessor.[104] In July 1603, the Venetian ambassador delightedly reported that 'the Levant Company is finally dissolved' and looked forward to the imminent withdrawal of the English diplomatic presence from Constantinople.[105] The dissolution was, however, no more than an endeavour to prove to the King that the trade's abandonment would be 'disastrous, not merely to private individuals, but to the commonweal, owing to the effect on the customs'.[106] That the merchants' stance ultimately won through demonstrates how Levantine money spoke to a King whose revenues were heavily reliant on customs duties. The merchants soon petitioned for the restoration of their charter and a committee appointed by the Council of State to look into the matter reported favourably on the idea.[107] By the following spring, vessels were

being prepared to voyage to the Levant under the auspices of the reconstituted Company.[108]

The period of open strife with the Crown, spanning the latter part of
Elizabeth's reign and the earlier part of James I's, came to an end with
the issue of a fresh charter on 14 December 1605. This was the charter
which was to provide the formal basis of the Company's trade for the
next half-century and it marked the beginning of renewed vigour in the
expansion of its activities in the Middle East. As the Venetian ambassador anxiously recorded, 'they are not only going to keep up the
company and its Consul at Constantinople, but they are going to enlarge
its numbers, and extend the field of its operations'.[109] Just as importantly,
it announced an uneasy accommodation with the Crown.

That is not to say that the war of words over taxation came to an end. It
was a disgruntled Levant merchant who prompted one of the great consti-
tutional set-pieces of Stuart England over the King's powers to fleece his
own people. In 1605, Mr John Bate refused to pay an increase in the duty
on currants which had no parliamentary approval. The judges decided
against him: the King could exercise his prerogative how he liked.
Members of Parliament, however, had naturally inclined to the merchant's
view; and in the period of commercial crisis witnessed in the 1620s, an
alignment could be seen between the intransigent stance of Parliament on
the one hand and the growing obstreperousness of the Company on the
other in the face of the monarch's attempts to squeeze ever more money
out of his subjects. In the same era as Parliament's refusal to grant tonnage
and poundage revenues to Charles I, a number of Levant merchants went
so far as to break into customs warehouses forcibly to liberate their
goods.[110] In 1628, a Levant trader was flung into gaol for publicly
complaining that merchants 'are in no part of the world so screwed and
wrung as in England' and (what seems to have provoked the most upset)
adding that even 'in Turkey they have more encouragement'.[111]

Even so, by the outbreak of the Civil War, there is good evidence to
suggest that the Company's sympathies were overwhelmingly royalist.[112]
If merchants had resented in earlier decades the manner in which both
James I and Charles I clawed into their profits to shore up crumbling
royal finances, they also had to admit owing a deep debt to the Crown.
Even at their peak, customs duties were a comparatively small price to
pay for its willingness to conspire in – and do much to enforce – the
Company's domestic monopoly over the trade. Moreover, the resources

of the state were applied to a limited degree to the capture and monop-
olisation of the trade even *beyond* England's borders. This was manifested most strikingly in the Navigation Act of 1615, which reserved
Levant goods to English ships and thus anticipated, by several decades,
the better-known Navigation Acts of mid-century.

Looked at from the perspective of those excluded from the growing
bonanza – not least the men of the provincial outports who felt increasingly marginalised by the fancy metropolitan elites thronging the Royal
Exchange – it was obvious that the Crown and the Company were quite
unfairly in cahoots. Parliament became a major channel for denouncing
the trading companies' cronyism. After all, as one Member of Parliament
pointed out in the 1620s, 'No Law here ever restrained any Subject to
trade freely': rather, the 'Restraint [has] grown by mere Monopoly
Patents . . . The Spanish Merchants have got a Company lately; so the
French . . . The Levant Seas restrained by the Turkey Company.'[113] The
Levant Company was somewhat less of a target than the joint-stock
companies and its abandonment of that status won praise – 'since the
Breaking of [that] Combination', it was claimed, 'there go Four Ships
for One'.[114]

Nonetheless, the chartered companies generally, whether joint-stock or
regulated, were regarded by many as a recipe for stagnation. 'The
engrossing of this traffic into these few men's hands,' it was complained,
'increases the price of these kinds of wines, raisins and commodities, the
benefit whereof goeth but to a few'.[115] There was a flurry of free-trade
agitation in the early years of the seventeenth century, which was renewed
in the midst of the commercial crisis of the 1620s.[116] But it was of little
effect in the face of a monarchy still potent and, more importantly,
desperately grappling for revenues. This was, after all, the heyday of
monopolies: by the dawning of the Civil War, as has been said by one
historian, the typical Englishman 'lived in a house built with monopoly
bricks . . . heated by monopoly coal . . . ate monopoly currants, monopoly
salmon [and] monopoly lobsters'.[117]

The voices of opposition were to be heard again. In the mean time,
perhaps the only means of cocking a snook at the Company's domination of the Levant trade was simply to circumvent its monopoly. This
was widely done throughout its history, sometimes with the complicity
of members, by sending goods to the Levant via such intermediary ports
as Livorno.[118] Interloping of various kinds was a frequent source of ire

among the Company's big-wigs; but these, when all was said and done, were men who could well afford a dent in their profits.

Embarking

On 20 October 1660, a warship and two merchant vessels hoisted their sails off the south coast and disappeared into the grey morning mist.[119] At their head was the *Plymouth*, charged with carrying Heneage Finch, third Earl of Winchilsea, and his bloated entourage to the Ottoman capital.[120] Stocky, whiskered and loquacious, Winchilsea struck Dudley as the very model of a 'jolly Lord' when he met him in Galata some years later. If this man appeared singularly cheerful amidst the gloom of the Channel, it was not without cause. Reaping the reward for staunch royalist convictions, during an extraordinary six months of preferment he had successively been appointed governor of Dover, Lord Lieutenant of Kent and ambassador to Constantinople. True, this last posting had been sought only with reluctance. Its hazards needed no introduction and Winchilsea hardly relished the prospect of the 'tedious winters voyage' which was its necessary prelude.[121] (In the King's impatience for his new appointment to arrive at the Porte, there seems to have been no question of waiting for the regular Levant convoys whose spring and summer sailings offered kindlier conditions.) But as well as being of considerable diplomatic eminence, this appointment offered to restore the Winchilsea

10 A portrait of the *Plymouth*, the ship which carried Winchilsea and Rycaut to Constantinople after the Restoration.

family's faltering wealth to equal terms with its late-won political distinction. So he found himself journeying to the Levant in the stormy season, as he put it, 'to make my selfe miserable that I might make my posterity happy'.[122]

It was also aboard this ship that Paul Rycaut first embarked for the Middle East, marking the start of his evolution into consummate Company professional – 'modest, discreet, able, temperate and faithful', as Winchilsea later praised him.[123] Paul would spend seventeen years in the Ottoman Empire, ten of them occupied in the post of the Company's consul at Smyrna, until one day he found himself 'affected with a passionate desire (which is natural I conceive to all persons) of seeing my owne country', and abruptly left.[124] From the comfort of his London armchair, he still participated after that in the world of Levantine commerce, trading in eastward markets through Jacob Turner, a man whom he had met whilst serving the Company and who earned his spurs, not only as a trader in Smyrna, but as a captive on the Barbary coast.

The *Plymouth*'s journey began amidst pomp and heraldry, 'many of the nobility and gentry' of the county turning out to see the great man off, some of whom 'lay aboard all night; his Countess, Lady daughters and attendance with him'.[125] The sea, however, was a great leveller in the seventeenth century, and within a fortnight of entering the Atlantic the ship had begun to fall apart. Broken buntlines were the first of several ill omens. Then, at the height of a violent gale, a crew-member pumping out seawater spied the mainmast 'split from the upper deck to the lower and . . . wrought until it spewed out like oakum and a cross crack beside'.[126] At a hastily convened conference the ship's carpenters offered assurances that it might be saved. But their repairs were botched and soon found out by twenty-four hours' atrocious weather. The captain, Sir Thomas Allin, had often sailed these waters as a privateer before the Restoration; yet, he observed, 'I never saw so much breaking and a ship so ill fitted out.'[127]

Robert Bargrave, still in his early thirties but an old hand of the Levant trade who had also boarded at Gravesend, was as inured to these vicissitudes as Paul was fresh to them. He had first visited Constantinople in 1647 as a nineteen-year-old apprentice – then, too, sailing in the company of a newly appointed ambassador, Sir Thomas Bendish, on a voyage which proved nearly as ill-fated. 'No sooner had we sett saile,' he described, 'but the wind grew exceeding boisterous making us fresh-water souldiers sensible of the sudden Change; so that we threw our very Galls in Neptunes face.' Bargrave's naivety of the sea in those days guarded him from full knowledge of how closely they had approached oblivion. 'I found my selfe in a strange world,' he recorded of the experience, 'the Seae beating sometimes into my very Cabin; & I tossd & tumbled, sometime my bed upon mee, & sometimes I upon my bed . . . all wett & dabbled, sick, hungry without sleep, & in a confusion of Torments.' The ship was eventually forced to return to the Downs; and when it set out again, he had to contend with chronic seasickness, a cloud of locusts and fire from the North African shore before finally reaching his destination.[128]

That sort of experience was an integral part of the pashas' world. It lay in store both for Dudley North, who departed for Smyrna in the spring of 1661, and John Verney, who sailed for Scanderoon almost exactly a year after that. As it had for Bargrave, the departure from Gravesend marked the end of their three years as London-based apprentices. For that reason, if no other, it would have been eagerly anticipated, preceded by months of excited packing, planning and fond farewells. Montagu North, Dudley's brother, went to the trouble of travelling down to the Kent coast to see off this young relative who was following in his footsteps.[129] 'I shall want for my voyage about three or four pair of sheets, half a dozen towels and as many napkins, and one or two cheeses that will keep,' Nathaniel Harley wrote to his mother at the same point in his career. 'I won't trouble you for a cake.'[130]

If those provisions suggest hopes of a comfortable journey, it was usually anything but. The passage involved spending two or three months shut up in a leaky wooden cage: perhaps a month to the straits of Gibraltar, then another two through the Mediterranean putting in at Livorno, Zante, Chios or Crete along the way, then onwards to the eastern corner of the Mediterranean or northward into the Archipelago.[131] It was Dr Johnson who, in the eighteenth century, compared life aboard ship to imprisonment 'with a chance of drowning besides'. That was a comparison which had long since suggested itself to Company traders. There were the heart-stopping storms that blighted Paul's outward voyage, of course; but for the most part, travelling this way consisted, as Dudley put it, of incessant 'lying a-bed', being rocked gently into nausea. It was an experience 'more tedious to me than any jail could have been', he wrote. 'Do but imagine what a condition it is and how miserable, neither to eat, drink, sleep, nor do any thing else, but with an absolute nausea and reluctance.'[132]

By the time of the *Plymouth*'s voyage, the English had emerged unmistakably as a power to be reckoned with on the Mediterranean sea. 'This was Themistocles opinion long since, and it is true,' as John Evelyn famously opined in the 1670s and his contemporaries took for granted, 'That hee that commands the sea, commands the trade, and he that is Lord of the Trade of the world is lord of the wealth of the world.'[133] From the start, ships had indeed played a leading role in the Company's story. In first seeking to persuade Elizabeth I to send an ambassador to Constantinople to promote their trade, the Turkey merchants had assured her that, besides its commercial advantages, 'The navy and mariners shall not only hereby be maintained, but also augmented with great and serviceable ships which this traffic doth require.'[134] Elizabethan and Jacobean governments recognised well enough the financial beneficence of the new trade both for the 'commonwealth' and the state coffers. Yet the energetic construction of merchant vessels which it stimulated, in turn readily convertible to naval use, was at least as powerful an attraction.

For if the tally of its ships was regarded as a major parameter of national might in the era of the Elizabethan sea dogs, the merchant marine always dwarfed the Queen's navy. In 1600, Sir Thomas Wilson estimated the former to be twenty times the size of the latter: 'This may well be conjectured,' he wrote, 'by this, that when there was a fleet of 240 ships of war sent into Spain and 4 other fleet of merchants to the Levant, to Russe, Barbary and Bordeaux, all at one time abroad, yet should you never see the Thames betwixt London Bridge and Blackwall, 4 English miles in length, without 2 or 300 ships or vessels, besides the infinite number of men of war that then were and ever are roving abroad to the Indies and Spanish Dominions, to get purchase, as they call it, whereby a number grow rich.'[135]

These vessels were treasured, of course, as much by merchants as by the Crown. Ships first carried factors to the Levant and on them their survival of the journey would depend. Forever afterwards, ships' comings and goings would also do much to dictate the pattern of their work and their fortunes. Safe arrivals would be a cause for rejoicing. 'Sir, yesterday morning I received yours . . . communicating to me the grateful news of your safe arrival [at] Scanderoon,' wrote a typical greeting from the Aleppo factory to an English ship's captain, 'which I most heartily congratulate wishing you increase of health & prosperity.'[136] Ominous reports of bad weather, or hostile vessels sharking the waters, might

11 An English merchant ship in an eastern Mediterranean harbour. In the foreground, turbanned figures mingle with soldiers carrying the flag of St George.

arrive in advance of the vessels themselves. They would send traders into a frenzy of betting on the hasty (and often extortionate) insurance markets which sprang up on such occasions. 'The storm as happened on your departure from England', one mariner was grimly informed after he had safely put in at Scanderoon, 'occasioned several of this factory to be very uneasy & some made insurance at 8 or 10 per cent.'[137]

Marauding pirates and privateers were a constant blight on the Company's business before the Civil War, at times seriously denting its prosperity. 'The Turkish pirates do great harm to our ships in the Mediterranean; if they are not destroyed, the Levant trade will be at an end,' it was declared in 1618.[138] By then, schemes were afoot to embark on a naval campaign to clear the seas of the menace. They were supposed to be paid for collectively, both by the great trading companies and the ports most afflicted by the scourge. Stubborn passing of the financial buck between city big-wigs, however, caused the plans largely to founder. In September 1620, Sir Robert Mansell sailed with six of the King's ships and twelve armed merchantmen for Algiers, charged with stamping down the corsair menace emanating from Barbary. The mission was partly funded by a large donation from the Company. Confronted with a well-fortified harbour, it was hopelessly underpowered even so and achieved little other than temporarily to satisfy London's merchants that something was being done.[139]

A cheaper, though not entirely popular, solution to the chronic insecurity encountered on the seas was found in the convoy system. This complemented the practice already favoured by the Company of 'general' shipping, whereby merchant vessels were chartered for use by the members and prohibitive duties placed on all sailings to the Levant other than its own. Hugely valuable items, ships themselves tended to be the property of wealthy mercantile syndicates.[140] The Company would negotiate time charters with their owners and agree detailed terms for the voyage, then open a subscription book in which members might book space for their goods. Convoys for Aleppo would sail usually in February and March to arrive in the summer, those for Constantinople and Smyrna in June and July to arrive in the autumn.[141] At times they could be very large indeed: the Levant-bound convoy which left the Downs in September 1670 was made up of two warships and no less than 110 merchant vessels.[142]

General shipping offered major attractions to the Company beyond merely safeguarding cargoes from attack. It helped to regulate the flows of trade to and from the Levant, eased the collection of duties and kept shipping readily accessible to the general run of Company merchants.[143] The Company was not ashamed to admit that at least one purpose of the system was 'to *raise* the Value of *English* Manufacture abroad, and Silk at *home*'.[144] Security was more than a pretext, however, and from the mid-seventeenth century the fleets were frequently accompanied by naval escorts. This convoy system was relied on at times of maritime hazard right down the decades. After the Restoration, as the threat of piracy eased but that of Dutch, Spanish or French attacks replaced it, the same methods were relied on to minimise the hazards.

Warships aside, both the distance and danger that were features of the Company's trade had always dictated the use of large and well-armed vessels. In the earliest decades, Levant ships were far and away the mightiest in circulation. In the course of the seventeenth century they would be surpassed only by the East Indiamen. Ships which were 'stronger of bulk' and well manned were far better able to defend themselves when unable to rely on naval protection. Although somewhat smaller vessels came to be used in the eighteenth century, the Company stemmed this trend by imposing minimum tonnage requirements. In the century before, they were typically twice or even three times that minimum and armed with scores of guns, even if unscrupulous masters might equip them with 'wooden gunes or scare crows'.[145] In this era, in which boarding was a decisive element in naval combat, manpower mattered as much as gunpowder and, again partly in response to the Company's exacting regulations, crews were dozens strong and routinely ran into the hundreds.

The appearance of such colossi on Mediterranean waters, matched only by the ships of the Dutch, has sometimes been portrayed as altogether transforming the balance of power on this historic sea. The northern invaders, it is said, easily out-gunned and out-sailed all home-grown ships and soon reigned over these waters. They were even able to ply a profitable trade ferrying goods between Mediterranean ports for Ottoman subjects, who craved the safety for their wares that only westerners could provide. Pirates simply steered away from English vessels, keeping their powder dry for easier targets. English ships sailed with impunity where Spanish and Italian shipping feared to venture.[146]

This has probably been exaggerated. The English remained one power among many on the Mediterranean and they did not yet predominate.[147] The carrying trade between Mediterranean ports in particular remained a cosmopolitan affair, despite the undoubted reputation of English and Dutch shipping for invincibility. Even so, it is evident that the pashas were more willing to assert themselves on Ottoman seas than they ever were in Ottoman lands. When Sir Kenelm Digby attacked Venetian ships off Scanderoon in 1628, the gunfire shattered crockery in the town and cracked the eggs of the English consul's carrier pigeons.[148]

If Britons newly arriving might show bombast at sea, though, they would soon find that doing business ashore called for them to adapt to the mores of an Islamic society and submit to its Ottoman masters.

3

People of the Book

❖

Expats

The *Khan al-Gumruk* is little changed from the place that John Verney found when he arrived there in July 1662. Then, as now, the ground floor served for warehouses, filled with 'fine cloth in odd colours, as orange, haire, lead, gold, strawe, rose, blacke, brimstone, olive, white willow green, which are now esteemed here & much worne'.[1] So they are today, though the fabrics once supplied by English counties will likely have been spun in Korea. The consul and many of Aleppo's Englishmen were arrayed across the courtyard, primed to greet him as the entourage set down. Quickly John's would have been eyes drawn upwards, to where (as one contemporary visitor recorded) 'the upper story [was] fitted up for their dwellings, by building between the pillars of the colonnade, which forms a long corridor; opening on which are a number of rooms, so that they much resemble cloisters'.[2] In time, he would come to know these diminutive homes well. They were comfortable enough inside, richly adorned if hardly capacious. New arrivals would find themselves besieged with offers of beds and furniture to deck them out, though experienced hands warned of the money that might be squandered this way. 'When I was there', Montagu North boasted, 'I had nothing but a pintado nailed about my bed and curtains tied back and everything as cheap as is possible.'[3] In summer, it had to be borne in mind, the indoors would be forsaken altogether, the pashas 'lying in the open air on the tops of our houses' in a bid to stay cool.[4]

John was led into the English consular house, in the midst of ambitious refurbishment by its occupant.[5] Taking up one whole side of the khan and boasting a long terrace overlooking the courtyard, this was

12 The entrance to the sixteenth-century *Khan al-Gumruk* as it appears today.

where newcomers would often be put up for the night.[6] Inside, he caught his first glimpse of the 'stately roome' that furnished the English with their chapel, Henry Maundrell's main haunt a few decades later.[7] Blithely mixing the sacred with the profane, another room of the house played host to the consul's sumptuous entertainments.

Contemporaries struggled to decide whether the factory's architecture, not to mention its way of life, should best be described as 'academical', military (for, to some minds, the khans resembled 'small forts') or monastic. 'They so much resemble the cells of a convent,' one visitor thought of the rooms, 'that I could not help fancying myself immured while I tarried in town, though I was always sure of enjoying such cheerful and agreeable conversation as is not to be found in a cloister.'[8] Either way, it seemed undeniably hermetic. After dark it was almost literally so: its iron gates, guarded by porters and each surmounted by a 'massy and strong portcullis', would be 'shut up . . . after the manner of colleges'. To get in or out after that, one would have to bribe the porters; and even that by itself achieved little, since beyond lay yet more locked gates, it seeming that 'every street, lane and alley' had one. 'It sometimes happens,' one account records, 'that the consuls, or other gentlemen of the frank* nations, after spending an evening out, have four or five gates to be opened for them before they get home.'[9] Within a few hours of arriving after the exhausting journey, then, John would be all but imprisoned here.

Aptly enough, the daily routine that he witnessed unfold was a tightly disciplined affair. Each morning would begin with communion, at which, Maundrell wrote years later, 'I am sure to have always a devout, a regular, and full congregation'. Beyond that were 'set times for business, meals, and recreations'.[10] The pace of work could be gruelling in busy trading periods. Its rhythms, dictated by the silk harvest and the comings and goings of ships, typically reached their most intense in the autumn. Much of the rest of the time, though, would be spent at study or leisure; and the summer, 'being commonly a season of little business', was given over almost entirely to relaxation.[11]

Spare hours were whiled away partly in reading and writing. 'The multitude of Books is one reason why I have so few,' wrote one of the Aleppo chaplains, for 'the report of a great Library here, kept me from

---

* The term 'frank' was used to refer collectively to the foreign Christians resident in the Ottoman Empire, primarily French, Italian and Dutch as well as English.

bringing any along with me'.[12] Amongst the inventories of factors' estates are to be found books of theology, history and literature.[13] John's father sent him out armed with such wholesome tomes as Taylor's *Holy Living and Dying*, Bishop Andrews' *Devotions*, and Gerard's *Meditation*. At least by the eighteenth century, though, less salubrious fare seems also to have abounded.[14] The pashas were keen to stay well apprised of the run of events in England, not least because high politics could still impact rather directly on their lives in the field. In 1705, the factory took subscriptions through a London agent for 'the London Gazettes, the Postmen, the Votes of Parliament, and the Sessions Papers twice every week' (as for 'the Review, or Observator', the consul recorded in a pronouncement that betrays what a serious-minded lot at least some of them were, 'they are such trifling Papers, that it is not worth the trouble to make them take so long a journey').[15] They read not only newspapers, but accounts of current affairs penned by friends and business contacts back home. 'You cannot certainly have forgot how grateful letters are to us, who live at this distance from our native country', one Aleppo trader pressed a retired colleague.[16]

Other cultural pursuits also found a prominent place. Musical instruments and libraries of musical works, like books, would commonly feature amongst traders' possessions. John Sanderson first felt the effects of the fever that very nearly killed him shortly after his arrival at Syrian Tripoli when he 'soncke downe upon a lute, that stode at the corner of my bourd, and broke it all in peces'.[17] An anonymous letter dating from 1699 describes another English trader's delight at making the acquaintance of Europeans in Aleppo who seemed 'to love musick as much as I do' – one a Dutchman and the other a German, both of whom had 'very good hands upon the Violin'. 'I give you my heart thankes for the case of providing my little Organ,' he adds, 'which will be now doubley welcome . . . I had them last week with me above 2 houres.'[18] John Verney brought with him to the factory his much-treasured viol, and his first letter home from Aleppo asks for a new bridge (the old one had been broken on the voyage) and spare strings: 'at least 5 Trebles, 4 seconds, 3 thirds, 1 fourth, 1 fifth, and 1 sixth'.[19] Robert Bargrave, likewise, kept friends and colleagues entertained with the performance of plays and masques: these would, as he wrote of several performances in Constantinople, always be greeted with 'the reward of great Applause'.[20] Bargrave also composed, writing songs to mark births, deaths and marriages, not to mention his own release from

13 Portrait of Henry Lannoy Hunter, an Aleppo consul in the early eighteenth century, portrayed in oriental dress and showing off the fruits of a successful hunt.

brief captivity in Smyrna ('Fortunes wheele is runn about, & has kindly turnd us out', it began).

There was plenty of sport, too. 'Bowles is a fine recreation,' one enthused, 'and wee have a very good ally here.'[21] In the winter there would be hunting 'in the most delightful campaign twice a week'.[22] The factory kept its own pack of hounds and most factors would own a horse. 'The English', a Dutch visitor wrote, 'have a pleasant way of Hunting with their Greyhounds . . . It begins a little out of Town, and ends about a League from thence, at a certain Hill which they call the *Green-hill*; upon which, when the Chase is ended they Dine under a great Tent which they bring with them. Every Person is obliged to bring his own Provision and Wine, and all being put together they make themselves merry after the sport is over.'[23] Nathaniel Harley kept a particularly extensive array of animals to feed his passion for hunting: 'Now that I have despatched away my horses, my dogs, and my hawks,' he wrote, shortly before returning to England, 'you may be sure I shall not long remain here.'[24] The lushness of the surrounding countryside ensured that there was 'plenty of game' to be had: 'quails, partridges . . . woodcocks and snipes', not to mention hares and boar.[25]

In the summer, the pashas would go just as often to 'divert ourselves under our tents, with bowling, and other exercises'. Another Englishman gave a fuller description of one such excursion:

This morning early (as it is the custom all summer longe) at the least 40 of the English, with his worship the Consull, rod out of the cytty about 4 miles to the Greene Platt, a fine vally by a river side, to recreate them selves. Where a princely tent was pitched; and wee had severall pastimes and sports, as duck-hunting, fishing, shooting, handball, krickett . . . and then a noble dinner brought thither, with great plenty of all sorts of wines, punch and lemonades; and at 6 wee returne all home in good order, but soundly tyrde and weary.[26]

But the pretext of sport was not always required to unleash bouts of communal gluttony. On New Year's Day 1676, the chaplain to the Smyrna factory preached on the text: 'It is always good to give thanks'; then 'the congregation adjourned to the dining room for a feast of "Turkye Woodcocke Francolins wild boare goose ducke mince pye plum broth", and after a card session supped on "mince meate severall wines" '.[27] Throughout the summer months it was the custom to dine under tents every Saturday, 'on some green spot on the banks of the river'. On such occasions, one traveller recorded, 'three or more gentlemen form a party, each, in his turn, sending the provision and liquors for one day, which is dressed on the spot under a small tent, called a cook's tent: sometimes there are five or six such tents pitched'.[28] Visitors to the Aleppo factory were perennially impressed by the feasting in which they would be invited to join, even if the Company's bean-counters were less enthused.[29]

The factors' culinary ambitions called for a taxing quest to source ingredients absent from the eastern Mediterranean market. One trader wrote home in 1725 to say that 'while he appreciated the shipment of bacon, tea, cider and beer which had recently arrived, he still missed butter and cheese'.[30] The arrival of a European ship would prompt a stream of demands from Aleppo to Scanderoon, where the Company's resident official might be instructed to get hold of 'the best butter good or none, & a cheese or two' (cheeses, John was somehow aware even before he left London, were held in 'great esteem' in Aleppo), perhaps also a barrel of oranges or of beef, and dispatch it east across the hills.[31] This stretch of the Mediterranean coast was also the source of their seafood. 'I would entreat you if there be any salmon, herrings, salt-fish, or other Lenten fare to be found,' an Aleppo consul wrote in a fairly typical entreaty, 'buy me what you think may be necessary for my family, and send it me by first caravan . . .'[32] Plates of fresh fish were regularly sent up from the coast as gifts to traders further inland, their couriers racing against the rot that descended rapidly in the heat and which was only imperfectly warded off by the ice brought down from the mountain-tops and sold amidst the souk's cool.

The greatest deal of effort, though, was reserved for keeping a well-stocked cellar. In Smyrna the non-Muslim communities were usually allowed to keep taverns, 'open all Hours, Day and Night'.[33] At least one was run by an Englishman, and much frequented by sailors disembarking from Company ships.[34] Drinking establishments similarly abounded in Galata: the Ottoman traveller Evliya Celebi (famed for his love of exaggeration) claimed in the late 1600s that there were 'two hundred taverns and wine booths [there] where the infidels divert themselves with music and drinking'.[35] In Aleppo, a greater discretion was called for and drinking seems to have been confined to the *Khan al-Gumruk* and Christian merchants' dwellings. Maintaining a constant supply demanded plenty of forward-planning, for it relied on imports from the Mediterranean islands, perhaps even all the way from home. 'My stock of Cyprus wine is quite out,' complained the consul one year, 'so if you don't stand my friend, and send me a supply, I shall be utterly spoiled for a Huntsman this winter.'[36] 'I understand Captain Ramsey had brought down some good French Brandy,' he was writing in desperation a few months later. 'If you can have it at a reasonable price, buy me 20 Gallons.' The arrival of an English ship at Scanderoon would foretell the appearance of barrels of beer at the factory within a day or two and scenes of drunken merriment.

With its hunting, cricket, roast pork and beer-swilling, this little community of expats at times seemed to display a 'Britishness' that was precocious for its times. There was much about the social life of the factory that could only be described as self-contained. Visitors from overseas were scarce. People generally came here for professional reasons rather than pleasure, and they expected their stays to be lengthy ones: this was, for most, simply too remote a spot for casual visits to be contemplated. Winchilsea was very much the exception when, long into his retirement, he slogged all the way back to Smyrna to see his old protégé, Paul Rycaut. Rarely was Aleppo a viable detour for those voyaging further east on business. 'The distance of the Port of Scanderoon is an obstacle to many of the sea faring people [en route to other destinations in the Mediterranean world] undertaking the journey to Aleppo,' was a complaint in the later eighteenth century, 'and unless it be a few gentlemen who cross the Desert, in their way from India, the English seldom have the pleasure of being visited either by their countrymen, or by other European travellers.'[37] In the seventeenth century, the journey to or from the Indian subcontinent was rarely undertaken by this route. The odd Briton making the pilgrimage to the Holy Land would spend a few nights in the factory during the seventeenth century. The injection of fresh blood to its diminutive society, though, relied almost wholly on the periodical arrival of apprentice factors, or traders relocating from elsewhere in the Ottoman lands.

If new arrivals were intermittent, death brought about a steady attrition in the ranks of those already here. Disease loomed large in daily life. Aleppo even had its own ailment: ' 'Tis commonly call'd *Il mal d'Aleppo*,' the Royal Society was informed in a scientific paper on the subject published in the later seventeenth century, 'and appears to be in the skin a small pustula or wheal, hard and red, the head whereof is scarce bigger at the beginning than the point of a pin; afterwards growing bigger, and being nourisht by 5 or 6 little roots or fibres, it goes on to its height for the space of about 6 months.'[38] It sometimes appeared on sufferers' arms or legs, but just as often – and more troublesome – it would spring up on their faces. This 'sort of Itch', one visitor thought, should be blamed on something in the town's air.[39] Others were convinced the problem lay in the water, which 'makes strangers, who drink of it, break out in blotches . . . nor is there any remedy found against it'.[40] Either way, it was notoriously hard to shake off and 'those that have a Spice of a Hectick Fever, or some such like Distemper, when they come to *Aleppo* generally dye of it in a short time'.[41] In 1669, disease claimed ten members of the factory within the space of a few months.[42] Three decades later, Henry Maundrell caught the 'small pox & purples', and was dead within the week.[43]

It was not unusual in summer for the factory to be abandoned altogether, traders taking to the hills to avoid an outbreak of plague, though the flight usually came too late to save some ill-fated English soul. 'I arrived in these mountains 4 days since, in Company of about 20 of our nation,' wrote the consul from the Bylan mountains in June 1705. 'We being forct to leave Aleppo on account of the Plague, which began to grow hot there, and those who remain behind, are shut up in their Houses, and permit no body to come near them, for fear of the infection.'[44] That particular year, the plague was so 'very hot in Aleppo . . . that not only the Christians, and Jews are fled to avoid it, but also several of the chief Turks, are gone to their gardens, and country houses, which is a thing I never yet knew in Turkey'.[45] Only the brave or foolhardy remained in the factory: they would lock themselves in and try to carry on business 'by means of a bell and trustie servants'.[46] They tried to inoculate themselves with alcohol: 'it is certain they that drank the hardest escaped best'.[47] The rest might camp outside the town for many weeks as they waited for the danger to pass. 'We live here under tents, after the manner of the old Patriarchs, with our flocks, and herds about us,' one trader described, 'and want nothing to make the scene complete but some Sarahs & Rebeccas to console us in our retirement.'[48]

The pashas' society was indeed an overwhelmingly male one. 'The female society is very confined,' it was noted later in the century, 'for the native Christian ladies know no other language than Arabic and only a few of the *Mezza Razza* speak French.'[49] The Company placed formal restrictions on bringing wives and families. The general expectation was for the Levant merchant to sustain bachelorhood until he had made his fortune, then marry upon his return. Sir John Finch wrote to recommend a 'Mr Berchen, an Aleppo merchant, and son to Captain Berchen, an eminent member of the Levant Company . . . He will make an excellent good husband I dare say; if you know any pretty young lady you could wish well disposed of, you cannot place her better.'[50] The successful factor would represent an eligible match, particularly if he could also boast gentry stock.

There are signs that, like many of the Company's strictures, the bar on bringing wives to the Levant was not universally observed.[51] A candidate for the post of Factor Marine at Scanderoon was passed over on this score early in the eighteenth century and in the same era a Treasurer lost his post for the same reason.[52] In 1703 a General Court of the Company complained of the 'unlawful keeping of women at Smyrna' and in 1664 ordered that 'such women as remained at Smyrna without husbands' were to be removed.[53]

High officials were always allowed a greater leeway. Sir Thomas Bendish brought his wife and children with him on his embassy: she apparently delighted all with her 'obliging carriage' and presided over an open table at the English palace in Galata where the embassy party resided.[54] Winchilsea was also accompanied by his wife on his embassy, until she suffered a miscarriage whilst in Constantinople and he reluctantly arranged for her return home. He would, he wrote, 'rather be deprived of her for a time, than to run any more the hazard to lose her for ever.[55] His children had remained in England, causing acute paternal guilt when his elder son formed an inappropriate liaison in his late teens. (Assured by his son that he had not 'lived as man and wife', the ambassador wrote a flurry of letters from Constantinople to the great and good in London trying to have the marriage annulled.) Early in the eighteenth century, Edward Wortley Montagu was accompanied on his embassy by Lady Mary. A decade later, the Earl of Kinnoull was informed by the secretary of state that the Company had 'taken umbrage at some women that they alledge are gone in the same ship as you to Constantinople' on his appointment as ambassador.[56] 'All the Women that I brought here with me', Kinnoull defended himself improbably, 'are servants – to clean my house & wash my Linnen and they are turn'd so idle here that I resolved to Send them all back before I recd. Yr. Graces letter.'[57]

Kinnoull's wife stayed in England, but his secretary brought his own.[58] Robert Bargrave was similarly accompanied on the *Plymouth* by his wife, who was left distraught at his death along the way. Aleppo consuls also tended to be accompanied by their wives from the eighteenth century onwards.[59] Nathaniel Harley reported from Aleppo in 1717 that 'our consuless has brought with her a great many pretty children, and is ready to lie in of another'. They were, he wrote:

> . . . a great diversion to me; scarce a day that I spend less than two or three hours in the nursery. It was a bold undertaking to venture upon so long a voyage with so many small children, but they are all come safe, though most of them had the measles aboard ship.[60]

On the other hand, local liaisons were regarded, at least publicly, as being strictly off limits. 'Many Evils have ensued upon the marriage of Englishmen with the Subjects of the Grand Signior,' departing ambassadors would be informed by the Company. 'We therefore pray your Lordship to discourage and discountenance that practice, it being prejudicial to themselves as well as to the public.'[61] The taboo seemed to be amply justified by the infamous saga which occurred after the death of one pasha who breached it in the late seventeenth century.

By the time that he succumbed to a fever at the age of fifty-two, Samuel Pentlow had spent long enough in Smyrna to outlive all notions of home, or so his fellow countrymen thought. For most of his life, there had been nothing very remarkable about the man.[62] But in his final years he found himself a wife, a 'Greek woman of mean extraction'; and that made him, as Sir John Finch pointed out, 'the onely man since our Trade into Turkey that ever married Here, and was worth any thing'.[63] Pentlow was, in truth, worth a lot. In the course of three decades in the eastern Mediterranean, he had amassed 'very considerable Riches', to add to an estate in Northamptonshire left him by his father. Having married abroad, though, it never occurred to him to take the conventional path of returning westward and living out the remainder of his days in landed comfort. There lay the nub of the problem when he came to die.

The other cause of the Pentlow affair was a law 'never heard of before, and peradventure will never be again'. That law, as Paul Rycaut paraphrased it years later, insisted that 'whosoever marries a Woman that was a Subject to the Grand Seignior, did by virtue of such a Match make himself a Subject to the Grand Seignior also'. The capitulations guaranteed – after a manner, at least – that Britons' fortunes would not be tampered with. As an Ottoman subject by virtue of his marriage, though, Pentlow's property would be ceded to the sultan when he died. Other foreigners, with much less to lose, escaped the force of this decree simply by hiding what wealth they had amassed outside the sultan's grasp. Pentlow failed to do this and no sooner had he drawn his last breath than Ottoman officials were despatched to seize the whole of his abundant estate. 'Sorry Sam a Christian Subject of ours being now dead,' as an Ottoman imperial command still sitting among the papers of the Company peremptorily states, 'his money, goods & estate, whatever it bee, wee doe confiscate.'[64]

When his two English executors, ever loyal to their departed friend, tried to stand in the way of the Turks, they were 'carried away immediately, and threaten'd with the Gallies, the Rack, the Wheel, and other Tortures', before being flung into prison, chained to a post with iron collars about their necks and manacles on their hands. To worsen their plight, the Ottoman officials had made a point of grossly overvaluing Pentlow's property. After 'a thousand Menaces of further Punishment', they extracted from the two Englishmen a promise to stump up the whole ninety-thousand dollars that it was supposedly worth in return for release from gaol. In the hurry to raise this money, the pair sold off Pentlow's goods too cheaply, leaving them with a shortfall of many thousands. Unable or unwilling to make up the difference, they were sent straight back behind bars, where they languished miserably for the next six months. In the meantime, an Ottoman official 'broke open the warehouses & sold all the goods, at his own prices, most of them to himself'.[65] The community of English merchants in Smyrna, deeply disturbed at the precedent this set, were left fulminating for months afterwards. Even a century later, marrying locally even to a 'Frank' would invoke fears of hard-won estates 'falling into the hands of the Turks'.[66]

The Company's prohibitory policy served, if nothing else, to ensure that any sexual relationships with Ottoman subjects were kept quiet. Nonetheless, the pashas' correspondence provides hints that the official rule may have been broken quite often. Paul Rycaut's brother James was forced to return home after being caught in a compromising situation with a local woman. When John Lethieullier departed for England, the Aleppo consul wished that he would find there 'a virtuous, and rich spouse, who may fix your rambling temper, and convince you by experience, that the charms of an English lady, do much surpass those of Miss Modesty at Scanderoon, or any of your Scio Madams'.[67] A London merchant wrote in the same era of a factor who had fled: 'He proved of the most rascally villains, that ever God let live, for besides the cardinal virtues of gaming, and drinking, he had so far intrigued himself with women, that it was not safe for him to stay longer here.'[68]

Behaviour of this sort was always a matter of deep concern to principals and Company big-wigs alike. In theory, the pashas were subjected to tight structures of discipline whilst in the Levant. The factories outside Constantinople were each presided over by a consul, appointed usually from an old hand amongst the factors, or from the ranks of career officials like Paul Rycaut. It was their job to enforce the instructions of the Company, communicated in a steady volley of letters issuing from London, which would be read out aloud to the assembled members of the factory. These officials were also charged with settling routine disputes between factors, the more serious matters being sent up to Constantinople to be dealt with by the ambassador. Higher up the chain of command, the ambassador himself possessed, at least on paper, an absolute authority over his charges. Both consuls and ambassadors had the power to imprison Britons, as well as to fine them. In cases of grave wrongdoing, they might despatch them home.[69]

Many of the Company's regulations imposed in this way were narrowly concerned with business matters. Yet, like the strictures on sexual relationships, they also extended to the pashas' moral welfare. 'If you shall find any of our Factors or others of the English Nation to be notoriously addicted to Gaming, Drinking, Whoreing, or any other licentious course of life, to the dishonour of God, the scandal of our Religion and Nation, their principalls' damage, and the ill example of others,' the Company instructed its ambassadors, 'wee doe straitly require and recommend to you to endeavour to reclaim them by your good admonitions or, finding them incorrigible, to give us speedy notice of such persons to the end some other course may be taken with them.'[70] The Company's concern for this aspect of their lives found expression, most obviously, in the practice of attaching chaplains to the Aleppo, Constantinople and Smyrna factories. Given the Company's notorious frugality, this represented a major outlay, but its necessity was not questioned. Soon after arriving in Constantinople as ambassador, Sir Thomas Bendish proclaimed that services at the factory there were henceforth to be held twice on every Sabbath, whilst a fine would be payable by anyone absent in the morning service 'longer than a psalm is singing'. For good measure, he imposed other penalties for blasphemy and swearing.[71]

Such pious social codes betrayed the puritanical bent of the times, whose influence extended widely into the regulation of professional life. Yet they also served a function that was rather special to the circumstances of this trade. Placing heavy reliance on factors charged with executing deals on behalf of principals located many months' sailing away, honesty was essential to its successful functioning. Since they traded in small-scale units, individual acts of duplicity could spell ruin at a stroke for all members of a firm. Trust was accordingly a treasured commodity.[72] Moreover, it was widely believed – and with some justification – that the general orderliness of the Company's operations in the Levant could do much to determine their commercial fortunes. As the ill-success of the French trade in the earlier seventeenth century seemed to show, infighting amongst factors quickly sapped profits and might make a mockery of the collective position of a 'nation' within Ottoman society.

It was such assumptions which recommended the tight-knit kinship networks permeating the Levant trade. More than that, though, they encouraged the streak of clubbishness and machismo so evident a feature of their social world. Hearty sports and earnest prayer spoke of a moral wholesomeness that, in the eyes of London principals, boded well for their probity as men of business. Sir Thomas Bendish's assault on the dissipation which he claimed to find at the Constantinople factory is a case in point. It extended not just to his demands that factors attend religious worship, but to his creation of a bowling green in the garden of his ambassadorial palace, intended to lure them away from gambling and other suspect pastimes. From London, and even from the embassy in Constantinople, the official policy of the Company was to encourage amongst the pashas a mode of living in the Levant that was as clean as it was self-contained.

Wilde Beasts of Mankind

That these men lived and traded in the Islamic domain of the Ottomans, of course, was seen to create an especial reason to fear for their spiritual well-being. Much of what could be read in English print at the time about the 'Turks' subjected them to an elementally crude chorus of bigotry. They were said to be a 'rude and barbarous' cabal of Scythians; a race, as another polemicist proclaimed, 'no better than dogs'; according to yet another, 'the wilde beasts of mankind'.[73] Aleppo's chaplains were numbered amongst those keen to shore up this seam of vituperation. Charles Robson, the very first chaplain to the factory, set the tone in 1628 in his *Newes from Aleppo, A Letter*. Writing about the use of the Aleppo aqueduct, he described how the water was either 'fetched for private uses, or forct to wash the stinking feet of the profane Turke before they enter into their bawling devotion'. Another chaplain, William Biddulph, was just as scathing, lamenting: 'Oh how happie are you in England if you knew your own happinesse! . . . if they were here in this heathen Countrie, they would know what it is to live in a Christian common wealth, under the government of a godly king, who ruleth by law and not by lust; where there is plenty and peace, and preaching of the Gospell.'[74] Henry Maundrell followed suit. 'In a word,' he wrote of the locals, 'lust, arrogance, covetousness, and the most exquisite hypocrisy compleat their character.'[75]

For such men, it was the Islamic faith, that 'brood of most lewd and impudent cozenage', which underpinned much of the animosity.[76] 'The basis of this government is the religion,' it could be said, 'which is so closely connected with the sovereign power, that it is impossible for the one to subsist without the assistance of the other.'[77] The ethnic and religious pluralism of the Ottoman realm meant that the simple equations routinely drawn between 'Ottoman', 'Muslim' and 'Turk' were misplaced. So far as the ordinary run of seventeenth-century Englishmen were concerned, though, 'Turk' and 'Muslim' were near-synonymous: in the contemporary vernacular, to convert to Islam was to 'turn Turk'. And when Englishmen thought of Islam, they would have thought primarily of 'Turks', only secondarily the Moors of the Barbary states; the rest of the Islamic world barely registered at this stage. Contemporary works like Fuller's *Historie of the Holy War* traced an essential continuity, moreover, between the Saracens and the Ottomans: the important aspect of both, at least in the minds of religious polemicists, was to ensure that the crescent and not the cross prevailed over the Holy Land.

Many accounts of Ottoman lands were accordingly told like Christian parables, struggling to accept the grim reality of these holy places having fallen into infidel hands. As one clergyman falsely apologised, 'if the thread of a Churchman' ran through his pages, his readers might thereby 'the more thankfully . . . reflect upon that most blessed and merciful providence' which had 'cast [their] lot in Christendom'.[78] The disturbing pace of the Muslim advance into the *dār al-harb* was itself often accorded a theological rationale. The early-modern mind detected in it (somewhat perverse though the logic may seem) evidence of the workings of God, 'punishing by this violent and wicked sect the sinful divisions of Christians'.[79] The Eastern Church was singled out for blame: as an early biographer of Muhammad put it, this Church 'having wearied the . . . long-suffering of God' by turning his 'Holy Religion into a Firebrand of Hell for Contention', he 'raised up the Saracens to be the Instruments of his Wrath to punish them for it'.[80]

Just as power on the world stage seemed the outstanding facet of the Ottomans, so it seemed of Islam itself. The success of Turkish arms provided a compelling reason to take an interest in the faith: the 'port it bears in the world', a sermon of the time recognised, demanded at least its 'consideration'.[81] The translator of a mid-seventeenth-century English Koran (out of butchered French rather than the Arabic original) made much of this in his preface. Since the Turks' territories border upon the dominions of Christendom, he argued, inevitably there had been 'continual wars, and will be still between us'. Therefore it concerned every Christian 'who makes conscience of his ways' to 'examine the cause, and to look into the grounds of this war . . . which cannot be known but by reading the Alcoran'. In this book, he added, 'we see the enemies of the Cross of Christ' and 'so many passages . . . repugnant to, and destructive of Christian religion', that Christian Princes were bound to oppose its believers.[82]

In a time of continued deference to authority, many contemporaries were content to limit their 'consideration' to the recycling of a bigoted medieval inheritance, much of it the product of the Crusades; indeed, the polemical style of this inheritance was well suited to the fighting purposes to which it was still often put.[83] The prime focus was on denigrating Muhammad himself, 'that famous imposter and seducer of the Arabians or Saracens . . . and inventor of the Alcoran and laws of that superstitious faction'.[84] The Prophet was said to be a person 'of no honest or honourable qualities', but having 'all the marks of an impostor; rebellious and perfidious, inhuman and cruel, lewd and lascivious'.[85] His motive was, so the conventional narrative went, the wholly base one of attaining political power and satisfying his lusts besides; and as for the '*Scheme* of that *Imposture*' by which he sought to achieve this, doctrinally it was described as a 'medley made up of *Judaism*, the several *Heresies* of the *Christians* then in the *East*, and the old *Pagan* Rites of the *Arabs*, with an indulgence to all Sensual Delights'.[86] Another contemporary put all this much more pithily: Islam was the 'scumme of Judaisme and Paganisme sod together, and here and there strewed over with a spice of Christianity'.[87] That this was a faith evincing the odd virtue its denigrators might be prepared to admit, tolerance and charity prominent among them. But these were merely 'daintie fruits growing out of a *Dung-hill*'.[88]

The medieval legends concerning Muhammad's deceptive ways also continued to have wide circulation. He was supposed, for instance, to suffer from epilepsy: 'Whenever this fit was upon him, he pretended it to be a *Trance*, and that then the *Angel Gabriel* was come from *God* with some new *Revelations* unto him'.[89] In the same vein, it was said that Muhammad had persuaded his followers that he 'had daily instructions from the holy Ghost' by training a dove to 'feed in his eare'.[90] However much Muhammad himself was so defamed, though, the painful fact of Islam's advance had to be confronted (all the more so since it was recognised as having 'chiefly seised on those Regions, where Christianitie in ancient time most flourished, both in Afrike and Asia, and partly in Europe').[91] As one account mused, it 'may justly seem admirable how that senseless religion should gain so much ground on Christianity'.[92]

How could its success possibly be explained in a (Christian) God-centred universe? One favoured theory we have already encountered: that its advance was no more than the circuitous playing out of God's will, his means of punishing wayward Christians. Other theories were put forward, though. The sheer skill, for instance, of this imposture's perpetrator was stressed, 'whose juggling tricks have so bewitched these infidels'.[93] In finding echoes of the supposed gullibility of their ancestors, hostile Britons could also find a stick with which to beat present-day Muslims. By the Turks' worship of saints and dervishes, a contemporary wrote, one 'may see how the Devill doth delude them still as hee did their Forefathers at the first by Mahomet's Machiavellian devices'.[94] Another oft-cited explanation for Islam's expansion was 'the sensuall libertie allowed by it'.[95] For the 'Moors' (by which this writer meant the inhabitants of seventh-century Arabia), it was claimed that 'nothing was more acceptable, than to have the indulgence of their vile affections to be made an article of their religion'.[96]

Again, this accorded with conceptions of contemporary Muslims, not least the supposed sexual predilections of the Turks. Turkish women were portrayed as louche and lascivious. Robert Withers' *The Grand Signior's Seraglio* typified a fascination with the Harem, full of 'young, lusty, lascivious wenches', and its 'carnal commerce with the King'.[97] On the other hand, women's treatment at the hands of Turkish men provided another indictment of their tyrannical polity: 'The Turks do not believe that women go to Heaven, and hardly account them rational creatures', complained Thévenot, a writer much read in Restoration London.[98] As for the efficacy of all this for proselytising the faith, it was 'no wonder if they get fish enough, that use that bait'.[99]

Yet none of these explanations quite solved the problem of those Christians who had been converted to the faith following Islamic invasions. Too much denigration of such people would embarrass by their one-time allegiance to Christianity. It was in this context that Islam was most often portrayed as the 'religion of the sword'. The advance of Islam was sometimes portrayed as comprising two stages: first, it caught on by playing to the base urges of a primitive people; then, 'being furnished with such champions', it 'diffused itself by rage and terror of arms, convincing men's minds only by the sword, and using no other arguments but blows'.[100] And yet, the suggestion had to be maintained that the Muslims did engage in religious coercion, so that historical accounts were peppered with allegations of atrocities. Thus an early biographer of Muhammad furnished this emotive description of what the Muslims' 'rage and terror of arms' might entail for its Christian victims:

> And [the Saracens] having fixed that Tyranny over them, which hath ever since afflicted those Parts of the World, turning everywhere their Churches into Mosques, and their Worship into a horrid Superstition; and instead of that Holy Religion which they had thus abused, forced on them that abominable Imposture of Mahometanism, which dictating War, Bloodshed and Violence in matters of Religion, as one of its chiefest Virtues . . . [Christians] were soon brought by the Sword at their throats to give up the whole in compliance to the pleasure of a Barbarous and Savage Conqueror.[101]

Schooled in rhetoric of that kind, it is hardly surprising to find Henry Maundrell insisting that 'as for our living amongst [the Turks], it is with all possible quiet and safety'. He was, like many, keenly aware of the spiritual unease of being 'a poor Christian in a heathen land'. On the journey out to Aleppo, he bored his companions by insistently saying prayers twice a day, singing them a daily psalm and preaching a sermon every Sunday.[102] In their bolder moments, providential Protestants liked to fantasise about recapturing these biblical lands from their Muslim masters. To live in the Middle East brought constant reminders of what a forlorn hope that was. 'Who can expect ever to see these holy places rescued from the hands of infidels?' Maundrell would ask wistfully on glimpsing Jerusalem.[103]

Yet there was an even more pressing concern for an English chaplain in Aleppo in this period: the spectre of his co-religionists and countrymen 'turning Turk'. If, as Maundrell claimed, the Turks were 'incredibly conceited of their own religion, and contemptuous of that of others', there were plenty of Christians who appreciated its attractions, and conversions to Islam occurred on a significant scale during the early-modern period.[104] For all the vitriol directed against Islam in print, in practice it was as frightening for its sheer allure. Some of these 'renegadoes', as a traveller earlier in the century put it, were the sort 'whom hard usage, and captivity brings in, rather than any ambition, or disgust at home'; altogether more disturbing, though, were the 'Atheists, who left our cause for the *Turkish* as the more thriving in the World'.[105] John Sanderson goes so far in his diary as to name names of those who had succumbed: 'Memorandum:' he wrote, 'that many Englishmen, old and young, have in my remembrance turned Turkes, as Benjamin Bishop, George Butler, John Ambrose, and others'.[106] Another Englishman came upon the circumcision ceremony of such converts in the same period: 'There were at least 200 proselytes made in these 13 days,' he wrote. 'It is our shame, for I believe all Europe have not gained so many Turkes to us these 200 yeares'.[107]

Charged with warding off a rival religion, whose temptations to the pashas proved real, perhaps the only viable response was for the chaplains to try to insulate their flock from the wider Ottoman world. 'Our delights are among ourselves;' Maundrell protested of daily life in the factory, 'and here being more than forty of us, we never want a most friendly and pleasant conversation'.[108] Yet his counterpart in Smyrna took a rather different view of his congregation: they were, he wrote, 'single men of uncontrolled liberty and violent inclinations accustomed to getting and bred up in the arts of gain'.[109] If tending a flock of Christian souls was one thing, the realities of trading in the midst of this souk were quite another.

Pax Ottomana

At the eastern corner of the Mediterranean, two worlds collided and their wandering nomads came to meet. Beyond its hectic and historic stretch of sea was a realm of Anatolian fecundity; eastward of that, one of sand and heat, stretching across the silken riches of Persia to embrace those of the Indies. To its west was one of salt water and soaking timber, encompassing the trade routes to the Italian city-states and, onward into the Atlantic, towards the emerging wealth of northern Europe. The bustling towns creased between these two great expanses gathered people and their wares from all ends of the earth. It is, at root, that broad-brush geography which provides a major clue to the significance of Middle Eastern emporia for the English economy during the period of concern for this book. This was the geography, moreover, which fashioned the extraordinarily heterogeneous culture of the Ottoman 'shared world' into which the pashas found entry in places like Aleppo.[110]

The city drew traders, whether from east or west, in much the same manner. Even the experience of journeying towards it from their opposing poles might not have been very different. 'Those that travel these [Arabian] Deserts must carry Provisions with them and direct their Course by the stars', declared an English map of the 'Turkish Empire' drawn up in the early eighteenth century. 'A Country that has neither Men, Beasts, Birds, Trees, Grass nor Pasture, and not any thing but sands and rocky mountains.' The intention was to conjure up something exotic and faintly Biblical for its London purchasers. Save for those last few words, though, it might as easily have described a north-western maritime world that was all too familiar to the pashas.

Like that of the first Islamic state, the Ottoman expansion had from its earliest decades brought large numbers of adherents to other religions within its borders.[111] Whilst Islamic law was uncompromising in its stance toward polytheistic faiths, it was fairly accommodating of fellow 'people of the book' – that is to say, Jews and Christians. The actual practice of toleration by Islamic polities varied greatly across the ages and continents, of course, but its theory was fairly clear, if subject to differing interpretation. So long as they accepted the political authority of the Islamic state, such non-believers – the *dhimmi*, as they were called – were allowed not only to practise their faith, but to participate with relatively little interference in its economic and social life. This indulgence came at a price beyond mere allegiance, in particular in the form of the *jizya*, the head tax levied only on non-Muslims. The price of religious freedom and protection was political submission.[112] Yet if these infidel lambs were to be fleeced, they were emphatically not to be slaughtered.

Some Islamic societies of past times (one thinks, especially, of Moorish Spain) have been painted as utopias of religious pluralism. That, perhaps, is too generous, if judged through the prism of modern liberalism. According tolerance to non-Muslims did not mean according them equality: the *dhimmi* were, through symbolic burdens and casual discrimination, left in no doubt of their inferior status in all these contexts. By the standards of western Christendom in early-modern times, even so, where apostasy might prompt roasting alive, mass expulsion or periodic pogrom, this Islamic doctrinal norm was rather impressive.[113] To a considerable degree, moreover, it found expression in the realities of Ottoman society.

14 This engraving, from the mid-eighteenth century, gives a rare glimpse of the interior appearance of the rooms lining Ottoman khans, where many of the pashas made their homes.

The pluralism of that society was an aspect which could not but strike English visitors, all the more so because they came from a decidedly closed and homogeneous one. Ottoman openness, as we have noted, was partly a function of the territory over which the Empire had planted its dominion since the very beginning, but such a policy was encouraged still further by the Empire's irresistible strategic position, once fully fledged, on major land routes of global commerce. Whereas the diversity of the Ottoman world was becoming all the more pronounced in the course of the sixteenth and seventeenth centuries as a result of the greater internationalism of its trade, England had broadly been moving in the opposite direction, the policies of its state doing much to rid the realm of the last foreign traders who still lingered in London or Southampton. In the religious sphere, the Reformation's orgy of repression could be witnessed most dramatically in burnings at the stake, but it was also manifested in a strict intolerance pervading all aspects of society. Restoration England fundamentally remained 'a persecuting society': this was, it has been said, 'the last period in English history when the ecclesiastical and civil powers endeavoured systematically to secure religious uniformity by coercive means'.[114] Even the so-called Toleration Act eventually ushered in by the Glorious Revolution of 1688 was altogether conservative in its concessions. In the late seventeenth and early eighteenth centuries, England was wrestling with the acceptability of tolerating sub-sects of the monarch's own Protestant faith, let alone its Catholics, atheists and Jews.

In the Ottoman Empire, by contrast, the rich kaleidoscope of the population, encompassing all manner of Christian dominations as well as Jews and Muslims, was irrepressibly visible. More than that, it was audible – for the cacophony of languages that one would hear was perhaps the most immediate marker of ethnic variation amongst peoples who might not necessarily *look* all that different. As Lady Mary Wortley Montagu wrote in the early eighteenth century, wallowing in the literary possibilities offered by rattling off this litany of nationalities:

In Pera they speak Turkish, Greek, Hebrew, Armenian, Arabic, Persian, Russian, Slavonian, Wallachian, German, Dutch, French, English, Italian, Hungarian; and what is worse, there is ten of these languages spoke in my own family. My grooms are Arab, my footmen, French, English and Germans, my Nurse an Armenian, my housemaids Russian, half a dozen other servants Greeks; my steward an Italian, my Janissaries Turks, that I live in the perpetual hearing of the medley of sounds, which produces a very extraordinary effect upon the people that are born here.[115]

Dudley North recorded similar impressions.[116] In Livorno, where he joined a Flemish convoy bound for Smyrna on his journey out, he found aboard his ship men of 'several nations of all sorts, French, Italian, Spanish, Dutch, Armenian, Greek, and what not; and as much variety of religions and languages'. Here was a world where the Englishman might swiftly feel himself the odd one out: even on this ship there were, he added, 'none wanting company to speak with in any language he pleaseth, except myself that am left to talk English all alone'.[117]

The instinct to fit in expressed itself often in the adoption of oriental dress. Views on the wisdom of this differed. Montagu North wrote, on his nephew's departure for Aleppo: 'I am glad to see my sister has stocked him with linen & you with one suit of clothes but I think an other new suit of clothes will be requisite for him and 2 or 3 hats and a dozen of shirts at least with crevatts, cuffs and handkerchiefs & stockings, being I would have him continue in English habit 2 or 3 years at least, as I did'.[118] It does not seem to have been the norm to do so, however, for Montagu warned Dudley that no sooner had he arrived than the factors would 'be putting you to go in Turkish clothes'. This, he said, 'need not be, only you must have a cloth vest to wear over all your clothes and so I always went and for a year or two you need doe no other'.[119] Perhaps the lavish oriental clothes that portraits from the time showed the pashas wearing, including turbans, were spurs to earn with time. Such headgear could also offer other advantages, as the balding John Verney discovered: '. . . pray do me the favour as to send me by the next shipping for this place a Periwig my own hair being already almost all come off suppose must go in the Turkish mode before it comes'.[120]

If such diversity was an aspect of Aleppo's trading milieu immediately striking to the seventeenth-century English mindset, so too was the policy of toleration which nourished it. In the midst of the religious cornucopia, as even one of Maundrell's predecessors in the chaplaincy was prepared to admit, all 'injoy freedome of their consciences', and, even more to the point, all were quite free to 'bring thither many kinds of rich merchandises'.[121] The merest glance at the architecture of Galata or Smyrna, places where Ottoman religious licence extended furthest, could attest to that.

Smyrna, whose Europeans visibly dominated the place by the mid-seventeenth century, its harbour dotted with northern European ships and its seafront dominated by its tavern-lined 'Frank street', offered perhaps the most remarkable vista of all so far as religious heterogeneity was concerned. Soon after the *Plymouth* had arrived there, a party of Englishmen climbed a hill next to the city. 'We had there a full view of the town', wrote Captain Allin of the sight that greeted them atop its summit, 'where is eleven mosques or churches round on the top and a small space or staircase for a man to go up to cry aloud to bring the people to church. We saw 2 synangogues, 3 canes, which are places to entertain all sorts of Armenians, Persians and other strange merchants.' 'They have churches', added a long-time English resident of the place, 'and all freedom in performing their ceremonies that possibly can be allowed them.' As for Galata, it was a place 'more Christian or Jewish than Turkish', as one observer in the late seventeenth century observed.[122] The 'suburbs of Pera, Tophana and Galata', another English resident observed, 'are collections of strangers from all countries of the universe'.[123] In addition to the three mosques there, the Greeks had numerous churches, the Armenians had three and the Latins five, while there were also two synagogues.[124] For the Turks maintained, Dudley soon concluded, that 'all men are to be saved by their own religion; so that neither Christian, Turk, nor Jew can curse either's faith, but upon complaint to the magistrate you may have them punished'.[125]

Acknowledging the Ottomans' toleration of others' religion involved a departure from the habitual vilification of their state. Yet it was one that many writers felt bound admiringly to make, even in pre-enlightened times. As early as the 1580s, Jean Bodin had written in approval of the 'great emperour of the Turks' for permitting 'neere unto his pallace' the religions of 'the Jews, that of the Christians, that of the Grecians, and that of the Mohametanes'.[126] Richard Staper, seeking to justify the continuance of the Levant trade to the court of King James, endorsed this kind of assessment in 1605: 'notwithstanding that the Turks in general be a most wicked people, walking in the works of darkness', he wrote, '. . . they permit all Christians, both Greeks and Latins, to live in their religion and freely to use their conscience, allowing them churches for their divine service, both in Constantinople and very many other places.' In that regard, Staper went on to point out, they compared very favourably with the stance of Christendom itself (or, at least, Catholic Christendom), where 'by proof of 12 years residence in Spain' as a trader he could attest to being 'not only forced to observe their popish ceremonies but in danger of life and goods . . .'[127] In the seventeenth century, similarly, Richard Knolles praised the licence accorded by Islam to Jews and Christians even as he lambasted the Empire: 'To give the Mahometans their due,' he conceded, 'they are generally good fellows on this point.'[128]

Making money in this trading world called on Britons not to conquer its Ottoman rulers – even had that been conceivable – but to negotiate a place at their table. To do that meant putting aside the instincts of national or religious chauvinism and to obey instead the rules of Ottoman-Islamic institutions, under whose auspices Christian and Jewish outsiders had for centuries been welcomed into the *dār al-Islām*. Nothing could have conveyed that truth more powerfully than the khan itself, where Aleppo's pashas found their accommodation amidst the souk. Much later, Enlightenment savants would eulogise markets as great levellers of men: Voltaire once remarked of the London Exchange that 'the Jew, the Mahometan, and the Christian transact together as tho' they all profess'd the same religion, and give the name of Infidel to none but bankrupts'.[129] Such a notion had a certain intuitive force even in this earlier period. As an anonymous writer put it in 1637, marking the visit of a Moroccan ambassador to London, trade 'acquaints each nation with the Language, Manners, Behaviour, Customers, and carriage of one another; so that by these meanes men are made capable of understanding and knowledge; and therefore preferred knowledge before wealth and riches, for the one soone fadeth, the other abideth for ever'.[130]

If the lifeblood of the pashas' trade was the Persian silk that would travel through Isfahan, Basra and Baghdad to the Turkish Mediterranean coast, from there to continue its journey westwards towards Spitalfields, it drew their business concerns into the heart of the Islamic lands. Agreements would have to be hatched in the souk to exchange English cotton and cash for the raw product, perhaps alongside mohair, cotton wool and yarn, carpets, drugs, spices, currants, indigo. Then factors and their warehousemen would have to supervise its cleaning and careful packaging for the journey; and arrangements would have to be made for transport to the coast, where it would be stored in the Company's warehouse, before eventually being loaded for onward dispatch. Ships' arrivals would presage toil. News of their putting in would reach Aleppo within hours, by carrier pigeon sent from Scanderoon: 'a small piece of paper,

15 A seventeenth-century etching showing one of the great caravans from Constantinople approaching Mecca.

with the ship's name, day of arrival, and what else material could be contained in a very narrow compass, was fixed so as to be under the wing, to prevent its being destroyed by wet.'[131] The ships might remain in the port for a matter of weeks; and during that time, the harbour would be a hive of activity, *mallems* (camel transporters) carrying letters back and forth over the coastal mountains, together with the parcels bringing bacon and beer from home. 'You little think what trouble we have in procuring camels to bring up the goods,' a typical complaint went. 'I some time have had cloth at Scanderoon 8 or 10 months after its arrival and was almost 2 years in getting up 600 slabs of lead.'[132]

In much the same way, Persian caravans setting down in one of the *bedestans* in the centre of town would signal a plethora of opportunities to come. 'Caravans of all sorts [of] goods dayly comeing in,' a trader scribbled enthusiastically one day, 'so doubtless, what comes next, will meet with very good encounters . . .'[133] The loss of a caravan might, conversely, signal lean times ahead, for the pashas as for the town. In 1701, not for the first or last time, the annual caravan of the *Hajj* pilgrims was attacked by Bedouin on its return from Mecca: ' 'tis a prodigious loss besides great damage to our trade . . . & may be the ruin of abundance of families', wrote one.[134] The indispensable ingredient of success in such a line of business was intimate knowledge of both sides of the trade – with the eastern as the western segments, with the camelloads of silk and ship-loads of cloth. It was the delicate equation between these two which would shape the appetite for doing deals and set the daily temperature of the market. Take this typical rundown of business, penned by two factors in the late seventeenth century for the benefit of their London principal, Sir John Lethieullier:

> Several caravans of silk have come in lately from the neighbouring towns . . . Severall French ships and barques are at Tripoly and more intends to go from Scanderoon shortly which causes the expectation of silk to jeep up high the merchants demands . . . Expect one Captain Savy in a French ship from Marseilles at Scanderoon. Mr Prescott writes . . . [that] caravans are coming from Persia with Iniggo, Indian linen and some silke . . . A considerable caravan went some time since from hence for Persia . . . The Isaiah Captain Bluet sailed from Scanderoon for Cyprus and London the 16 past and the Cotton Captain Pocock the 17th intends to proceed from Cyprus by the first good conveyance for London.[135]

From the eastern Mediterranean shore, English contacts kept traders informed of commercial developments as far afield as Libyan Tripoli in one direction, Isfahan (in Iran) in another – and, of course, London in yet another. They might write as often as weekly to their principals in England telling them of the latest developments.

Successful traders could not confine themselves to socialising with men of their own 'nation', for their business required them to gather information relentlessly. 'As to imploy yourself when at Aleppo,' an apprentice factor was advised, 'your chiefest business is to get the language, which you must apply all your spare time in.'[136] 'I must confess to be esteemed a spy is an ill character', wrote one factor, 'but amongst the Turks in these parts 'tis no great crime to discover secrets so that hardly any thing passes at the Seraglio, or Mackimae, but what is advised the Consuls & other Franks . . .'[137] One's friendships should ideally extend right down to the level of the camel transporters, for to them was entrusted the conveyance of highly valuable cargoes to and from the coast. 'Pray invite the mallim on board & make him a present of some gunpowder he is a civil young fellow,' an Aleppo trader entreated of Captain Robinson, commander of a vessel that sat in Scanderoon at some point in 1702.[138] 'Sir, These accompany a Grecke & 2 Turkes as designe for Cyprus passengers on your ship . . '. wrote this same trader on another occasion. 'Pray receive them at the terms as customary & treat them kindly as their poor circumstances may deserve . . .'[139]

The pashas' primary commercial contacts were brokers, who in the Persian silk trade would generally be Armenian and, in the domestic Ottoman trades, Jewish.[140] That might be taken to reflect, in part, a standing presumption against dealing directly with Muslims, in turn encouraged by their domestic indoctrination against the religion. More straightforwardly, though, it was also a consequence of the general domination of international trade in the Ottoman Empire by non-Muslim diasporas. Armenians, in particular, heavily dominated the overland silk trade with Persia. Their shared Christianity did not necessarily win them much affection: 'Pray be careful of those vermin,' a consul in Aleppo wrote of them, 'who you may depend upon it, will cheat us of what they can.'[141] The Earl of Kinnoull described the Greeks as 'the most despicable people under the sun' and far worse than the Turks.[142] In the diary kept by his butler at the Palace, expressions of contempt are reserved for Catholics rather than Muslim Turks. Later in the Company's history, international networks of Jewish traders, plying an indirect trade from the Levant to London through intermediate ports such as Livorno, represented a major source of competition. The Jews, Lady Montagu declared, 'have drawn the whole trade of the empire into their hands'.[143]

In spite of the greater cultural hurdles standing in the way, the call of profits also drew the pashas into contact with the Ottoman Empire's Muslims to a far greater degree than often suggested. The correspondence of the Aleppo factory speaks of frequent commercial engagement, at times in the silk trade, but more especially in the lucrative but risky sphere of money-lending. The intrigue which John Verney saw unfold during his time in Aleppo, prompted by the 'running away of two of our Factory with 40000 dollars of the Turkes money (besides some of our own nation's)', was all too common.[144] The pashas' work also plunged them into contact with an administrative Ottoman bourgeoisie which was heavily comprised of Muslims.[145] Friendships with Muslims ranking high on the social scale would represent highly valued assets. 'I further acquaint you I have a friend Turke merchant of Antioch', a typical boast of an Aleppo factor went, 'as in the season usually brings 7 or 8 good bales [of] Antioch silk hither . . .'[146] Ottoman business contacts occasionally appeared in the factory itself, or were put up by English factors in their chambers and houses. 'Omeir Chellibee is now with me & shall continue so long as pleases', wrote one English trader of a Muslim contact in 1701; '[and] when finds himselfe any wayes uneasy with our way of living will lodge him at Causim aga in a pleasant seraglio & good entertainment . . .' The business of hosting such guests was not without its cultural sensitivities. Omar Chellebee, the Englishman wrote a week later, 'continues with me & is of such an excellent quiet disposition as have not met the like & am of opinion will manage your business extraordinary well . . .'[147] But the following year, the prospect of a similar arrangement attracted censure:

When the Tchoadar comes as you have dispatched about your business to Adana I will advise you of his success, & afford him my best assistance in his occasions here, but for the future must entreat you not to recommend any in such a manner as to be lodged with me very unwilling to be subject to the like besides no wayes convenient to have Turkes with Christian servants for when wine is to be procured occasions disorders . . .[148]

Avoiding social awkwardness in this instance meant calling on a further stock of non-European acquaintances: 'when that Tchoadar comes', continued the letter just quoted, 'I hope you will not take it amiss if I lodge him at Optarraman Aga or Causim Aga, both have fine houses & entertain strangers with much civility . . .'[149]

Hospitality was meted out more commonly in private residences. Dudley attached great importance to the *sopha* room in his house in Constantinople, where he might 'receive and entertain the Turks that came to visit him after their own way'. He would regularly dine with a high-ranking Ottoman official, with whom he had formed a close bond of friendship.[150] The Chevalier d'Arvieux described how, in Smyrna in the mid-seventeenth century, he was 'one of those who used to assemble on most evenings at the house of M. Edouard, a well-known English merchant . . . [His wife] was young and beautiful . . . Often there was a dance, and afterwards supper. Greek ladies were invited . . . came, and enjoyed it . . . Turkish guests, who were at first greatly shocked at these goings on, became accustomed to them.'[151]

Such entertainment was also reciprocated. John Covel describes rambling about Smyrna en route to Constantinople, during which one of the fellow passengers on his voyage, a Levant Company trader, took him to 'a rich Turkes house, who was one of his old acquaintance'. There they found the Turk already at Supper; and he 'very earnestly prest us to sit down, which we did . . . crosse leg'd, for we saw neither chair, nor stool, nor anything else but the floor cover'd with carpets'. 'We tasted of his good cheer,' he adds, 'which was good, plain, wholesome food.'[152] Robert Bargrave, similarly, records the entertainments regularly offered to the English traders of Constantinople by 'our noble Patron Mamout Effendee' at his 'faire Country Pallace' outside the Ottoman capital. In the gardens there, he wrote, 'the great number of Nightingales invite . . . many great Persons to theyr Melody'. These Turks would often bring with them their 'great Families of Concubines to recreat themselves' who would not be contented 'unless they saw the Franks Chambers . . . & there entertaining themselves & us, with Dauncing, Leaping, & roaring like wild persons let out of a Prison'.[153] Even a chaplain, Robert Frampton, would habitually engage in wine-drinking binges with the *kadi* (local magistrate) during his time in Aleppo.[154]

Muslim hospitality might also be encountered on the road. At the very end of the seventeenth century, Edmund Chishull rode with a companion into a conurbation near Smyrna, intending to remain there for the night, and they began to be troubled for lack of a place to receive them. Their distress was observed, he wrote, by 'an *effendi*, who saw us pass under his window, and therefore courteously acquainted us by his servant, that if we want accommodations, we might be welcome to his house'. They gladly accepted the invitation and were conducted into a house consisting of a large *sopha* room, a kitchen and an open *kiosk*, with a beautiful fountain in the middle:

> The *effendi* himself came down, and welcomed us to our apartment . . . [and] bid us freely make use of what this place afforded . . . By our *dragoman** he likewise informed us, that the *cadi* of the city was at that time making him a visit, before whom it might not be improper to shew ourselves; but at the same time not to come empty handed. According to this motion we waited upon the *cadi* with two *okes* of sugar, and as many of coffee. He received us and our present very obligingly; and upon the *effendi*'s invitation, we there drank a dish of coffee in the company of several Turks, who seemed to be of the better rank, and behaved themselves gentilely, that is, according to the genius of this haughty people, with an agreeable mixture of civility and reservedness. This ceremony performed, we returned to our garden, and there entertained ourselves at supper with just and grateful reflection on the great courtesy and hospitality of our land-lord, whose name we had now learnt to be *Mahomet effendi*.[155]

In much the same vein was the experience of a group of pashas who, at the end of the seventeenth century, set off from the Aleppo factory to trek to the banks of the Euphrates. Reaching the river, they met a chief who 'had some acquaintance with our nation' and treated the party to a 'handsome supper after their manner'. To give the Turks their due, one of the party was moved to write by this, 'the world does not afford a more hospitable people to travellers amongst them'.[156] But it was far from the last of the Muslim hospitality marking their journey, for a little further on they encountered a man named Sheikh Assine, 'to whom we were recommended by one of the factory his intimate acquaintance'. He gave them a lavish entertainment, fed their horses and took them hunting. They reciprocated by inviting him to dine in their camp, rustling up 'as

---

* Borrowed from the Arabic term *tarjuman* (interpreter), these men were generally Armenians, Italians or Jews and were employed by the English factory not only as translators but as general guides to the mechanics of the Ottoman state and world.

handsome a treat as the place & short time would admit of', even if high spirits on the English side were tempered by the consideration that good manners 'obliged us to drink no wine in his company'.[157]

Such conviviality was one facet of the pashas' encounter with Ottoman Muslims. Another, often less cordial, facet consisted in direct dealings with the apparatus of governmental power. As we shall see in a later chapter, the pashas' business plunged them into the intricacies of both Ottoman law and politics. From London, the Company imagined that the guarantees enshrined in the capitulations would enable them to keep their hands clean of such entanglements, tainted as they were with the mark of Islam. Disputes were supposed to be remitted to the ambassador, to be dealt with through peremptory diplomacy in the corridors of the Porte. Yet such detachment was, in practice, wholly unrealistic. The pashas were, to a large extent, absorbed into the Ottoman world: one among many interest groups vying for status and commercial success. Any idea that they could rise above the power structures of this Islamic society – and, above all, the mighty Ottoman polity – could not survive the realities of living and trading amidst its great emporia and centres of power.

PART TWO

———— ❖ ————

CONSTANTINOPLE

4

Galata

❖

Seated for Sovereigntie

When, in 1845, a wooden bridge first linked Eminönü with Karaköy, on opposite sides of the Golden Horn, it tilted the Ottoman capital's cultural geography toward its northern faubourgs and drew the city's soul westward into Europe.[1] Into the later nineteenth century, darkness still sank after dusk onto old Stamboul south of the Horn. North of it, though, gas lamps nightly cast their glow over the boulevards from the mid 1860s, beckoning people over the bridge onto the funicular railway up to Pera.[2] Even by day, as the new guard saw it, the old city slept, wallowing in Asiatic backwardness, wood and dirt. It was Galata, skirting the shoreline of the Golden Horn, and Pera, newly cast out of stone and iron into a self-consciously Parisian mould, which were dragging the place into 'modernity'. Here, clustering around *La Grande Rue* and jostling for space, were the principal hubs not just of commerce, but also of fashion and diplomacy. Here were the western embassies; here, the financiers' headquarters and the merchants' storehouses. Here, too, were the plush hotels and the brothels, the parks and the squares with their pricy street-cafés.

Galata, alongside the rather bourgeois district on the hill above it that was Pera, had long been known as a commercial enclave for non-Muslims. When the Ottomans conquered Constantinople in 1453, they allowed the city to retain something of the autonomy it had enjoyed in Byzantine days as a city-state under Genoese sovereignty. For the three centuries thereafter, it remained a Christian island in an Ottoman-Islamic sea. Geographically, it might have been held apart from the great metropolis only by a narrow stretch of water 'not above half so broad as the broadest part of the Thames'. Culturally speaking, though, it clung to its distinctive Italianate milieu throughout the early-modern era, resisting the allure of the great 'anti-Europe' and Islamic 'counter-Christendom' on its southern doorstep. It seemed, even to an eighteenth-century visitor, 'no more a suburb of Constantinople than Westminster is a suburb to London'.[3] Into the nineteenth century, parts were still surrounded by a defensive wall. True, large chunks of this fortification had been knocked down in 1453 at the Ottomans' insistence. Its remnants, though, seemed to proclaim Galata's separateness centuries later, no less stubbornly for their military obsolescence.

So it was fitting that, within twenty-five years of the bridge going up, this wall should have all but come down. The mode of resistance for which it stood no longer had much place. The effect of building the

16 The view over the Galata bridge in today's Istanbul.

106

land-link across the Golden Horn might have been to help Constantinople finally to merge with her diminutive neighbour (for nowadays, we tend to think of 'north of the Horn' as no less a part of Istanbul than its southern side). Yet by the second half of the nineteenth century, the magnetic pull across the sliver of sea had come to seem irresistible. The old Stamboul would follow the path of westernisation that Galata was beating.[4] It was anybody's guess who was absorbing whom; and plain, at least, that Galata could never be regarded as a mere suburb of an enlarged city. Brimming with the self-confidence of its European ways, it seemed nothing less than 'the St. James's of the Capital'. In the decades ahead, it would often lay claim to be its heart.[5]

In nineteenth-century Galata, the growing hold of western Europe on the Ottoman Empire – cultural, economic and ultimately political – would be plain to behold. Yet in the pashas' heyday, Galata's distinctive character owed more to the Ottomans' impervious might. The English, French, Dutch and Italian outsiders who gathered there, hovering close to Stamboul's all-powerful and Islamic orbit, could not forget that they remained at the sultan's pleasure. From the Royal Exchange, London's merchants might boast of how their commercial empire encompassed the world; and it was true enough that their direct routes into the eastern Mediterranean were well entrenched by the seventeenth century. Yet the reach of Atlantic capitalism extended into the Middle East long before it drew the region into anything like subservience. It lived alongside an Ottoman Empire which remained vibrant and still expanding. Britons' political and economic muscle there was meanwhile slight, all but powerless to challenge the Ottomans' command. Only in Georgian times would a pattern of western domination unmistakably emerge. The pashas, then, were no proto-colonists: the only Empire that counted within their trading universe was the Ottomans'. Far from seizing their realm, the Britons living within it bowed to a polity whose lustre in many regards seemed to outshine their own.

On 17 January 1661, three months exactly after it had left the chalk cliffs of Kent behind, the *Plymouth*'s crew caught sight of the Yedikule Fortress along Constantinople's city wall.[6] The final leg of the journey from Smyrna had proved the most hazardous of all. A storm despatched the main sails 'like paper blown away' and even their replacements were ripped by the hook of the anchor. Robbed of the means to set its own course, the ship struck a rock five times and appeared destined for 'totall wrack and ruin'. Paul Rycaut, the Earl of Winchilsea, and the rest of its beleaguered passengers found themselves, 'with cast up eyes, and stretched out arms . . . [thinking] of no other but of our last and final port'.[7] But miraculously, when the ship finally got clear, it was barely scathed.

After their brush with doom, the final approach along the Marmara coast felt like blessed release. 'You begin to approach *Constantinople*, which you behold to the left hand,' as one visitor taking this route described, 'and to coast along by the Walls, which reach from the Castle of the seven Towers to the Point of the Seraglio.' Rounding the promontory, Galata's shoreline would appear, stretching 'with considerable breadth, from the opposite shore of the *Haven*, much above an *English Mile*, with steep ascent, even to the very *summit* of the Hills, which overlook the City.'[8] Closer at hand, the full profile of the Topkapi Palace slowly revealed itself, then the Haghia Sophia and great Ottoman mosques of the city skyline, 'each gilded Crescent and each antique spire'.[9] It was 'certainly that part of the Universe above all others, where the eye most deliciously feeds itself with a prospect every way delightful', this visitor recorded; and 'for my own part, when I arriv'd there the first time, methought I was entring into an Inchanted Island'.[10]

From the moment of the *Plymouth*'s arrival, the posturing of diplomacy began, Winchilsea still possessed of his metropolitan delusions of grandeur. Informed that the sultan was seated in a summer house of the palace looking out over the Bosporus, the ship ceremoniously sailed past, 'our Flaggs and Ensigns . . . displayed, our Guns and Wastcloths out'. The Ottoman sovereign, said to be impressed with the sight of the vessel, sent word inviting its captain to fire a salute. With her sails swelling in a gentle gale, the swiftness of her motion slowed by the current, the ship fired sixty-one guns. She could not have appeared with better advantage, Paul enthused, 'had she been described by the Hand of the most skilful Painter'.[11] The sight of such a vessel, the new ambassador boasted to the King, had 'not only done honour to me as your Ambassador, but affected the great Emperor himself with an apprehension and terror of his Majesty's navy'.[12]

This pageantry complete, the ship anchored in the bay and, after a pause, Winchilsea rowed to Galata's shoreline. Not least for its popularity with foreign merchants, Galata enjoyed a real commercial importance in its own right. The teeming Bosporus supplied its most time-hallowed fare, the seafood raucously traded in the market along its waterfront. Behind, clusters of commercial buildings forged out of wood and stone marked the *Perşembe Pazari* covered market and the environs of Sinan's *Rüstem Pasa Han*, where meat and handicrafts were traded outside the sun's glare. Past that, the narrow streets leading to the fourteenth-century Galata Tower were 'formed', as one visitor wrote, 'by shops and magazines for articles of European commerce'.[13] But it was the voracious consumption of the Ottoman court and, more generally, the Empire's capital city which set the pace of this trade. The goods laden onto foreign ships moored in the harbour would have made their way through Stamboul's markets.[14] As today, the real hub of shopping lay in the alleyways of the Grand Bazaar, amidst its cornucopia of the earth's riches.

The source of Galata's appeal was as a sort of communal pied-à-terre. This was a place, as one English merchant put it, where he and his fellow merchants could 'passe very commodiously with pleasure, love and Amitye among themselves, wearing our own Countrie habitt, Provision, fruit and wine very good varietye and plenty'.[15] It was a commonplace that Galata was 'very much inhabited by Christians, and by all the Europeans'; and as for Pera, the haunt of the ambassadors, it was 'almost entirely inhabited by Franks and other Christians'.[16] The European, Christian milieu was firmly imprinted onto the architecture. It appeared more Italian than Ottoman until at least the end of the eighteenth century, just as it would take on Parisian airs in the next. Visual marks of its inhabitants' Christian convictions also abounded, even if the ringing of church bells had been prohibited ever since Constantinople fell to its Muslim masters. 'The Greeks have three churches in Galata,' it was noted in the mid-eighteenth century, 'and the Armenians two: The Jesuits, Dominicans and Franciscans have each of them a convent in this place.'[17] Galata was home to several synagogues, as well as to mosques.

A little further inland were the embassies, where Winchilsea now wound his way in a procession through streets thronged with crowds. The arrival of new ambassadors would always be marked by Galata's Franks with public feasting, affairs that were good-natured enough until 'all the low people were made drunk' and fistfights broke out.[18] The climb up to Pera, where these residences clustered, was rewarded with space and verdant tranquillity. Istanbul's diplomatic buildings today, standing much where they have done for four centuries, are hidden amidst tall nineteenth-century boulevards. In early-modern times, though, the area was renowned for its views over 'the port, the city and the seraglio and the distant hills of Asia, perhaps altogether the most beautiful prospect in the world'.[19] Close by the French, Venetian and Dutch residences, the English maintained a fine palace, with its own chapel 'almost after the model of that at Windsor'.[20] The building itself was fashioned out of wood in the Turkish style, set in a large garden planted with carnations, roses and jonquils and surrounded by a wall.[21] As one occupant wrote of it:

> As to the House in itself, it affords no great aspect to the eye without, but truly it is very convenient within, and I think it gives great content to [the ambassador], as I am sure it does to me. We both taking a great delight to set in our chairs and see the birds in the court lodge upon the cypress tree with as much alacrity and security as the malefactors fly into a church in Italy or a publick minister's house . . . we have little wrens which begin to learn to fly first from bough to bough, then from tree to tree, then from tree to the top of the house and so back again, and all under safe protection.[22]

The milieu of homeliness this side of the Golden Horn extended even to the inhabitants' dress. There was no need to conform to Turkish modes and it abounded with people 'who wear hair and hats upon their heads'. If some of the European women wore veils, that was for reasons of fashion – 'to show their beauty to more advantage' – rather than out of force of necessity.[23] 'Amongst the inhabitants of Pera there is nearly an equal mixture of European and Oriental manners,' it was commented by a later resident. 'The men almost universally wear the dress of their own nation, but the ladies blend the French fashions with the Greek, and produce a style by no means ungraceful.'[24] This was a telling mark of the wider freedoms that prevailed. For in Galata, the Franks enjoyed '*almost uncontroul'd*, an envied liberty, which very rarely, any *Turk* presumes to make Encroachments on, tho' some have often *insolence* enough to threaten it'.[25]

On the other side of the Horn, matters were different. There, it was usually thought, safety demanded adoption of oriental disguise. One visitor at the beginning of the eighteenth century relates how, walking 'to the Shore [south of the Horn] with several *European* Gentlemen, all dress'd according to the *Christian Fashion*', they 'receiv'd a thousand barbarous Affronts as we were landing from the Boat'. This was nothing out of the ordinary, he says, and he relates how they were forced to beat a hasty retreat through the crowd.[26] The same author penned another anecdote, telling of an English merchant who, whilst in the streets of Constantinople, had accidentally 'let Fall his *Turbant*'. Having thus revealed himself a 'Frank', he had to run 'swiftly thro' the Street, while all the *Boys* he pas'd by, seeing him disorder'd, and Bareheaded, and *besides*, Alarm'd by the repeated exclamations of the *Turks* he broke away from, who Cried out *an Infidel, an Infidel*, as loud as they were able, gather'd round him, and with *Dirt*, and *Stones*, pursued him thro' the City'.[27] Robert Bargrave, rather more plausibly, complained of the 'dayly hazards' on the southern shore of 'being stabbd by the drunken . . . Turkes'.[28]

Yet if Stamboul instilled fear where Galata stood for comfort, it was also the place which evoked by far the greater fascination. The lure of Galata might, in the nineteenth century, come to surpass that of Constantinople herself, but in this earlier era, the fount of Ottoman power across the water was first and foremost what drew the pashas to these parts. Galata was where they spent the bulk of their time, but in their writings it rarely merits more than the barest of mentions. Instead, they dwell endlessly on the prospect of Constantinople's skyline. The view of it from the hills of Pera was much the most common scene to be depicted in English engravings of the time. From there, it was agreed, the skyline presented itself quite spectacularly:

The unequal heights make [Constantinople] seem as large again as it is (though one of the largest cities in the world), showing an agreeable mixture of gardens, pine and cypress trees, palaces, mosques and public

17 The prospect of Constantinople, much as it would have appeared to ships first approaching the city from the Marmara Sea in early modern times.

buildings, raised one above another with as much beauty and appearance of asymmetry as your lady ever saw in a cabinet adorned by the most skilful hands, jars showing themselves above jars, mixed with canisters, babies and candlesticks.[29]

As they do today, visitors would take trips into the Bosporus purely for the views it afforded, 'rowing upon the canal of the sea here, where for twenty miles together . . . the most beautiful variety of prospects present themselves'.[30] 'We embarked in a vessel which we had hired of a Turk at Tophana,' one account from the later eighteenth century describes. 'A few minutes' sailing gave us a perfect external view of the seraglio, encircled with lofty embattled walls, with its domes and kiosques clustered in splendid confusion, and intermixed with gigantic cypresses . . . rising in the sea.'[31]

It was hardly any wonder that Stamboul should have so far outshone Galata in its estimation by contemporaries. Even now, tourists might warm to Beyoğlu's churches and merchants' houses, its restaurants and stores; but in all likelihood it will have been Sultanahmet and its skyline, Aya Sophia and the Seraglio, which brought them to this city, their first and most eager port of call. If Stamboul's ample trade was the major draw for many of the pashas, it outshone Galata on this measure as well. This latter was an aspect of its appeal deliberately fostered by the city's Muslim masters. Sultan Mehmed II started to build the Grand Bazaar within a few years of the city's capture.[32] Like Aleppo and Smyrna, it was renowned by the seventeenth century as a place where fortunes might be made. '[I have received a letter] bringing me advice of your changing Smyrna for Constantinople where I heartily wish you much success and prosperity', wrote one Aleppo factor to a friend. 'The place where you now are, is certainly the best to get an Estate in, which I think is the only good reason that can be given for any man's living in this country.'[33] It was, as a later observer put it, difficult to exaggerate 'the advantage to be made by trade in that great city, and with the court and with the dealers that came together and resided for the sake of trade there, from most parts of the world . . . there not being a greater emporium upon the face of the earth than Constantinople'.[34]

This cultural topography says much about how the pashas experienced the might of the Ottoman Empire as merchants within its realm. The vitality of its trade itself seemed to signal the Empire's rude health even into the mid-eighteenth century. 'Built upon a neck of land between two seas,' it was declared, 'it seems to have been formed for the seat of empire';

but, just as notable, 'its secure and spacious harbour invites the most remote nations to resort to it, profiting by the advantages of a flourishing trade'.[35] As for the 'Provision of *Constantinople*,' another added around the same time, 'there is no want of any thing, Wheat, Wine and Flesh of all sorts, being there in great abundance and cheapness'; there was also the reputed fish, of which, it was added, 'there are always great quantities . . . and those very good'.[36] A similar sense of commercial dynamism was conveyed by the city's architecture. 'The exchanges are all noble buildings,' it was said by one visitor early in the eighteenth century, 'full of fine alleys, the greatest part supported with pillars, and kept wonderfully neat.' Much the same could be said of the markets, 'most of them handsome squares, and admirably well provided, perhaps better than in any other part of the world'.[36] Many were struck, too, by the cleanliness of this city (in stark contrast to the Victorians, who were forever harping about the supposed filth of the place that mirrored, as they saw it, its inhabitants' degraded moral condition). Although its paved streets might not be 'so clean as those at the *Hague*', as one visitor admitted, nor were they so dirty as those in London.[38]

Yet the city's forms also evoked, with an immediacy that Aleppo's could not, the Ottomans' potency in the world as a political force. Constantinople allured all the more because it seemed to be bathed in the full glow of imperial glory. That perception was emblazoned on all contemporaries' sense of it. To write that 'of all places, that I ever beheld, Constantinople is the most apt to command the world' was to voice a sentiment that had entered the realm of cliché by Hanoverian times.[39] This was, as another English visitor wrote, a 'Citie by destinie appointed and by nature seated for Sovereigntie'.[40] 'This city', yet another wrote, seemed to be 'built to command all the World'.[41] Indeed, some such expression will be found in almost every account published by an English visitor at any point before the middle of the eighteenth century. 'This city with the glory of this great Empire I hold much better worth seeing than all Italy,' as Winchilsea himself wrote to Sir John Finch.[42] Here was a metropolis fit to crown the 'terror of the world' which, to many of its early-modern observers, the Empire still appeared.

Blood and War

A new century, another ambassador. In the winter of 1717, Christian Europe ended somewhere north-west of Belgrade. Precisely where its

18 A skirmish between Ottoman forces and Hapsburg cavalry in the early eighteenth century.

edge lay was never easy to say: in 1683–4, it had stood for a second time outside the gates of Vienna after a seemingly relentless march westwards; since then, it had been pushed back east, and the spring would carry it further still into one-time Ottoman heartlands. For the present, though, travellers would know if they were in its vicinity, because the earth would begin to throw up the unburied dead. Even where the snow was piled thick, whole clutches of them might be seen jutting out against the horizon, jarring the stillness of the winter landscape. The previous August, during one 'Glorious bloody day' (as it seemed to an English traveller), perhaps thirty thousand Janissaries were cut down here by the Hapsburg army as the Ottoman cavalry fled. 'We took no more than twenty prisoners,' an Austrian officer wrote, 'because our men wanted their blood and massacred them all.'[43] In the hot months, decapitated bodies and severed limbs were quick to fester. The battleground had been abandoned in haste for fear of disease descending on the living (even the victorious dead were considered too perilous for burial and left to their shallow graves). With the turning of the seasons, nature's decay shuddered to a halt; the earth froze over and putrefied flesh became sealed in

Honble S^r:
Dudley North K^t:
3^d Son of Dudley L^d:
North & Ann his Wife

19 A portrait of Dudley North at forty, his fortune already made.

ice, as if sculpted to remind all who travelled there of what had passed.
So it was that when the English embassy party crossed these fields in
January 1717, they found them still 'strewn with skulls, carcasses, horses
and camels'. Warriors, both Christian and Muslim, lay side by side
largely as they had fallen, united at last in martyrdom.[44]

Such visions of horror were hardly unexpected among the
Englishmen who ventured this way. It was not just that news of the
Hapsburg victory had already fanned out across western Europe. (There
were celebrations on the streets of Vienna, where the new ambassador to
the Porte had been accorded an audience with the triumphant Hapsburg
commander, and in Rome the bells rang out on the orders of the Pope.)
For centuries now, to embark on this journey, running south-east from
the Hapsburg capital across the Balkans, through Belgrade and on
towards the Ottoman capital, had been to enter a vale of Christian
sorrow. Heading towards Smyrna or Aleppo atop the oceans might bring
to mind the lucrative possibilities of trade with the Ottomans. The land

route to Constantinople reminded of the political and military might of their empire, leading across countless sites of holy war.

This latter was, perhaps, no longer the dominant paradigm for viewing the relationship between the Ottoman Empire and Christian Europe. The 'common corps of Christendom' straitjacket had long since been in decline. Even so, the accounts of those who travelled the continental land-route before the mid-eighteenth century often read like litanies of religious humiliation, peppered with the sites of ignominious Christian defeat. Travelling alongside a Hapsburg Embassy just after the 1684 siege was beaten off, for instance, John Burbury described the field outside Vienna where Suleyman the Magnificent pitched his tent as he laid siege to the city; further east, the wood where the King of Hungary fell under the weight of his armour as twenty thousand of his troops perished; a little further east still, a city which, in happier times the seat of a Bishop, had changed its master twenty times in little over a century. Not far from the City, 'a sad Spectacle was seen, to wit, many Heads of poor Christians pil'd up on a heap, which exceeded a thousand. They were taken at *Barchan*, and kill'd in cold blood by the *Viziers* command, who to satiate his unquenchable thirst of humane slaughter, had them pickt out one by one, and kill'd before his face, as he lay in his tent.'[45] Taking this same route in the 1660s, Paul Rycaut found the heads of Christian prisoners of war 'thrown up into a heap, the beards and hair of those that lay underneath still growing; the earth which sucked in their blood, became thence stenched up and barren, and the white bones and carcasses of their bodies lay dispersed and scattered in a large field'.[46]

Such defeats were still etched into the English consciousness well after the battlefields were cleared, but equally, long before they had entered the realm of literary Romanticism as harmless and distant fantasy. When Daniel Defoe, for instance, wrote of 'the infidel House of Ottoman' and its destruction of Christianity in 'above three-score and ten Kingdoms', when he described the 'Green Ensigns of Mahomet and the Turkish Halfmoon on the Tops of their Spires, in the room of the Cross', these words had a directness of meaning which they could not for, say, Sir Walter Scott writing a century-or-so later. For this was an empire commonly thought of, in the oft-cited words of its best-known seventeenth-century historian, as 'thundering out nothing . . . but Bloud and War, with a Full persuasion in time to rule over all, prefixing unto itself no other limits than the uttermost bounds of the earth from the rising of the Sun to the setting of the same'.[47]

This was psychological baggage which Britons, from humble apprentices to pompous ambassadors, would carry with them to the Middle East. The immense scale of the 'Formidable Empire of these Successful Infidels', even in the later seventeenth and early eighteenth centuries, is perhaps not now as widely remembered as it might be.[48] Yet it was deeply impressed on the minds of contemporaries. 'So prodigiously have they spread their Conquests,' Aaron Hill wrote in his illuminating 1710 account of the Empire's 'Present State', 'that they now enjoy a free and unmolested Possession of the Noblest Parts of *Asia, Europe*, and the Remoter *Africa*.' He went on to delineate, in painful detail, the '*Western* Part of its *European* Dominion', which then extended to 'the very Borders of the once-lost *Hungary*' and was only 'bounded on the *South* by the *Mediterranean Sea*'. Then he dissected the extent, no less impressive, of its '*Asiatick* Territories', containing 'that vast Tract of Land between the *Euxine, Cilician*, and *Aegean* Seas; *viz. Bythynia, Pontus, Phrygia, Galatia, Lycia, Cappadocia, Pamphylia, Cilicia*, and the vast Extent of *Armenia Minor*... *Babylonia, Mesopotamia, Phoenicia, Caelosyria*, and *Palestine*, [which] are altogether in the *Turks* Possession, as are the vast Dominions of the Three *Arabias*'.[49]

So far as the Empire itself was concerned, its 'equal Division between *Europe* and *Asia*' – planting the Turkish hobnail boot, as it were, firmly in both camps – was a particularly troubling aspect of its world-power status in the eighteenth century. On both sides, the Ottomans seemed to be placed 'in the Center of the Surrounding World', so that they were 'ever ready to enlarge their Conquests either way'.[50] Their empire, as another account agreed, 'stands almost in the middle of the World' and is 'thereby capable of performing commands over many Countryes, without any great prejudice of distance'.[51] Indeed, this extraordinary strategic position spanning Europe and Asia was a feature seen to be vividly crystallised in its capital above all, a metropolis planted squarely at the fault-line of 'Europe' and 'Asia'. An English map produced in the middle of the eighteenth century underscores the point particularly well: 'Europe' and 'Asia' are penned boldly into the respective landmasses occupying its wings, whilst the Bosporus, running perpendicularly down the centre, appears like a great chasm holding them apart. And there, in the centre of it all, seeming to hang rather awkwardly off Europe and reach towards Asia, is Constantinople herself. 'In less than a quarter of an Hour,' it had elsewhere been pointed out, the Porte 'can dispatch its

Orders from *Europe*, wherein 'tis situated, into *Asia*, which seems as it were to come so nigh it in order to be subject to its laws'.[52]

It is, though, little wonder that we have been inclined to forget the Ottomans' immense power to intimidate English souls throughout the early-modern era. For it is only recently that writing on the Ottoman Empire has cast aside the prism of 'decline' through which its history was so often told.[53] In the colonial era, it suited westerners well to paint the Middle East as a site of interminable decay. Decline, they suggested, was a function of oriental despotism. Here was a victim of corrupt and effeminate political regimes, fostered by a hot climate, which was therefore ripe for occupation. Yet narratives of Ottoman decline long pre-dated these nineteenth-century embodiments. Probably the earliest emanated from critics of the establishment writing within the Ottoman Empire itself, dating even from the era of Suleyman the Magnificent.[54] At roughly the same time, a Christian eschatology was emerging which, however optimistically, predicted imminent Ottoman collapse as part of the unfolding of God's grand scheme for the world.[55]

From the early seventeenth century (admittedly a time of Ottoman crisis), English accounts were routinely declaring that the Empire's power had 'exceeded the observed period of Tyrannie' and was perhaps near an 'extreme precipitation' – for 'the body' had by now 'grown too monstrous for the head; the sultans unwarlicke, and never accompanying their armies in person; the souldier corrupted with ease and liberty, drowned in prohibited wine, enfeebled with the continuall converse of women, and generally lapsed from their former austerity of life, and simplicity of manners'.[56] The 'Lion is not so fierce as he is painted', another author of the same era agreed, for 'the Turks head is lesse than his turbant, and his turbant lesse then it seemeth; swelling without, hollow within'. Because 'luxurie' had at last 'found the Turks out', there was 'just cause to hope that the fall of this unwieldy Empire doth approach'.[57] 'It may stand, but never rise again', Thomas Roe predicted in Jacobean times.[58] That pronouncement was frequently echoed by other ambassadors to Constantinople in the century which followed.

These diatribes might seem to give the impression that an incipient western arrogance towards the Islamic world was visible by an early date. That impression is, however, misleading. The political backdrop against which they were written swiftly exposes how wishful was their thinking. Britons at this time belonged to a state with virtually no means, whether cultural, economic or military, to challenge Ottoman hegemony in the Middle East.[59] To be sure, the balance of power between the English and the Ottomans on the world stage could be regarded as tilting somewhat more towards the former by the later seventeenth century. As a spiritual challenge, Islam, in its Ottoman guise, probably worried the early-moderns less than it had done some of their forbears. When Thomas More wrote his *Dialogue of Comfort Against Tribulation* in the 1530s, it seemed natural to set its theological themes against the backdrop of an impending Turkish invasion. This would not have resonated nearly so powerfully by the Restoration.

Old mental habits nonetheless died hard.[60] As far as one major strand in the pashas' collective thought was concerned, for decades after the Ottomans' second retreat from Vienna, the Ottomans were first and foremost people 'grown Terrible to Christians, and Formidable to all the World'. 'If ever race of men were borne with Spirits able to beare downe the world before them,' another contemporary wrote, 'I thinke it to be the *Turke*.'[61]

There were, moreover, good grounds for viewing the Ottomans and Islam as a still-expanding global contagion throughout the seventeenth century. 'Arabia was indeed the Nest, that bred and fostered that uncleane Bird,' a fascinating early survey of the Islamic world proclaimed, 'but from Arabia that poison hath in such short time dispersed it selfe through the veines of Asia, that neere the one halfe, is at this day corrupted by it.'[62] The Ottoman Empire encountered a series of crises at the end of the sixteenth century and into the earlier part of the seventeenth. Most historians now agree that it ultimately adapted well to its straitened circumstances, however. Under the firm grasp of the Koprulus, a particularly effective dynasty of viziers, it flourished once more in the second half of the century.

Ottoman incursions westward into central Europe, accompanied by spats with the Hapsburg Empire or Venice, were several even in the first decades of the eighteenth century. In consequence of the 'Incursions of this cruel Enemy', it was lamented in 1666, 'in the last war not three English miles from Vienna many poor people have been surprised, and fallen into the hands of the Tartar and the Turk, and sold afterwards into perpetual slavery'.[63] The Peace of Karlowitz in 1699, signed with the Hapsburg Empire and inflicting a profound humiliation on the Ottomans, is sometimes treated as if it marked an absolute turning point in European history, from which time the Turkish 'threat' posed to its eastern flank wholly evaporated. But that is putting it much too strongly, at least so far as contemporary English perceptions were concerned.

Vienna might never have looked in danger afterwards, although the tenor of the celebrations which the city witnessed in 1717 suggest that even that was not taken entirely for granted at the time. Consider, though, Belgrade. For most English visitors heading eastwards across Europe by land, this was one of the first places which they encountered to appear distinctly 'Muslim'. Its fate over the course of these years points to how fluid was the frontier of 'Turkey in Europe', as also to its aptness still to move west as well as east. Having been conquered by Suleyman the Magnificent, it was lost by the Ottomans in 1688 to the Austrians; recovered by them in 1690; then lost again in 1717 (notwithstanding that it was, as Lady Mary Montagu recorded in that year, 'fortified with the utmost care and skill the Turks are capable of, and strengthened by a very numerous garrison of their bravest janissaries'); then recovered once more in 1739.[64] As Aaron Hill put it (and it should be underlined that he was here writing late in the first decade of the *eighteenth* century):

> Notwithstanding the Inglorious Reigns of several Modern Emperors, have added nothing to their Territories, they still continue in full Possession of their former Acquisitions, and are not only able to Defend *their own*, but Conquer *other* Countries, shou'd the Warlike Spirit of some more Active *sultan* once lead 'em out to *Action*.[65]

Even should the 'United Arms of Warlike Christendom' now be 'bent against them', Hill added, still 'they are not yet so sensibly Decayed, as to become an easy Conquest'.[66] At the least, the Ottomans' vast dominion appeared fundamentally stable from the perspective of the Company's merchants. To a greater extent than ever before and quite possibly since, individual encounters between Britons and Ottomans took place against a backdrop of something like equality in the global power wielded by their states. Within the Ottoman Empire itself, the balance still seemed to tilt firmly against Britons' own. The smug certainties of military superiority over the Ottomans would have to await the arrival of a later era.

Trusting

Dudley North took little persuading to give up Smyrna in the late 1660s for 'the seat of a vast empire . . . where a merchant of spirit and judgement cannot fail of being rich'.[67] His abilities had by then caught the eye of William Hedges, treasurer of the factory at Constantinople. In partnership with the sottish John Fairfax, Hedges was at the time running one of the most celebrated English commissioning houses in the Ottoman capital. The *ragione*, to use the Italian term by which such houses were usually known, had the backing of leading merchants on the Exchange. With Hedges concentrating his energies on embassy affairs, however, it had increasingly fallen into disarray. Not only were its account books outdated and poorly maintained, but large sums of money under its care had been poured into hazardous loans. Meanwhile, overheads were running out of control, not least through its occupying sprawling premises amongst the grand merchant houses north of the Golden Horn and retaining a small army of servants, secretaries and helpers to maintain them. When Hedges returned to London in 1670, with high hopes of climbing the greasy pole of city politics, the partnership was denuded of its founding force.

It offered just the opportunity that the ever-ambitious Dudley needed. By then, Hedges had already brought him in as a partner in the *ragione* and, with the older man's departure from the Levant, the way was clear for him to take over its management. Initially he tolerated the ineffectual Fairfax, who at least possessed the virtue of a long list of contacts and an established reputation both in London and the Levant. In late 1674, however, North dissolved the partnership and went into business with his brother Montagu. This was a bold step indeed, requiring him to write to each of the *ragione*'s contacts in London and ask them to side with him against the better-established Fairfax. The gamble paid off. The North partnership threw off the excesses of the Hedges-Fairfax combine, while the more frugal regime which followed quickly squeezed out unprecedented profits. With Fairfax off the scene, Dudley was well on his way to making the glittering fortune on which he had always set his sights.

Such a public parting of ways had nonetheless represented a gamble. In the far-flung Levant trade, where the line dividing triumph from ruin was a fine one for all concerned, trust was a priceless commodity. The trade relied heavily on credit, in the reputational sense as much as the

20 Portrait of a successful Company trader and his companion, on his sofa in Constantinople, dating from the earlier eighteenth century.

financial one. Men had to be entrusted with authority to act on others' behalf in affairs played out many hundreds of miles away. Here was a classic embodiment of the difficult nexus between principal and agent, and it afflicted the whole gamut of relationships in which the pashas found themselves entwined. Whitehall struggled to direct its envoys at the Porte, whilst ambassadors bitterly complained at the lack of instructions issuing from home. Suspicion was meanwhile rife among the capital's merchants – and not without cause – of the motives harboured by their servants in the East. They feared that many were pocketing profits rather than passing them on, or devoting energies to trading on their own accounts rather than enriching distant metropolitan masters. Even amongst the pashas themselves, money-lending frequently led to strains within the factories. The tendency for the Ottoman authorities to visit the blame for individual debts on the whole community of Englishmen (notwithstanding the capitulations' categorical assurance to the contrary) made the pashas forever vulnerable to their fellow countrymen's misjudgements and greed.[68]

Tussles which were at root about who was to control the trade emerged as a perennial theme in its history. Partly this was a matter of the relationship between Levantine outposts and the London metropolis. The nub of the problem lay in the long distances over which it was conducted (it would be no less prominent a feature of British trade in India). That alone rendered tight control from London, whether by the Company or the Crown, well-nigh impossible given the limited regulatory apparatus which early-modern institutions had at their disposal. The conduct of diplomacy raised identical difficulties: 'it is none of the smallest misfortunes', Winchilsea wrote, 'to be so far from home, where the distance of the place, will not admit of speedy interactions, & in a country, where the alterations are so frequent, & extreme, that the perfect preparations to an action seldom arrive the opportunity'.

During the era of the Civil War, there had been almost total breakdown in the Company's authority overseas. In 1646, King Charles I instructed his ambassador to Constantinople, Sir Sackville Crow, to seize the property of the English traders under his charge so that it might be poured into furthering the royalist cause. Crow found some success at winning the support of the Ottoman authorities for putting this ruse into effect, even in the face of the merchants' bitter opposition. In London, the court of the Company responded by enlisting Parliament to its cause and embarking on an aggressive propaganda campaign to discredit Crow. It then forced the weakened King's hand, securing his agreement to despatch Sir Thomas Bendish in his stead. When Bendish arrived in Constantinople, Crow stubbornly refused to recognise him. His removal required a posse of Ottoman soldiers and servants, who one day seized him in his garden, 'dragged him through the streets of Galata, displayed him before an English throng who jeered at him from the windows of Bendish's residence . . . and dumped him unceremoniously into a small *kayik* bound for San Stefano'.[69]

Bendish would still face continued challenges to his authority in the decade that followed, as the domestic fractures of the Civil War infected communities of Englishmen abroad. Henry Hyde made a concerted attempt to usurp his position, issuing warrants supposedly on the authority of the King and proclaiming to the pashas that they need not obey the 'usurped and scandalous government of Sir Thomas Bendish and his rebellious complices and impudent incendiaries'.[70] For a time the loyalties of the English were split down the middle and the factories' government broke down.

This predictably wreaked havoc on the Company's commerce. The Restoration brought renewal of the Company's charter and, abroad, Winchilsea arrived with firm instructions to revive the 'dying trade' by urgently restoring the lines of authority between London and its Middle Eastern factors.[71] Amongst his first actions was to administer, at the Company's bidding, an oath requiring the pashas to swear that henceforth they would accurately record the volumes of goods being despatched for home on carriage documents. Designed to put an end to the practice of circumventing Company levies through creative accounting, it was reluctantly acceded to.[72] Similarly, in March 1688, the Company ordered that each factor was to declare under every entry that he made no personal benefit on any goods he shipped to England for his principal.[73] Such regulations were given teeth by a convoluted mechanism of fines, extending to 20 per cent of the value of goods improperly traded. It would be the job of the ambassador and factory treasurer to levy them; the Company offered to these enforcers a generous chunk of the proceeds.[74]

The effect of all this was to lend the Company a surer institutional presence in the Middle East. Even so, minor corruption remained endemic, albeit less acutely so after 1660. The Company had difficulty enough at home, installing its own man in the Customs House to scrutinise all imports and exports in a largely vain attempt to stamp down on interloping.[75] The means by which London sought to govern its interests outside domestic shores were necessarily weaker still. They rested on the individual loyalties of ambassadors, consuls and other officials. In the marts and palaces of the Ottoman Empire, neither Whitehall nor the court of the Company could wield clout other than through these men. Efforts to stock their ranks with slavish loyalists met with only mixed success.

It did not strengthen the metropolis' enfeebled hand that the pashas lacked any strong devotion to a 'British' cause. Ties to fellow members of their 'nation' (the word they used themselves to refer to the communities of Englishmen in each of the factories) were undoubtedly key in forging their social and business lives. But if at times they were impelled by loyalty to these men, to their king or to their religion, at others they were swayed by kinship ties to London principles, or long-cherished relationships with French, Dutch or Ottoman commercial contacts. Their identities were tractable, but no force proved so consistently powerful as the drive to enrich themselves.[76]

The respective places occupied by the Company and the Ottoman state in regulating this quest, in fact, were surprisingly similar. The pashas could feel they were members of a commercial culture that was shared by London and the cities of the Levant. Core business practices like double-entry bookkeeping, an Arabic import to England, were common to the merchants of both. The courtyards and colonnades of the Royal Exchange in many ways brought to mind those of the souk and the *bedestan*. The gossip in both, not to mention the coffee houses flourishing in their midst, was of price movements, security of routes, political intrigues and natural disasters. Nor was the manner in which these markets were governed so different. Policies were commonly built on an intrinsic conservatism, assuming that economic exchange should be tempered by strong professional ethics. The guild structure into which Ottoman trades were organised had parallels with the form of the regulated company. The Company and the Ottoman polity were twin poles of authority, which together set the framework for the pashas' trading world. Each as rapacious as the other, each might also be harnessed to benefit their mercantile cause.

Perhaps most importantly of all, the effectiveness of both was hampered by an absence of modern bureaucratic forms. Opportunities for nest-feathering, well beyond officials' salaries or factors' basic commissions, were ruthlessly exploited from the top downwards. 'Any ambassador that is not an honest man (if that he be not a foole)', as Winchilsea wrote, 'may deceive the company in great matters, and all the witt they have, and theire factors, will never be able either to find it out or to prevent it.'[77] Sir John Finch had to lay down a £10,000 bond with the Company as security for performance of his promises, in the manner of a humble apprentice.[78] Even that was not sufficient to prevent a spat later breaking out, when he was accused of abusing his position to extract money from the merchants. 'The Consul of Aleppo on my arrival sent me a horse,' he defended himself, 'and the factory there in gratitude for the great service I had done them made a public subscription for me to buy a ring. Mr William Hiet gave me a horse; they at Smyrna two or three carpets; Mr Jacob Turner, a Scio quilt. Besides this, in the space of more than six years I never received the value of a penny from the factorys of Smirna and Aleppo, and from those at Constantinople not one asper in my life; indeed from Smirna they yearly send me wine, and I in lieu of it as constantly send them bacon.'[79] The volley of directives issued by the Company trying to curb such practices (and proscribing wholesale any involvement in trade on the part of officials) were more honoured in the breach than the observance. It was the unfortunate official who found himself being sent home for failing to abide by these rules, although this did happen on occasion.[80]

The Company's efforts were frustrated by political realities. On the one hand it was notorious for its frugality; the Crown hardly less so. On the other, ambassadors were no less inclined than merchants to regard their posts first and foremost as routes to personal wealth. Not that they always succeeded. Winchilsea left having 'lived in Turkey for so many years as with good fame and reputation to have gained a considerable estate'.[81] Four decades later, Edward Wortley Montagu was less fortunate. When he fell victim to a change of administration at Westminster, the revocation of his appointment was backdated. By the time he got wind of it, he had already expended a small fortune in equipping himself for a lengthy diplomatic mission away from Constantinople. Appeals to George II on his return for reimbursement seem to have elicited some sympathy, but no cash.[82] Ambassadors might also find the legitimacy of their estates challenged upon return. Sir John Eyre, like Finch, found himself accused of extorting more from the merchants than his due: his 'extortions and ill speeches abroad' had 'well nigh overthrown [our] trade', the court of the Company complained.[83] Eyre defended himself on the ground that, since the Company had failed to pay his salary, he had every right to extract recompense from the merchants.

If the Company tried to reach factors directly by issuing oaths, it could not assume that they would willingly swear them.[84] Even the authority of the ambassador over the factories was at times weak. Early in his embassy, Winchilsea took the step of removing the Smyrna consul from his post. This man was mischievous but well connected: he had a good deal of support within the factory and, more importantly, amongst the members of the Company. For a time he flatly ignored Winchilsea's order removing him and persuaded the Company to issue a rebuke to its ambassador. Political spats like this suffuse the pashas' correspondence. The tight discipline which the Company liked to think characterised factory life was a forlorn hope. In truth, divisions were rife. Individual factors might be difficult to control even by the consul on the spot, let alone the ambassador in Constantinople or the Company in London.

The Company conceded to the reality of its own partial control by permitting factors and even apprentices to trade on their own 'account'. Far more dangerous to its interests, though, were the pashas' dalliances beyond the core silk-for-cotton business in the quest for greater returns than the latter could afford. For all the skill with which Dudley revived the fortunes of William Hedges' *ragione*, he made his real money by selling jewels to the Ottoman court and lending money at eye-watering rates of interest to Muslims. He succeeded through his consummate skill at fitting into the Ottoman world and cultivating its elites. Yet such lucrative activities were also fraught with risk. The illicit status of usury made lenders vulnerable to Muslim borrowers simply disclaiming their debts and, where this occurred, there was often little that could be done to retrieve them. The fingers of many men less politically astute than Dudley were severely burned in this way.

In consequence, the Company had a particularly abiding fear of credit arrangements.[85] In 1672, it required all factors to take yet another oath swearing not to 'trust', or sell goods on credit. All ambassadors were instructed to enforce it without mercy. At the beginning of the next century, mounting evidence reached London that the oath was being flouted. A tougher wording was swiftly introduced, in the hope that it would prove more daunting. Yet it is doubtful whether the rule, which was stubbornly resisted by the factors, ever achieved much effect. Even when the letter was obeyed, merchants found ways to circumvent its spirit. Often, they would simply hand the money paid by Ottoman merchants straight back to them, in exchange for promissory notes that became due when the next caravan arrived.[86] Such arrangements were made unavoidable by an abiding shortage of currency, which in turn propelled lending as well as monetary speculation into hugely profitable enterprises and major temptations to the pashas.

An incident in 1705 which nearly brought down the Aleppo factory altogether casts light on why the Company felt such concern at their involvement in such activities. When Samuel Harvey first got into financial difficulties, his fellow English merchants were willing to rally to his support. His story seemed typical enough. He had, he claimed, lent cash to a guileful Muslim, who had then denied the debt and, even worse, sued him in the Aleppo court claiming that Harvey owed *him* money. The factory voted to treat this as an *avania** visited on the English

---

* '*Avania*' was the word used to describe the embroils which required money to be paid to Ottoman potentates in bribes or fines. As the English portrayed it, these payments were always forced on them under a false pretence.

nation as a whole and to bail Harvey out with public funds.[87] It soon became apparent, however, that Harvey had not been telling the whole truth to his fellow countrymen. Over the past decade, he had created an elaborate and lucrative money-lending business, which had now gone badly awry. Trying desperately to borrow and speculate his way out of trouble, he had become entangled in a web of colossal debts, both to his fellow pashas and to local Muslims. When the consul went to argue his case before the local authorities, he found an angry mob of local creditors waiting to seize Harvey. 'If we had not rescued him,' the consul recorded, 'I doubt not that they would have torn him in pieces.'[88]

In the following year, one Hajji Mahomet Ebyr Ishmael even travelled to London, apparently with Harvey's encouragement, to petition the court of the Company to compensate him for the 5,262 Lion Dollars which he had lost at the Englishman's hands. As soon as he arrived, the Muslim suffered a 'fit of sickness', which prevented him from presenting his case for forty days. When eventually he did, the Company offered him £10 for his troubles, but insisted that the Company was 'not a joint-stock company, but every member trades on his own behalf' and that, both in English and in Turkish law, no man was liable for another's debts. Since Harvey was now in Turkey, it declared, he should be prosecuted there.[89]

By then, Harvey had already been thrown into a 'damp stinking prison', where he was denied the consolation even of wine.[90] That did not resolve the issue of how his creditors were to be repaid, though, and the threat that the factory would eventually have to foot the bill rumbled on. Recriminations began to fly. The consul was charged with failing to warn Harvey's principals of quite what trouble their factor was in. He was even accused of accepting a bribe from the Ottoman authorities to do their bidding. Facing similar situations to Harvey's own, pashas were known to convert to Islam to escape the arm of the Company's justice.[91]

Saddled with a dishonest factor willing to exploit the manifold opportunities for evasion offered by Ottoman society, there was little a London merchant could do to limit his exposure to ruin. The Company voiced an understandable paranoia when, in 1661, it declared itself 'well nigh ruined by the factors, who have been so long their own masters and will not submit to honesty and reason.'[92] If this was a trade involving 'masters of the universe', they were nowhere to be found in London.

By the 1660s, the reach of the Company's business stretched across the Middle East. The odd Briton would find himself living in conditions of almost total isolation as a result. A letter book extant from the later seventeenth century among the Company's records establishes that there was, even then, a factor resident in Syrian Tripoli (on the modern-day Lebanese coast). This was a place which, for a time, had served as Aleppo's primary seaport and supported an English consulate, but it had long since been deserted by its community of Company traders. Most miserable of all such outposts was malarial Scanderoon, where there was a lonely English counting-house on the shoreline, squalid as it was indispensable for the Aleppo trade. The chief qualification for employment in the port seems to have been a strong physical constitution. On a replacement being sought for the resident post, whose previous occupant had (like so many before him) prematurely expired, warm words issued from Aleppo in favour of a certain Mr Wilson, 'a person unquestionably qualified for your services, as well in respect of his great experience, as his long residence at Scanderoon, whereby he is in a manner habituated to the air of that place, and of consequence likelier to live, than any person that can be sent from England'.[93]

In this central period of the Company's existence, though, by far the greater part of the commerce was done from one of the three main 'Scales': 'Constantinople in the Northern Part; Smirna in the middle part, and Aleppo in the southern part of that Empire.' The significance of places like Chios and Patras had declined along with that of currant imports. By now, it could be declared that these three alone served 'the whole Turkish Empire with all the Native Commodityes of England that Empire can vent: and afford us the exportation from thence of all that Empire and Persia too, affords of Merchandise'.[94] The English trading communities in each place were large, highly developed and deeply entrenched.

The *Plymouth* arrived at the outset of a prosperous period for the trade. In the space of six years after 1662, the value of their imports to the Ottoman Empire as a whole grew by well over a quarter, exports by nearly 15 per cent. In the period 1666–71 an average of 13,672 cloths were imported every year. By 1672–7, this figure had climbed to 20,075 per annum, a level which was sustained for the next half-decade.[95] Meanwhile, annual silk imports from the Levant to England climbed during the 1660s to around 280,000 pounds per year, representing by far the greater part of the total.[96] Twenty years later, Paul Rycaut could declare from his desk in the consulary house at Smyrna that he lived in a time when English 'navigation [i.e. sea power] is in a higher esteeme, then that of all nations together, so is our trade in like manner & I believe greater then ever it was known, though being overlaid by quantities of Goods, & multitude of Traders, it becomes liable to those complaints which are common in all great Marts of the World'.[97] The general shipping fleets by now routinely numbered into the hundreds and, in the same era, Sir John Finch boasted of the 'vast trade we now drive'.[98] The Company's fortunes were reaching their zenith.

5

Ambassadors

❖

Palaces

More than a month after the *Plymouth* laid anchor in the Ottoman capital, the day appointed for Winchilsea's audience with the sultan arrived. Before first light he emerged from the English palace, still suffering from fever and a cyst behind the ear picked up during the voyage. The retinue of officials, pages, dragomen and merchants, their number swelled by locals hired for the occasion and bedecked in imported English livery, stood ready for departure.[1] Mounting his horse (the coach that he had shipped out for these occasions proved treacherous on Pera's hill and he despatched it straight back to London), Winchilsea fixed his gaze on the famous skyline ahead and trotted forth.[2] The train of Englishmen, 'richly clad & bravely mounted' and one hundred strong, advanced first through mansion-clad vineyards then, as Stamboul's domes and turrets loomed larger, along streets swelling with the bustle of daybreak.[3] Slowing to a halt at Galata's waterfront, they boarded a long boat and headed into the Golden Horn, joining the 'many thousand *Boats*' which were 'perpetually rowing up and down, call'd *Kaicks*, of *long* and *narrow* form, a little rising at each end and *widening* in the middle; not unlike an open'd *Bean-shell*'.[4] Their vessel put in at one of the waterfront outhouses used for the sultan's galleys on the opposite shore, where a squadron of messengers from the Ottoman court waited to meet them. From here they were spirited inshore, past pine and cypress trees, then onto the wide stone thoroughfare that wound past the Blue Mosque and Haghia Sophia and up finally to the Great Gate marking the threshold of the Topkapi Palace.

On occasions like this, every sight was a spectacle. Winchilsea's audience had been timed to coincide with the day when the sultan, in an elaborate display of imperial might, paid his famed legions of Janissaries. Riding across the first court, the Englishmen dismounted at the Gate of Salutation and walked past its guards. In front of them unfolded a courtyard which, as William Harborne had enthused decades earlier, was twice the size of St Paul's Cathedral.[5] Along one of its perimeters, rows of petitioners would queue to seek the sultan's justice meted out from the divan on its far left-hand side. Tucked into the corner next to it was the entrance to the Harem, where in Elizabethan times Thomas Dallam had once lingered too long in the hope of glimpsing its 'young, lusty lascivious wenches'.[6] Opposite, five thousand uniformed Janissaries now stood, 'drawn up in a body, and ranged on one side of the courtyard'. There was, Paul Rycaut recalled, amongst them 'that silence, that the least whisper, noise, or motion was not heard; and as their Janisar Aga, and other commanders passed, the bowings they made in salute were so regular, and at the same time, as may well testify the exactness of their discipline, and admirable obedience, which that in a great measure contributed towards their conquests and enlargement of their Empire'.[7]

If the Ottomans were consummate masters of political theatre, the Topkapi was their grandest stage. Alongside the Empire's military prowess, its wealth was paraded in front of the distant northern visitors. In the divan, bags of gold were heaped up under the gaze of the Grand Vizier, from where Janissary captains stepped forward to harvest their platoons' pay. Winchilsea himself was now ushered into this building, its floors covered with ornate carpets laid in his honour. At its upper end sat the Grand Vizier, flanked on the right by five Viziers of the Bench, amongst them the Lord High Admiral, and on the left by the Chief Justices, the Lord Treasurer and other dignitaries.

The Empire ruled the world, but these were historically the men who had ruled the Empire. In council meetings held in this room on most days of the week, decisions would be weighed beneath a globe hung from a chain, symbolising unashamedly the Ottomans' mastery of the universe.[8] The English guests were brought a succession of coffee, sweetmeats, sherbet and perfumes as they exchanged greetings, then treated to a meal. Scores of dishes, passed by hand along a great line stretching towards the imperial kitchens on the other side of the courtyard, were placed in front of them. Once served up, the food was quickly snatched away, so that the feast was brief as it was ostentatious. Next, ceremonial vests were exchanged, those given by the English a present from the King and paid for grudgingly by the Company, consisting of 'fifty vests, *viz.* ten of velvet, ten of satin, ten of cloth of gold, ten of tabbies, and ten of fine English cloth, [which] were brought forth and displayed in the open court by fifty men which carried them', as well as four English mastiffs. The Company might as well have spared its gold, for the mastiffs proved 'more acceptable to the Grand Signior than all the rest'.

Drawing up in line with the Great Vizier at their head, the dignitaries next processed to the Gate of Felicity, which guarded the way to the private realm of the Inner Court. Two Chief Porters of the Gate, carrying long silver staves, took Winchilsea under each arm and conducted him forward, followed by Sir Thomas Bendish, Sir Thomas Allin, the English dragoman, and lastly Paul Rycaut, clutching the ambassador's letters of credential made up in a purse of cloth of gold. These were the chosen few

21 The sultan receives an English ambassador in the audience room of the Topkapi Palace.

who would be allowed into the sultan's presence. The gate was flung open to reveal forty eunuchs standing in its porch, clothed in vests of satin and gold cloth. In the silence of the parade, the gurgling of the fountain in the sultan's garden was distantly audible. They advanced the short distance up to the Chamber of Audience, stepping over floors covered with crimson velvet and embroidered with golden wire. The sultan sat in his throne, raised a little from the ground and supported by gold-plated pillars, topped with gilded balls and laid with cushions beset with jewels.

The two porters, still gripping Winchilsea's arms in a lock, led him to the middle of the room, laid their hands on his head, and forced him to bow until he touched the ground with his forehead. Raising him again, they dragged him backwards into the corner of the room, then took each of the Englishmen in turn through the same ritual. This orchestrated obeisance was ostensibly to safeguard the sultan from assassination. In practice, by far its more important role was to force envoys into total prostration before him. In the drama of the court's formalities, foreigners were cast as clients of a supreme sultan. Resistance was worse than futile. When, later on in Winchilsea's spell as ambassador, the Grand Vizier failed to rise to receive the French ambassador who had come for an audience with him, the Frenchman loudly demanded that the Ottoman potentate show him more honour. The Vizier is supposed to have replied furiously: 'Do not I know that you are an . . . Infidel, that you are a hogge, a dogge, a turde eater.' In the argument that ensued, the Frenchman was assaulted and imprisoned, only narrowly escaping with his life. In the same era, a Dutch official who offered a 'rash answer' to the Grand Vizier received 184 blows on his bare feet in sight of the divan, from which it was justly feared that he would 'be crippled all his life'.[9]

Winchilsea was wise, then, to submit to his allotted role in the perform-ance. The ambassador's letters of credential from the King having been presented, his dragoman read a brief declaration in Ottoman Turkish:

First, declaring how the King of Great Britain our sovereign Lord and Master, was restored to the throne of his ancestors without war, or any conditions: and the great clemency of his Majesty in pardoning all, but those who had a hand in the murder of his father. Secondly, recom-mending the Merchants and their interest to the continuance of his usual favour and protection. Thirdly, begging the freedom of all English slaves, as a particular testimony of favour, and grace to this new ambassador.[10]

This done, and without a word from the sultan, who preserved his haughty silence throughout, the Englishmen shuffled backwards and slowly departed. As they crossed through the Second Court back towards the shore of the Golden Horn, they passed yet more soldiers, 'a very flourishing militia of young men, robust, and well clothed; many of them running with bags of money on their shoulders, and all of them cheerful'.[11] Within the hour, they were restored to the familiarity of Galata.

From the beginning of the Company's history, the post of ambassador to Constantinople was one of undoubted prestige. The attempt to enlist Ottoman support for Queen Elizabeth's crusade against Catholic Spain in the late sixteenth century, moreover, immediately set bold ambitions. Yet high diplomacy at the Porte thereafter struggled to get off the ground and remained tentative during the century that followed. In part that was owed to the ambassador's uneasy status. For until the government finally took over wholesale responsibility for the post in 1803, he was the creature of both the Company and the King. Which of these two masters held the upper hand was to remain a source of contention throughout the seventeenth and eighteenth centuries. 'The principal part of your employment is to protect our merchants in their lawful trade & to assist them in the orderly government thereof', even Winchilsea's instructions from the Crown had admitted in 1660.[12] Yet if the Company of merchants from the outset shouldered the burden of paying the ambassadors' salaries, amounting to the princely sum of £150 in the mid-seventeenth century, it did not necessarily call their tune.

For one thing, the Company encountered the perennial difficulty that the post's occupants preferred the glamour of a high political mandate to mundane commercial responsibilities. 'They think', one complained of the Company, 'their commands can control his majesty's commission, and the orders that come out of their counting-house equal to those of the Privy Council.'[13] Diplomats looked with horror on the notion of being no more than a 'grand factor for the merchants'.[14] From William Harborne's time, foreign envoys had tried to undermine the English influence at the Porte by painting its ambassadors as mere hired guns for petty cabals of traders. That they instead spoke for a mighty, if distant, monarch, was a message which the ambassadors tried tirelessly to convey to the Ottoman court, simultaneously playing down their role as a mouthpiece for merchants. In 1679, the Aleppo factory wrote to Sir John

Finch demanding that he complain to the sultan of abuses being suffered by English merchants there and threatening that, if he did not, the Company would order him to do so. Dining together at the palace some time afterwards, Finch told Dudley, Paul and others in passing of this, then insisted that they were:

> . . . not to mention so much as by whisper any such thing, for if it should take air, it would cut the throat here of the interest of the Company . . . for should the Vizier by any means to know that the ambassador, whom he justly looked upon to come to audiences to him by order of his Majesty, did ask them by virtue of the orders of merchants, he would despise the ambassadors as much as he does the merchants themselves; giving no honour to any ambassador but upon account of his prince . . .[15]

If the slur of being glorified trade lobbyists tended to bite, that was because it contained a large dose of truth until at least the Restoration. True, the capitulations governing the pashas' trading rights were the product of negotiations between princes, not merchants. Yet the greater part of their time was absorbed by the responsibility to 'do all things requisite for the honest and orderly government of our subjects' in the Ottoman Empire, as Elizabeth I had instructed Harborne.[16] With the odd exception (in the 1620s, for instance, Sir Thomas Roe managed to stir up Bethlen Gabor of Transylvania against the Emperor Ferdinand and ally him with Christian of Denmark and the Protestant princes of Germany), the ambassadors' successes were scored in protecting the Company's trade, rather than projecting the power of the English state on any more squarely political footing.[17] In an era when that state lacked any conception of a trade policy, this reflected an absence of diplomatic ambition – still less imperial ambition – on the part of the English within the sphere of Ottoman influence.[18] As the secretary of state informed Winchilsea, batting off his demands for a government allowance to fund the gathering of intelligence, 'there hath never used to be allowance given to any ambassador at Constantinople for intelligence, and that place is soe remote, as any intelligence from hence hither (it's conceaved) can be of little use here'.[19] Whitehall even managed to despatch a missive to the sultan which addressed him by the wrong name.[20]

For most of the seventeenth century, indeed, the English state recognised few interests in the region worth pursuing. What diplomatic imperatives existed still bowed to the hoary mantra of religious solidarity. References to the interests of 'Christendom' abound in diplomatic despatches. In a small nod to the future, Winchilsea's instructions spoke of preserving the balance of power in Europe. They gave greater weight, though, to the 'especial care' to be given to 'the welfare of all Christian princes in general, particularly those that border on the Turkish Empire'.[21] Set against Ottoman might, England was both a puny and timid player in Middle Eastern power politics.

Keen to make something more of his office, Winchilsea strove to banish such attitudes. 'You may, perhaps, reckon the information of affairs here, by reason of the distance, the little intercourse between the two Crowns, and the negotiation of former Embassadours (which was nothing antiently but the support of merchandise and trafficke) to be impertinent to matters of state in England;' he wrote indignantly to the secretary of state, 'yet, I can assure you it was always a grosse mistake, and the interest of his Majestie might as well have beene promoted here as in the more neere parts of Christendome.'[22] His appointment as ambassador itself revealed the tide to be turning. He was the first peer of the realm to occupy the post. He was also, as he was too fond of boasting, the first to be conveyed to Constantinople aboard a navy warship.

There were good reasons for the place of Ottoman affairs in English diplomacy to restore its Elizabethan prestige somewhat after the Restoration. Through its *'European* dominion', as described by Aaron Hill (see p. 117), perhaps, the Empire no longer preyed on English minds as it had done in the sixteenth century as a direct military or spiritual threat. Its *'Asiatick* Territories', on the other hand, were now assuming for Britons an unprecedented salience. That was so for the simple reason that, increasingly as the seventeenth and eighteenth centuries progressed, Asia was an important sphere for their direct trade and nascent imperial ambitions. An Ottoman (or, more generally, Islamic) military threat could impact on England's interests here rather directly. As he began 'to extend his dominions in the Mediterranean sea', Winchilsea told the King in a reference to the short-lived English colonial possession of Tangier after 1662, he was 'becom[ing] a dangerous neighbour' to the Ottomans. At the same time that the Turks were besieging Vienna for the second time in 1683–4, this was being evacuated because it could no longer be defended against its North African assailants.[23] By the same token that the King was becoming a dangerous neighbour, Winchilsea might have pointed out, he was himself acquiring one in the sultan, to whom a fresh regard would have to be paid.

As for the Ottomans' '*European* dominion', the role it might play in the interminable wrangle for mastery of western Europe was gaining some recognition. Winchilsea planned to foster war between Austria and the Ottomans, in the hope of diverting Hapsburg attentions from English interests in Spain.[24] He struggled to gain his political masters' support for the ploy and it achieved little. Yet it illuminated a feature of the Ottomans' strategic position which would soon catch London's attention, namely its capacity to sap the forces of the Hapsburg Empire.

The consequences of this latter would not turn out as Winchilsea had foreseen. In general, war between the Hapsburgs and Ottomans suited French interests well and, for that very reason, English ones badly. Between the late seventeenth century and the onset of the Seven Years War, the rule was that the French would try to foment war whilst the English fostered peace on the Empire's western frontier. In the wake of the Glorious Revolution particularly, William III developed a concerted *Ostpolitik* aimed at drawing the Ottomans and Hapsburgs to a peace, in the interest of furthering his Protestant crusade against France. Sir William Trumbull was instructed to achieve just that in 1690 and, for the best part of a decade thereafter, the policy was determinedly pursued, culminating in the peace congress at Karlowitz in the autumn of 1698 which was presided over by the English ambassador to the Porte, Lord Paget, together with his Dutch counterpart.[25] Paget's successor, Sir Robert Sutton, devoted much of his attention during his long stint in the role to counteracting French intrigues aimed at fomenting war between the Hapsburgs and the Ottomans and thus weakening the allied position in the War of Spanish Succession.[26] Sir Edward Wortley Montagu, Sutton's successor in turn, oversaw yet another peace congress, which ultimately brought the Austrians and Turks to a renewed peace.[27]

English high diplomacy at the Porte, then, flourished as never before in the Company's heyday, though its importance still tended to be regarded as minor in London. By the later seventeenth and early eighteenth centuries, high affairs of state increasingly predominated in ambassadors' missives from the Porte. As their mandate representing the English (or, soon, British) state burgeoned, though, it sat all the more awkwardly with their responsibility to champion the wants of merchants. The two charges often pulled in quite contrary directions. The Company had its own interests to protect in questions of war and peace, though where those interests pointed was not always easy to say.[28]

On the one hand, war would always stimulate demand for England's military exports – its tin for munitions and wool for uniforms. Whenever they encountered a dispute with the Ottoman authorities over trade, the English drew comfort from 'knowing that no nation could furnish [the Ottomans] with tin or lead but [themselves], nor with cloth so good as that of England, unless they stole English wool'. That alone, they reckoned, would ensure the 'impossibility of the Turks subsisting' without the Company's trade.[29] On the other hand, both Ottoman and European wars tended to decimate markets key to the Company's prosperity. Perennial Ottoman conflict with Persia on the eastern frontier, heavily disrupting the silk routes, was a favourite gripe of traders in Aleppo. Though they were largely beyond the power of the Company to influence, English wars against the French or the Dutch visited even more calamitous consequences on volumes of trade, primarily by rendering sea routes hazardous and ships more costly to insure.

Ever eager for reassurance that he was their man in Constantinople and not the King's, the Company endeavoured to keep the ambassador

22 The view from the Dutch embassy in Constantinople, near the English one. Pera's wooden houses clutter the foreground.

on a tight rein. Nor was it shy to extend its demands into overtly polit-ical territory. Sir John Finch once complained of receiving orders from the Company so entirely at variance from those of the King that they were an invasion of the royal prerogative, and presupposed a power the Company 'could no more exercise then the whole city, nor neither of them more then a company of cobblers'.[30]

The question of control over the ambassadors was fought out most bitterly over appointments to the post. These were in the hands of the Crown, but the court of the Company would make plain which candidate it favoured and in the early years its preference tended to be respected. The breakdown of this arrangement was epitomised by the wrangle over the appointment of Sir Thomas Phillips, emphatically a creature of the court. The merchants wished to keep on Sir Thomas Roe, who had already served as ambassador to the Mughal court in Delhi and showed an undoubted flair for the role. The Company petitioned both the Privy Council and the House of Commons, but to no avail.[31] It then insisted that it would not pay his expenses or confide its interest to a person 'so incapable and untrust-worthy' as the King's candidate. The impasse was only resolved when Phillips unexpectedly died.[32] Sir Peter Wyche, who was despatched instead, was regarded by the Company with little more enthusiasm.

With the strengthening of the ambassador's squarely diplomatic role, the Crown's hand was broadly strengthened. By 1679, Sir John Finch could declare that 'the Company had no more authority to choose ambas-sadors then his servant had'.[33] The Whig ascendancy, however, allowed the Company to reassert some autonomy and a pattern emerged whereby a compromise candidate would be appointed after a flurry of horse-trading.

The Company and ambassador themselves tussled over the appoint-ment of lowlier officials in the Levant. The embassy maintained a size-able staff: grooms, porters, butlers, cellar-keepers, ladies-in-waiting, as well as dragomen, secretaries, chaplains and doctors. The former of these were mostly supplied by 'Greeks, Armenians and other people of the country'.[34] The Company paid the salary of the ambassador's secretary, the role in which Paul Rycaut began his Levantine career, and therefore 'pretend[ed] a right to choose him'.[35] Ambassadors, moreover, might regret being too free with the scope for patronage which other embassy posts offered. 'You will have great applications made to you to entertain the sons or relations of gentlemen in order to their preferment or to make their fortune,' Sir William Trumbull was warned, 'and perhaps you will not be able to resist their importunities . . . but you must know that when these gentlemen have been some time with you, and find that matters there do not correspond with their expectations, they will then desire to return home at your expense and perhaps with various complaints against you'.[36] The most important appointments were to the consulships of Aleppo and Smyrna. The ambassadors were determined that these should be in their hands, but the Company was forever loathe to agree.

The cost of the embassy was a significant one for the Company to bear. If it became a well-worn tradition that the Company had to cough up for it, this left plenty of room for dispute with the Crown over the bill for the various accoutrements. There was, for instance, the vexed question of presents: a vital element in getting anything done, since 'in this Empire the authority of a foreign minister is but faint which is not armed with some other weapons than the bare commission of his Prince'.[37] Harborne set the pattern, arriving in Constantinople with thirteen dogs, a mass of silver plate and a silver clock studded with jewels.[38] It thereafter took years to agree the arrangements that would lead to the despatch of Thomas Dallam to Constantinople at the end of the sixteenth century. He took with him a famous royal gift, the mechanical organ which stood for some years in the garden of the Topkapi Palace, until it was smashed by the iconoclastic Ahmed I.

Further difficulties were occasioned by the sultans' prolonged sojourns in Adrianople. The Company routinely refused to bear the expense of the elaborate journey to the court required to carry out weightier diplomatic negotiations. It would do so only on its own, rather than state, business.[39] Ambassadors demanded funds from the Crown for such journeys, in the absence of which they flatly refused to go.[40] The Company instructed Lord Chandos, Sir John Finch's successor, to do all he could to avoid having his audience with the sultan in Adrianople for all the cost it would incur.[41] The Company's parsimony perennially hampered English diplomacy. Merchants in London were slow to grasp a vital truth: how indispensable was the pashas' engagement in Ottoman politics for the health of their trade.

Capitulating

It all began when a mule tumbled down William Harvey's staircase. Perhaps, as Harvey later claimed, the corpse which appeared in his cellar in Aleppo one morning really had been 'purposely thrown there to ground a pretence'.[42] But when Harvey, a long-standing member of the English factory in Aleppo, sent its dragoman (translator) to demand an order from the local magistrate (*kadi*) that the beast's owner drag the body off, the order was readily granted and a Muslim merchant turned up at Harvey's door to lug the animal, bone-achingly and begrudgingly, to an unceremonious burial.

The tale might have ended there, had not the Muslim's aggrieved business partner bumped into the dragoman in the souk and threatened to exact revenge. This dose of intimidation was taken as a serious affront by the English traders. If their translators were allowed to be brow-beaten, they reasoned, 'none of them for the future will dare to serve us as they ought'. It fell to Consul George Brandon, who occupied the Aleppo post for five years and by now felt altogether self-assured in the Ottoman world, to respond. His first thought was to drag the offender before the magistrate. Success in such a case, however, would require witnesses to testify against a Muslim, something which Christian outsiders were not permitted to do. Muslim witnesses, conversely, were always difficult to enlist where rich and powerful adversaries were involved. So it was unavoidably the Muslim merchant who won his case.

Brandon next went to the governor, local figurehead of Ottoman imperial authority, and secured on the basis of the capitulations that the dispute now be heard before the sultan's divan in Constantinople. When the magistrate heard of this, he fell 'into a great rage . . . [and] publicly curst the Grand Signior for granting, & me for obtaining such a command'. To rub salt into the wound, Brandon then returned to the governor, reported the magistrate's slighting of the sultan's authority, and despatched the dragoman back to the Aleppo court to tell the magistrate what he had done.

This only deepened the magistrate's rage. He demanded to know how the English could dare to go to the sultan's court without his own leave and, having threatened him with execution, flung the dragoman into gaol. Brandon did not hesitate to report once again this man's 'violent & unjust manner of proceeding' to the governor, who had already dispatched a soldier forcibly to break open the gaol and free the prisoner. Brandon, having complained of 'the violation of our capitulations in imprisoning our drugorman', now insisted that the magistrate 'might be drubbed in my presence'. He also wrote to the ambassador in Constantinople, Sir Robert

Sutton, asking that a man be sent down to help the English cause. The case called for a high Ottoman official, he wrote, who might yield the necessary clout; and so that his sympathies might not be in doubt, he asked that 'the Aga who is sent down, may take up his Quarters at the house of one Ibrahim Beg, son of Ahmet Pasha of Cyprus, who is my particularly good friend, and will faithfully inform me, in case the . . . Cady should endeavour to corrupt or bribe him'.[43]

In the event, this envoy never materialised. By early in the next month, though, Sutton had prevailed on the Grand Vizier himself to despatch a letter to the Ottoman governor ordering that he 'drub [the magistrate] severely, and banish him to Baghdad'. News of this prompted the terrified magistrate to pay sufficient bribes to have the punishment suspended. In hopes of getting off the hook altogether, he also offered to host a day of entertainment for the entire English factory. So it was that one Thursday in April 1704, the English merchants of Aleppo, accompanied by their French and Dutch counterparts, rode to a garden out of town, where in front of the assembled company, in a 'very humble submissive manner, [the magistrate] craved pardon for his faults'.

Brandon thought he had triumphed. 'This Sir,' he trumpeted to Sutton, 'is such a prize of Justice, as I presume was scarce ever granted to any Ambassador since our first settlement in Turkey, and has so scared the Great Men here, that I believe they will hardly have courage enough to attaque us for the future.' As for himself, he continued, 'I may without Vanity say, I have gained some Reputation by my conduct in this matter, which I presume will be talked of when I am dead and gone.'[44]

Set against stories of life in the Levant typical of the period, Brandon's hubris is not difficult to understand. One tells of an English merchant who, when an Ottoman officer 'expressed himself a little disrespectfully in contempt of the *Christians* in the Merchant's Company', dared to return 'the Salutation as roughly as it was sent him'. The officer 'order'd the Merchant to be taken from his Horse, and undergo the Punishment of One Hundred and Fifty Bastinadoes [beating on the soles of the feet] . . . Complaints were altogether useless.' The merchant was so sorely beaten, supposedly, that he was not able to stand upright for a long time after. (There turns out to be a 'Jest' to this latter story, we are told: the unintended outcome of the merchant's punishment was to cure him of his crippling gout.)[45]

George Manwaring, one of the earliest English visitors to Aleppo en route to Persia, described a Turk nearly pulling off his ear and dragging him around the streets 'with much company following me, some throwing stones at me, and some spitting on me'.[46] Another, early in the seventeenth century, describes how, whilst walking in the streets of Constantinople in the company of a Janissary, an old woman took him for a captive to be sold and asked his price, '. . . who for his mirth entertained her offer to buy me and another gentleman . . . but because I was very slender and leane after my long sickness he could not induce her to give more than one hundred aspers for me . . .'[47] William Biddulph had this advice for Britons intent on travelling in Islamic lands: 'Neither if a man receive a box on the eare at any of their hands, must he give one bad word, or looke frowningly upon him that smote him: for then he will strike him againe, and say, What, Goure [infidel]? Dost thou curse me, and wish that the Devil had me? But hee must kisse his beard, or the skirt of his Garment, and smile upon him, and then he will let him passe'.[48]

All this is remarkably frank in the way it puts surrender at the heart of Britons' experience of Ottoman lands. Albeit that some of these tales were no doubt fabrication, they did reflect a certain reality. Captivity as slaves in the Muslim world, the postlude to attack by Barbary corsairs, is a subject much favoured by historians.[49] Freeing English captives within his dominions was, as we have seen, one of the three grovelling requests that Winchilsea addressed to the sultan at his audience with him. Ambassadors would frequently be implored from London to secure the release of prominent victims of Mediterranean piracy and it was a perennial object of North African diplomacy.[50] A short period of being slung into an Ottoman gaol on land was nearly as common a fate to be suffered by Company traders. We have already noted John Sanderson's confinement in Jerusalem and Samuel Harvey's in Aleppo. In Smyrna, it was one which also befell, amongst others, Montagu North, whilst Robert Bargrave, in the midst of a particularly intractable dispute with local notables, was thrown into the 'dismall, darke, & noisome Dungeon' of Smyrna's castle, where the air was filled with a horrid stench and the 'musique of monstrous rats'.[51]

Surrender, however, was also called for in a sense at once more subtle and pervasive than that of submitting oneself to being clapped into manacles. In the nineteenth century, the 'millet' system – under which foreign communities were, to a large extent, self-governing within the

Ottoman polity – would become synonymous with western Europe's thoroughgoing humiliation of the Ottoman regime. If you visit Galata today, it is possible to dine in a British prison dating from that era, distantly visible even from the Topkapi Palace. This was a place symbolising the power of the British to decide whom it would imprison for 'wrongs' committed on Ottoman soil – and, more importantly, whom it would not, cocking a snook at the sultan's authority to reign in the misdemeanours of his capital's western Europeans and their Christian clients. In this earlier period, the connotations of the distinctively Ottoman regime that licensed foreign communities' presence on their soil were quite different.[52]

We have seen that precepts of Islamic law underpinned the toleration of the non-Islamic subjects of the Ottoman Empire.[53] They also informed the capitulations, which licensed the presence of non-Muslims who were not so much as subjects of the sultan. Classically, traders from the 'abode of war' – those parts of the globe where Islam did not hold sway – might be granted an *aman*, a temporary safe-conduct which spared them from the enslavement to which they might otherwise be liable. The immediate model for the capitulations came from Byzantine practice rather than Islamic law, but it also strongly echoed this Islamic doctrine.[54] Its application to the pashas, as to other northern-European merchants, involved a considerable fudge. Unlike the *dhimmi*, such outsiders owed no allegiance to the sultan. And whereas an *aman* was supposed to be a short-term expedient, a mere prelude to subjection as a *dhimmi* or conversion to Islam, the capitulations became the diplomatic and legal underpinning of a centuries-long European presence in Ottoman lands.

Partly as a result, their meaning was never anchored and often argued over. Even in early-modern times, the capitulations might be said to raise their foreign beneficiaries to a status of privilege over the non-Muslim subjects of the sultan – sparing them, not least, the indignity of the *jizya* (poll tax levied on non-Muslims). Even so, if they might come to signify Britons' arrogant autonomy by the nineteenth century, in these earlier times they did more to illuminate their dependence on the sultan's patronage and the degree to which their very presence in Ottoman lands was on the Ottomans' terms. It was in the very nature of the *ahidname-i hümayun* ('imperial pledge'), as the Ottomans called the institution of the capitulations, that it represented a munificent and one-sided dispensation from the sultan, not a binding treaty with a foreign state which he might regard as tying his hands.[55] In a symbolic affirmation that it was his patronage alone which sanctioned their presence, the sultan would even fork out an allowance to the ambassadors of foreign princes at the Porte. It was this status which the ambassadors were compelled to play out in their enforced prostrations before his throne. 'Ambassadors and ministers should remember,' Sir James Porter advised in the later eighteenth century, 'that they are received only conditionally at the Porte, as guests to the Grand Signor.'[56]

Throughout the Company's history, the English capitulations continued to resemble the text obtained by Harborne, in turn modelled on the French one. It became apparent early on, though, that the various pledges extracted by Harborne were by no means immutable. In 1581, a brazen act of piracy off the coast of Greece, inflicted by the English *Bark Roe* on two vessels crammed with Ottoman subjects, very nearly derailed the new trading relationship altogether. When news of the incident reached the Ottoman court, it prompted an immediate imposition of sanctions, lifted only when the Queen herself was prevailed upon to write a letter of apology to the sultan. Conversely, Harborne was later able to amend them to the English advantage, securing a preferential rate on customs duties of 3 per cent rather than the 5 per cent which had hitherto prevailed.

Improving the capitulations' terms would be a favoured ambition of ambassadors until the later seventeenth century. In its mid-part they went through a flurry of reconfirmations. When, after more than five months of negotiation and successive rounds of bribery, Sir John Finch obtained in 1675 the revision which would endure for the remainder of the Company's history, he declared the renewed articles 'farr the greatest Present that ever was made to the Company since the first forming of this Trade'.[57] This was hyperbole, but the English negotiating position was nonetheless strengthened in a number of significant aspects, particularly as to the basis on which the customs duties levied by the Ottomans were to be charged. Finch's effort to persuade the sultan henceforth to refer to the King of England by the grand title of *Padishah*, on the other hand, flatly failed.

For all their humbling overtones, the capitulations were nonetheless regarded by the English as holding an elemental importance. At home, the old slur of 'oriental despotism' had at its heart the claim of Ottoman lawlessness.[58] The pashas were all too keenly aware of the untruth of this idea: the very existence of the capitulations as a set of legal rights formally accorded to Britons, and to varying degrees observed, exposed the hollowness of the polemic. Ottoman-Islamic law, in truth, both underpinned the pashas' presence in the region and did much to shape their everyday experiences of it. Given the pashas' wholesale inability to draw on military force, the capitulations were regarded as the legal guarantees standing between them and total vulnerability in the Ottoman world; and accordingly, they strove to protect them with vigour. As the ambassador Sir John Finch boasted of his dealings with a particularly intransigent Ottoman regime: 'Though we cannot brag of our usage, yet we may justly say we have fared better than any other Nation. For hitherto though in the worst of Times, I have maintained all the Capitulations Inviolable.'[59] He could not sleep soundly, Finch had elsewhere declared, without the capitulations stowed under his pillow.[60] In a typical instruction from the Company, Sir Daniel Harvey was told to uphold 'the protection of all the priviledges & immunities of our subjects of the Turkey Company, for whose good & benefit you are most especially to reside there, by preserving firm & inviolable to them the Capitulations . . .'[61] They had, the merchants declared, 'ever been the safeguard of our estates'.[62]

Yet if the text of the capitulations was one thing, their enforcement was quite another. In 1583, one of the Company's ships sent to Libyan Tripoli was seized and its crew enslaved, both fates from which the capitulations supposedly offered protection.[63] Harborne did eventually manage to obtain redress from the Porte, but only by means of a tortuous effort of diplomacy.[64] Fending off 'violations' would become a well-worn theme in the Company's history. It was rarely achieved by anything so straightforward as the assertion of a right, however unambiguously it might seem to be accorded by the text of the capitulations. How valuable could these assurances be, a later ambassador was moved to wonder, when they were 'like a piece of paper that may be stretched in any way'?[65]

The capitulations' legal guarantees were mediated by political realities. Much depended on the character of the administration which happened to hold sway. When Sir Daniel Harvey was sent as ambassador to Constantinople in 1668, he was made to wait a full year to receive a first audience with the sultan. The notorious era presided over by Kara Mustapha, the Grand Vizier who failed at the second siege of Vienna in 1683, coincided with a series of particularly vicious diplomatic spats. By the middle of the 1680s, by contrast, Lord Chandos felt able to write to the secretary of state that 'wee live in extreame peace & quiet at present', for the Turks had 'an excellent chimacham that governes the citty of Stambole, who is a great favourer of all Christians, [and] we have no cause of complaining'.[66]

Even when a favourable regime prevailed at the Porte, though, the capitulations' force outside the capital would stand or fall on the authority of the sultan. The distribution of political power in Ottoman society was nothing if not complex. Regional elites routinely challenged the authority of both the sultan and his representatives scattered around the Empire. The Aleppo consul still complained in the early eighteenth century of Sir John Finch's failure decades earlier to tailor the capitulations to Aleppo's circumstances: unlike Constantinople and Smyrna, where the trade was well regulated, they were 'exposed to the mercy of every litigious Mohasil, who might embroil us at pleasure'.[67] If the sultan's command 'happens to fall into the hands of a Bashaw, who has been himself Vizir, and is consequently experienced in the various turns of government', another ambassador acknowledged, 'he seldom pays any regard to the demands of the Porte, but as he himself happens to be disposed; nor will he assist or execute, without being gained beforehand by the golden motive, which with the Turks is all-prevailing'.[68]

This problem tended to worsen as time wore on. A provision of the 1675 capitulations was designed to cure it by allowing all valuable disputes to be dealt with at the sultan's divan in Constantinople. As the Harvey affair demonstrated, though, that provision in itself might or might not secure the obedience of provincial notables. The Porte's authority over the further reaches of its dominions during the seventeenth and, even more so, eighteenth centuries was at times fragile.

We should be attentive to the fact that this latter has been a favoured theme of historians keen to trace the Ottoman state's supposed 'decline' and arguably overplayed as a result. Pretenders in a variety of guises, there is no doubt, emerged to challenge the will of the centre from the late sixteenth century onwards. Yet if nationalists have sometimes painted these figures as expressions of a nascent Arab identity, bucking against the yoke of Turkish imperialism, there was a fine line between political struggles conducted within the framework of the Ottoman state and wholesale challenges to its legitimacy. The Ottomans, generally skilful at co-opting local elites into their system, never did impose a monolithic political structure on their vast empire. Its subjects' outbursts of intractability were, perhaps, not in all instances symptomatic of a growing weakness on the part of the state.

Still, that could do little to blunt their impact on the pashas' lives. Even in Constantinople, the force of imperial edicts might be undermined by the vagaries of court politics and rivalries of elite households. Syria was especially prone to rebellion. In Aleppo, the pashas lived through episodes of outright defiance of Constantinople and even armed rebellion against it. In 1606–7, the Kurdish chieftain Canboladoğlu Ali called his tribe to arms in revenge for the death of his uncle Hüseyin at the hands of an Ottoman potentate. His forces were eventually crushed in the following year, but in the meantime the Ottomans had been forced to placate him by appointing him governor of Aleppo and he appeared to threaten a separate state in northern Syria.[69] A further serious revolt took place in mid-century, this time centred on Damascus.

Through it all, the House of Osman managed to retain a considerable prestige in the city.[70] Yet engaging with the intricacies of local politics was rendered an especially important aspect of the pashas' business there. 'The merchants at Aleppo, being far from the Court,' Paul Rycaut observed,

23 A portrait of an Ottoman court official dating from the early seventeenth century.

'are more subject to troublesome Avanias than others, who are nearer to the Head or Fountain, from whence Justice should proceed . . .'[71] Pleading the sultan's patronage was a tactic on which consuls frequently relied to avoid them. Any notion that spats with local potentates could always be resolved by resort to diplomacy at the sultan's divan, on the other hand, could not long survive the realities of Ottoman life.

Ensconced in London, the Company stubbornly refused to acknowledge this truth. In more chauvinistic moments, it liked to pretend an almost total autonomy to rise above the authority of the Ottoman state, its system of law and regional politics. Winchilsea was instructed by its court to uphold merchants' rights with uncompromising severity: 'You must not forbeare to tell [the sultan] plainely', they stated, 'that Justice will be the only Expedient to help him in possession of [the advantages of the British trade], which by the extortion & oppression of his ministers will be lost inevitably.'[72] The impracticability of that mandate was swiftly exposed. Shortly after Winchilsea's arrival in Constantinople, a merchant ship commanded by one Captain Robert Hudson was requisitioned to transport the sultan's troops to Crete. 'I opposed it,' Winchilsea informed London, 'by declaring it, to be against the capitulations, a discouragement to the English trade in this place, & some affront to me, to have my first coming entertained with so unpleasing a welcome.' But those feeble protestations fell on deaf ears and it was quite clear to the ambassador that he could push his point no further. 'Perceiving that there was Turkish fury, & obstinance in the resolution;' he wrote, 'I contended as far as with discretion & prudence I might, rather conniving at a small breach, then to make a total rupture in the whole, & to permit one man to suffer, rather than the generalitie to be ruined.' So off went the English ship carrying Turkish troops to war against Christendom, not for the first or final time.

On occasions like this, the most powerful weapon which Britons could unleash against their hosts was unilaterally to cease their trade – 'battulating', as they called it.[73] This was, of course, a deeply self-mutilating form of attack. Whenever put into effect, it tended to demonstrate how little the Ottomans depended on their commerce in this era. The temporary loss of revenues visited on the Porte was always unlikely to bring it to its knees, and it never did.

Less adversarial tactics succeeded better. In practice, Aleppo merchants made recourse to local courts notwithstanding the Company's disapproval.[74] Though some voiced their contempt, there is evidence of a grudging regard for Ottoman-Islamic law. 'I have sent you an authentic attestation that in case a Frank dies in Turkey indebted to several persons of different places, those who are actually present, and ready to prove their debts, will be first satisfied, without having any regard to those who are absent,' one missive from an Aleppo consul reads. 'This sir the Turkish law doth positively order, neither can any Frank magistrate avoid complying therewith, seeing we have nothing in our capitulations that does exempt us from it . . . since the custom here is different, I know no remedy; neither ought it seem very strange that we are obliged to conform to the laws of the country, in which we live.'[75] Dudley North became especially conversant with its ways. As his eighteenth-century biographer described: 'As to the law part of his business, it was so much as in the end gave him a competent skill in the rules and methods of the Turkish justice; whereby in common incidents he could advise himself and assist his friends . . .' For Dudley, arguing cases before the local court seems to have become a major part of his work. 'I have heard our merchant say,' the same writer added, 'that he had tried in the Turkish courts above five hundred causes; and, for the most part, used no dragomen, or interpreters, as foreigners commonly do, but in the language of the country spoke for himself.'[76]

Fighting the pashas' corner called for considerable skill not just in the courts, but outside them, in playing off the powerbrokers of Ottoman society. The pashas were in that sense indistinguishable from the profusion of other groups vying for influence in the Ottoman world. The capitulations now and then offered them a trump card: invoking the sultan's authority might allow them to slap down local notables. Yet this tactic did not always prevail. The interests of their commerce drew them into the full complexity of Ottoman politics.

Consul Brandon's wrangle with the *kadi* would, in the end, prove a case in point. For if the Aleppo consul thought that he had scored a triumph when the Porte promised to banish his Ottoman adversary, a week later nothing had happened. As he wrote nervously to the ambassador, 'the people of the Country begin to flatter themselves, that he may yet continue in office'. What made it worse, he recorded, was that he had already boasted of the English 'success' in securing his removal. The tables now turned, Brandon soon found himself with no choice but to make peace with the magistrate, by forking out an eye-watering bribe to his adversary. He had to consider, not least, the several merchants who had 'large summes out [in loans to Turks], which cannot be recovered but by Turkish Justice'. And in the last resort, he lamented, this humiliating surrender was simply 'the best that could be obtained'.[77]

Friends and Rivals

It was 'the finest fleet that had appeared on the *British* seas, in the memory of any man then living'.[78] Around four hundred vessels, both Dutch and English, departed the Isle of Wight on 30 May 1693, the richest of them bound for Smyrna. With war raging against the French, the merchantmen were accompanied by a squadron of warships under the command of Sir George Rooke. It was known that the French had been assembling at Brest, so the main English fleet accompanied the convoy until it had safely rounded the Breton peninsula, before turning back to guard the Channel. Yet this intelligence was woefully outdated. The Brest and Toulon squadrons had long since departed the French coast and, after uniting off Cadiz, now lay in wait in the Bay of Lagos. When the allied convoy rounded Cape St Vincent, the French sprung the trap.[79] Rooke's squadron found itself hopelessly outnumbered. The French commander, blessedly slow to close in on his beleaguered prey, allowed a good number of the ensnared vessels to make their escape.[80] Both on the Royal Exchange and in the factories of the Levant, though, the French attack was greeted as a monumental catastrophe. In London, the losses were thought to equal those sustained in the Great Fire, amounting to as much as a million pounds.[81] In Aleppo, the news seemed grimmer still. Writing from the factory, Nathaniel Harley bemoaned the years of toil undone in a few brief hours:

> This last misfortune of our ships is truly a great loss to the nation, but to the traders hither the greatest they or any other society of merchants ever felt at one blow . . . You cannot think me exempt from so general a calamity, in which I have but too great a share, but possibly less than others, who have lost not only the labour of ten or twelve years but are deprived also of all future hopes.[82]

The Smyrna fleet disaster marked the beginning of an upsurge in French competition which, after more than a century of dominance, would eclipse the pashas' trade. From the outset, though, they had lived alongside traders from other states of northern and western Europe. The presence of these fellow 'Franks', who were at different times their bitter rivals and kindred allies, would prove a major force in shaping their daily lives, as well as the progress of their trade.

The forces which impelled the grant of the first capitulations to Harborne were, for the most part, peculiar to the English. Yet the appearance of an organised English trade in the eastern Mediterranean had coincided with a 'rush' of similar dispensations to other Christian powers beyond the Italian city-states.[83] In retrospect, the late sixteenth century seemed to be witnessing unmistakable signs of a structural shift, by which the well-worn patterns of Mediterranean trade were first wrought open to 'northern, Atlantic, international capitalism'.[84] Northern ships, Fernand Braudel memorably (if melodramatically) described, now 'swarmed into the Mediterranean like so many heavy insects crashing against the window panes'.[85] It was hardly surprising that the incipient English presence provoked intense opposition from the diplomatic missions of the Venetian incumbents, as well as the French, themselves relative newcomers and occupying an intermediate status between the Mediterranean *ancien régime* and the Atlantic interposers. Both saw in the English a serious threat to their trade and prestige in the arena.

The English position accordingly came under sustained pressure from the diplomacy of other states even before the capitulations were obtained.[86] A series of worried missives, penned to their respective capitals by the Imperial ambassador to Constantinople and the Spanish ambassador to London, attended Harborne's first arrival at the Porte and tracked his every move. It was the French, in a foretaste of their eighteenth-century ascendancy, who were most effective in blocking the growth of his influence. No sooner had Harborne departed Constantinople for the first time than their ambassador succeeded in securing the revocation of the capitulations. On his return, armed this time with presents to the sultan and formal recognition from the English monarch, he managed to restore them. He did so, however, only after a renegotiation fraught with further intrigue.[87]

All this set the pattern for an intense rivalry between the merchants of the different Christian powers and their diplomatic representatives played out in the decades to come. The fears of the English harboured by the French and Venetians would prove well placed. The story of the Company's success in the first century of its Ottoman trade might largely be written, indeed, as the story of its skill in overtaking these two rivals, whilst holding at bay the threat posed by a third in the guise of the Dutch. Between the late sixteenth century and the beginnings of the eighteenth, it acquired and broadly held onto a pre-eminent position among the western trading nations active in the Levant.

The most immediate victims of the English newcomers were the once-mighty Venetians.[88] Venice was in the throes of a generalised decline by this date, the result of such diverse factors as demographic changes, shortages of shipbuilding materials, fluctuations in real wages and the debilitating effects of Mediterranean piracy.[89] With the birth of the Company, the death knell was permanently sounded for the direct trade once plied by Italian merchants between eastern Mediterranean and English ports.[90] The indirect trade for Levantine goods reaching London via the Venetian entrepot was similarly dented. There was worse to come, however, for after 1600 the Company's competition also wreaked severe damage on Venice's lucrative export trade to the Ottoman Empire. Its manufacturers of fine goods had long enjoyed a loyal following among well-to-do Ottoman buyers.[91] The purchasing power of this market was hit hard by a series of Ottoman financial crises at the turn of the seventeenth century.[92] At the same time, the arrival of the English shook the foundations of the monopoly which the Venetians had built up over cloth sales in the eastern Mediterranean. The Company found itself pushing at an open door into this market by the simple device of churning out imitations of the Italian real article at much lower prices. Faced with far higher labour costs than those prevailing in the underdeveloped English economy and lacking its mercantile dynamism, Venice struggled to hold ground in the sustained price warfare which the English now embarked upon. By 1635, its bailiff at Constantinople was declaring:

> . . . the English devote their attention to depriving our people of the little trade that remains to them in the mart of Constantinople, as they imitate Venetian cloth and make borders after the Venetian manner; they also have plates and wheels sent from their country, and although there is no market for these it shows they are trying to imitate everything and despoil our merchants of all of the trade they have left.[93]

It did not help that the Ottomans' advance during the seventeenth century correspondingly weakened Venice's political hold over the islands of the eastern Mediterranean. The long period of warfare between Venice and the Ottomans, above all that over Crete between 1645 and 1669, seriously impeded their trade. Meanwhile, England's growing commercial and maritime presence was strengthening its own prestige within the sea, partly at the Venetians' expense. It was reported as early as 1624 that Zante and Cephalonia were 'reduced to great penury by reason of the English merchants who at present have the trade to themselves and accordingly control it and turn it to their interests, to the grave prejudice of [Venetian] subjects'.[94]

Up to that date, the Venetians held their heads high and hoped that it all might be a passing phase. 'Although it is quite obvious their trade in the Levant entirely depends upon the courteous permission to use the Venetian post both for Venice and Aleppo,' the Senate complained of the English, 'yet they act as though they were under no sort of obligation and Venice was in duty bound to serve them.'[95] This sort of thinking, however, was increasingly wishful. By the time that Venice finally emerged defeated from the war over Crete in the later seventeenth century, it was clear that its declining industry could make no pretence of being able to keep pace with its northern competitors.[96] The Venetian contingents in the trading emporia of the Ottoman Empire would fairly soon melt away as serious contenders.

Until the Glorious Revolution, the French proved similarly tractable rivals. France's trade was seriously hampered into the middle of the seventeenth century by its lingering domestic strife, which also nourished Ottoman suspicions of French sympathies for its Hapsburg enemies and so weakened its diplomatic standing. Compared with the English Levant Company, moreover, the French lacked a well-structured institutional framework for organising their trade. Even Colbert's attempts to remedy this deficiency in the later seventeenth century conspicuously failed. A lack of organisation rendered the French trade all the more vulnerable to the aggressive and co-ordinated undercutting by which the English had broken into the Ottoman cloth market so effectively.

So too did the inferiority of France's shipping to the great Atlantic vessels now criss-crossing the Mediterranean. Designed for speed, French ships connecting Levantine ports with Marseille sacrificed both the capacity and intimidation factor which made for the success of their heavily armed Dutch and English counterparts. They enjoyed more favour in the Mediterranean carrying trade, where Ottoman merchants made widespread use of craft operated by small-time Provençal owners.[97] In spite of their well-deserved reputation for near-impregnability on the seas, the merchant ships of the Atlantic powers did not in the seventeenth century achieve the same dominance in this sphere of trade that they had in the transoceanic one (the Company tried to prevent English participation in it altogether, though these injunctions were, as ever, disregarded).[98] Nonetheless, even here the French encountered serious competition from Greek shipowners under Ottoman sovereignty.[99]

The most enduring obstacle to French success, however, was discord amongst its traders. Their presence might have been voluminous, but it was remarkably unproductive. As an English observer wrote in 1672:

> At Smyrna . . . there are above a Hundred [French] Merchants; and yet the Truth is, that in some Years the Effects that came out of France consign'd to all those Merchants did not amount to above Four Hundred Thousand Crowns Stock: Besides that they agree but very badly together, as being a sort of people that Love to harbour Division and Contention one among another.[100]

In part the problem lay in the absence of a proper system for paying their ambassadors and consuls a salary. In the first half of the seventeenth century, this propelled the French traders into internecine quarrelling, as officials sought to make amends on their pockets by imposing levies on the merchants.[101] An early French ambassador brought catastrophe to the French factory in Constantinople by running up huge debts on their behalf.[102] That the office of consul was a venal one inclined its occupants all the more strongly towards preferring their own interests to those of their charges. The French factory in Smyrna was thrown into disarray when its consul insisted that he should have precedence over the merchants in loading valuable Valencia acorns onto a home-bound ship.[103] Lacking any legitimate hierarchy of command, Ottoman officials in Istanbul and Smyrna were regularly called upon to arbitrate feuds between representatives of the French state.[104]

A more serious threat to English supremacy before the late seventeenth century seemed to be posed by the Dutch, who sprang onto the scene of Levantine trade not long after the grant of the English capitulations.[105] At first they traded without any capitulations of their own, relying on the protection of the English and the French. Nor was their trade much to speak of in this initial phase. Lacking any substantial domestic textiles industry, they were disabled from entering the three-way competition between the English, French and Venetians for domination of the cloth supply market, relying instead on silver to fund their Levantine purchases. This rendered them all the more vulnerable to the onset of Spanish economic warfare against them, which seriously hindered their progress at the outset of the seventeenth century. It took a truce with the Spanish in its second decade to reveal the true Dutch potential. The forces propelling them to dominance across large swathes of the world economy – above all, the combination of low freightage rates, born of formidable sea power, and access to Iberian silver – were a similarly propitious mix in the Mediterranean. The grant of capitulations to the Dutch in 1612, which put their customs rates on a par with the favourable ones secured by the English, marked their full emergence as a force to be reckoned with in Middle Eastern trade.[106] A network of consuls across the Ottoman Empire was swift to follow.

This provoked immediate alarm among the pashas.[107] 'It is now some years that the Dutch have frequented the Levant with a large number of ships and have tasted the profits of that trade,' as the Venetian ambassador in England reported in 1612. 'We may be sure that they will draw a large part of it to themselves.'[108] The Dutch and the English, both dynamic northern Protestant powers set on actively expanding their overseas trade, were natural rivals before they joined forces. If both were playing at the same game, moreover, in the seventeenth century there was no doubt that the Dutch were doing so with far greater global success.

Still, the Dutch emergence damaged the English position in the Levant less than it might have done. Principally this was because there was not a complete overlap in the markets on which they set their respective sights. Whilst the Dutch quickly seized the Mediterranean spice trade from the Venetians, this was of fairly minor consequence to the Company, which had by then conceded that the Mediterranean route for such goods was obsolete. The Dutch were markedly successful in the cotton trade, centring on Cyprus, but they were less so in the field of Persian silk, where the English concentrated their energies and continued to hold sway. Furthermore, the Dutch emergence was dealt a decisive blow with the return of economic conflict with the Spanish early in the 1620s. For the next quarter-century, their trade remained in eclipse.[109] In 1644, Amsterdam merchants complained that the Dutch Levant trade was ruined 'so that in many years we have had no ships sailing to or returning from there, the English having wholly taken over that commerce'.[110]

The arrival of peace with Spain three years after this lament coincided with a moment of particular English vulnerability brought about by the Civil War. The second Dutch emergence which now occurred was both sudden and dramatic. This time, moreover, their trade incorporated the sale of Dutch fine cloth of domestic manufacture, rather than relying wholly on imported currency. When Winchilsea arrived for the first time in Smyrna he found 'four great Holland ships in the bay, and more expected', and wrote of his fear that they would 'get away all the trade'.[111] On the other hand, it remained the case that the focus of the Dutch and English Levant trades differed. This was apparent, not least, from how small the Dutch presence remained at Aleppo: 'one house, & two, or at most three factors' in Lord Chandos' time. They still remained there under the protection of the English, at other times the French.[112] Similarly, there were only three or four Dutch trading houses in Constantinople in the early 1670s.[113] Their trade was almost wholly concentrated on Smyrna,

24 A Dutch depiction of Smyrna in its prime, a diplomatic audience taking place in the foreground.

where they bought mainly mohair yarn manufactured locally, rather than Persian silk imported along the caravan routes.

The damage which the Dutch inflicted on English trade was also mitigated by the support which the government lent to the Company's cause, albeit that it would prove a rather mixed blessing. The introduction of fresh Navigation laws in mid-century, restricting foreign imports to English ships, quickly halted the reappearance in the Royal Exchange of Levantine goods which had reached English shores only by way of Dutch entrepôts. Anglo-Dutch naval conflict swiftly followed, in which the Royal Navy seized every opportunity to attack Dutch Smyrna fleets. This might have demonstrated the superiority of England's naval puissance, but it did few favours for the pashas' trade. Insurance rates for Levant voyages out of London quadrupled after the outbreak of the Third Dutch War. This was not owed to the threat of the Dutch navy. Rather, as one factor wrote to his London principal in August 1672, 'the Dutch finding themselves unable to deal with our Royal fleet makes them fall to privateering, having of late done considerable damage to the traders of our nation'.[114] It suited the Company well when conflict gave way to union after the Glorious Revolution. The Ottoman market offered riches enough to share.

Indeed, one can question how far a picture of cut-throat commercial rivalry between the various Christian states trading in the Levant would have been recognisable to the pashas before the eighteenth century.[115] 'Nation' (in the narrow sense in which they understood it) was, as we have seen, but one focus of their loyalty. At times, a common identity as 'Franks' could seem more important still. There is some evidence of co-operation between western European merchants in attempts to manipulate the market. In 1617, for instance, the English, French, Dutch and Venetian consuls hatched a plan to make a joint approach to the Grand Vizier, Halil Pasha, then on a visit to the city, to complain of increases in duties and the behaviour of the customs farmers.[116] In 1632, a more extensive arrangement was enjoined to desist from buying silk and galls already sold on the market in Aleppo, in order to keep prices down. The experiment, it must be said, proved short-lived and both the English and French failed to be as good as their word.[117]

If such economic co-operation did not really get off the ground, though, the possibility only suggested itself because these merchants' social lives drew them into close interactions. That tendency was most visible in Smyrna, whose 'Frank Street' gathered their warehouses, churches, homes and consulates into the space of a few hundred feet. Across the Middle East, though, each nation's ceremonials often drew in the whole community of Franks, who would join the processions, answer warships' salutes in kind, or share in feasting and drinking (even if the latter was a frequent source of diplomatic spats as drunken mobs fell into fighting). Common subjection to *avanias* might bring them closer together still, diplomats frequently putting rivalries aside to make intercessions on behalf of fellow victims. There was no counterpart in the annals of the Levant Company's history to the Amboyna massacre, when the Dutch brutally murdered their competitors in the English East India Company. The sort of open conflict between the English, Dutch, French and Portuguese routine in South Asia was absent from the Ottoman Empire, where the building of forts was never on the cards.

Cordial relations were possible in part because identities were so fluid. National consciousness of a recognisably 'modern' kind, along with the oppositional identities it implied, was nowhere to be seen until well into the eighteenth century. By then, ironically, Europeans were becoming all the more united by their shared self-image as superior beings to Asiatic Turks.

6

Objects of Enquiry

— ❖ —

A Mahumetan Philosopher

In 1674, *The Philosophical Transactions of the Royal Society* announced publication of a short volume of Arabic and Latin prose in the name of the 'Learned Dr. Pocock'.[1] It related a curious tale. A baby appears on a deserted island somewhere in the Indian Ocean, born of the earth, perhaps, or brought there by the sea. Suckled by a gazelle, for a time he lives a feral existence. But as infant matures into child, the realisation dawns that he is not like the other creatures. He alone can reflect on what he sees around him; and by shining reason on his world, he quickly becomes its master. He gathers leaves and feathers to keep warm, learns to make fire, fashions weapons for hunting food. Yet his science eventually fails him: when the beloved gazelle grows old and dies, grief sends him on a metaphysical quest to understand the spirit of life and in time he single-handedly infers the existence of God. Then another human arrives, whose religion comes from the books of the prophets. The newcomer is startled by what he finds. For it seems that reason unaided has brought the island's marooned inhabitant to greater wisdom than could the revealed, priest-ridden faith of his own civilisation.

The story is that of *Hayy ibn Yaqzan*, work of the twelfth-century Andalusian physician and philosopher, Ibn Tufail. For many seventeenth-century English readers, its messages seemed peculiarly contemporary.

The impression that Arabic literature made on modern western culture through *The Thousand and One Nights*, first introduced to western Europe in Antoine Galland's edition early in the eighteenth century, might nowadays be much better remembered.[2] Yet this very different work of translation, foreshadowing Galland's French publication by more than three decades, was in its way perhaps as influential. Sinbad, Aladdin or Ali Baba, it is true, played better to the taste for eastern exoticism permeating fashionable Parisian *salons* (as latterly Hollywood studios). Through *Hayy ibn Yaqzan*, on the other hand, a philosopher of medieval Islam spoke to the avant-garde of the European Enlightenment at its most high-minded, right at the fulcrum of western intellectual modernity.

The Enlightenment has received a poor press in recent decades for the demeaning attitudes towards the 'Orient' which it is said to have spawned. How far those claims ring true depends partly on which 'Enlightenment' one speaks of. In the period of the Napoleonic invasion of Egypt, certainly, some *philosophes* were overtly complicit in the hardening of attitudes towards the 'Turks'. Much of the imagery favoured in that period was hardly new, but it was systematised as never before to cast them as cruel, effeminate, despotic and altogether inferior beings. Yet a different legacy emerged from the intellectual movements coinciding with the Company's prime in the later seventeenth and early eighteenth centuries. This was an Enlightenment whose centre of gravity was England rather than France, and whose dominant theme was an empiricism characteristically softer-edged than the thought of the Revolutionary period.[3] Even if it shared some of the latter's penchant for encyclopaedic classification, moreover, the attitudes it nourished towards other cultures were typically gentler.

The influence of this earlier Enlightenment on the pashas' mentalities was most keenly felt in their growing insistence on the claim of truth-telling. Late in the seventeenth century, Daniel Defoe foresaw what a potent intellectual concoction trade and travel might prove in the realm of knowledge:

Every new voyage the merchant contrives is a project, and ships are sent from port to port, as markets and merchandizes differ, by the help of strange and universal intelligence; wherein some are so exquisite, so swift, and so exact, that a merchant sitting at home in his counting-house, at once converses with all parts of the known world. This and travel, makes

a true-bred merchant the most intelligent man in the world, and consequently the most capable, when urged by necessity, to contrive new ways
to live.[4]

If none of this should be taken at face value, there was more than a
measure of truth to it as a description of the pashas. 'Mere curiosity of
learning some things abroad whereof I thought we had but slight knowledge at home,' as a letter penned from Pera in the later-seventeenth
century declared, 'was one of those motives which brought me hither.'[5]
Collectively, they spawned unprecedented volumes of print concerned
with the Ottoman Empire during the seventeenth and eighteenth
centuries. Company officials and their companions – the likes of Sir Paul
Rycaut, Robert Bargrave, John Covel, Henry Maundrell, Lady Mary
Montagu and Sir James Porter – set down their impressions for a wider
audience. Alongside such figures as these, the early Enlightenment also
encouraged a new breed of traveller to the Ottoman Empire, who came
to assume a growing prominence within the pashas' universe.[6] Their
appearance broadly coincided, moreover, with a flurry of print circulating
in London whose significant reappraisal of Islam owed much to the
traffic in manuscripts which the pashas had animated.

These revisions never displaced the vitriolic clichés of old, whose
popular purchase seems to have remained strong. Nor would their
moment last long. Coinciding with the Company's pinnacle in the second
half of the seventeenth century and early part of the eighteenth, by the
mid-part of the eighteenth century their brief flowering was already
beginning to be overshadowed, as a darker Enlightenment took hold.

Hayy ibn Yaqzan might have been amongst the most striking, but it was
only one of the myriad Arabic texts that by now had found their way
westwards out of eastern bazaars – first to England, then into English. A
traffic in such manuscripts was an important counterpoint to the more
purely commercial ventures pursued in the Middle East. Aleppo,
acknowledged a pre-eminent centre not just for trade but also of
learning, was a natural focus for their collection by Britons. The substantial exchange in them united, in a sense, these two contrasting aspects of
the city: these were at once valuable decorative commodities and invaluable repositories of Arabic thought. A somewhat similar alliance of
culture and commerce was visible on the English side of the trade. For

the complicated and costly business of purchasing them was, from the first, intricately bound up with the Levant Company's wider operations.

The quest for Arabic manuscripts began almost simultaneously with the beginnings of an English trading presence in Ottoman lands. In 1611, Paul Pindar, English consul in Aleppo and subsequently Ambassador to Constantinople, presented the Bodleian with a number of manuscripts which he had obtained in the East.[7] Sir Thomas Roe (better known for his embassy to Delhi) did likewise after returning from his embassy to Constantinople, in all donating twenty-eight manuscripts.[8] In the same period, George Strachan travelled to Aleppo and was employed for three years as physician to Emir Feyyad, acquiring manuscripts all the while.[9] The chaplains to the Aleppo factory were among the most prominent agents of the literary sub-trade.[10] Robert Frampton was one notable collector.[11] Robert Huntington, chaplain to Aleppo throughout the 1670s, was another.[12] 'When any of the Books . . . fall in your way,' he wrote to his counterpart in Pera, 'pray shop them upon my account, & charge the money to any of the nation that have dealings with you, it shall be paid to you without more ado.'[13]

But the practice received much its most important boost when it attracted the interest of William Laud – Archbishop of Canterbury, Chancellor of Oxford University and with it all a man of considerable oriental enthusiasms. Laud even used his political influence to try to impose a sort of 'knowledge tax' on the Company. Every ship which returned to England from the Levant, so the idea went, would be required to carry with it an Arabic or Persian manuscript. The document which placed this scheme for consideration before the court of the Company, where it was detested instantly, sets out its rationale in revealing terms: 'There is a great deale of Learning and that very fitt and necessary to be knowne, that is written in Arabicke,' it maintains. Yet, 'there is a great defect in both our Universityes, very few spending any of theyr time to attaine to skill eyther in that or other Eastern Languages'. The blame for this is said to lie 'not soe much to the fault of the Students there', as with 'the great scarcity and want of Arabick and Persian Bookes, in which they they might spend theyr paines'.[14]

The ruse was, in the event, not destined to meet with much success. Regarded understandably as a menace by the merchants in the field, it was half-observed for a brief time and quickly fell with the archbishop's own fortunes. Instead, it was through the offices of another of Aleppo's chaplains, Edward Pococke, and harnessing the archbishop's financial backing, that Laud's most sustained and successful collecting endeavour would be made.

Pococke's mere presence in the city is testimony enough to a powerful streak of ambition. He would prove to be on the threshold of a meteoric rise to prominence as an Oxford don, followed by equally rapid eclipse during the Civil War as he paid the penalty for close ties to Laud's regime. Long before all that, though, in Aleppo, he had spent his days commissioning a local scribe named Ahmad al-Darwish to prepare transcriptions wherever Arabic manuscripts could not be bought in their original copies. Where they could be bought, the Muslim man also acted as his broker. Transcription was much the more painstaking task, hampered by the perennial dinginess of the place and, in summer months, its close heat, even under the protection of the souk's stone-covered roof. It was al-Darwish who did the real work, but the Englishman would take it upon himself to oversee the whole fraught affair, right up to the finished product's despatch into the hands of the *mallems* for the journey to Scanderoon, and the making of arrangements that would take it thence across the sea. So it was a partnership of sorts, and it seems to have brought the two men to a genuine closeness. Nor did it end with Pococke's departure for Oxford in 1636. 'God be praised we are well and safe,' a letter al-Darwish penned to him in Oxford read, 'and we trust in God, you are in like manner.' The letter then proceeded to business:

> We have gotten Echwans Sepha . . . As for the history of Al Jannabi, the *Kadi*, of which I saw some pieces, you told me that we should tarry till the transcribing it was finished, and when it was finished we should buy it, if the most high God please. The commentary on Gubstan is also finished, which we will send you; and, if it please God, we will do our endeavour to send you the history of Ebn Chalecan; and any book that we shall see, which is convenient for you, we shall send to you. And you must needs send us an answer to these letters, and some little token of what your country affords.[15]

Pococke served as the Aleppo chaplain for six years; and during that time, the consul there wrote, he 'made Arabb his mitresse' – 'soe amorous' was he of it that he was 'not willinge to part with any booke' in the language.[16] He was, as well, acquiring new ones at a rapid rate. As his eighteenth-century biographer described,

25 An image from one of the manuscripts acquired by Pococke in Aleppo and now held in the Bodleian Library, Oxford University.

He bought up whatever manuscripts in that language [Arabic] he could meet with [there], and employed his friends . . . to procure the like from other places, waiting the opportunities of the caravans from Persia, and other countries. When he could not obtain the books themselves, he took care to have them exactly transcribed.[17]

These activities, combined with his dogged study of the Arabic language, caused him to be among those who strayed beyond the confines of factory life. He recruited a native speaker called Hamid to be his personal attendant, and also made an arrangement to study literary Arabic with a Muslim 'shaykh' named Fathalla.[18] His successor in the chaplaincy wrote to Pococke, in his first letter to him from Aleppo, of how 'your old sheikh [now dead] was always mindful of you, and expressed your name with his last breath. He was still telling the good opinion he had of you, that you were a right honest man; and that he did not doubt but to meet you in paradise, under the banner of our Jesus.'[19] Then there was the friendship with al-Darwish, which seems to have been closer still. The correspondence between the pair after Pococke's return from the East was quite regular and the Englishman continued to rely on his services as intermediary in the buying of books. When he returned to Ottoman lands some years later, this time residing in Constantinople, al-Darwish visited him there.[20]

The trade in books was apt to raise particular sensitivities. As was true of that in silk, there seems to have been a general presumption against dealing directly with Muslim sellers. Pococke's biographer records that during his second trip to the East, his companion, John Greaves, urged him to buy manuscripts on his behalf in Constantinople, 'not only by soliciting the assistance of their common friends at Galata, but even by going over the water himself to the Bezars, and shops at Stamboul'. This, he supposed, 'might be done without hazard, provided a due caution were used about such books as relate to religion'.[21] That Greaves felt the need to deny the risk of engaging in such activity suggests, at the very least, that it was far from run-of-the-mill. When in Constantinople himself, he was quite prepared to admit its outright danger:

> In my enquiry after Turkish and Arabick books I have been a little more fortunate, than in those of Greek, tho' with some danger. For finding my selfe often cheated by the brokers . . . I ventured once or twice to the shops, where the Turks sell them, where I have bought some few, tho' at excessive prices, and might have had many more choice copies, if I had had sufficient money to have disbursd.[22]

Like spices and silks, the riches of eastern manuscripts were apt to bring greater rewards when reaching England by more direct routes. An older route of intellectual traffic had transported 'Arabic learning' to England via dubious translations made on the European continent, introducing much corruption along the way.[23] By the accession of George I, though, contemporaries had no doubt that the Bodleian Library in Oxford was 'the best furnished with oriental manuscripts of any in Europe'.[24] For this transformation the Company's trade could lay claim to much of the credit.

As the indispensable revisions of the historians Nabil Matar and Gerald Toomer have underscored, regard for aspects of Arabic learning was a notable feature of the Renaissance; and this primarily scholarly phenomenon had reached its zenith by the end of the seventeenth century, as its esoteric connotations came into conflict with the empirical methodology of the new science.[25] This was also the era in which the exotic oriental tale began to gain popularity, most famously in Galland's publication of the *Arabian Nights*, emblematic of the patronising western discourse towards the Islamic East that was to be the hallmark of modern times.[26] To Matar, it was therefore the closing decades of the seventeenth century which were decisive for ushering in a maleficent and uniform stream of modernity: here was the moment when a 'centrifugal force' triumphed and it became inevitable that 'Britain was to become opposed to, and apart from Islam' throughout modern times.[27]

But there is reason to prefer a somewhat different chronology, for the century after 1650 as a whole probably marked the most benign period in English attitudes towards Islam before the later twentieth century. The decline of Arabic studies in the ivory towers only presaged a more popular interest in Islam during the next few decades. This, in fact, was the moment when print was disseminating a small but forceful strand of pro-Islamic views to a wider audience. It co-existed with a wider discourse which, if not wholly sympathetic towards the religion, adopted a stance of greater moderation and moved away from the older mode of outright contempt. As a result, Islam was a faith being freshly scrutinised in all its aspects – talked and written about to an unprecedented degree and amongst an expanded public. It came in some instances to be harnessed to the cause of reason itself, deployed and championed by prominent trailblazers of the English Enlightenment in their self-conscious quest to forge a distinctively 'modern' world.

Whereas the contrast should rightly be drawn between early-modern mentalities and the condescension of a later, imperial age, we should also be attentive to the contrast which all this marked with a still *earlier* period. Removed from its heretical place in the divinely ordered universe of old, Islam would now be set instead against the distinctively enlightened yardstick of reason. Placed there, for the first time it came to strike at least some contemporaries as a religion surpassing their own. For many more, who would certainly not go that far, it was acknowledged to possess a host of admirable attributes, if not for being equal to Christianity. Even that was sufficient, in turn, to allow Islam to assume a prominent role in casting the light of 'reasonableness' over their own faith. This reappraisal of Islam sprung on one level from the shifting of English thought in the direction of celebrating the fruits of observation and reason. The great expansion in contacts that the Levant trade especially brought with Muslim polities and peoples, though, was itself a necessary factor. It was in the material culture of manuscripts – like the one bringing *Hayy* before its modern, 'western' audience – that these two forces perhaps most visibly met. Once there, these texts would be translated, printed, circulated, discussed and, above all, read.

Translations

Just as the collection of Arabic manuscripts was not tied to any conscious attempt at reappraising the religion, the same was initially true of their reception. The seventeenth century was a prosperous time for the study of the Arabic language generally and that owed much to the influx of books from the East.[28] William Bedwell, 'the first Englishman after the Middle Ages to undertake the serious study of Arabic', was also the first to make use of the resources which the eastern trade provided for obtaining Arabic materials, and it was this which really set his work apart.[29] Conversely, the pace with which their availability flourished meant that by the time his long-delayed dictionary of the language came to completion, it had already been surpassed. Pocock himself embodies the ongoing nexus between the collection of oriental manuscripts and their domestic study: on his return to England in 1636, he swiftly became Oxford University's first Professor of Arabic (a post his patron Laud had endowed, making him a shoo-in for the role).

The universities acknowledged in the Renaissance that Islamic civilisation had played a decisive role in rescuing Hellenic philosophy in an age of European barbarism. That many of the venerable works of the Athenian golden age had been preserved only through their translation into Arabic provided a rationale for the careful study of commentaries and translations in the language, if only as routes to understanding the great originals of Greek extraction. Arabic developments on Aristotelian themes by the likes of Avicenna were also regarded as somewhat worthy of study in their own right. So too were selected achievements of Arabic science – physical, medical, astronomical – as well as a whole host of Arabian esoteric lore, mostly dating from the same medieval era.[30] The earliest citations of Avicenna in England are to be found in the writings of Oxford scholars dating back as far as the last decade of the twelfth and first decade of the thirteenth centuries. At least some Arabic texts, usually already in Latin translation and stemming originally from Spain, had made their way across the European continent and could be perused in England from that point onwards. For the late Renaissance humanists, the study of Arabic had become 'an indispensable component of [their] philological endeavours', put to purposes of scriptural analysis and their broader confessional enquiries.[31]

For all their age's characteristic and deeply held hostility to Islam and its threatening Ottoman adherents, scholars had managed to summon a degree of grudging acquiescence towards aspects of Arabian literature and learning, sufficient to persuade them that it was worthy of their attention. This had been achieved through consciously downplaying the Islamic origins of such works. By these means, an intellectual regard for aspects of Arabic learning and an unwavering religious hostility were quite able to coexist. As an account from the end of the seventeenth century makes clear, Averroes' stock in this earlier period had plummeted when he increasingly became 'charged with the Whimsies and Visions of the *Alcoran*'.[32] The Islamic associations of Arabic texts were downplayed, even as their fruits were enthusiastically plundered for their medical or astronomical worth.

The strength of suspicion with which an Islamic text could be regarded in early-modern England is well illustrated by the controversy prompted in 1649 by the first Koran to appear in English: 'Englished', as its title-page declared, 'for the satisfaction of all that desire to look into the *Turkish* vanities'.[33] Though a poor rendering usually ascribed to a hack polemicist who elsewhere had described Mahomet as 'a transcendant Arch-heretick', a successful petition was made to Parliament for the book's suppression. Soldiers were promptly despatched to the city, to 'make Search for the Press, where the Turkish Alcoran is informed to be now printing'.[34] In the event, publication was eventually allowed to proceed, but a strongly worded 'caveat' had to be added to the end of the work. This was framed for the benefit of those who 'desire to know . . . if there be danger in reading the Alcoran' – a 'poison', it was said, 'that hath infected a very great, but most unsound part of the Universe'. 'Set aside some grosse idolatries of the church of Rome, & their Tyranicall government,' as Cambridge University's first professor of Arabic had written only two years earlier, 'the onlie pressure on the bodie of the Church of Christ is Mahomets Alcoran.'[35]

The Levant trade provided a real impetus to the study of Arabic itself, not just by improving the supply of books in the language, but also by raising its practical worth. Bedwell made much of the fact that this tongue was 'the only language of religion and the chief language of diplomacy and business from the Fortunate Islands to the China Seas'.[36] The Sir Thomas Adams Chair in Arabic at Cambridge University was endowed not long after the creation of its Oxford counterpart, in the hope that study of the language would 'tend not onely to the advancement of good literature . . . but also to the good service of the King and State in our commerce with those Easterne nations . . .'[37] Orientalists like Simon Ockley found themselves able to pick up much-needed income by undertaking bits of Arabic translation for diplomatic purposes.

It was, even so, confessional purposes which continued to strike early-moderns before the mid-seventeenth century as the most persuasive rationale for studying the language. To their way of thinking, the East offered itself above all as a rich resource for examining abstruse theological questions. 'The present Practice and Language of the Mahometans,' one Arabist wrote in this vein, 'are the best Comment upon the Old Testament extant in the World.'[38] This commentator also felt able to proclaim (though hardly a neutral observer) that 'without some degree of competence' in oriental studies, 'no man has ever achieved true greatness in theology, nor ever will'.[39] Arabic study was, in its infancy, indisputably a Christian theological affair.

As a result, the learned in Arabic were just not that interested in Islam in this period. Indeed, they were especially prone to the hostility towards it that was endemic to their times. Insofar as the religion entered the picture at all, it did so mainly as a target of confutation. Other than his dictionary of the language, the only work Bedwell produced based on it was one whose title speaks for itself: *Mohammedis Imposturae: That is, a Discovery of the Manifold Forgeries, Falshoods, and horrible impieties of the blasphemous seducer Mohammed*. In bolder moments, there could even be the suggestion of a missionary rationale for cultivating Arabic proficiencies. The Sir Thomas Adams Chair also manifested a hope that 'in God's good time' would be seen 'the enlarging of the borders of the Church, and propagation of Christian religion to them who now sitt in darkness'. Pococke showed the potential for this sort of application by translating into Arabic a missionary tract written by Grotius in Latin. It was duly shipped out to Levant Company chaplains for them to distribute. Doing so in the event proved 'downright dangerous', and many copies seem just to have sat around in one of the warehouses lining the *Khan al-Gumruk*. Still, none of this scholarly and not-so-scholarly activity encouraged serious study either of Islam or of Islamic civilisation.

It was in the later seventeenth century that this changed, in tandem with a rapid decline in the older tradition of scholarly interest in Arabic texts. The sort of regard for eastern learning familiar to the Renaissance fell naturally with the birth of the new science, which insistently substituted the authority of empirical enquiry for that of the written word. That, inevitably, lessened the demand for Arabic texts to shine light on the word of God or of Aristotle. It also fuelled the enthusiasm for texts which would illuminate the Islamic religion and the societies that had adhered to it. With this development, the manuscripts entering onto the stage of earlier seventeenth-century England could underpin a significant reappraisal of Islam played out in its later decades.

Pococke's own writings were the first in which the shift of focus became evident. He voiced no great sympathy for Islam. His publications concerned with the religion nonetheless marked an important moment in the emergence of its study from the distortions of medieval polemic. His major work, the *Specimen Historiae Arabum*, an annotated translation of one of the manuscripts which he had obtained in Aleppo, offers a detailed account of the religion that is both informative and uncontroversial – albeit in Latin – and, crucially, it is one compiled from Muslim sources. Within its pages, the first challenges were mounted to a number of the fables traditionally surrounding the Prophet's life, such as the story that he trained a dove to feed from his ear in a bid to feign a miracle. In a nice clash between Christian evangelism and donnish impartiality, he unilaterally decided to cut these bits out of Grotius' missionary pamphlet when he came to translate it from the Latin into Arabic. When the two met some months later, Pococke demanded to know of the author what his grounds could possibly have been for ever including them (even Grotius was unable to offer a satisfactory reply).

The mark of a greater objectivity became pervasive in writings to touch on Islam during the latter part of the seventeenth century and into the next. Even fervent anti-Islamic polemicists felt obliged to dispense with the more flagrant parts of their propaganda. More than that, they now criticised those who 'esteem'd it a Merit to invent all the Calumnys they could, in order to discredit both *Mahomet* and his Religion'. It had to be accepted, as one put it, that it was 'but fair' to follow 'the Accounts of the *Arabian* authors themselves', even if that meant dispensing with many time-hallowed elements of the Christian polemic.[40] The likes of Humphrey Prideaux, who authored a profoundly derogatory biography of the Prophet Muhammad early in the eighteenth century, nonetheless claimed to rely on the work of Pococke and his fellow luminaries. The grosser fables of old, such men now told themselves, had never really been necessary to establish the superiority of the Christian religion: 'There need no such pitiful and unfair Methods to expose this Deceiver, and his Reveries, to the Laughter and Contempt of all the sensible part of mankind.' Instead, the man who set out to dispute with Islam was well advised, it was pronounced in the late seventeenth century, first to 'learn the *Arabick* . . . to get the *Eastern* Writings, and to see with his own Eyes'.[41] A tone of greater objectivity and scrupulousness, it seemed, was being forced on all.

If the defenders of medieval polemic claimed they could harness the new scholarship to their own cause, more usually it would force a greater moderation. Take Adrian Reland, a scholarly Dutchman much read in England in the early-eighteenth century. He was, unshakably, a Christian evangelist. Yet, whilst taking the view that his own religion was clearly superior to Islam, he did not feel the need to paint Islam as the fruit of the devil. The universal spread of Christendom was a desirable ideal, he thought, but he could still admit that Islam was at least superior to paganism, and might be a staging-post on the road to his New Jerusalem.[42] This was a notion which, as we shall see, would become widespread.[43]

Some of these publications, wrenching Arabic texts out of libraries and laying them before a nascent reading public, also attained real popularity. Simon Ockley's *History of the Saracens* – a work whose composition early in the eighteenth century had taken the Cambridge don who authored it to Oxford, there to burrow through the 'invaluable collection' of Laud's in the Bodleian Library brought west from Aleppo and Constantinople in the previous century – quickly went through several editions.[44] 'A man might as well undertake to write the History of France, for the time, out of our Newspapers,' Ockley wrote, 'as to give an account of the Arabians from Christian Historians.' Elsewhere, he excoriated the 'Folly of the westerlings' in 'despising the Wisdom of the Eastern Nations, and looking upon them as Brutes and Barbarians; whilst we arrogate to our selves every thing that is Wise and Polite'.[45]

His account of the Saracens is full of sympathetic vignettes which speak of his subjects' wisdom and humanity. These were people who had, he wrote, 'performed as considerable actions, as any other nation under heaven'. If their military achievements are, for him, a clear source of admiration, there is also much on the subject of their intellectual pursuits, which he felt compared very favourably to those of his own time, as well as their traditions of toleration.

This sort of work existed alongside more overtly radical reassessments of Islam. 1671 saw the publication of *Hayy ibn Yaqzan*, but it may also have been the year in which Henry Stubbe embarked on his equally remarkable book offering 'a vindication of [the Prophet Muhammad] and his religion from the calumnies of Christians'.[46] It was a vindication which could not have been written without the recent flood of Arabic translations (though neither is Stubbe afraid to fill the gaps in his knowledge with sheer invention). He specifically acknowledges his debt to 'the late improvements in the Oriental Learning', and Pococke is the authority from whom most material is drawn.[47] His life of Muhammad is, he boasts, 'extracted out of the best Authors, Arabians and others' and he has 'justly rejected a good deal of fabulous, ridiculous trash, of which most of the Christian Narratives of him are stuff'd'.[48] He tells with relish the story of Pococke's challenging Grotius on his use of fables, and denounces the Koran translated by Alexander Ross: 'Our English translation follows the French, and the French is very corrupt, altering and omitting many passages.'[49] He criticises any attempt to produce a translation without first mastering the 'Arabian tongue' and becoming proficient to draw on the 'Arabic, Persian and Turkish commentaries'.

Stubbe's book demolished several of the shibboleths of Christian dogma: 'It is manifest', he declared (to take but one example), 'that the Mahometans did propagate their Empire, but not their Religion, by force of Arms.' In doing so, his polemic targeted his fellow countrymen's religion as much as it did their attitudes towards Islam. It was wider currents of enlightened religious radicalism, indeed, which were responsible for spawning the more forcefully positive accounts of Islam to appear from this time onwards. Its cheerleaders might find in the teachings of Muhammad powerful support for their denial of the Trinity. Prominent anti-Trinitarians, such as John Toland and Stephen Nye, churned out a consistent strand of intensely pro-Islamic discourse throughout the final decades of the seventeenth century and the first decades of the eighteenth, giving much greater currency to the attitudes embodied in Stubbe's work. In January 1682, a 'cabal of Socinians in London' went so far as to attempt presenting the visiting Moroccan ambassador with an address of theological unity.[50] A yet more radical and later strand of Enlightenment sages relied on Mohammad to advocate their deist cause. This association featured most notably in an approving biography of the Prophet penned by the Frenchman Boulainvilliers, which was swiftly translated into English and published in 1731.[51] Stubbe had called Muhammad 'the Wisest Legislator that ever was'; Boulainvilliers developed the same theme and went further, eulogising him as 'a very extraordinary Personage: one who from an able Merchant, became a wise Politician, and renowned Legislator. In a word, a Great man, a Great genius, and a Great Prince.'[52] In featuring prominently in such debates, Islam had become a live issue in the intense battle of ideas that attended the early Enlightenment.[53]

In 1734, eighty-five years after troops had marched up Ludgate Hill to seize Ross's effort, the Koran was 'Englished' once more. This time, the days of licensing long gone, there was not a hint of interference by the authorities. The frontispiece proudly bears the name of the book's printer and there is even a dedication to a distinguished patron. 'I imagine it almost needless', the translator writes in his preface, 'either to make an apology for publishing the following translation, or to go about to prove it a work of use as well as curiosity.'[54] George Sale's work of translation – made 'immediately from the original Arabic', as its title-page boasted – illuminates how far the prevailing view of Islam had journeyed in the preceding decades.

Gibbon called him 'half a Musulman', but the 'explanatory note' with which he prefaced the Koran's actual text displays neither the polemical tone nor the radical stance that suffuse the writings of a Stubbe, Toland or Boulainvilliers.[55] To be sure, its leanings are decidedly sympathetic towards its subject matter, but its manner is also measured and detached. There are extensive footnotes, revealing the full use that he made of Arabic sources, alongside the flurry of European commentaries. His appraisal of Islam itself exhibits the same moderation. Whilst denouncing acid-tongued critics, he is careful to rank it below his own religion. Many of Stubbe's revisions are certainly endorsed ('they are greatly deceived', Sale pronounces, 'who imagine [Islam] to have been propagated by the sword alone').[56] There are even nods in the direction of the deist canon:

Muhammad was a wise law-giver, he says, and in seeking to bring the people of seventh-century Arabia to the 'knowledge of the true God', his designs were certainly noble. But he portrays the Islamic religion, unlike his own, as emphatically a product of human design, not divine intervention.

This was a near perfect exposition of a consensus emerging among the enlightened. For now, it was a view that still had to be evangelised. So to complement the measured prose of his 'explanatory note', it may well have been Sale himself who was responsible for publishing, in the following year, an anonymous set of *Reflections on Mohammedism and the conduct of Mohammed* – a work 'occasioned', as the title made clear, 'by a late learned translation and exposition of the Koran'. The arguments which it put forward were near-identical to those of Sale's preface, but from the outset, the flavour of this subsequent work is decidedly controversialist. 'Our prejudices run so strong and so unreasonable against Mohammed and his Law', it complains, 'that scarce any passions are more violent than those which commonly inflame us at the bare mention of either.'[57] In its scheme, as in its virulence, this pamphlet resembles Stubbe's work of the previous century, dissecting the derogatory portrayals of Islam familiar to early-modern times with a ruthless methodical approach. And yet, also in common with Stubbe's book, this work of forceful persuasion feels obliged to acknowledge its debt to Pococke and his fellow academicians: until these men carried out 'their candid and learned labours', it says, 'we were next to quite ignorant of the genuine Mohammedism'.

The harnessing of 'reason' in this way made life increasingly difficult for the opposite corner. A refutation of Prideaux's attack on Muhammad, which appeared in 1720 under the pseudonym 'Abdulla Mahumed Omar', made the point well: 'It is no new matter to find a Christian author railing against the Prophet,' it declared in its opening paragraphs, 'and heaping together a company of false and scandalous reflections, to render him and his religion odious to their own people.' What follows is a brilliant exercise in making this putatively Muslim author stand as the voice of enlightenment itself, pitting it against Prideaux's shrill and bigoted Christianity. Even the methodology of the new science is harnessed to aid Islam's cause: 'This Gentleman's bare Assertion, without any Proof,' the narrator insists, 'will never be able to pass with men of reason.' He then launches into a lengthy exposition of Islam's own rational virtues.[58] Reason, this clearly asserted, favoured the revisionists. Theirs was a sympathetic stance towards Islam which had, by now, emerged from Arabic manuscripts, from out of the ivory towers, and from out of the limiting contexts of religious radicalism. Meanwhile, a new set of attitudes was being carried east into Islamic lands.

Grand Tourists

Almost a century after Winchilsea's first audience with the sultan, James Caulfield, first Earl of Charlemont, departed Pera to visit 'the first and most pressing object' of his curiosity, the Topkapi Palace. Charlemont, whose travels had led him south through Italy, Greece and Egypt to the Ottoman capital, possessed an aristocratic pedigree sufficient to earn his board in the English palace. The ambassador, Sir James Porter, even made the journey down to greet him as he arrived at Galata's shoreline. Typifying the British 'grand tourist' now much in evidence across continental Europe, he was just eighteen when he embarked upon his travels, dispatched by an anxious mother who hoped to forestall her son's descent into rakishness. He and Porter had more than a little in common. Both Irish-born, they were loyal denizens of enlightened culture. Porter's love was astronomy: he would spend his evenings noting down planet movements from the garden of the ambassadorial palace. Charlemont's were travel and poring over the ancient ruins of Europe and the Near East. For either, life offered no higher pleasure than to discuss learned papers among like-minded men – a penchant which they indulged as members respectively of the Royal Society and Royal Irish Academy in later life.

26 The Topkapi Palace as it appeared from Galata. The rowing boats that ferried passengers back and forth across the Bosporus and Golden Horn are visible in the foreground.

Travel accounts, along with a panoply of other works describing the wider world, were already gaining popularity in England by the mid point of the seventeenth century. They would advance to still greater prominence within the culture of the expanding public sphere in the century to come. Such books were to be considered 'the chief materials to furnish out a library', wrote that supreme arbiter of the new politeness, Anthony Cooper, the third Earl of Shaftesbury, in 1710. The library of John Locke, tutor to Cooper's grandfather and briefly his own, was stocked full of them.[59] Nor was it by coincidence that the 'age which saw the rise of the Royal Society, the publication of Newton's *Principia* and Locke's *Essay*, the age, in other words, which conceived the world of nature and of man as machine-like in its construction, governed by laws discoverable by man and, when known, immeasurably conducive to his advantage', should equally have been an age which 'raised the traveller to an eminence he had never before enjoyed'.[60] The torch of empiricism (as contemporaries would have seen it) enlightened them all.

That mantra also infused the manner in which travel would be undertaken and written about. In the Ottoman context, it encouraged journeys undertaken purposely to seek out encounters with Muslim 'Turks', to elicit understanding both of their 'manners' and religion. The distinctive mark of these encounters was a self-proclaimed mode of curiosity and two-sided exchange. The evolving balance of power between the Ottoman Empire and Christian Europe made it an opportune time for the spirit of enquiry to show itself. If the direct military threat posed by the Ottomans was somewhat on the wane, that made it easier to jettison the traditional mode of contempt born of outright fear. On the other hand, as I have argued, their empire retained its status as a world power sufficient to merit considerable esteem. More than that, many aspects of its society could not help but strike Britons as impressive.

Until the mid-eighteenth century, travel accounts describing Ottoman lands almost always had close associations with the pashas' trading world. Often, their authors had gone there on the Company's business, whether as traders, officials, chaplains or companions. Such observers reckoned that, through their extended stays, they could lay claim to deeper insights than the fleeting impressions gathered by tourists-cum-travellers. Even those falling into the latter camp would tend to seek out the pashas' protection and guidance in the Middle East. The grander amongst them would, like Charlemont, be put up in the palace in Pera, or the consuls' houses in Smyrna and Aleppo, and even the lowlier might find lodging in a merchant's house.

In the mid-eighteenth century, Constantinople remained a fairly rare destination. Yet Charlemont, regarding his morning's call on the home of its Ottoman rulers rather like a levee in Grosvenor Square, wrote of being impressed first of all by the 'wonderful manners' which he found everywhere at the Porte. He was shown first of all to the apartment of the Reis Effendi. Sitting on his sofa, the official welcomed his guest 'with the most cordial, easy, and unaffected politeness'. They conversed on the subject of Charlemont's travels: where he had been, where he meant to go, his impressions of Constantinople. Then he was served iced sherbet and coffee, carried atop a silver vessel filled with a sort of perfumed marmalade, which he ladled in generously with a golden spoon. A servant showered rosewater out of a silver bottle onto his hands and clothes. Another presented him with a silver urn:

> This, it seems, was full of burning perfumes, but as I did not well know what to make of it, I unluckily laid my hand on its cover, and burned my fingers, at which ridiculous accident the Reis Effendi laughed heartily, and with great good humour told me that he was pleased to see me begin to accommodate myself to their customs, to which he hoped I should not be long a stranger.

The tour did not end there, for he was next introduced to a succession of high dignitaries, by all of whom he was 'most politely received' and entertained with the same heady mix of coffee, sherbet, perfumes and small talk. The manner of these great officers of state, Charlemont enthused, could only be described as 'dignified in the highest degree, and yet as pleasing as possible'. They seemed to possess an air of unassuming superiority, which commanded 'respect without their seeming to demand it'. How different all this was, he observed, 'from the petulance of France where every coxcomb assumes a superior air which turns his very civility into rudeness and insult!' Grace seemed to be 'a native of the East and to degenerate as she travels westward'. Returning to Galata that afternoon, the Englishman felt 'not a little pleased and surprised at having found such amazing and much more than Christian politeness among a people whom I had been taught to believe a little less than barbarous'.[61]

The picture of bonhomie and Ottoman clubbability which Charlemont painted could hardly differ more from the oppressive display of might with which Winchilsea was met by the court of nine decades earlier. Yet Charlemont's account might be fitted into a tradition of describing cultural encounters in the Ottoman world which by now stretched back for more than a century. Take Sir Henry Blount's visit to the Ottoman capital in 1634. Shunning Galata, he chose to lodge 'with the *Turkes*, in the *Hane* [*Khan*] of *Mehmet Basha*' in Stamboul, wearing oriental dress and shifting into '*Christian* habit' only when eventually he crossed over the Golden Horn. The result of this boldness was, he wrote, that in the '*Seraglio* I saw as farre as Strangers use, having accesse into the second Court'. Such discoveries were, this pioneer of English coffee-drinking seemed to imply, the preserve of those who braved the crossing between cultural boundaries.[62]

Blount explicitly declared his Baconian outlook in the travelogue which resulted from these experiences, the *Voyage into the Levant*. He wrote that he had set out to discover how far, 'to an unpartiall conceit', the Turks lived up to their stereotypes in domestic print.[63] Those accounts already set down he derided as 'not only in great part false, out of the relaters mis-information, vanitie, or interest', but also hopelessly slanted to suit the predilections of their writers, so that 'the reader is like one feasted with dishes fitter for another man's stomacke, then his owne'. Ocular and aural experience were, he insisted, the only sure route towards true knowledge: 'A traveller rakes with his eye, and eare, only such *occurents* into observation, as his owne apprehension affects.'[64] So that the assiduous Blount, 'desiring somewhat to informe my selfe of the *Turkish* Nation', would not just 'sit down with a booke knowledge thereof, but rather (through all the hazard and endurance of travel), receive it from mine owne eye not dazzled with any affection, prejudicacy, or mist of education'.[65]

Such claims to expose the gap between slanted perceptions, as embodied in the now-suspect books of the past, and oriental realities became widespread. ''Tis a particular pleasure to me here to read the voyages to the Levant [by Dumont],' wrote one such traveller early in the eighteenth century, 'which are generally so far removed from truth and so full of absurdities I am very well diverted with them.'[66] 'Certain it is,' Sir James Porter was himself still writing of the Turks in the middle of the eighteenth century, for all the quantities of ink by now dedicated to their scrutiny, 'that we have hitherto very imperfect accounts of their religion or of their manners.'[67]

Complaints such as these served, in part, to advance the claim to novelty that was highly prized by the cultural marketplace of the times. 'I will not tell you what you may find in every author that has written of this country' would be a typical boast of the early eighteenth century.[68] Yet it also went hand-in-hand with a re-evaluation of inherited attitudes towards their subject matter. It became a commonplace to declare at the outset of accounts of the Turks, of which a voluminous number were being published by the later seventeenth and into the early eighteenth centuries, that 'these people are not so unpolished as we represent them'.[69] This is demonstrated in the dedication to Paul Rycaut's *Present State of the Ottoman Empire*, published a few decades after Blount's work:

[The Turks] may be termed barbarous, as all things are, which are differentiated from us by diversity of Manners and Custom, and are not dressed in the mode and fashion of our times and Countries; for we contract prejudice from want of familiarity. But your Lordship . . . will conclude that a People, as the Turks are, men of the same composition with us, cannot be so savage and rude as they are generally described; for ignorance and grossness is the effect of Poverty, not incident to happy men, whose spirits are elevated with Spoils and Trophies of so many Nations.[70]

Difference was more to be comprehended than condemned in the version of the mechanistic world view which this declaration typified. That shift brought such accounts into line with those on the subject of early Islamic history, whose domestic presence we have already noted. Unlike in the God-centred universe of old, the Turks' characteristics were to be explained in terms of natural circumstance: 'The customes of men are much swayed by their naturall dispositions, which are originally inspired and composed by the Climate whose ayre, and influence they receive,' as Blount wrote.[71] In the Augustan age, moreover, that was also frequently attached to an assertion that all men were at root 'of the same composition' with each other. 'The same variety of Humour and Morality', Aaron Hill opined in 1710, 'now reigns in Turkey that is found in Christendom, and that the numerous Mahometans are like our selves divided into Good and Bad.'[72] 'There are many in Christendom who believe that the Turks are great devils, barbarians, and people without faith,' Thévenot agreed, 'but those who have known them and who have talked with them have a quite different opinion; since it is certain that the

Turks are good people who follow very well the commandement given to us by nature, only to do to others what we would have done to us.'[73] 'Human nature is everywhere one and the same;' as Charlemont himself declared, 'and, however she may be checked and thwarted by physical and by moral causes by the influence of climate or by the shackles of unnatural manners she will be endeavouring to return to herself, and instances of the success of her endeavours will never be wanting.'[74]

It had once been de rigueur to meet the spectre of Ottoman success with contemptuous derogation, of the people and still more so of their religion. No longer tied to the workings of divine providence, the early Enlightenment encouraged the notion that temporal success was instead to be taken as an indication of a civilisation's worth. That success might now be frankly admitted. 'I was of opinion', Blount had written, 'that he who would behold these times in their greatest glory, coulde not finde a better *scene* than *Turky*.'[75] It followed that the '*Turkish* way' may not be 'absolutely barbarous, as we are given to understand', but rather 'an other kinde of civilitie, different from ours, but no lesse pretending'.[76] 'All things being so different from our own way of living did very much surprise me with wonder and delight,' wrote John Covel in the later seventeenth century. 'I am now got into a new world, where everything appears to me a change of scene,' Lady Montagu wrote a few decades later. 'I write to your ladyship . . . hoping at least that you will find the charm of novelty in my letters.'[77] Such novelty could increasingly be assumed to bring delight, both to Britons travelling in Ottoman lands and their domestic readers.

What of Islam itself? It is a mark of his times that Blount was careful to draw the distinction between the Turks, on whom he lavished praise, and their religion, for which he evinced only contempt. The reappraisal of Turks as 'Muslims' represented a thornier act of volte-face than their reappraisal as merely secular beings. Nonetheless, where Islam had impelled the vicious polemic of travellers in the early part of the seventeenth century, it became a frequent focus of their enquiry in its later decades. Just as Arabic manuscripts were coming to be scrutinised at home, travellers to Islamic lands now assumed that their questions concerning the religion were best put to Muslims at first hand.

'The Articles of their Faith and Constitutions of Religion,' Sir Paul Rycaut boasted of his account of the Turks, 'I have set down as pronounced from the mouth of some of the most learned Doctors and Preachers of their Law, with whom for Money or Presents I gained familiarity and appearance of friendship.'[78] Most travellers were agreed that such information was not easy to come by, something which was blamed on the Turks' reticence. 'Forasmuch as the Turks are reserv'd and close in communicating any thing that relates to their Religion to those who they call Infidels,' as one traveller put it, 'it is the hardest thing in the World to get any thorow information from them, unless you give them some Hopes of becoming a Mussulman.'[79] This is a version of events which has won some endorsement from Ottoman historians.[80] True or not, however, the mere perception of it gave rise to a series of carefully manufactured encounters with Muslims which peppered the travel accounts of this era.

Take Lord Sandwich, another aristocratic visitor to Constantinople who made his journey there a decade before Charlemont's own. 'During our stay in this vast metropolis,' he wrote, 'I applied my whole thoughts towards informing myself of the maxims and customs of a people so different from those, which I had till then been conversant with.' There were, he accepted, 'many authors who have taken upon them to inform the public of every particular relating to the government, religion and manners of this nation'. Yet most such accounts could not be relied upon, he claimed, since their writers were 'unskilled in the Turkish language' and hence were incapable of gaining more than a 'superficial' insight into these matters. As to himself, he had the 'good fortune to get over' these disadvantages through 'an acquaintance with a person, who, together with a thorough knowledge of the Oriental tongues, had been for the greatest part of his life conversant in the most eminent Turkish families, and been himself employed in many very important state transactions'. There follows a lengthy and, for the most part, objective and dispassionate account of Islam.[81]

From the later seventeenth and earlier eighteenth centuries, accounts of the Ottoman world commonly described visits to mosques. Charlemont's praise for the 'grace' of the East, for instance, is immediately followed by a description of an incident which had occurred when he visited one of Constantinople's mosques. Whilst there, he wrote, he saw 'an Imam, or Turkish priest, expounding the Koran to a circle of devout Turks' and 'was so struck by his action and manner of speaking that I found myself perfectly fascinated by it, and though all he said was unintelligible to me I could hardly tear myself from him'.[82] Porter, meanwhile, describes conversing on the subject of the Koran 'with a learned *Effendi*, who was known to have [it] by heart; a chapter from Sale's translation was explained to him in the vulgar Turkish dialect: the old Turk, in a sort of rapturous surprise, followed the interpreter; repeating verse by verse in the original Arabick. He remained astonished and amazed; and asked with some emotion, how we could have so perfect a translation, the sense so justly preserved?'[83] Richard Pococke, author of the highly popular *Description of the East* (and distantly related to Edward), relates in a similar vein how he 'entered publickly into such of the mosques as I desired to see, and sometimes even on Fridays, just before the sermon began'.[84] Edmund Chishull, chaplain for a time to the Constantinople embassy, offered a lengthy account of a visit to a mosque, during which he had, he wrote, 'the liberty to view several copies of their *Alcoran*, and other books of Mahometan prayers, all curiously written and adorned with golden figures'. He described the interior:

> The windows are with excellent painted glass, full of flower work and religious inscriptions; and from the roof hangs a multitude of lamps, together with bright balls contrived to reflect the light, all of them well ranged in a beautiful and artificial manner.[85]

In the late 1670s, Sir Thomas Baines held a particularly remarkable audience with '*Vani Effendi*, the great preacher among the Turkes'. Baines was attached as physician to the Constantinople embassy of Sir John Finch between 1674 and 1680. He and Finch had become acquainted whilst students at Cambridge University, and remained close friends and possibly lovers ever afterwards. Both devoted to the new science, both were early supporters of moves to create a Royal Society in London. If Baines shared with Maundrell membership of the new guard of empiricists, the physician was wholly unlike the cleric in his willingness to turn Baconian maxims to the more objective scrutiny of Islam.

It was the Muslim, an 'old huncht-back man, very gray, [with] a crabb'd countenance', who invited the Englishman to visit him. Having duly 'come to him and set down', Baines straight away 'ask't liberty of discourse', to which he was informed that he might 'say what he pleased, nothing would be taken amiss'. He proceeded to put to the effendi a series of testing questions about his faith: 'whether all soules were equall of men, women, children?'; 'whether women shall be in Paradice?'; 'what people might be suffer'd to live amongst the Turkes?' The resulting exchange was set down in an account penned by the embassy's chaplain, who had accompanied him there.

It was the last of these questions which gave rise to the fullest exchange. For it spawned a discussion of whether, supposing Islam were 'the onely perfect law', it could possibly be fair to deny paradise to those who had never had the fortune to be exposed to it. Baines put forward a metaphor to convey his meaning. Suppose you had lost a jewel and sent two children to find it, he said, and 'one being more successful than the other finds it; the other notwithstanding being very industrious, and leaving no stone or stick unturned', does not. 'Shall this son be blamed for his ill successe,' he asked, 'notwithstanding his endeavours were as much, perhaps more, than the other?' To put it another way, he, by virtue of being born English, had heard 'many things which he now found not truly reported of [Muslims]'. He had even, he added, gone so far as to read their Alcoran, which 'he now sees wrongly translated'. He could hardly be blamed for the misconceptions in which all this had resulted, just as he could not help the prejudices of the society into which he had been born. Even so, it was quite understandable that they should have 'rather prejudic'd him [than] furthered him in his belief [in Islam]'. And then, of course, there were 'many there are who never heard of [Islam] at all'. Surely neither they nor he should be denied the possibility of God's grace? And to complete his defence, Baines 'told what kind of Christian he was . . .'

> . . . viz., he would rather dye then worship either crosse, Pictures, Images, or the like. He adored onely one true God, and lived in his fear onely; he believed a Musselman, living up to the height of his law, may be undoubtedly saved. He thought himself obliged (though it was never so absolutely in his power to do it) not to touch a hair of a Mussulman's head for his difference in religion, but rather to help, assist, relieve and cherish them in every good office that he was able to do for them.

On this, according to the clergyman's account, the Muslim 'wept, and said he could not believe any Christian came so near true Musselmen'; and that the 'standers by (which were many) cryed out *E Adam* – he was a *Good Man*'. But just as the Muslim pressed 'the perfection of his law, and the necessity of turning to it', Baines insisted that he was now 'about 55 years of age, and his bones were dryed and hardened to their forme; and his understanding was in like manner settled by long practice of his own religion, and it would be a hard task . . . to unrivet his notions'.[86]

Baines' particular enquiries about Islam, like those posed by Stubbe and Sale, closely reflect the wider concerns of the early Enlightenment. The dilemma of the fate of 'those millions who had not heard the Word' was one that would much preoccupy Locke in *The Reasonableness of Christianity*, published two decades later. He, too, would reach for analogy – though in his case in the form of the parable of the talents. Even his answer to the dilemma was the same one that Baines' question to the effendi had plainly implied: that 'the Lord would not expect ten talents from him to whom He had given but one'. As Locke's position has been summarised: 'Independently of revelation, man was governed by the law of reason, and he should make use of "this candle of the Lord, so far as to find what was his duty".'[87]

The same elision of Islamic and contemporary themes is visible in a somewhat similar encounter described by Lady Mary Wortley Montagu, much the best-known and celebrated of English travellers to the Ottoman Empire during this period. Whilst in Belgrade, the English embassy party was put up in the house of Achmet Bey – 'a title something like that of a count in Germany' – whom she found to be a man 'educated in the most polite eastern learning, being perfectly skilled in the Arabic and Persian languages, and . . . an extraordinary scribe, which they call *effendi*'.[88]

He dined with them every night, and her conversation with the Turk supplied her 'only diversion' during their stay. She boasted that they gave her the means of 'knowing their religion and morals in a more particular manner than perhaps any Christian ever did'. Like Baines, she assimilated his religion with some of the more radical ideas circulating the coffee-houses of London. 'The ridicule of transubstantiation appeared very strong to him,' she wrote. She also defended Muslims from the charge of atheism being directed at radical religionists at home. 'The most prevailing opinion if you reach into the secret of the effendis', she instead declared, 'is plain deism . . .'[89]

Charlemont followed suit. 'There was nothing I more ardently wished for during my short abode at Constantinople,' he wrote four decades later,

. . . than to be made acquainted with some sensible Turk, unprejudiced and well informed, from whose conversation . . . I might be able to gather much more information with regard to the real character of this people than I could possibly expect from those Greeks and Franks of whom our society was almost wholly composed.

After a great deal of 'importuning our ambassador', an audience was arranged with Mustapha Effendi, the 'Turkish Secretary to the English nation'. It was the Englishman who opened the conversation: 'My high esteem for the Mussulmans,' he declared, 'makes me desirous to be authentically informed of every circumstance which may in any way concern them.' As the effendi's opinions must, he continued, 'undoubtedly be those of the wisest of your nation, I would wish to trouble you with a few questions, if I might do it without offence'. 'You may ask what you please,' the Muslim replied, 'and take what license you choose in your queries, for, though a good Mussulman, I am not fool enough to be offended at any question you may please to ask.' There proceed a series of questions and answers:

Question.
Do you believe in astrology or the influence of the stars in enabling men to foretell events?

Answer.
I do not, but think it a foolish science. For whilst a man pretends to foretell events and to read the heavens he does not know what his own wife is doing.

. . . Question.
There are in all religions many things which should be understood metaphorically. Do you believe literally those relations in the Koran, of Mahomet's ascent into heaven, etc., etc.?

Answer (with a smile).
Do you believe that Christ came from heaven, and is gone thither again?

The question repeated.

Answer (by the Turk).

I am obliged to believe what is written in the Koran. I believe the world was created, because, when I see smoke, I am sure there must be a fire. I have read a translation of the New Testament and believe the miracles of Christ ... Whatever is attested and confirmed to me by a sufficient number of witnesses, that I believe, even though it be contrary to my reason and to the natural and usual course of things.[90]

Ottoman Islam had evolved, in at least some English eyes, from a heresy into a religion of reason. Yet it would not be long before a different Enlightenment, together with the wholesale change in the global balance of power visiting the later eighteenth century, consigned it once more to the realm of 'fanaticism'.

PART THREE

❖

ALEXANDRIA

7

Antique Lands

———— ❖ ————

Gunboats

The engraving with which the artist David Roberts adorned the third volume of his work _The Holy Land_, published in the mid-nineteenth century, could leave no doubt that a new era in Britain's relationship with the Middle East had arrived.[1] It portrays an 'interview' granted in 1839 to Colonel Campbell, the British consul-general, by Egypt's modernising ruler, Muhammad Ali Pasha. Behind the uniformed Briton, warships amass in Alexandria's bay. If they might seem to cast his diplomacy as unashamedly of the gunboat kind, closer inspection reveals this fleet to be Egypt's own. Rebuilt in a western mould after its destruction by Britain and other powers at Navarino in 1827, Muhammad Ali declared it 'the most magnificent . . . ever owned by a Mahomedan power'.[2] Aping Europe's military technology, however, could only gain him so much. The mere appearance, some years later, of a flotilla of British ships beneath his Alexandrian arsenal was sufficient to convince Muhammad Ali to abandon his designs on ousting Ottoman sovereignty from Syria.[3] This was not an isolated intervention. Britain's political influence in Middle Eastern affairs was by now a potent one, backed up routinely by displays of armed might.[4] Meanwhile, the twin objectives of its modern policy in the region – securing and improving the gateway to its Indian empire on the one hand and creating markets for exports

27 The Victorians arrive: David Roberts' *Interview with the Viceroy of Egypt.*

of British-manufactured goods on the other – had assumed their definitive form.

It was the quest for speedier routes between the Mediterranean and Red Sea, spurred by the first of these aims, which provided the occasion for Roberts' canvas. It depicts Campbell urging on the Egyptian ruler a scheme, expounded on maps sprawled across his sofa, to build a railway spanning Egypt's length. Lieutenant Waghorn, the Briton who dreamed it up, had hopes of creating a mail service which would bridge India and Europe, to be operated in its Arabian segment by Bedouin couriers trekking between desert staging posts. Such grand designs were the height of fashion among imperialist visionaries, the same impulse finding expression a few decades later in the construction of the Suez Canal (albeit, to Britain's chagrin, under the direction of Frenchmen).

Yet Britain's imperial aims in the Middle East were not confined to forging paths across its landmass. Its industrialists also saw in the region a promising outlet for the fruits of England's cotton mills, whose industry now aspired to supply 'shirts for black men and brown men and for the muslim world'.[5] The prising open of Ottoman markets to cheap cotton goods – a primary item of consumption for large masses of the Ottoman population – would be trumpeted as a victory for free trade.[6] In truth, a good measure of this success was owed to the flexing of political and military muscle.[7] With the region's transformation into consumer of the West's manufactories and supplier of its cheap raw materials, nonetheless, its modern economic fate was sealed. 'It is . . . this capability of supplying raw material at a low price and of excellent quality', it was being openly declared by 1860, 'which gives to Turkish commerce that importance and consideration in which it is held by the European powers.'[8]

It was not by coincidence that this era also witnessed a prolific output of depictions of the Middle East – of Egypt and its antique ruins especially – by British writers and artists.[9] Suddenly, Britons thronged the byways of the Middle East. 'It is scarcely possible to turn the corner of a street without meeting an Englishman recently arrived, either from the borders of the Red Sea, the cataracts of the Bile, or the ruins of Palmyra,' a journalist complained in 1826, while 'interviews with the Beys and Pashas of the empire of Mohamet have now-a-days succeeded to the usual presentations at the courts of the Continent'.[10] Roberts made his journeys to Egypt and the Holy Land in the late 1830s, churning out drawings (mass-produced ever since) of the sites forming the litany of the modern tourist trail. In the decade following, John Frederick Lewis donned oriental costume and lived the 'life of the languid lotus eater' in Cairo, meanwhile painting his famous scenes of harems and domestic interiors.[11] It was the mid-part of the nineteenth century, in fact, which spawned the quintessential 'orientalist' corpus still feeding the West's clichés about the Arab world.[12] Thomas Cook's tours down the Nile would not be long to follow.[13] Nor would long-term British occupation, which began in 1882 and lasted for no less than four decades thereafter.[14]

By the time Britain's presence assumed this unambiguously colonial character, the pashas had long since disappeared from the scene. Even before the arrival of the Victorian imperial moment, its Georgian prelude had wrought an unmistakable shift in the balance of power between 'western' traders and their Ottoman hosts. Prefigured in the latter half of the eighteenth century, the contours of a new relationship became clear in the wake of the Napoleonic invasion of Egypt in 1798. This transformation precipitated the decline of the pashas' trading world and the Company's eventual disbandment in 1825. By the mid-nineteenth century, British goods were rapidly conquering the region's markets again, helped along by the political dominance of their imperial state and unhindered by the Company's strictures. But this new invasion bore few of the hallmarks of the older pattern of commerce with the region: a commerce which, after long sickness, had finally expired more than two decades earlier.

Though contemporaries would not acknowledge it, the Company's fortunes had proved to be closely tied to those of the Ottoman state. Both lived ill with the distinctively modern forms of western political and economic penetration emerging onto the Middle Eastern scene. Its own presence had been built throughout its history on firm allegiance to Ottoman sovereignty. To be sure, the pashas individually were willing to buttress their position by also doing business with a variety of local figures, some of whom might openly defy the Porte's authority. Yet none contemplated the Company's factories ever rising above their subordinate, client status within the kaleidoscope of Ottoman political life, whether in provincial cities or at the imperial court. This overriding political caution (the Company, one contemporary complained, was 'unintelligibly prudent') was equally expressed in a stubborn refusal to countenance trade outside a small number of well-established centres, where its presence had been sanctioned for centuries.[15]

As the authority of the Ottoman state itself plummeted within the Middle East and that of various local notables grew, this policy fell increasingly out of step with the times. It was the arrival of more forceful western players, though, which did most to make it appear archaic. The pashas lost out on the one hand to the French, who were energetic in strengthening their political hold in places like Smyrna, whilst extending the tentacles of their commercial interests into manifold smaller locations across the region. On the other hand, the Company's commerce was being sapped by the East India Company. This latter was a corporation which shunned its Levantine parent's conservatism, gradually embracing the mantle of political sovereignty and sheer violence within its trading world. The nabobs' superior political clout meanwhile helped them to flood London with cheaper Bengali silk, closing off the lifeblood of the pashas' business. Moreover, Britain's rising imperial fortunes, above all in the Indian arena, were forging a fresh strategic role for the region. With that came the inevitability of the Company's usurpation by a powerful newcomer to Middle Eastern politics: the British Empire.

The shifting of sands was plainest to see in North Africa, the first scene of nineteenth-century colonial incursion into the Ottoman

Empire. On the fringes of the sultan's authority, it had also been an arena where the British openly attempted (and failed) to establish their position through military force. Meanwhile, the weakness of the Ottoman state there caused the Company's efforts at establishing a commercial presence largely to founder. Britons' Victorian arrival in Egypt, unlike elsewhere in the Ottoman sphere of influence, altogether lacked a 'pre-colonial' history of engagement. Only with the decisive change in the global balance of power, which saw Britain's ascent to the status of a mighty imperium, was it able to gain a foothold. But with this rise, the curtain at last fell on the pashas' story.

A quarter of a millennium beforehand, at the dawn of the Company's history, Egypt's significance in English eyes was overwhelmingly a commercial rather than political one. Perhaps more markedly than it would again become (with the opening, that is, of the Suez Canal in the later nineteenth century), it represented one of the great siphons of the East–West trade, connecting Europe with the famed luxuries of the Indies. Spices and drugs reaching the English Channel by this way would have wended their way up to Suez, then on to Alexandria, from whence they were conveyed into the Mediterranean. This flow of goods lured the Company into concerted efforts from its earliest years to gain a foothold in the port, and for a time direct shipments from Alexandria supplied London on a significant scale with such goods as pepper, ginger, varnishes and gum arabic.[16] In 1585, John Sanderson and his fellow merchant William Shales were despatched there on a reconnaissance mission, finding passage aboard a galley belonging to the city's Ottoman governor. The lengthy report which they conveyed back to the Company's court enthusiastically endorsed its commercial renown.

Still, it also hinted at some of the obstacles to doing business in Egypt which were to form staple complaints of the next two centuries. Britons were forced to vie with the Venetians and, of greater future importance, the French, for a stake in westward traffic. It was also formidably expensive: 'no place to live in', Sanderson wrote, 'without trading to some purpose, so great is the charge thereof every way'.[17] The problem was not just the everyday costs of living. The favourable duties from which the pashas benefited under the terms of the capitulations did not apply.[18] Nor did the Company's own rapaciousness much help. 'I note what you write about the charge on Goods,' one trader wrote much later to a correspondent in Cairo, 'but must still be of opinion they are very high, & much discourages trading to your place but what troubles me most, is the Consolage since we have that privilege from the Company not to pay any for that ship from one port to another in Turkey, since the Company regulate the trade of your place in another manner must have patience.'[19]

More than that, however, the humiliations that Christian merchants might labour under were infamous. 'At Gran Cairo,' Sir John Finch recorded, 'none are suffered to ride on horseback but publick ministers, amongst the Christians; the rest ride upon asses; and he that goes with the asse tells them when they come near some moscheas [mosques], for then they must walk on foot, and if they doe not, they are layd down and drubbd to 200 blows, as the French frequently are for non-observance of this duty.'[20] Local potentates were particularly inclined to exploit their unbridled power over the trade by imposing *avanias*. Hakluyt reprints a number of commandments which the Company extracted from the sultan, directed at curbing local officials in Alexandria.[21] But the familiar strategy this embodied, of turning to the Porte for protection against all manner of abuses suffered far from Constantinople, proved less effective in the Egyptian arena than it had in Smyrna or even Aleppo.[22]

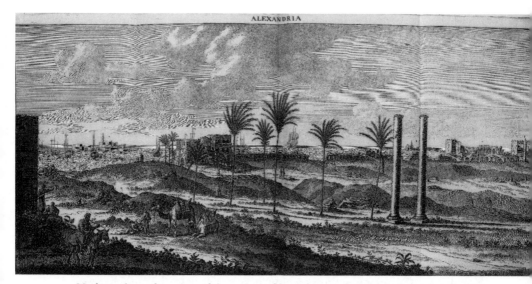

ALEXANDRIA

28 An early modern view of the coast at Alexandria, predating any signs of an English presence.

These impediments long encouraged the pashas to stay away from Cairo and Alexandria. Their abstention was also encouraged by a certain hiatus in Egypt's geopolitical stature coinciding with the Company's prime. The ultimate success of the English and Dutch in diverting the spice routes away from the Middle East did much to undermine its status as a vital emporium of world trade. An English observer noted in the second decade of the seventeenth century that the Egyptian spice trade 'is now discontinued by the Portuguese, English and Dutch who bring home such wares by the back side of Africa, so that the traffic of Alexandria is almost decayed'.[23] The Yemeni coffee taking fashionable London by storm, commonly funnelled through Egypt, could only take up some of the slack. On the other hand, Britain's Indian empire was not yet sufficiently advanced for serious thought to be given to developing lines of communication between the Mediterranean and the Red Sea on that score. Furthermore, the heavy English cloth which found favour in the cooler climes of the Levant made little headway in North African markets. From Sanderson's day, conducting trade in Egypt had called for the import of large amounts of bullion, a serious indictment of its worth in the eyes of mercantilists.

Alexandria nonetheless remained a caravan city of real significance, Cairo hardly less so. The growing visibility of the French even during the seventeenth century caused merchants to question the wisdom of whole-sale abandonment. By the middle of that century, an Englishman was again present in Cairo, claiming to be his nation's consul. It seems that he may have enjoyed the support of the ambassador, Sir Thomas Bendish, but certainly he lacked the Company's blessing. When it found out about his presence, it insisted that it 'never held it fit to settle a consul there' and would have nothing to do with the man.[24] Bendish himself sought appointment as consul in Cairo after his recall from Constantinople, but this scheme was again rebuffed by the Company.

For the next four decades, much the same pattern repeated itself. Egyptian trade would attract enthusiastic support from Britons in the Levant, but deep suspicion from the Company. The ambassador wrote to the secretary of state in January 1688 urging that 'if the Levant Company shall make any instances to Your Lordship [secretary of state], to re-assume their Trade into Egypt (which of late yeares having been abandoned by them, has been carried by particular ships of other nations, contrarie to their *Desires*), I most humbly beg your Lordships countenance

& protection in their behalf . . .'[25] No such 'instances' were forthcoming, however, though by the beginning of the eighteenth century, William Harvey for one was corresponding with two Levant Company merchants based in Cairo, Thomas Vernon and John Goodman.[26] For the next several decades, a handful of merchants again plied a trade there.

Even so, the Company was destined never to secure a commercial foothold in the land of the pharaohs to compare with its presence in Anatolia and Syria. 'As to our intermeddling with the trade of Alexandria,' its Court testily declared in 1688, 'we have had so many costly experiments of the desperate hazard which attend it that we have resolved that nothing shall tempt us to engage in it.'[27] It was not by coincidence, moreover, that the position of the sultan, who nominally remained Egypt's master throughout the Company's existence, often appeared little surer during these years.

We have seen that, for all the power of local politicians to resist Constantinople's demands, the Ottoman sultanate nonetheless retained an unrivalled prestige in places like Aleppo. Whether the same could be said of Egypt was less clear. Even if prone to rebellion, Syria had been fully subjected to the *timar* system, the classic instrument of Ottomanisation, in the decades following its conquest in the early sixteenth century, and an Ottoman-speaking Turkish elite consequently became entrenched. In Egypt, by contrast, power was allowed to remain vested in the Mamluk households, who retained a memory of an independent sultanate predating that centred on Constantinople.[28] Syria and Egypt were alike in witnessing their share of outright rebellions against Ottoman rule down the centuries. Yet that similarity arguably obscures an abiding weakness of Ottoman authority in the latter province during the seventeenth century (and thus well before the direct challenges which Muhammad Ali mounted to it in the eighteenth century) which was absent from the former.

Further west in Africa, the Ottomans' position was all the more precarious. The incorporation of Egypt and Sinai into the Ottoman Empire was, as we have seen, a consequence of the great conquests in the era of Selim I which brought the House of Osman to dominance over the Middle East. Its extension into more westerly parts of North Africa, though taking place in a similar period, was of a markedly different hue. Hayreddin Barbarossa turned to the Ottomans for protection sometime between 1517 and 1520, bringing Algiers into the Empire as a semi-autonomous province. In 1534 he overthrew the Hafsid rulers in Tunis, but in the following year Charles V, the Holy Roman Emperor and King of Spain, conquered the city. Then, in 1574, within just three years of the naval victory of the Holy League against the Ottomans at Lepanto, an Ottoman expedition retook Tunis from the Spaniards. By 1580, Tripoli (in Libya rather than Lebanon), Tunis and Algiers were all provinces under at least the nominal authority of Ottoman governors, though even in that era it has been said that 'local leaders continued to put their own parochial interests first, and undermined any notions the Ottoman central government might have had of bringing the administration of these provinces in line with the bureaucratic norms elsewhere in the empire'.[29] Morocco remained substantially beyond the Ottomans' reach, in spite of serious attempts to unsettle the Sa'adian dynasty there in the mid-sixteenth century. Ottoman North Africa as a whole retained a frontier character, wherein the authority of the Ottoman court was tenuous at best.

All this impacted fundamentally on the Company's trade. It feared to tread where the sultan's patronage lacked authority to legitimise the pashas' status. Yet whereas commerce as a result struggled to get off the ground on the North African fringes of the Ottoman sphere of influence, it represented one theatre in which British military force was brazenly deployed.

It was here, indeed, that Britain made its first squarely colonial foray into the Islamic world. The Portuguese garrison of Tangier, the wedding gift which sealed the marriage of Charles II to Catherine of Baraganza in May 1662, fell into English hands through foreign bounty rather than conquest. The acquisition nonetheless spawned a brief wave of jingoism in London. This would, it was roundly declared, mark but the beginning of the King's Protestant empire in Africa.[30] In reality, the puny band of Britons sent to inhabit it were on the back foot from the first, encountering in the Moroccans a well-armed and organised adversary. Facing the sobering truth that merely to retain its African foothold would represent challenge enough, for an English state whose capacity to project strength into this region was still severely limited, expectations were rapidly downgraded. Tangier was, the King instead declared, to play the role of 'a good port of entry of the Meditarranean', and thereby serve the interests of Britain's trade in the sea.[31] Lacking a safe harbour to protect vessels from the adversities of the Atlantic, though, it was ill suited even to this.[32] At vast expense, Sir Hugh Cholmley embarked on the construction of a mole intended to make up for the latter short-coming. But it was a project which would soon appear vain as it was bold.[33] The colony never became a hub of any significance. Meanwhile, its protection from Moorish assailants sapped both treasure and lives at a rate that was increasingly hard to stomach. Cholmley's mole was finally completed in 1677, but by the middle of the next decade, his creation had been demolished as the English scuttled their position. The costly adventure had lasted barely two decades.

The Tangier episode demonstrated that the Ottoman Empire was not the only Islamic power in the Middle East able to match British arms in this era. Yet it also revealed a colonial ambition absent from the Company's dealings in the heartlands of the Ottoman Empire. Outside the Porte's realm and on its fringes, indeed, gunboat diplomacy was commonplace after the onset of the seventeenth century.

The pattern was set as early as 1620 by Sir Robert Mansell's attack on Algiers, the first in a string of ineffectual attempts to stamp down on the piratical menace emanating from the Barbary states. For a time there-after, policy oscillated between punitive expeditions in this mould and efforts to engage the Barbary states in the sort of treaty-based diplomacy

29 English ships join battle with Barbary corsairs in the later seventeenth century.

successfully practised with the Ottoman Empire. Shortly after Mansell's fruitless assault on Algiers, Sir Thomas Roe concluded a treaty with the Algerines before taking up his post as ambassador to the Porte. The rapprochement was supposed to provide a foundation for trade. As in Egypt, however, Britons' political vulnerability exposed them to demands for large bribes, which undermined the profitability of their commerce.[34] Moreover, piracy had soon resumed, in spite of the Algerines' assurances that it would be reined in. Thereafter, making a visit to the North African coast en route to Constantinople became a routine jaunt for the Company's ambassadors, as they sought to repair the perennial inadequacies of the status quo. Instructed to do just this, Winchilsea paused offshore aboard the *Plymouth* and despatched Paul Rycaut and Robert Bargrave to conduct negotiations. They were, they reported, received by the Algerines 'in their rude manner'. Quite unable to persuade them to relinquish a clause which gave an unfettered right to search British vessels, hopes of a fresh treaty had to be abandoned.[35]

In any case, treaties with the Barbary states became notorious for their observance only in the breach. In the face of a persistent corsair menace, a policy of outright violence came to predominate. Even as Winchilsea's envoys negotiated with the Algerines, he spied on the city's fortifications and dreamed of their destruction:

> The Mold [of Algiers] where ships lie is defended by 2 forts (though now a third is a building) easy enough to be assaulted, and the ships that lie under their protection to be fired and destroyed. For as Captain Allin informs me whom I sent purposely on shore, to survey their works, that their forts being but small and round, and the posts but little, they cannot come to traverse above 4 guns at the same time . . . That a fleet of ships, taking advantage of a southerly wind, fire their broadsides on the forts, they may quickly make their defendants retire; at which time boats well manned may fire their ships which will be so great a damage to that city that forty years will scarce repair.[36]

A little over a decade later, Sir John Narborough led a nocturnal attack on Tripoli. Entering the port, he seized a guard boat, then boarded a group of Tripoline ships and set them in flames. This served to 'utterly destroy them all, some turks and moors slain', he recorded, whilst his sailors had all 'behav[ed] themselves, as became Englishmen'.[37] Such outright violence had always been shunned by Englishmen inside the Ottoman Empire. In other parts of the world, its use had long been deployed as a means of asserting their colonial presence. From the North African frontier of the sultan's domains, that strategy would in time spread to encompass whole swathes of the Ottoman world.

Returns

Dudley North returned to London in 1680 laden with silks, jewels and potash, grogram yarn, balsam and boxwood.[38] For the successful among the pashas, there were myriad ways to redouble fortunes made in the Levant trade from the comfort of the city's coffee houses. Dudley remained active in the Levant trade. A routine feature of prosperous merchants' portfolios before the mid-eighteenth century, it was all the more attractive for a man whose years of overseas service armed him with powerful Levantine connections. His good standing at home was affirmed by appointment to the Company's court of assistants.[39] Abroad, he continued to do business with erstwhile colleagues in the Middle Eastern factories. Neither was he forgotten by Ottoman commercial acquaintances. His brother, Roger, relates how two dervishes one day appeared on the Royal Exchange enquiring after him. Finding him there, the trio conversed in Turkish, then repaired to Roger's house to dine on pilau. The younger of the Turks took opium, whilst the elder 'drank wine plenty and beating his fingers on the table for a tambour, sang divers merry songs', Dudley all the while interpreting for his brother's benefit.[40]

Yet he also branched out. He traded diamonds and other jewels with the Indies. He invested in shipping, chartering vessels for East India as well as Levant-bound voyages. He loaned money to both companies. As earlier in the century, the men who grew rich from the international trade passing through London were a tightly knit group, their networks and commercial interests densely intertwined. Institutional loyalties were fickle, quickly unlearned when fresh opportunities to profit were espied.

For all this individual promiscuity, though, relations between the trading companies themselves were caustic as ever. Dudley's return coincided with the culmination of a long-running dispute between the Levant and East India Companies, into which he would soon find himself drawn. The traffic in raw silk had allowed the pashas to prosper in spite of losing the spice trade to the long-distance maritime routes falling within the East India Company's monopoly rather than their own. Yet the silk trade was itself vulnerable to suffering the same fate. As the East India Company saw it from an early date, an obvious opportunity presented itself to siphon off the Levant Company's pan-Iranian trade, by shipping the product direct to London from the Persian Gulf at lower cost.[41]

By the second decade of the seventeenth century, they were already forming designs to divert Iran's entire silk output, 'henceforth by sea [to be] carried and dispersed throughout Christendom and not more through Turcky ... transported'.[42] Though Levant traders serving on the East India Company's court tried to discourage such notions, their protestations were to little avail. The peril to Levant traders was heightened by the policies of the Persian Empire, then at the peak of its ambition under the mighty Shah Abbas. From the turn of the seventeenth century, precisely the sort of diversion envisaged by the East India Company was being actively promoted in European capitals by the Persians themselves. Their motivations had less to do with profiteering than hopes of denuding the coffers of their Sunni rivals, the Ottomans. The very fact of the protracted warfare which raged between these two empires lent further attraction to the idea, since overland supplies to the eastern Mediterranean were regularly hampered by fighting. When, in 1624, Baghdad fell to the Persians, the Ottomans' command of the silk route linking the producing regions to the Mediterranean reached a low ebb.

In part through the efforts of the Shirley brothers, colourful Englishmen who entered the service of the shah, England had by this point come close to reaching a formal arrangement with the Persians.[43] It seemed for a while, indeed, as if the East India Company's ambitions might be fully realised. In 1618, the Venetian Ambassador to London reported that: 'The East India Company have arranged with the King of Persia to bring their silks by the Persian Gulf, which will ruin the Turks and much enrich England.'[44] In the years after the opening of negotiations with the shah in 1615, a number of ships did arrive in London carrying Persian silk laded in the Gulf. Politically, the high point of the Anglo-Persian entente was reached in 1622, when English ships co-operated with Persian forces in an attack on the Portuguese at the Gulf port of Hormuz.[45]

For a variety of reasons – ill-timed hiatuses in the Persian-Ottoman conflict, the tendency of Shah Abbas to overplay his hand, the skill of the Levant Company in scotching the plans, a perennial lack of ready money among the East India Company's traders – the sort of flourishing commercial venture which some had envisaged never quite materialised. For now, the East India Company's presence in the Gulf did relatively little to dent the English trade in silk through the Levant. It is estimated that in the 1620s, as much as 90 per cent of Europe's raw silk consumption passed through Aleppo.[46] By mid-century, the East Indian Company had largely abandoned its designs on directly importing Iran's silk.

If it never achieved the comprehensive rerouting for which its directors once hoped, however, it had nonetheless by then built up a significant commercial network within the shah's territories.[47] Having early planted roots in Bandar Abbas and Isfahan, a factory also appeared in Basra in 1638, shortly preceding the last major shipment of silk direct to England.[48] Even after these factories gave up trying to buy silk, they continued to see in Persia an attractive market for selling England's broadcloth. Disappointing Indian sales of the latter had played a role in first bringing this market within the East India Company's purview.[49] This traffic of itself posed a threat to the Levant Company's interests, since a good deal of the cloth sold by its own traders was ultimately destined, via Armenian peddlers, for the same consumers in Iran. Moreover, the market was fairly small and readily saturated. By selling cloth directly to the region, the East India Company undermined the barter for silk further west on which the pashas' business depended.[50] The problem was exacerbated by a requirement placed on the East India Company, under pressure from mercantilist dogma, to export a certain volume of the finished product each year. As the Levant Company complained: 'Not finding an advantageous vent for [it] in India, they have transported a great part thereof to Persia . . . formerly supplied with draperies from the Turkey Company's factories at Constantinople, Smyrna and principally Aleppo.'[51]

Meanwhile, the East India Company discovered another source of silk, which came to pose a graver threat to its importation via the Middle East. Bengal, where the British gained a bridgehead in the second half of the seventeenth century, was a substantial producer of the raw material – poorer in quality than Persian silk, certainly, but also temptingly lower in price. Yet it also produced silk textiles, which soon did a roaring trade amongst the fashion-conscious of London.[52] Their intrusion onto the English market set the scene for the furore of 1680, when the rivalry between the East Indian and Levantine combines burst into the open. In his role as a Levant Company assistant, Dudley was assigned to a committee given the task of drawing up petitions in support of its cause.[53] The struggle between the two companies, indeed, would be conducted largely by means of a pamphlet war. In August 1681, the Company presented a catalogue of grievances – 'The allegations of the Turky Company and others against the East India Company' – which was swiftly published and did the rounds of city cognoscenti.[54] It was not long before the East India Company had churned out an equally cantankerous reply.

Much favoured by the King, the latter's eventual victory was never much in doubt. Still, the Levant Company cleverly allied itself with both the gripes of the textile manufacturers and the predilections of the mercantilists, each of whom resented the East India Company's tendency to export bullion in order to import finished textiles when people might instead buy British. The Levant Company's trade was a far more virtuous one in these men's eyes: they exported English wares to the Levant worth £500,000 every year, taking in exchange raw silks, galls, grogram yarns and cotton, all of which being worked up in England, 'afford bread to the poor of the kingdom; whereas the East India Company export immense quantities of gold and silver with but little cloth, bringing back calicoes, pepper, wrought silks, and a deceitful sort of raw silk'. These manufactured goods were, Dudley's committee wrote, 'an evident damage to the poor of England and the raw silks an infallible destruction to the Turkey trade'.[55]

Such protectionist cries have, of course, echoed down the ages. Many of the arguments advanced against the East India Company's trade sound more than a little contemporary. It would, one speaker said in a House of Commons debate, 'in the end be the destruction of the [domestic] manufactory trade . . . because the people in India are such slaves as to work for less than a penny a day; whereas ours will not work under a shilling; and they have all materials also very reasonable and are thereby enabled to make their goods so cheap as it will be impossible for our people to contend with them'.[56] But this was not a straightforward clash between free trade and blinkered self-interest. The bargain prices of the East India Company's imports reflected not just India's comparative advantage in silk production. They were also a factor of the East India Company's political presence in the producing regions, very different in kind from the Levant Company's in the Ottoman Empire. For the establishment of a British presence in Bengal, one of the factors spelling gradual doom for the Middle Eastern silk trade, coincided with a growing appetite among East India Company directors for the deployment of brute force.[57]

This development was associated above all with the name of Josia Child, first elected governor of the East India Company in 1681. Child believed not only that the Company must seek formal recognition from the Mughal Emperor of its right to trade as a sovereign power, but that this right must be upheld by the establishment of a fortified settlement in Bengal.[58] The person despatched to the Mughal court to implement the new stance was none other than Dudley's old mentor, Sir William Hedges. Like Dudley, he had served for a time as an assistant to the Levant Company after his return from Constantinople. Then, in the same year that Child became governor, he was appointed to the East India Company's court of committees. By July 1682, he found himself in Hooghly, a little to the north of what would become Calcutta, with instructions to renegotiate the terms of the company's operations in Bengal with the emperor, Aurangzeb.

Hedges shared Child's belief in the necessity of a fortified settlement in Bengal. His background in the Middle East had nonetheless taught him an ease with the conventions of a Muslim court, as well as fluency in Turkish and Arabic, which won him the regard of the nawab of Dacca, Shaista Khan. His own assessment was that the negotiations which he entered into with this potentate might have scored a minor triumph for British interests. The nawab proved agreeable, in return for various sureties, to petitioning the emperor for a renewal of the customs exemption then enjoyed by the company. If that prospect seemed an enticing one, however, it was soon snatched away again, for Hedges was drawn into a spat with the abrasive Job Charnock, kingpin of the local nabobs, which culminated in Hedges' summary dismissal by edict from London. In December 1684, he left for home, visiting old friends in the Aleppo factory along the way.

With Hedges' departure, policy in Bengal drifted away from fairly malleable diplomacy towards outright confrontation with the Mughal emperor. By the autumn of 1686, three companies of British infantry had arrived at the mouth of the Hughli river.[59] 'You see what a mighty charge we are at', Child wrote in the midst of the ensuing war, 'to advance the English Interest and make this Company a formidable Martial government in India which formerly the Dutch despised as a parcel of mere trading merchants or Pedlars as they used to miscall us.'[60]

This latter comment is revealing of the audiences that Child intended for his display of military might, encompassing not just the Mughals, but also the East India Company's European rivals. Even so, 'Child's War' served to underscore how, if there were similarities between the processes of change experienced during the seventeenth and eighteenth centuries in all three of the great Muslim empires of Asia – the Mughal, Safavid and Ottoman – by the end of the seventeenth century, the English presence in the Mughal Empire was markedly different in kind from that in either the Safavid or Ottoman ones.[61] The war itself was an ignominious failure. The East India Company deployed, as a Victorian historian decried, '308 soldiers to make war on an empire which had at that moment an army of at least 100,000 men in the field'.[62] The grandiosity of Child's delusions rapidly exposed, the company was forced to grovel to the emperor and sue for peace. Yet its appetite for sovereignty nonetheless remained. By the third decade of the eighteenth century, the company would repeatedly make the point in disputes with local governors that it 'traded in India by right and not by any favour of the [Mughal] imperial officers'.[63]

In one sense, Child's own assessment of the Levant Company's campaign against the east Indian silk trade had been spot-on. 'The truth of the case at bottom is this,' he wrote, '[that] the importation of better and cheaper raw silk from India may probably touch some Turkey merchants' profit at present, though it doth benefit the kingdom and not hinder the exportation of cloth.'[64] Yet it also embodied, however unwittingly, the defence of an older and more egalitarian mode of exchange against an incipient western imperialism in the Islamic world.

Once it was thought that there had been an Asian trade 'revolution' in the sixteenth century.[65] That idea, as has long since been pointed out, is hard to square with the vitality of overland spice routes for decades thereafter. Maritime and landward routes became locked in protracted competition, in which the new-fangled sailing ship at first lacked a decisive superiority over the desert caravan.[66] Yet even as the former did triumph, silk went a long way to take its place and shore up patterns of trade between Europe and the Middle East. Mostly despatched in raw form to be weaved in England, it was nonetheless a high-value product, enriching many eastern hands as it passed along its westward passage.

Looked at from this point of view, the East India Company's arrival in Bengal emerges as the most portentous moment of all in signalling the end of a pattern of trade which, for centuries, had brought luxuries through Middle Eastern markets into English homes. So much would have been no more than faintly visible to contemporaries in the latter part of the seventeenth century. During the eighteenth century, though, the scale and dominance of imports from India (coming to include silk deriving from as far east as China) progressively grew. By its mid-part, moreover, the essential features of a new economic relationship had been born.[67]

Retreat

In 1749, Sir James Porter sat down at his desk in Pera to brief London on what had gone wrong.[68] Since arriving in the post as ambassador, he had been beset by complaints of haemorrhage in his charges' profits. Nor, for once, was their growing despondency without cause. The Company's trade entered a sharp period of contraction after the second decade of the eighteenth century. Wide fluctuations were par for the course in the Levant trade no less than in any other. Even serious downturns, like that occasioned by the War of Spanish Succession in the early years of the eighteenth century, might be long-lasting without signalling any secular trend.[69] The Cassandra-like among the pashas had foretold the imminent doom of their business throughout the centuries of its history, on grounds as various as the rerouting of the spice trade, the Dutch arrival, the exactions of Stuart and Ottoman sovereigns, or the depredations of pirates. Their 'lamentable complaints of a bad market' hardly abated even in the most prosperous of times.[70]

By the middle of the eighteenth century, though, the grim sooth-saying seemed increasingly to be borne out by reality. In the first quarter of that century, the value of imports of raw silk from the Ottoman Empire to Britain had grown by a quarter. In the twenty-five years that followed, they fell back by no less than a half. True, the traffic in other goods was more resilient and there was even some recovery in imports of cotton and fruits. This, however, could bring but scant cheer to traders whose business had long since become heavily dominated by raw silk.[71] The last decade before 1750 had witnessed a particularly sharp drop, whilst the decade to come would bring yet another. Export volumes to the Ottoman market told a similar story. Official figures for tonnage show a steady decline as the century proceeded.[72] So if commerce tended in the natural course of things to have 'its ebb and flow', as Porter wrote in 1768 after finally returning from the Ottoman Empire, by then it nonetheless seemed plain that 'this branch has sunk to such a degree that the channel remains almost without hope of replenishing'.[73]

Its decay owed a good deal, among other things, to the disruptive effect on the long-distance silk route of a fresh round of warfare between the Ottomans and Persians, combined with a weakening in the purchasing power of Ottoman consumers. An extended dearth of the Iranian product stimulated production in Anatolia and Syria. The inferior substitute which these regions offered, however, struggled to find favour on the London markets, particularly in the face of Indian competition.

This squeeze on the goods available to send back home itself had knock-on consequences for exports from England. Bills of exchange were used to enable imbalances of trade within particular factories – above all, the perennial surplus yielded by Constantinople – to be levelled out.[74] Across the Ottoman Empire as a whole, though, some semblance of balance had to be attained, largely through the exchange of cloth for silk alone. 'If we can have no silk we can sell no cloth, that is to say, no considerable quantity;' as one trader explained, 'for all the other Returns are trifling compared to the silk, neither is there any such thing as a sale of cloth for Ready Money to any Quantity worth speaking of . . . without the silk there are no Returns to be had, no Exchange being negotiated there to any part of the world; nor could it be brought in specie, because of the baseness of the Grand Seignior's coin'.[75]

Other than the encroachments of the East India Company on its turf, though, one cause more than any other was the focus of the pashas' recriminations. This was the rising commercial fortunes of the French, who, Porter wrote, 'have left no stone unturn'd within these 50 years to grasp [the trade] from us'.[76] Their return in earnest as large-scale importers of cloth to the Levantine market was first noticed at around the turn of the eighteenth century.[77] Within three decades, they had decisively overtaken the English. The textile trade in Constantinople set the pattern for elsewhere. Volumes of goods arriving from England fell precipitously, from around a thousand bales in the 1720s, to half that number in the following decade, then to just four hundred by midcentury.[78] Meanwhile, the French not only wrested their place as the leading nation in the western trade of the Ottoman capital during the early decades of the eighteenth century but, by its middle, accounted for as much as two-thirds of the total.[79]

To some extent, their success spoke of nothing more than a superior ability to supply the Ottoman market with its wants. The French, Porter explained in his memorandum of 1749, offered a cloth that was thinner and softer than the English product, and as a result more brightly coloured. There was greater demand in Turkey for Languedoc cloths than for any other sort. Not least, the Turks would clothe their servants twice a year in loose garments; for this purpose, the light French cloth was considered quite strong enough.[80] Many attempts had been made in England to imitate its patterns. Yarn had been introduced, but the fineness of the materials and of the spinning which were required posed insurmountable difficulties.[81] By storming onto the market with a cheaper imitation of the English real article, the French were doing nothing that the English had not done with brilliant success a century earlier for the sake of displacing the Venetians. By the eighteenth century, however, the lean pretender of that period had fattened into the behemoth.

The ascendancy of the French over the English was also associated with a more profound shift taking place in the politics of Ottoman markets. With it, there emerged sure signs of the unequal power relationship between the Middle East and western economies which was to characterise modern times. Even before the Napoleonic invasion of Egypt at the turn of the nineteenth century, the French ambassador felt able to declare the Ottoman Empire 'one of the richest colonies of France'.[82] Nor was that boast entirely crass. It seemed by then to have assumed many features of the archetypal role at the periphery of the world economy, supplying raw materials to French factories and lapping up their finished goods.[83]

This does not, however, quite capture what had changed about the Middle Eastern markets' relationship with western Europe by the Revolutionary era. To be sure, the growing salience of cotton exports on the one hand and colonial imports on the other were important straws in the wind. Yet Aleppo actually came to sell more finished goods than it imported in its growing commerce with France in the later eighteenth century.[84] Not until the nineteenth century did Europeans systematically dump manufactured goods onto Levantine markets, strangling local crafts and manufacture in the process. More fundamentally, the English Levant trade was always one predominantly involving an exchange of eastern raw materials, for most of its history in the form of silk, for western manufactured goods, in the form of woollen cloth. The Company, well aware of the public relations asset contained in that fact, frequently cited it against domestic critics of its monopoly. But there was nothing intrinsically unequal in this trade.

Even unspun, after all, the silk business was (akin to the spice trade before it) a high-value one, implying profits for both participants and fiscal authorities along its Middle Eastern routes. Not unlike the invisible earnings by which the British Empire enriched London's capitalists, the Ottoman Empire's role as a channel for luxurious commerce helped to foster prosperity. Crucially from the point of view of its rulers, the influx of foreign traders and goods swelled the state coffers.[85] So far as its own businessmen were concerned, the traffic created rich pickings for intermediaries, even if it must have appeared to Muslim eyes that too much of them flowed into the pockets of Jews and Armenians. Meanwhile, the import of English manufactures was on too small a scale seriously to harm the position of local craftsmen: even in the market for cloth, there remained a healthy space for indigenous manufactures.

All this serves to underscore that the incorporation of the Ottoman Empire into an Atlantic-centred 'world economy' did not from the first cast it into the role of an exploited underdog of the West. Into the early eighteenth century, it is probably fair to say, the East–West exchange of the Levantine world was conducted on terms roughly approximating to equality. Only thereafter did it tilt palpably in favour of western Europeans. The most significant factor in bringing this about was not so much any change in the structure or make-up of the trade, as the numerous subtle ways in which western traders were able to bring political muscle to bear in strengthening their commercial hand. In one sense this was, once more, just a continuation of what had always gone before. From the first, western traders had jostled for political position in the Ottoman world for the sake of bettering their trade. Yet gradually, they did so with the implicit backing of an economic, diplomatic and military might, which was both categorically modern and a source of power which other groups in Ottoman society could never match.

The difficulty of pinpointing precisely when western Europeans thereby gained the upper hand is well illustrated by the ambiguities inherent in Smyrna's development during the seventeenth and eighteenth centuries. The *Plymouth*'s brief station there en route to Constantinople had given Paul Rycaut his first introduction to a city which he would come to know intimately. It was also the place where Dudley North made his first Ottoman home, serving out the remainder of his apprenticeship and

30 Smyrna's harbour in the late seventeenth century, bustling with merchant ships from northern Europe.

earning his spurs as a fully fledged Levant merchant. Robert Bargrave, too, had passed through it more than a decade earlier during his first voyage to Constantinople. Then, he had been left with a rather idyllic impression of the place, for upon arrival, the ambassadorial party had been 'invited by the Nation to a Generall Enterteinment, in a wood about :6: miles distant from the Toune: where they treated us *Alla Turchesca* to the height'.[86]

If that speaks of the pashas' accommodation with the culture of their Ottoman hosts, a greater assertiveness was nonetheless apparent on the part of English, Dutch and French traders in the city than elsewhere in the Empire. Before reaching the castle that guarded over the entrance to the city's bay, the *Plymouth* announced herself with the firing of five guns; and even before it had come to anchor, Bargrave recorded, 'the merchants and commanders came aboard in great number; 15 or 16 boats brought my Lord refreshings, although we needed it not'. Then, the next morning, 'about ten of the clock the Consuls came aboard in their scarlet with a great company of the chiefest merchants in town, near 60, and after an hour's discourse my Lord went ashore in a pinnace and the Consuls, where there was a great entertainment made, both eating and drinking for all that went ashore'. Meanwhile, the posturing at sea continued: 'We fired [21 shots] and the English next us, the Dutch and French in order firing all the war ashore, and our trumpets sounding before all the boats, being near 20.'[87]

This sort of grand ceremonial was by now routine. Paul boasted of the size of the procession which accompanied his reception as consul to the

Company factory there seven years later: 'The whole factory . . . met me,' he wrote, 'and having made a hansome collation, conducted me with about a hundred horse, and six trumpteres before, through the streets of Smyrna, which was such an appearance, as hath never before been seene of Franks in that place since this Empire fell into the hands of the Turks.'[88] When Britons departed, likewise, it was a custom 'time out of mind' to hold celebratory dinners aboard ships anchored in the bay, to fire cannons and liberally drink the King's health.[89] Their bombast was generally tolerated by the powers that be, even if in 1687 it caused a minor diplomatic incident with the French, when celebratory cannon fire was mistaken for an act of outright aggression.[90] Similar such behaviour in Constantinople, by contrast, risked provoking the sultan's wrath, with all the diplomatic consequences that would inevitably follow.

On Smyrna's 'Frank Street', a contemporary wrote, we 'seem to be in *Christendom*; they speak nothing but Italian, French, English or Dutch there' and everybody 'takes off his Hat, when he pays his respects to another'.[91] Running along the waterfront, this street was where the western merchants built their homes, incorporating quays for loading or unloading ships at night and outside the gaze of the taxman.[92] Somewhat like Galata, but without Stamboul's taming presence alongside, the city had emerged as the Hong Kong of the Ottoman Empire. The merchants of northern European states crowding into it dominated the 'western' side of the Levantine trade from the city, just as they dominated the street running along its seafront. 'Smirna has of late so thrived by the English, Dutch, & French Traffick, that it is restored to be a place of Consequence, & neer as great in Riches now, as it was formerly for Religion', wrote Bargrave on his first visit there just before mid-century.[93] Its rise to prominence from the outset arguably reflected the Ottomans' reduced ability to direct the Empire's economy in support of its traditional concerns, above all that of supplying the needs of Constantinople. A melee of western merchants was instead able to forge new patterns of trade, directing Anatolian products to their own markets.[94]

Even so, at no point in the seventeenth century was Smyrna's trade on a scale nearly sufficient to effect a major dislocation in the Ottoman economy. Its expansion as a hub of international trade was soon positively encouraged by the Porte, in recognition of the fiscal windfall which this promised.[95] In the era of the Koprulus in the later seventeenth century, the sultan clawed back a good deal of his authority over the city, so that his own coffers were among those to share in the bounty. The failure of Smyrna's Franks to prevent the Porte building a castle there after mid-century, its purpose to enforce pecuniary exactions on their trade, served to declare that the sultan's word remained the last.[96]

By the middle of the eighteenth century, it was far harder to say whether that was still the case. Undeniably, much had changed about Smyrna. For one thing, the city now dominated the Ottoman Empire's westward trade. The city's growing ascendancy over Aleppo was owed above all to the decline of the traffic in Iranian silk. The caravans of yore entirely disappeared from northern Syria after mid-century.[97] For a time, Smyrna directly benefited from the disruptions to the traditional silk routes to the south, which found themselves partially diverted into Anatolia as a result. Soon, however, Persian supplies had dried up altogether. Some of the gap was filled by more local alternatives, grown in Bursa and elsewhere in Turkey and Syria, but Aleppo was nonetheless robbed of its former geographic significance, whilst Smyrna became the more natural hub for trade with western merchants.

Smyrna's rising fortunes as the eighteenth century wore on, however, owed most to a product whose export on a large scale was quite new: cotton. Whereas foreign exports still consisted mainly of silk in the first two decades of the century, cotton dominated thereafter. The trade in it was, in turn, the province overwhelmingly of the French. Britain's supplies of raw cotton came mainly from further-flung colonies, but the French West Indies found themselves unable to meet France's industrial needs. Already by mid-century, cotton accordingly represented a third of all French imports from the Levant.[98] It was thereafter, though, that the real explosion of shipments from Smyrna to Marseilles took place.[99] At the end of the century, their value had increased more than eightfold since its beginning, to reach almost 13 million *livres*.[100] By then the French routinely accounted for over half of the city's entire foreign trade.[101]

It took the industrial revolution and Napoleonic invasion of Egypt to usher in a fully fledged 'colonial' commerce, as we shall see. Nonetheless, this new pattern of trade did much to prefigure it. Although Smyrna's exports of raw materials for western Europe at times represented less than half of its total exports in the early part of the century, after 1718 their share was never less than 55 per cent and often topped 90 per cent.[102] Its connotations of a nascent imperialism were heightened by the fact that, among the goods shipped out in return by the French, there were growing volumes of colonial re-exports: sugar, coffee, spices. The ancient caravan trade, it seemed, had now been well and truly reversed by the sailing ships of the Atlantic.

This eighteenth-century trade, then, already hinted at a changing balance of power between the Islamic world and the West. With a gusto that the British did not match, the French exploited altered political realities to entrench their commercial gains. Their merchants were backed by the diplomatic and administrative labours of a weighty bureaucracy, 'from the Marseilles Chamber of Commerce to the Ministry of the Navy in Paris', with which the Company could not compare.[103] How the might of their state could be turned to mercantile advantage was shown by the new set of capitulations extracted from the Porte in 1740. These were presented as a quid pro quo for the helping hand accorded to the Ottomans by French diplomats in their treaty negotiations with the Austrian Hapsburgs in the previous year. Unlike all capitulations that had gone before, but redolent of the parasitic place that Europe's merchants and financiers would assume in the nineteenth-century Empire, their concessions were for the first time 'born of an Ottoman political "obligation" '.[104]

Emerging victorious from the Seven Years War (1756–63) not long afterwards, Britain's global eminence could easily rival France's own. Snatching the latter's West Indian colonies also enabled it to gain ground on the French in the colonial re-export trade to the Levant. Yet Britain showed no sign of following the French example of squeezing wide-ranging concessions from the sultan. The pashas still traded on the basis of the capitulations obtained by Sir John Finch in the later seventeenth century. This was a direct reflection of the Company's continuing hold on Middle Eastern commerce. For the time being, Anglo-French imperial rivalry across the globe was doing little to encourage the British state to make a concerted arrival in Ottoman affairs. Sir James Porter's plea that British merchants be lent the 'public assistance' which seemed to underpin the French commercial success fell on deaf ears.[105] A half-century later, Napoleon's decision to invade Egypt would change all that.

8

The Last Pashas

❖

Drinking of the Nile

Alexandria, 1801. They lead him, parched and blindfolded, towards the line. The dust kicked up by his boots is buoyed by the late-afternoon heat, hovering above ground and marking his trail from the distant fortifications. Every now and then a blast of artillery sails overhead, or a sharpshooter's bullet flies by, each unanswered from beyond the walls. His advance feels unconscionably slow, a white flag his only protection on perilously open ground. Yet for the Frenchman, who has been told what is coming, capitulation is sweet. Hustled at last into a tent, he hands over the letter which it was his mission to deliver, then awaits the guns' silence. In the two months since news of Cairo's capitulation to the British, the only talk among French troops has been of this city's inevitable fall. Even now, a contingent of Indian soldiers hurries from the south. Their arrival will come too late to fulfil the British generals' design of 'making a Bengal sepoy shake hands with a Coldstream Guard on the bank of the Nile', but that matters little. Within the week, the King's grenadiers and dragoons will enter Alexandria, their drums and fifes blaring *The Downfall of Paris* and *God Save the King*. The defeated invaders, leaving their warships and much of their artillery behind, will abandon North Africa. So this man's heart-pounding walk across no-man's land, a little over three years after Napoleon's entry to Cairo,

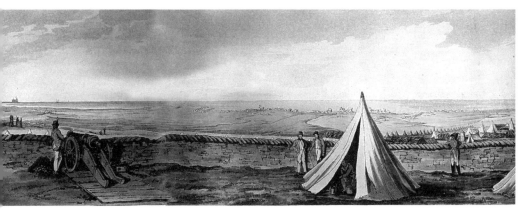

31 A British military encampment outside Alexandria at the turn of the nineteenth century.

signals that the French occupation of Egypt is irreversibly at an end. Britain's – the first, as it will turn out, of many – is about to begin.[1]

Even as Robert Clive's armies had swept triumphantly across Bengal four decades earlier, the Levant Company still quivered before Egypt. In the mid-eighteenth century, it summoned back its consul on account of the danger of doing business there.[2] The French, meanwhile, were enjoying a roaring commercial success. At first they purchased Yemeni coffee from its Cairene hub; then, by the third decade of the century, they discovered an even surer source of profit, by flogging cheaper substitutes shipped in from Caribbean plantations.[3] The General Court in London was unperturbed by all this. True, the odd Englishman resolutely traded from Alexandria or Cairo. Yet the Company consistently refused either to encourage these men or to accept responsibility for their fate.[4] Those who chose to 'fish in those troubled waters', it reckoned, had to take their chances.[5] Without political backing, those few Britons who ventured to Egypt lived uncomfortably, if not in actual fear. The growing self-assurance evident in a place like Smyrna showed no signs of emanating this far south. When the explorer James Bruce arrived in Alexandria in 1768, he sought safety behind the disguise of a wandering fakir.[6]

The Company's attitude towards Egypt epitomised the narrowness of its horizons even amidst the rising ambitions of an imperial age. It never would produce a Sir Josia Child, still less a Clive. The notion of asserting the pashas' position by force, rather than through entreaty with an

Islamic state whose sovereignty they took as an article of faith, was never seriously entertained. Neither were more subtle means of projecting political vigour much in evidence. Unmoved by Britain's rise to global eminence, the Company's abidingly conservative outlook held sway. It refused, even now, to countenance expansion outside the well-established factories in Aleppo, Constantinople and Smyrna, where (as the Company's big-wigs saw it, at least) the sultan's patronage firmly established the legitimacy of its presence.[7] The French, by contrast, were willing to seek footholds in new centres and spread their networks aggressively outwards. If their trade was consistently more dispersed than the English one, in the eighteenth century they established merchants anew in Ankara and considered doing so in Baghdad.[8] Suggestions of similar initiatives on the part of the pashas were consistently rebuffed.

This timidity came to be mocked at home. In 1695, the East India Company pointed out that the Levant Company had 'been settled above a hundred years, and had not established any trade but at Smyrna, Aleppo and Constantinople'; a hundred years later, a critic asserted that they never made any effort to 'deviate from the footsteps of their fathers'.[9] It was, in truth, worse than that, for the Company actively blocked factors' attempts to broaden the geographical scope of their trade. 'I approve very well of your design of settling an Englishman at Sydon in company with yourself,' wrote an Aleppo consul to one trader with an eye for an opportunity, 'which would effectually mortify the French . . .'[10] That kind of attitude was common among its agents in the field, but the Company did its utmost to discourage their expansionary ambitions. Admittedly, it had countenanced a fleeting attempt in 1686 to establish a mercantile community at Erzerum, designed to draw the silk trade away from the Armenian networks.[11] However, the project soon ran into difficulty and three years later the court of assistants decided that the settling of a factory there would be 'of very great prejudice to the trade of the Company by bringing a disreputation upon our manufactures and forestalling the markets at Aleppo and Smyrna'.[12] Similarly, it was pronounced that settling new factories on the Syrian coast was 'very prejudicial' to the trade of Aleppo.[13] Around the turn of the eighteenth century, factors who tried to establish themselves at Erzerum, Baghdad and Trebizond were summoned back.[14] No more successful was the English presence briefly established at Ankara in the early eighteenth century.[15]

The Company justified its caution on the ground that its factors could live in the existing settlements 'with more honour, reputation, and safety' than the scattered French, who 'in many places have such mean persons and trade as rather makes them contemptible'.[16] The real nub of its concern, though, was borne out in 1750, when Sir James Porter sought recognition for an attempt to open a trade to Baghdad. The forestalling of the main centres of trade by its removal inland would, the Company insisted on that occasion, 'be setting a price by some factors', which by degrees would necessitate further advances into the interior. This would necessarily provoke trouble with the Ottoman authorities, who would never allow the English to trade on better terms than their own subjects. The Company did not prohibit the proposed trade with Baghdad, but it refused to accept any responsibility for the protection of those engaged in it.[17] Indeed, this was no more than its policy already provided for. Factors who chose to reside outside the established scales had to pay for their own protection.[18] This was not just a question of overheads. More fundamentally, the capitulatory agreements with the sultan must not be upset.

Such a policy was, in part, forced on the Company. Lacking a joint stock, its means were perennially limited. It said much about the meagre state of its resources that, until late in its history, it had no permanent home. The East India Company had quickly acquired plush premises on Leadenhall Street (East India House, humiliatingly enough, was where the Levant Company would sometimes hold meetings of its own general court). In the early decades, most Company business was simply done in the drawing room of its governor, and it was well into the seventeenth century before a more permanent arrangement was reached to make use of the Ironmongers' Hall in the city. Levant merchants could tell themselves that the bureaucracy called for by the East India Company's trade, born of its need for a state-like apparatus of control, would have been superfluous in their own. Yet placing fortifications in the sultan's realm would have posed problems of affordability even before ones of military feasibility, and there is no evidence of the idea being so much as discussed. The trail blazed by the East India Company, of swelling into a imperial leviathan, was unimaginable to an organisation of the Levant Company's ilk.

Incapable of exercising brute force, accommodation with local rulers was the necessary alternative. The Company's overriding loyalty to the sultan, on the other hand, had long flattered the extent of his own authority over the Ottoman Empire. If that was arguably true even in

Harborne's day, the Empire's centrifugal tendencies were unmistakable by the eighteenth century, as both ambassadors' and consuls' despatches frequently warned London. They were being exacerbated by the presence of western traders themselves. As the Porte's ability to command obedience declined, bolder strategic games came to be played on the Middle Eastern chessboard. They emanated not just from the French, but from the East India Company and the British Crown.

Egypt and, more particularly, the isthmus of Suez proved the initial focal point for the intensifying competition between these imperial rivals. In the aftermath of the Napoleonic invasion of 1798, Warren Hastings would write that 'my official situation in India led me, many years ago, to contemplate Egypt as affording, by the position of the isthmus of Suez between the two seas, which form the communication with the Atlantic and Indian Oceans, greater commercial advantages than any other land upon the globe'.[19] Truth be told, though, the voicing of such sentiments was rare before the very end of the eighteenth century. This was partly owing to the strong stance taken by the Porte against European access to the Red Sea. 'The Sea of Suez', it would declare in 1779, 'is destined for the noble pilgrimage of Mecca.' The sultan issued a stern warning to his own subjects accordingly: 'To suffer Frank ships to navigate therein, or to neglect opposing it, is betraying your Sovereign, your religion, and every Mahometan.'[20] The Levant Company, it is no surprise to discover, willingly submitted to this command.

It was nonetheless a Levant merchant who pressed most forcefully for a more proactive line. George Baldwin, born to a London hop merchant, was trading from Cyprus by his early teens and buying silk from Acre in his twenties, picking up fluent Arabic along the way.[21] Gutsy and opinionated, in Smyrna he wooed his commercial agent's daughter, a famed beauty who became a darling of London society years later. But his real passion was reserved for a commercial vision: that of opening a British-led trade which would link India with Suez. It is telling that, in spite of his existing connections with the Levant Company, it was to the East India Company that he turned for support in implementing this design.

Having arrived in Alexandria by July 1775, by his own account he 'succeeded very prosperously' in reviving direct trade between England and Egypt. But this was just the beginning. Since the route from India right up to Suez had been amply explored, he declared, there was 'a fair prospect . . . of seeing my plan of establishing a commercial communication between

Egypt and India equally successful'. For three years, between 1776 and 1778, ships were simultaneously arriving at Alexandria from England on the one hand, and at Suez from India on the other, goods being ferried overland between the two. Baldwin basked in his triumph. 'We composed our bowl of the Ganges, the Thames, and the Nile,' he wrote, 'and from the top of the pyramid drunk prosperity to England.'[22]

The Levant Company's officialdom was less enthused.[23] Even its ambassador in Constantinople, Sir Robert Ainslie, complained that Baldwin's disobedience of the sultan's injunction against venturing into the Red Sea endangered merchants who legitimately traded to Alexandria, however small their number may be.[24] As for the Company itself, Baldwin recorded that its merchants 'cried out that they would be ruined'.[25] Just as predictably, the venture provoked the fury of the Porte, which saw all manner of commercial, political and religious objections. Still, Baldwin's success for several years demonstrated just how little any of their opinions really mattered. What eventually sealed the fate of his enterprise was the withdrawal of support by local potentates. The consequences of *that* were felt immediately: in 1779, a caravan attempting to pass from Suez to Cairo was attacked in the desert, its valuable English cargo plundered and its passengers left stranded in the sand, where a number of them perished in the heat.

This event might have spelled Baldwin's permanent ruin. He was fortunate, however, that his return to London in the 1780s coincided with French efforts to open up the same route, which were causing some alarm to the newly established Board of Control for India. It was explicitly this French threat to Indian security which persuaded the Board, in 1786, to despatch Baldwin back to Alexandria as a consul-general, where he was to speak for the Crown, but also to advance the cause of the East India Company. The howls of protest which such blatant incursion onto its turf prompted from the Levant Company were dismissed with little ado.

The Board's belief in Egypt's strategic importance for now remained a minority one. What changed British political outlooks on this corner of the world, quite suddenly, was the worldwide war which erupted in the wake of the French Revolution. Imperial interests scattered across the globe became primary objects of the Anglo-French struggle, to a degree unmatched even in the Seven Years War or the American War of Independence.[26] With the Napoleonic invasion of Egypt, moreover, far bigger beasts than Baldwin turned their attention to Britain's geopolitical interests in the Middle East. Henry Dundas summed up the line of thinking now well represented in the highest echelons of government when he declared that 'the possession of Egypt by any great European power would be a fatal circumstance to the interests of this country'.[27] Not just the land of the pharaohs, but the whole sphere of Ottoman influence, had become a theatre for great power rivalry.

This proved a watershed in commercial as much as in political attitudes. In the mid 1790s, the ambassador to the Porte expressed the fear that control by the French might envelop the whole of the Ottoman Empire's trade, and in doing so provide them with a base from which to extend the tentacles of their influence into India.[28] Drawing this sort of connection between commercial and diplomatic concerns was emblematic of the jeremiads of the period. The Napoleonic invasion, moreover, transformed the prospects of British trade, both in Egypt and across the Middle East, in a number of concrete respects. In the first place, it disposed of the French at a stroke, at least for the time being. At the end of September 1798, the French diplomats resident in Constantinople were flung into the Seven Towers.[29] Its merchants' property was seized across the Empire, much of it never to be recovered. Meanwhile, Britain had concluded an alliance with the Porte. The market, long hampered by entrenched French interests, was thrown open. British merchants were not slow to spot the opportunity this offered. 'I happened to fall in yesterday, with a person who is a very good judge of the temper of the city,' Pitt was informed in the midst of the war. 'He considers that the opening of the trade to the Levant and the Turkish dominions will give a great spring to commerce and that the war is really become popular with the manufacturers and the merchants.'[30]

Secondly, Britons in the Middle East now found themselves with the implicit backing of unprecedented political and military might. The French invaders of Egypt propelled Britain into a lasting commitment to preserving the territorial integrity of the Ottoman Empire, by military means if necessary. On the eastern Mediterranean sea, meanwhile, Nelson's victory at the Battle of the Nile in 1798 lent the British an unimpeachable naval supremacy.[31] Command of the waves remained fundamental as ever to the prosperity of Middle Eastern trade and the withdrawal of the British fleet from the Mediterranean in the mid 1790s had caused it to suffer greatly. The blessings which Britain's unprecedented maritime prowess might confer on merchants were instantly felt, for the trade embargo imposed by Britain on its Continental competitors in the period of the war had a crippling effect on their cotton industries.[32] Yet there was a more subtle and long-lasting consequence. Britons suddenly found themselves possessed of the sort of prestige which had by now buttressed French commercial ambitions for decades.

How this might serve to open up markets hitherto regarded as too hazardous was nowhere more apparent than in Egypt itself, where Britons made a concerted commercial arrival in the decades after their troops had ejected Napoleon's. A string of consuls was now appointed to Alexandria – by the Crown, not the Company – who shared Baldwin's enthusiastic vision for the possibilities of direct trade with Britain. Agreement was also secured with Egypt's rulers for opening up the Red Sea passage to India.[33] In Alexandria itself, British vessels were allowed entrance to the safer eastern harbour previously reserved for Ottoman vessels.[34] The counterpart to these political measures was seen in a substantial growth in the volume of trade. In the second quarter of the nineteenth century, there was a dramatic increase in British exports of cotton goods to Egypt, increasing more than twelve-fold to reach the substantial value of around £350,000 by mid-century.[35] Exports as a whole were worth not far off double that amount by the same date. By the 1830s, Alexandria's Maydan al-Tahrir would be a scene of 'flag-poles and consulates', of 'flaming signs and mammoth posters, publishing, forsooth, nothing but – "Overland Route to India" – "Opera, to-night, Ernani", or "English Circulating Library" '.[36]

As this preponderance of cotton goods indicates, the nineteenth-century pattern of trade with Egypt fitted snugly into the 'colonial' mould. Egypt became a quintessential supplier of agricultural raw materials for Europe's industries, exporting long-staple cotton whilst importing cotton cloth. There was no doubting on whose side the balance of advantage accordingly lay. As one contemporary put it:

> Trade which consists in the exportation of manufactures made of the produce of our own country is highly advantageous because here the balance of industry is entirely in our favour. Should the returns for such an exportation consist in the importation of raw materials, to be manufactured here, such a trade would be doubly advantageous.[37]

This sort of pattern had, as we have seen, been prefigured during the eighteenth century. What now gave the region's trade a different character, not just in Egypt but across the Middle East, was the sheer volume of British imports bursting onto its markets. Those imports at first emphasised cotton yarn, already a major import to the Ottoman Empire by the turn of the nineteenth century and on which the cloth weavers of Aleppo, Damascus, Izmir, Bursa and Istanbul were dependent during the early decades of the century.[38] Like in Egypt, imports of finished cloth across the eastern Mediterranean also grew sharply and by mid-century were penetrating the internal markets of the Ottoman Empire. In the three decades after the Battle of Waterloo, the annual average value of exports to Turkey quintupled, with cotton goods predominating and by themselves reaching a value of nearly £2 million by mid-century.[39] It was thus the sheer profusion of goods which spoke of Britain's industrial revolution touching these faraway lands. Its factories were churning out cottons that were lighter and more brightly coloured than anything their rivals could offer.[40] But above all, these goods were simply cheaper than those of all competitors.

It is in this way, argues the *grand maître* of Ottoman history, Halil Inalcik, that Britain's industrial development provided the key to its new-found success. As had so often happened before, cheap imitations trumped the pricier genuine article, leaving local artisanal fabrics with little appeal over the imitations churned out by the factories of northern England. The difference this time was the manner in which technological advance allowed Britain to churn out bargains, notwithstanding its high labour costs. To Inalcik, the British therefore achieved a comparative advantage which, even if competing on a level playing field forged by free trade, would always cause them to win through. The real surprise is that the Ottomans, whose economic concerns were still focused on maximising fiscal revenues, put up no ideological resistance to the free-trade mantra to safeguard its industries.

That may be so, but Britain's industrial advantage was brought to bear so effectively only by political means. Imperial muscle was carefully deployed to advance the cause of free trade in the decades ahead. Its dominant commercial position by the mid-nineteenth century, moreover, secured for it longer-term advantage. As Lewis Farley could already declare by 1860: 'Turkey is no longer a manufacturing country.'[41] The economic relationship between western core and eastern periphery was by then firmly entrenched.

Yet even as British trade with the Middle East flourished at the beginning of the nineteenth century, the Company was marginalised.

Unwilling to adapt to the emerging modern pattern, it found its role blithely usurped by the sinews of the imperial state.

Another Enlightenment

If Dudley North succumbed to the allure of the City's gold-paved streets on his return, Paul Rycaut's mind was set on higher things. Apart from a brief diplomatic posting on the Continent, preferment passed him by. His name was mooted for the embassy in Constantinople, but he lacked the social clout of his aristocratic rivals.[42] He came up with a plan for a peace mission to Algeria, which got so far as to win the blessing of the King. Just as it was to be implemented, though, news arrived that a treaty had already been concluded by the naval commander on the spot.[43] Yet if high office remained frustratingly elusive, Rycaut could count on his reputation as a savant on Turkish affairs to keep him busy dining and opining

32 Sir Paul Rycaut in later years.

at the tables of the great and the good. In the course of his long writing career his pen spawned, among other things, encyclopaedic accounts of the Armenian and Greek churches, an exposé on the Jewish pseudo-Messiah Sabbatai Zevi, and memoirs of his own time in Smyrna. The work that made his name more than any other, though, had been written years before his homecoming. The tripartite and tome-like *Present State of the Ottoman Empire*, drawn on by no lesser figures than Montesquieu, Locke and Gibbon in years to come, won him prompt election to the Royal Society and near unbridled praise from the intelligentsia of his day.

It was not so much this work as a whole, as the notion of 'oriental despotism' standing at its heart, which so caught his contemporaries' eye. Yet its success should certainly not be taken to mean that there was any great novelty in the idea. The Ottoman Empire, to take one much earlier description by an English visitor, spanned parts of the globe that had once been . . .

> . . . the seats of most glorious and triumphant Empires the places where Nature hath produced her wonderfull works; where Arts and Sciences have been invented, and perfited; where wisedome, vertue, policies and civility have been planted, have flourished: . . . where God himselfe did place his own Commonwealth.

Even such places as these were said to have become 'the most deplored spectacles of extreme miserie', for the Turks had 'broken in upon them, and rooted out all civilitie'.[44] In their wake, he continued, the ground had become 'waste and overgrowne with bushes, receptacles of beasts, of theeves, and murderers', while 'large territories [were] dispeopled . . . goodly cities made desolate; sumptuous buildings become ruines'. Social disintegration matched the demographic and architectural morass: 'All Nobility [was] extinguished; no light of learning permitted, nor Vertue cherished.' In sum, the Ottoman advance ushered in a regime of 'violence and rapine insulting over all'. And the first cause of it all was 'the pride of a sterne and barbarous Tyrant . . . aiming only at the height of greatness and sensuality'.[45]

Here we find, in short order, all the hallmarks of the 'orientalist' canon most usually ascribed to the eighteenth-century Enlightenment: decay, depravity, contemptuous disinterest in non-western humanity and, running through the whole, that notion of 'oriental despotism' so beloved of Montesquieu and his fellow *philosophes*. All this, too, is commonly said to denote an easy assumption of superiority over the Orient within European culture, an assumption which prevailed by the Napoleonic era and was a reflection of its military, economic and political dominance in the Middle East. Except that the passage quoted above was first published in 1615 – a date when Ottoman expansion still had much further to run and predated any hint of the western ascendancy which would one day engulf the Ottoman sphere of influence.

In truth, the cliché of eastern despotism had ancient vintage. The Greeks perceived the rulers of Persia as oriental despots around 400 BC. It was revived by the Florentine Renaissance, most famously by Machiavelli, then routinely wheeled out by early-modern Europeans in circumstances of perceived susceptibility, not superiority. It was the mid-seventeenth century which supplied its foremost English exposition, Rycaut's own. The last years of the sixteenth century saw perhaps its most succinct – Francis Bacon's aside that 'where the Ottoman's horse sets his foot, people come up very thin'. The eighteenth century might have produced Montesquieu's systematisation of the theory, but it also spawned critiques of those who had 'injuriously misrepresented . . . the government of the Turkish empire', said to be 'censurers' who 'either from habit and the prejudices of education, or from presumption and opinion, are apt to think their own government the best'.[46] That view, as expressed by Sir James Porter in the mid-eighteenth century, also found endorsement from such luminaries as Voltaire and Burke.[47]

Oriental despotism was not alone among the modern tropes about Turks and Muslims to be recycled from older times. Accusations that Ottoman women were, at once, lascivious beasts and silent victims, for instance, were no less integral to how they were painted in Elizabethan times. Much the same could be said of the obsessive interest in Middle Eastern antiquities apparent during the eighteenth century. For the early seventeenth century likewise had witnessed lamentations on the decline of Ancient Greece, where 'the barbarousnesse of Turkes and Time' had 'defaced all the Monuments of Antiquity', its people like 'prisoners shut up in prisons, or addicted slaves to cruell and tyranicall Masters: so deformed is the state of that once worthy Realme . . .'[48]

This fondness for recycling renders it all the more difficult to demarcate change. And yet, there can be no doubt that change was indeed afoot in the late eighteenth century. If that era witnessed a watershed in political and economic relations between the Middle East and the West, so did it witness a cultural watershed whose consequences were no less momentous. The older note of mutability was heard with increasing rarity, whilst social categories became hard and fast. If the derogatory clichés still directed at the Turks were of old vintage, they were systematised as never before. The new flavour was well captured in the words of Lord Baltimore, an aristocratic traveller to the Ottoman Empire a half-century after Charlemont's journey:

> The religion, laws, and customs of the *Turks* are as much as they can make them, in direct opposition to ours . . . they eat, write, sleep, and sit low, we high; their dead they carry out head, we feet, foremost; their cloaths are long, ours short; they have many wives and mistresses allowed by law, we only one; they have few who—s, we have a multitude; they believe in one God, we in the Trinity.[49]

Such an oppositional outlook provides an important key to what had shifted in Britons' mentalities. As the pashas increasingly defined themselves as both British and European in the course of the eighteenth century, their identities were rebuilt on rigid distinctions from the non-Christians of Ottoman society. The Enlightenment's initial impetus towards valorising common humanity, even as it demarcated difference, was replaced by haughtiness towards 'others'. No beauty is to be found in the Ottoman Empire, as Lord Baltimore went on, because such beauty was only to be found in those countries where literature, arts and sciences abounded. They certainly did not abound here, for 'the good old Mussulman will not . . . for these advantages lay aside his Alkoran, or be inclined to quit his pipe, his sofa, or his girl'. That owed much, he thought, to their being 'enthusiasts in their religion . . . they look on those who differ from them as despisable as dogs, hogs, and devils'.[50] As this passage indicates, such difference was likely to be described in words tinged with contempt.

It was probably only in the latter part of the eighteenth century that Britons began to take on recognisably 'colonialist' airs, reflecting a change in perceptions – on both the British and Ottoman sides – of their respective places in the wider world. The Ottomans came to believe their inferiority to Europe as political humiliations mounted. Until some years ago, one visitor observed late in the eighteenth century, 'no Frank could walk in Constantinople without the risque of incurring insult, and the merchants of Pera were usually protected by a janissary'. But nowadays, he went on, 'no molestation is to be feared, at least by a person who is prudent enough to give the upper hand to a Turk'. This favourable change, he thought, was owed to a series of recent Ottoman military defects, which had produced 'a wonderful effect in reducing the insolence and ferocity of their national character'.[51]

Meanwhile, Britons' perceptions of their own global eminence were dramatically buoyed in the latter half of the seventeenth century by the string of victories accompanying the Seven Years War. Three decades later, Mather Brown's image of the Turkish embassy of 1793 stooping before prime minister and King, the latter emblazoned in divine light, poignantly reverses the rituals of deference enacted by Winchilsea and his fellow ambassadors before the Ottoman court. By the era of the Napoleonic Wars, there could be no doubt that Britons had developed, as Edward Said famously put it, a 'style for having authority over the Orient'. They began to walk through the Ottoman Empire sure in the knowledge that its rulers were beholden to the naval frigate and the maxim gun, not to mention Britain's cotton mills and, soon enough, its bankers.

By the dawn of the nineteenth century, moreover, the significant interest in the people of the Ottoman world which had accompanied the pashas' heyday was becoming scarce. Instead, the Middle East was newly imagined as a wasteland, a site of moral and physical decay whose sole interest consisted in its extensive ruins of classical antiquity. Where any attention was paid to its people, they were firmly subordinated to those of the West, a tendency which only increased as the nineteenth century wore on. As *Baedeker* reminded its readers in 1878: 'The Egyptians, it must be remembered, occupy a much lower grade in the scale of civilisation than most of the Western nations.'[52] In the politics of the Eastern Question, Islam in particular was being defined as a retarding influence. 'Did I wish to appear as an apologist for Russia I might point out', Lord Cromer opined, 'that it is somewhat unworthy to allow our political jealousies to retard the progress of civilisation in Central Asia . . . Russia is in a backward condition but I cannot but think that so much as the Bible teaches a purer and more humanitarian religion than the Koran, by so much does Russian civilisation bears with it a potentiality for progress . . . superior to any that is possible under the effete and decaying laws and institutions of

Mahomedanism.'[53] It was a short step from this type of pronouncement to the shrill rhetoric denouncing the 'Terrible Turk' in the late-nineteenth and early-twentieth centuries. Here was a new world which had no place for the pashas.

Eastern Questions

On 29 January 1807, the British merchants of Constantinople, wrapped in their evening finery, boarded rowing boats and pushed off from Galata's shore. They were bound for the deck of the *Endymion*, expecting to fill an evening with feasting and mirth, to toast the King and return tipsy to Pera. No sooner had they clambered aboard, however, than the anchor was hauled, sails hoisted, and the frigate slipped from the sultan's view. For the first time in its history, Britain was drifting towards war with the Ottoman Empire. Fearing the fate which had befallen his French counterpart a decade earlier, the ambassador, Charles Arbuthnot, had unilaterally decided to scuttle the British position. Whether or not he saved his countrymen from confinement in the Seven Towers, he precipitated another of the misfortunes to have befallen the French in 1798, for British merchants' property was now seized across the Empire.[54] For all his abundance of caution, moreover, Arbuthnot's plans had made provision neither for their wives and children nor his own, all of whom remained trapped in the Ottoman capital for the duration. Arbuthnot spent the following weeks torturing himself with thoughts of the horrors which might lie in store for them.[55]

The ambassador's abrupt evacuation marked yet another reversal in London's relations with the Porte. Before abandoning his post, he had sent word for forces to advance on Alexandria and, less than two months later, there began the second British occupation of the city in less than a decade. Its object, the government claimed, was 'not the conquest of Egypt but merely the capture of Alexandria', this for the 'purpose of preventing the French from regaining a footing in that country'.[56] Yet it also formed part of a grander scheme to cow the Ottoman Empire in support of Britain's imperial aims. A squadron of warships had accordingly been despatched to bombard the Porte and deliver the message that either it must accede 'to all our propositions, or Constantinople be in ruins'.[57] No longer confined to the North African periphery of his empire, British gunboat diplomacy was now being carried to the sultan's doorstep.

33 European sovereigns vie for slices of the Turkish feast in a nineteenth-century satirical print.

The Company's decay had spanned a century, but the end itself was swift. With the rising political importance of the Middle East, the merchants' voices were increasingly ignored by their government. The embassy's dual control by the Company and Crown had, as we have seen, long been a source of strain. It can be argued that the fundamental shift had occurred as long before as the Glorious Revolution in transforming 'a commercial agent masquerading as an ambassador into a servant of the Crown sent primarily for political and diplomatic business'.[58] Thereafter, it is true, high political concerns came to predominate in ambassadors' despatches, whilst there were growing signs that the Crown had wrested from the Company the upper hand in the partnership which it had hitherto enjoyed. Still, for a century more, the Company felt only mildly short-changed (as it always had) in its support of the embassy and tolerably able to steer the ambassador's energies towards its own concerns. The likes of Sir James Porter, when not entertaining aristocratic guests or gazing at the night sky, heeded carefully the concerns of the pashas' trade.

Once more, it was the Napoleonic invasion of Egypt which marked the real turning point. A few months after the French victory in the Battle of the Pyramids, Lord Elgin was moved to volunteer his services as ambassador to the Porte, in part by the consideration of 'how essentially the future greatness of France may be obstructed by our firmly establishing and maintaining an interest' there. This imperative, he suggested, demanded 'an English representative equal in rank and situation to the Imperial and French ministers at that court'.[59] In advancing this line, he was pushing at an open door. The government despatched him to Pera without so much as pausing to seek the Company's view. It was intended that the existing ambassador would remain to look after the latter's affairs. Not surprisingly, however, a power struggle broke out between the two men, resulting in the incumbent's return to London. The Company's firm backing had proved of little worth set against Elgin's clear mandate from the King.

As Elgin's had been, diplomatic appointments to the Ottoman Empire in the aftermath of the British expedition to Egypt were made with little or no reference to the Company.[60] With Arbuthnot's appointment in 1803, the Crown formally removed the embassy from the Company's hands. Its political role would now be confined to supporting the network of consuls across the Empire. It was no coincidence that Arbuthnot thereafter embarked on a concerted policy of preferring the interests of high diplomacy to those of the Company. This culminated in the flight of 1807, which for a time seemed to have undone all the commercial gains made against the French since the turn of the century.

As the state's diplomatic presence swelled in the Middle East, it was all the more difficult to formulate a convincing rationale for the Company's existence. At the turn of the eighteenth century, one contemporary had suggested the following typology for the organisation of trade: 'If we trade to countries able to defend us, and that are governed by stated laws, as Spain, France, Holland and such-like, I think an open trade best; but where the governments are able to defend us and the rule is arbitrary, as in Turkey and Russia, I am for a regulated company, for they must raise money for presents and several other occasions; but where they are absolute, diverse, independent and are not able to defend us, and we have Principalities of our own I see no way to manage but by a joint stock.'[61] This identification of the Ottomans' 'despotism' as the element calling for political protection of Britons trading within their realm was a commonplace, still referred to a century later as the basic justification for the Company's role. 'The Turkish government being essentially different from any other in Europe, perfectly despotic in its nature, and approached only like that of all Oriental people ancient and modern, through the medium of present and particular influence,' it was explained in the year of the Company's disbandment, 'no intercourse can be carried on with the natives with any security unless under certain regulations called capitulations, agreed upon by the respective courts.'[62]

Its domestic privileges were accordingly painted, as they had been since Elizabethan times, as the quid pro quo for the expensive overseas presence for which all this called:

> Now as it was the policy of the government of England to throw the whole weight of paying those officers and establishments on the Levant Company, it was but reasonable to confer on them the appointment and management of those whom they had to support, and it is clear that this power would be nugatory, unless the British subjects resident in Turkey were made amenable in a certain degree to their authority. It was to this end that the charters and acts restricted the trade to controllable numbers of the company, permitted them to make laws for its regulation, enabled them to resist avanias . . . authorised them to levy duties to pay the expenses of the protecting establishments and finally empowered them to send refractory persons out of the country to England . . .[63]

Special pleading of this kind was voiced against a backdrop of growing hostility to monopolistic practices. Criticism of the Company on the ground that it directed the trade's lucre into the hands of the few rather than the many had a long pedigree, as we have seen. Such cries came mostly from those whose own pockets seemed to be depleted directly in proportion to the Company's gains, most notably the provincial merchants excluded from its ranks. By the nineteenth century, though, such opposition was buttressed by a powerful ideological underpinning, as the tenets of classical political economy gained acceptance. By its final years, the Company's monopoly was flatly out of kilter with the economic orthodoxies of its day. No more would mercantilists ride to the rescue with declarations of its beneficial effect on the bullion supply.

Nor were influential mouths stuffed with gold as readily as in the past, for the Levant business ceased to be among those trades where London's successful merchants were likely to have interests. Increasingly from the mid-eighteenth century, those who had once traded with the Middle East shifted their spheres of interest to the Atlantic or South Asia.[64] The old school of Levant merchants stayed rich, but their circles became ever narrower.

Opposition to the Company found ammunition not just in economic dogma. There was mounting evidence that its monopoly was indeed hampering British commerce by its closing decades. So much seemed to be borne out by the success of the French in the later eighteenth century. Early attempts by Colbert to create a monopoly for the French trade (in an era when it would almost certainly have done some good) had been successfully batted off by the Chamber of Commerce of Marseilles.[65] Their trade remained a relatively open one compared to that of the British. One consequence was that French merchants were simply much more numerous in places like Smyrna during the eighteenth century.[66] Europe's mechanised manufactories were, at the same time, turning sheer numbers into an unassailable virtue. In the same year as Napoleon's invasion of Egypt, William Eton accused the Company of a comprehensive lack of enterprise and energy, especially in its failure to make the cottons of Lancashire and cutlery of Sheffield popular in Turkey.[67] This, however, was rather to miss the point. The very existence of an organisation in the Company's mould was, by its nature, ill suited to trading on the scale which the twin forces of industrialisation and imperialism now invited.

For all the criticism still directed at it in the nineteenth century, important inroads had by then been made on the Company's monopoly. Parliament stepped into the fray in 1753 by passing an Act which imposed a relaxation of membership requirements. This equipped Sir James Porter, in a valiant defence of the *ancien régime* some years later, to argue that the consequent expansion of numbers had not caused any discernable improvement to the Company's sagging fortunes.[68] He could no longer claim as much by the early decades of the following century, however. The growth spurt then being witnessed in the volume of Middle Eastern commerce could not have been conceived of had it not been for the swelling roster of the Company's merchants. These were, moreover, emphatically 'new men', of a very different hue from their predecessors and encompassing substantial numbers of provincial merchants and retailers. The old guard sneered at them, but the momentum of change was becoming unstoppable. Even the Company's refusal to branch out and establish trading posts outside the main factories was reversed in the final years and establishments sprung up in locations as diverse as Beirut, Patras, Acre and Bucharest.[69]

Piecemeal loosening of the Company's constraints might have bought it some time, but in the end only seemed to confirm the logic of wholesale abolition. By the time the axe fell, any thought of resistance had long since been abandoned by the members. The immediate trigger for disbandment was the outbreak of the Greek War of Independence, which once more placed the Ottoman Empire at the centre of Britain's foreign policy concerns. In 1825, George Canning wrote to the Company, informing it that the government had decided to assume control of its network of consuls. 'The Company being thus relieved from the charge of maintaining their establishment,' he wrote, 'the duties and consulages levied under the authority of their Charters upon the trade to the Levant will of course be repealed.'[70] If Canning could deprive the Company of its revenues, only Parliament could remove its time-honoured privileges. Alongside a thinly veiled threat to procure this, however, the foreign secretary invited the merchants voluntarily to give them up: 'I cannot refrain from suggesting to you, for your consideration, whether it may not be expedient to give up the remaining privileges of your Charters, which being no longer connected with the public interests, may be deemed, by Parliament and the public, to be useless and injurious restrictions upon Trade.'[71]

The loss of the consular role denuded the Company of any remaining pretence that it existed for the public good. Without a dissenting view being so much as voiced, the General Court voted unanimously to bow to what was only inevitable. As the ageing governor said in his address to the assembled merchants, the monopoly was 'in your former position . . . both necessary and just; those who bore the burthen of protecting the commerce could alone claim to share its benefits. But it will become wholly useless when you shall be relieved from the duties and expences in contemplation of which it was originally created.'[72] So, with a whimper, ended the quarter-millennium of its existence.

Britons involved in trade with the Middle East, though, had eyes only for the future. A new breed was amassing untold wealth: the traders flocking to the Maydan al-Tarir and Galata's Parisian houses, the cotton magnates of the north-east, the gentleman capitalists of London ('this great metropolis of the commerce of the world', as it could now truly be declared).[73] Free trade, the Levant Company had to admit during its final meeting, was animating the 'greatest commercial empire, which the sun has ever yet enlightened'.[74] As for the Middle East, the European powers pulled their noose around it ever tighter, as they fought the greater game for India.

Crescent Empire

❖

On the first day of January 1877 Queen Victoria was publicly proclaimed Empress of India in a feast of pageantry. The viceroy, Lord Lytton, marked the occasion with an 'imperial assemblage' in Delhi, whose culmination would display the majestic power of the *Raj* as never before to its nearly 300 million subjects.

Everybody sensed the coming spectacle would be something momentous and extraordinary. In the weeks before, sixty-three ruling princes, joined by three hundred dignitaries hand-picked from the 'flower of the Indian nobility', converged on the former Mughal capital from far-flung parts of the Empire: the Princes of Tanjore and the Taluqdars of Oudh; Arabs from Peshawar and Sikh Sardars from Amritsar; the Khan of Khelat and the Begum of Bhopal. British officials had spent months literally preparing the ground for the invasion. One hundred villages were cleared to make way for the rulers' vast entourages of courtiers and their clusters of tents, which after dark illuminated the surrounding plains with constellations of bonfires mirroring the stars in the night sky. New roads, water supplies and bazaars were installed to cater for the 84,000 visitors expected to swell the city streets, and extra provisions brought in to feed their elephants, horses, camels and livestock. For the viceroy, a grandiose temporary residence was erected out of canvas, its pavilions arranged into neat rows interspersed with grass and flowers to impart a flavour of home. At the centre of the imperial camp was an expansive durbar tent, where Lytton spent much of the final week of 1876. Sitting stiffly on a raised platform, he received a string of princes who came to pay homage, as the Queen's stern visage gazed down from the royal portrait fastened to the wall behind him.

When the great day arrived it was blessed with clear skies. During the morning, the outskirts of the parade ground began to fill with the fifteen thousand red-coated sepoys tasked with lining the ceremonial route, mingling with onlookers, camp followers, and street hawkers doing a brisk trade. At the appointed hour, the princes began to arrive. They processed towards the arched spectator stand on elephants, to which shield-shaped banners had been attached, fashioned especially for the occasion from Chinese silk dyed and embroidered with heraldic crests. Then, to the overblown strains of brass fanfares and the overture from *Tannhäuser*, the viceroy made his appearance. He ascended to a throne placed atop an enormous hexagonal daïs decked out with intricately patterned flags and friezes. When his opening address drew to a close, an artillery salute of 101 salvos and rifle *feux de joie* was fired, casting a cloud of smoke over the remainder of proceedings and setting off a stampede of elephants and horses which crushed several bystanders in its path. Seemingly undaunted by the mishap, the Maharaja Scindia sprung up in what Lytton noted approvingly as a 'spontaneous' display of loyalty to the British monarch, and recited ecstatically in Urdu: 'Shah in Shah, Padshah, May God bless you.' This was, the viceroy recorded, the crowning moment of his personal and very public triumph.[1]

One week later, at nine o'clock prompt, the viceroy stepped onto the platform at Aligarh, an unspectacular station on the railway line from the former Mughal capital to Agra, almost midway between the Ganges and the Yamuna. Lord Lytton was here to lay the foundation stone of the Mohammedan Anglo-Oriental College, the fruit of many years' work by the influential Islamic reformer Sayyed Ahmad Khan and a committee of local Muslims. Their idea was to bring the spirit of Harrow and Cambridge to Muslim India, without sacrificing the pillars of Islamic religious observance and learning. It was an ethos that found expression in the college cricket team and the 'Siddons Union Club', a debating society fashioned by an idealistic young principal, Theodore Beck, after those of Oxford and Cambridge Universities. This distinctive ethos also infused its architecture, like the tall construction which came to dominate the main quadrangle, Strachey Hall, marrying the oriental arches of its façade and the neighbouring Mosque with the occidental plainness of a pavilion-style roof. It was even visible in the students' uniforms – long academic gowns, modelled on those worn in Oxbridge colleges, combined with the somewhat more indigenous headwear of a fez.[2]

Looked at one way, the viceroy's visit here to celebrate the college's foundation marked just another modest version of the pompous durbar of the previous week. One of scores which were scheduled for the months ahead, he was well used to the routine: stepping onto the platform in full ceremonial dress, he tersely shook hands with the civil officers and local dignitaries lined up to greet him, and transferred to the carriage which would parade him through the bustling streets up to the unfinished gates of the college. He took up his place at the front of a large shamiana that had been assembled to house the rows of witnesses to the ceremony. Then, after uttering a few warm words from the podium, he knelt to place a bottle containing scrolls and coins into a cavity below the new buildings, and hammered the foundation stone into place above it.

Yet the viceroy's description of this day as symbolising 'an epoch in the social progress of India under British rule' was not entirely hollow. Once more, the occasion drew representatives from distant corners of India: they came from the Punjab, the Deccan and Lower Bengal; from Agra, Delhi and Calcutta. For all the diversity of their origins, though, in British eyes these were members of a distinct 'community', united by their shared faith. In his words to those assembled before him, moreover, this was a religion and a civilisation for which the Indian viceroy expressed apparently heartfelt words of sympathy and admiration:

> Not only have [Muslims] given to a greater portion of this Continent an architecture which is still the wonder and admiration of the world, but, in an age when the Christian societies of Europe had barely emerged out of intellectual darkness and social barbarism, they covered the whole Iberian Peninsula with schools of medicine, of mathematics and philosophy, far in advance of all contemporary science.[3]

The previous week's spectacle had been staged to show the unity of the *Raj* to its countless millions of subjects. Hardly less important, today's proclaimed the special status of the Queen-Empress' eighty-million Indian Muslims.

At its height, the British Empire came to span the Islamic world even more completely than it did the world entire. A new relationship between Britain and the 'Turbaned Nations', as John Locke referred to the Islamic polities of his day, had become unmistakable with the large-scale British expansions into India during the latter half of the eighteenth century. A Muslim ruler like Tipu sultan of Mysore could still pose a serious military challenge to their presence, and his defeat at Seringapatam did not come until that century's very end. It was not until the latter half of the nineteenth century that Britain's crescent empire acquired an air of invincibility inside India and gathered scale beyond.

Thereafter, the late Victorian and Edwardian expansions were rapid and unrelenting. The perceived threat of a Russian invasion of India through Central Asia had long ago ignited the 'Great Game', played out on her North-West Frontier towards Afghanistan and Iran. But in the half-century after Victoria's proclamation as Queen-Empress in 1871, the goal of safeguarding their South Asian prize suddenly pushed the British much deeper into the heartlands of the crumbling Muslim empires. To the west of the Arabian Sea, armies were sent into Egypt. From this new North African base, they advanced down the Nile into the Sudan, home of the Quranic state of the charismatic Mahdi. Further south still, in Somaliland, they waded into a protracted campaign against the 'Mad Mullah', while on Africa's opposite coast, they penetrated the swamps of Hausaland and turned its Muslim Fulani rulers into enforced tributaries. It was the eastern campaigns of the First World War which then brought extensive Middle Eastern territories under British sway. With the fall of Jerusalem in 1917, where this book began, and with Damascus, Cairo, Delhi and Baghdad already in their hands, they had achieved a political unity over the abode of Islam unprecedented since the days of the early caliphate. Britain was now 'the mightiest and most beneficient of Eastern powers', one contemporary trumpeted.[4]

For so quintessential a colonialist as Lord Cromer, mankind was divided squarely between the British and mere 'subject races'.[5] In truth, though, Britons' attitudes towards their subjects were rarely so Manichean, even when the tide of bigotry ran as high as it did in the later nineteenth century. Muslims continued to occupy a special place on their mental map of mankind, even if it had moved fundamentally since the era of the Levant Company's prime. This lent the diverse Muslim subjects of their empire a certain coherence in British eyes. A Muslim from Aligarh was seen to share an identity partly in common with, say, a Muslim from Cairo or Kabul, or indeed with the Islamic populations of any number of places across south-east Asia, the eastern Mediterranean and North and West Africa to where the Empire's tentacles ultimately extended. The contours of their outlook on the religion were shaped by countless local encounters taking place across these disparate continents. Yet, for all that, they continued to bear the stamp of a far longer history of contacts with Islam, which extended back into the period scrutinised by this book, when the British Empire familiar to Victorians and Edwardians was not yet born. This pre-history differentiated Muslims from most, if not all, other subjects of the British crown.[6]

By the later nineteenth century, this prompted imperial officials to ask one question above all others. Were they, a slim volume of prose penned by a civil servant named William Hunter asked, 'bound in conscience to rebel' against the Queen-Empress Victoria? Hunter's influential, if non-committal, argument was that no single answer could be given. On the one hand, there were 'saintly' Muslims, the true inheritors of a great and glorious imperial civilisation. These were men capable of assimilation to the Empire through English-style education and they might be conciliated and engaged. On the other hand, there were rebel ones, the fanatical and the fierce, members of revivalist jihadi groups who were engaged in a 'chronic conspiracy' to undermine British rule. For them, there could be no such indulgence: they must be subjugated or else annihilated.[7]

This formulation, eerily familiar today, was just as characteristic of the Janus-faced aspect which Islam at large presented to the British throughout modern times. It also exposes how little either the decline of the Islamic empires, or Britain's altered political relationship with the Muslim world, by now appeared to have done to extinguish the perception of an 'Islamic threat'. Colonial masters the British might have been; at times, nonetheless, the peril was to their eyes no less direct, their vulnerability no less real, than ever it had been in pre-colonial times. The danger that Muslims were seen to pose within the Empire, albeit of a different kind from the threat of old, was routinely the starting point for Britons' estimation of Islam.

If that needed demonstrating for Hunter's contemporaries, the Indian 'Mutiny' of 1857, an intensely violent uprising which for a time brought the *Raj* to its knees, had done so in dramatic style. For it dragged into the open, as many saw it, 'all the ancient feelings of warring for the Faith' which were seething inside Muslim souls, 'reminding one of the days of the first Caliphs'.[8] Thereafter, the British were forever seeing signs of a Muslim 'rebel colony' in their midst, culminating in their hyper-inflated belief in a pan-Islamic conspiracy during the run-up to the First World War, an episode which reinvigorated fears of a specifically Ottoman threat. Though they had never been absent from the imperial mindset, it was in the later nineteenth and early twentieth centuries – at the very 'climax of an empire' – that such attitudes reached their zenith.[9] Islam, one prominent intellectual declared in the 1920s, was 'the most dangerous of subject civilisations'; for there was, he wrote, a 'clash of civilisations – Christian, Muslim and Oriental'.[10]

So whilst late imperial Britons' increasingly contemptuous outlook on Islam is often explained in terms of their post-Enlightenment convictions of superiority, it also owed a surprising amount, even then, to perceptions of outright vulnerability. That furnished some continuity between pre-modern and modern contexts for viewing the faith. Naturally, these Britons linked the present-day Muslim threat with the Ottoman one remembered in their history books. It was just as inevitable that the same hostile stereotypes should have been resurrected and wheeled out to meet it. This was, after all, a time-hallowed vocabulary, tailor-made to describe the very emotions of fear which they still encountered in the face of the religion.

If modern times recycled the bigotry of old, what of the more reverent attitudes towards Islam also traced in this book? As both Hunter's book and the construction of the Aligarh college exemplified, the heritage of the early-modern Islamic empires was seen to imbue at least some Muslims with a potential, exceptional among non-western peoples, to attain a position of greatness in the scale of civilisations. This was associated with a markedly more sympathetic strand of ideas towards the faith and its adherents. But such expressions of sympathy were, of course, always deeply and inescapably loaded in the colonial context of their times. Whether or not it occurred to Sayyed Ahmad Khan or Theodore Beck, the experiment at Aligarh fostered a Muslim separatism which helped to entrench British rule. Similarly, the well-known Arab sympathies of the likes of T.E. Lawrence and Gertrude Bell conveniently furthered Britain's military ends against the Turks. Political circumstances could not but taint the motives for their advocacy of cross-cultural embrace. No matter what the substance of such attitudes might be, moreover, they took for granted a racial hierarchy, in which the ultimate superiority of white, Protestant Britons was axiomatic, the standard for which lesser mortals had to strive.

With the hardening of attitudes in the late eighteenth century, the brief flowering of cosmopolitanism came to an end and rigid categorisation of this kind became universal. Britons and Muslims might still wander through souks, share coffee on sofas or dine al fresco in desert tents, and give all the appearance of inhabiting the same world that the pashas had done for centuries. That their empire was lording it over the locals, militarily, economically and culturally, unavoidably lent such encounters a different character from those of earlier times. The unequal might of civilisations pulled against the meetings of individuals which had once been possible.

By rights, our post-imperial times should promise a return to the more fluid cultural boundaries that the colonial interlude destroyed. If the proto-globalisation of the pashas' day initially encouraged a more open-minded outlook on mankind, however, closer integration in our own time has seemed instead to stoke oppositional religious and ethnic identities, and to push us again towards an overt 'clash of civilisations'. Meanwhile, the balance of power between western powers and the Middle East has rarely appeared so unequal. In some eyes, the spectre of colonialism has not disappeared from the region. Meanwhile, the Islamic tradition of religious toleration plays a dwindling role in its politics. It is a depressing reflection that, in part through these centrifugal factors, it does not necessarily strike Britons today as less remote and dangerous than it did their ancestors of three centuries ago.

Set against that background, the pashas in some ways inhabited happier times. Their history underscores that the intensifying web of global connections, at the heart of the modern experience, did not from the first involve the West plundering and subordinating this part of the East. Nor was a world of opposites inherent, like some worm in the bud of western modernity, in the empirical habits of thought changing mental worlds in the seventeenth and eighteenth centuries. In that alone, unlike too much of what has come since, there lies some hope. Too often, it has been obscured by the ghosts of Britain's imperial past. Like the elemental voices in E.M. Forster's vision, the nineteenth-century ones seem to denounce the clasp of friendship between Britons and Muslims: 'They said in their hundred voices, "No, not yet," and the sky said, "No, not there".'[11] The pashas remind us that once upon a time there was a peaceful and mutually enriching encounter between Britons and the still-troubled Middle East. We can only hope there will be again.

Notes

❖

Preface

1. In illuminating the contrast between early encounters with the wider world and those of the nineteenth to mid-twentieth centuries, their stories resemble those explored in, amongst others Linda Colley, *Captives: Britain, Empire and the World 1600–1850* (London, 2002); Maya Jasanoff, *Edge of Empire: Conquest and Collecting in the East 1750–1850* (London, 2005); William Dalrymple, *White Mughals: Love and Betrayal in Eighteenth-century India* (London, 2002), all of which are of major influence on the interpretations advanced here.

2. The 'Levant', a word used by contemporaries, refers usually to the eastern part of the Mediterranean. The phrase 'Middle East', first coined by an American admiral in 1902, would not have been known to them, but nonetheless better captures the geographical sphere of the pashas' trading interests both around the eastern Mediterranean and further inland in the eastern part of the Ottoman Empire.

3. A.C. Wood, *A History of the Levant Company* (London, 1935), which provides an excellent institutional account of the Company's history, focusing on its political and economic affairs. Another broad account from the same era is contained in the unpublished PhD thesis of Gwilym Ambrose, 'The Levant Company, 1640–1753' (1932). For the period before the Civil War, these can be supplemented by M. Epstein, *The Early History of the Levant Company* (1908) and Chapter 4 of Kenneth Andrews' *Trade, Plunder and Settlement* (Cambridge, 1984). A brilliant study of the Company's domestic affairs of more recent vintage can be found in Robert Brenner, *Merchants and Revolution* (London, 2003), especially Chapters 1 and 2, which treat the Company's history insofar as it relates to the author's thesis about the transformation of London's merchant community in the century after 1550. An account of various aspects of the Company's activities in its central period can be found in Sonia Anderson's very fine monograph, *An English Consul in Turkey: Paul Rycaut at Smyrna, 1667–1678* (Oxford, 1989). The nature of the Company in its Ottoman context is further explored in the important work – of considerable influence on the present book – of Daniel Goffman, *Britons in the Ottoman Empire, 1642–1660* (Seattle and London, 1998), which focuses on an

incident in the period of the English Civil War to reveal the traders' engagement in local politics. Finally, the mechanics of the Company's trade in the eighteenth century is explored both authoritatively and entertainingly in Ralph Davis' work, *Aleppo and Devonshire Square* (London, 1967). Also dealing with the later period, Ina Russell, 'The Later History of the Levant Company, 1753–1825', Manchester University unpublished PhD thesis (1935).

4. See, for instance, Miles Ogborn, *Global Lives: Britain and the World 1550–1800* (Cambridge, 2008); Alison Games, *The Web of Empire: English Cosmopolitans in an Age of Expansion 1560–1660* (Oxford, 2008).

5. In particular, Matar's trilogy, *Turks, Moors and Englishmen* (New York, 1999); *Islam in Britain, 1558–1685* (Cambridge, 1998); and *Britain and Barbary* (Gainesville, 2005).

6. Bernard Lewis, *What Went Wrong?: The Clash between Islam and Modernity in the Middle East* (London, 2002).

Prologue

1. This account is based on John D. Grainger, *The Battle for Palestine 1917* (Woodbridge, 2006), pp. 200–225; W.T. Massey, *How Jerusalem Was Won* (London, 1919), pp. 195–210; Lowell Thomas with Kenneth Brown Collings, *With Allenby in the Holy Land* (London, 1938), pp. 101–27; Michael Yardley, *Backing into the Limelight* (1985), p. 116; David Fromkin, *A Peace to End All Peace* (London, 1989), pp. 312–13; Vivient Gilbert, *The Romance of the Last Crusade: With Allenby to Jerusalem* (New York, 1923), *passim*; James Barr, *Setting the Desert on Fire* (London, 2006), pp. 207–9.

2. The phrase belongs to Lloyd George himself: David Lloyd George, *War Memoirs of David Lloyd George*, vol. ii (London, 1936), p. 1092. C.E. Carington wrote that the supremacy of British armies throughout the world of Islam from 'Stamboul to Singapore . . . was perhaps the most astonishing consequence of the war'. Cited in Robert Holland, 'The British Empire and the Great War, 1914–1918', in Judith M. Brown and Wm Roger Louis (eds), *The Oxford History of the British Empire* (*OHBE*), vol. iv (Oxford, 1999), p. 135. See also Francis Robinson, 'The British Empire and the Muslim World', in *OHBE*, vol. iv, p. 407.

3. Thomas with Collings, *With Allenby in the Holy Land*, p. 125.

4. Sir William Foster (ed.), *The Travels of John Sanderson in the Levant, 1584–1602* (London, 1931). The Ottomans had extensively rebuilt Jerusalem's dilapidated city walls in the earlier sixteenth century and tasked the deputy district governor with keeping the gates locked from sunset to daybreak: see Amnon Cohen, *Economic Life in Ottoman Jerusalem* (Cambridge, 2001), pp. 2–3.

5. *A True and Strange discourse of the traveiles of two English pilgrimes: What admirable accidents befell them in their journey to Jerusalem, Gaza, Grand Cayro, Alexandria, and other places* (London, 1603), p. 6.

6. How early it entertained serious aspirations to territorial sovereignty remains controversial. See K.N. Chaudhuri's classic account in *The Trading World of Asia and the East India Company, 1660–1760* (Cambridge, 1978), especially Chapter 6; I. Bruce Watson, 'Fortifications and the "Idea" of Force in Early English East India Company Relations with India', *Past and Present*, 88, 1 (1980), pp. 70–87; Philip J. Stern, 'Politics and Ideology in the Early East India Company-State: The Case of St Helena, 1673–1709', *The Journal of Imperial and Commonwealth History*, vol. 35, issue 1, March 2007, pp. 1–23. Sir Josia Child, who dominated official policy in the 1680s, believed that the Company 'could only operate effectively from secure forti-fied settlements, outside the control of any Asian ruler' (P.J. Marshall, 'The English in Asia', in *OHBE*, vol. i, p. 280) and the English fought a little-remembered and inglorious war against the Mughals in India as early as this period. See Chapter 7.

7. Cited in Brenner, *Merchants and Revolution*, p. 4.

8. Roger North, *Lives of the Norths*, ii (London, 1826), p. 3.

9. I first came across this image by way of Drohr Wahrmann's book, *The Making of the Modern Self* (New Haven and London, 2004), p. 103. It is also discussed in Roxan Wheeler, *Complexion of Race* (2000), p. 36.

10. Paul Rycaut, *The History of the Turkish Empire from the year 1623 to the year 1677* (London, 1680), preface to 'The Memoirs of Paul Rycaut, Esq.'.

11. That is, in the openness which was accorded to the world's merchants. It is not suggested that this policy was founded on any ideology akin to liberalism: the Ottomans' policy was motivated primarily by the hope of fiscal gain (see Halil Inalcik, 'The Ottoman Economic Mind and Aspects of the Ottoman Economy', in M.A. Cook (ed.), *Studies in the Economic History of the Middle East* (London, 1970), pp. 207–19), while the Ottoman economy was in general a tightly regulated one.

12. Henry Blount, *A voyage into the Levant. A brief relation of a journey, lately performed by H.B.* (London, 1636), p. 1.

13. Henry Stubbe, *Account of the Rise and Progress of Mahometanism, with a life of Mahomet and a vindication of him and his religion from the calumnies of the Christians . . . From a manuscript copied by Charles Hornby of Pipe Office, in 1705 'with some variations and additions.' Edited, with an introduction and appendix, by Hafiz Mahmud Khan Shairani* (London, 1911), p. 182.

14. James Boswell, *Life of Samuel Johnson* (Oxford, 1904), p. 67. It should be pointed out, though, that Johnson – a man who dared to be inconsistent – elsewhere spoke of the 'Turks' as 'a remote and barbarous people' about whom 'none desire to be informed' (cited in Samuel Chew, *The Crescent and the Rose – Islam and England during the Renaissance* (New York, 1937), p. 112).

15. The standard work was for a long time Chew's *Crescent and Rose*. Brilliantly corrective is the more recent trilogy by Nabil Matar, *Turks, Moors and Englishmen*; *Islam in Britain*; and *Britain and Barbary*. Similar directions, though with a greater focus on literature, are explored in two works by Gerald Maclean, *The Rise of Oriental Travel: English Visitors to the Ottoman Empire, 1580–1720* (London, 2006) and *Looking East: English Writing and the Ottoman Empire Before 1800* (London, 2007). For a richly suggestive interpretation of the encounter in the context of corsairs on the Barbary Coast, see Linda Colley's *Captives*. Early-modern English writing bearing on Islam has received a good deal of attention from students of literature, much of it with strongly theoretical bent (and showing an influence of post-colonial theory): see, for instance, Daniel Vitkus, *Turning Turk: English Theater and the Multicultural Mediterranean, 1570–1630* (New York, 2003); Matthew Birchwood, *Staging Islam in England* (Cambridge, 2007); Emily Bartels, *Spectacles of Strangeness: Imperialism, Alienation and Marlowe* (Philadelphia, 1993).

16. Numbers cited by contemporary travellers routinely referred only to numbers of 'factors' and not to servants, wives and so forth. Some histories have tended to imply the same by citing numbers from factory meetings (where only the names of factors were recorded). There is little evidence on which to come to a reliable figure as to the number of these other English men and women here.

17. Edward Said, *Orientalism* (London, 1980). For a helpful overview of the 'orientalism' debate, see A.L. Macfie, *Orientalism* (London, 2002). Examples of the growing chorus of books which, in various ways, challenge the assumptions of Said's thesis are John Mackenzie, *Orientalism: History, Theory and the Arts* (Manchester, 1995); Robert Irwin, *For Lust of Knowing: The Orientalists and their Enemies* (London, 2006).

Chapter 1: Peace and Trade

1. Sir Thomas Herbert, *A Relation of Some Yeares Travaile begunne Anno 1626. into Afrique and the greater Asia, especially the Territories of the Persian Monarchie, and some parts of the orientall Indies . . . of their religion, language, habit . . . and other matters concerning them* (London, 1634), p. 5. For secondary accounts of Aleppo in the Ottoman period, see especially Bruce Masters, *The Origins of Western Economic Dominance in the Middle East – Mercantilism and the Islamic Economy in Aleppo, 1600–1750* (New York, 1988); the chapter by Masters on Aleppo in Edhem Eldem, Daniel Goffman and Bruce Masters (eds), *The Ottoman City between East and West – Aleppo, Izmir and Istanbul* (Cambridge, 1999); and Abraham Marcus, *The Middle East on the Eve of Modernity – Aleppo in the Eighteenth Century* (New York, 1989). On the city's architecture, see Heghnar Watenpaugh, *The Image of an Ottoman City: Imperial Architecture and Urban Experience in Aleppo in the 16th and 17th centuries* (Boston, 2004).
2. The National Archives, State Papers ('TNA SP') 105/110, fos 41v, 44r; Charles Robson, *Newes from Aleppo* (London, 1628), p. 11; Daniel Goffman, *Izmir and the Levantine World, 1550–1650* (Seattle and London, 1990), p. 67. It was also owed, though, to intrigue at the Porte by the Sayfa governors of Syrian Tripoli, who sought to restore the trade to there and hence benefit from the customs dues: see Masters, *Origins of Western Economic Dominance*, pp. 15–17.
3. Wood, *Levant Company*, pp. 110–11; TNA SP 110/23, fo. 124.
4. TNA SP 110/23, fo. 58; Henry Teonge, *The Diary of H. Teonge, Chaplain on board his Majesty's Ships Assistance, Bristol, and Royal Oak Anno 1675 to 1679 . . . With biographical and historical notes* (London, 1825), p. 112.
5. Robson, *Newes from Aleppo*, p. 11.
6. Teonge, *Diary*, p. 112; cf. Peter Mundy, *The Travels of Peter Mundy in Europe and Asia, volume 1, 1608–1628* (Cambridge, 1907), p. 19 and Abraham Parsons, *Travels in Asia and Africa: including a voyage from Scanderoon to Aleppo . . . and a journey from Suez to Cairo and Rosetta in Egypt* (London, 1808), pp. 16–18.
7. Kornelis le Bruyn, *A Voyage to the Levant, or, Travels in the principal parts of Asia Minor . . . done into English by W.J.* (London, 1702), p. 265.
8. Parsons, *Travels*, p. 1; TNA SP 110/23, fo. 85. Nathaniel Harley, though, writing of Aleppo itself, recorded that the 'cold breezes' rendered tolerable the 'very severe' heat of summer which could otherwise 'scarce be borne': Historical Manuscripts Commission ('HMC') *Portland*, vol. ii, p. 242.
9. Michael G., Brennan (ed.), *The Travel Diary of Robert Bargrave, Levant Merchant 1647–1656* (London, 1989), p. 87. This edition offers an excellent editorial introduction.
10. TNA SP 110/23, fo. 145. In 1771, General Sir Eyre Coote declared this building 'bomb proof': Parsons, *Travels*, p. 10.
11. TNA SP 110/23, fo. 141.
12. Robson, *Newes from Aleppo*, p. 11.
13. Richard Pococke, *A Description of the East and some other countries*, vol. ii (London, 1743), p. 265.
14. Though estimates vary considerably: Alexander Drummond (for many years an Aleppo consul) in the mid-eighteenth century, for instance, cites a time of thirty-five hours: Alexander Drummond, *Travels through different cities of Germany, Italy, Greece and several parts of Asia* (London, 1754), p. 287. John Verney's progress was more rapid: John Verney to Ralph Verney, 22 October 1662 (Verney MSS).
15. Parsons, *Travels*, p. 21.
16. Drummond, *Travels*, p. 181.
17. Parsons, *Travels*, p. 23.

18. Teonge, *Diary*, p. 156.
19. Parsons, *Travels*, p. 3. Dudley Foley was advised by a more experienced merchant to 'apply your self to the factor Marine to get a horse and forward you to Aleppo', but on no account to 'lye a shore at Scanderoon nor sleep there' (Cobbold MSS, Box 17).
20. Drummond, *Travels*, p. 181. In summer, the route often became too treacherous for camels to embark on: Additional Manuscripts kept in the British Library ('BL Add. MSS') 10623, fo. 5.
21. Woodbine Parish, 'Diary of a Journey with Sir Eyre Coote from Bussora to Aleppo in 1780', *Journal of the Royal Geographical Society of London*, vol. 30 (1860), pp. 198–210, at p. 210.
22. Minutes of Levant Company Court, 25 March 1630, cited in J.B. Pearson, *A Biographical Sketch of the Chaplains to the Levant Company, maintained at Constantinople, Aleppo and Smyrna, 1611–1706* (Cambridge, 1883), p. 55. Maundrell travelled to Aleppo in company with, among others, Richard Chiswell, who wrote a full account of it: see BL Add. MSS 10623.
23. On Maundrell, see David Howell's introduction in the 1963 fascimile reprint of Henry Maundrell, *A Journey from Aleppo to Jerusalem in 1697* (Beirut, 1963); Pearson, *Chaplains of the Levant Company*; and Robin Butlin, 'Maundrell, Henry (*bap.* 1665, *d.* 1701)', *Oxford Dictionary of National Biography* ('*ODNB*') (Oxford, 2004).
24. Jonathan Haynes, *The Humanist as Traveller: George Sandys' 'Relation of a Journey Begun An.Dom.1610'* (London, 1986), p. 14.
25. Richard Drayton, 'Knowledge and Empire', in *OHBE*, vol. ii, p. 232.
26. R.W. Frantz, *The English Traveller and the Movement of Ideas, 1660–1732* (Lincoln, NE, 1934), p. 17. The correspondence between Maundrell and his uncle, Sir Charles Hedges, survives in BL Add. MSS 24107.
27. Howells, 'Introduction', in Maundrell, *Journey from Aleppo to Jerusalem*, pp. x–xi.
28. Matar, *Islam in Britain*, Chapter 3.
29. Maundrell, *Journey*, p. 164.
30. Blount, *A Voyage into the Levant*, p. 41.
31. Charles Perry, *A View of the Levant: particularly of Constantinople, Syria, Egypt and Greece* (London, 1743), p. 26.
32. Teonge, *Diary*, p. 175.
33. Pococke, *Description*, vol. ii, p. 150.
34. Le Bruyn, *A Voyage to the Levant*, p. 238.
35. Ibid.; Pococke, *Description*, ii, p. 150.
36. Ibid., p. 151.
37. Teonge, *Diary*, p. 176; Parsons, *Travels*, p. 55.
38. Parish, 'Diary of a Journey', p. 211; Pococke, *Description*, ii, p. 150.
39. Alexander Russell, *The Natural History of Aleppo and parts adjacent* (London, 1756), p. 15.
40. Pococke, *Description*, ii, p. 150.
41. Russell, *Natural History of Aleppo*, pp. 14–15.
42. Drummond, *Travels*, p. 184.
43. Davis, *Aleppo and Devonshire Square*, p. 4.
44. Mundy, *Travels of Peter Mundy*, p. 60.
45. On the Islamic world system and interconnectedness of the Safavid, Mughal and Ottoman empires, see C.A. Bayly, *Imperial Meridian: The British Empire and the World 1780–1830* (1989), pp. 16–21; the three volumes of Marshall Hodgson's *The Venture of Islam* (Chicago, 1974); and Amira Bennison, 'Muslim Universalism and Western Globalisation', in A.G. Hopkins (ed.), *Globalisation in History* (London, 2002).
46. Donald Quataert, *The Ottoman Empire, 1700–1922* (2nd edn) (Cambridge, 2005), p. 17.

47. Cited in André Clot, *Suleiman the Magnificent* (London, 2005), p. 1. General accounts abound, but particularly recommended introductions are Philip Mansel, *Constantinople: City of the World's Desire* (London, 1995); Halil Inalcik, *The Ottoman Empire – The Classical Age 1300–1600* (London, 1973); Colin Imber, *The Ottoman Empire, 1300–1650* (London, 2002), or for a very incisive account, Norman Itzkowitz, *Ottoman Empire and Islamic Tradition* (Chicago, 1972). For an up-to-date treatment of the three centuries thereafter, see Quataert, *Ottoman Empire*. On the period before Suleyman the Magnificent, Metin Kunt, 'State and sultan up to the age of Suleyman: frontier principality to world empire' in Metin Kunt and Christine Woodhead (eds), *Suleyman the Magnificent and his Age* (London, 1995) and the seminal work by Cemal Kafadar, *Between Two Worlds: The Construction of the Ottoman State* (Berkeley and Los Angeles, 1995). Also excellent is Halil Inalcik with Donald Quataert (eds), *An Economic and Social History of the Ottoman Empire* (Cambridge, 1994). For a one-volume, very well written and enjoyable recent account, Caroline Finkel's *Osman's Dream: The Story of the Ottoman Empire 1300–1923* (London, 2005). Focusing on the Arab segments of the Ottoman Empire, see P.M. Holt's classic *Egypt and the Fertile Crescent, 1516–1922* (London, 1966), which has recently been updated by Jane Hathaway's *The Arab Lands Under Ottoman Rule, 1516–1800* (London, 2008).

48. Fernand Braudel, *The Mediterranean and the Mediterranean World in the Age of Philip II* (New York, 1992), vol. ii, p. 667.

49. Inalcik, *Ottoman Empire*, p. 34; pp. 56–7. A number of such ceremonial locks and keys can still be seen amongst the museum displays at the Topkapi Palace in Istanbul.

50. The 'warlike' view finds academic expression in such works as that of Paul Wittek, *The Rise of the Ottoman Empire* (London, 1938) and Stanford J. Shaw, *History of the Ottoman Empire and Modern Turkey* (Cambridge, 1976) (the first volume of which was entitled 'Empire of the Gazis'), but also more popularly in such works as Jason Goodwin's *Lords of the Horizons: A History of the Ottoman Empire* (London, 1988). For critiques, see Kafadar, *Between Two Worlds*; Heath W. Lowry, *The Nature of the Early Ottoman State* (Albany, 2003); and see the discussions in Daniel Goffman, *The Ottoman Empire and Early Modern Europe* (Cambridge, 2002) and Metin Kunt, 'Introduction', in Kunt and Woodhead, *Suleyman the Magnificent*. For a revisionist view of the Ottomans putting the quest for economic success at the heart of its policies, see Palmira Brummett, *Ottoman Seapower and Levantine Diplomacy in the Age of Discovery* (New York, 1994).

51. Imber, *Ottoman Empire*, p. 62. The northern half of the Red Sea suffers from unfavourable winds. Before the era of steam, it would be normal for vessels to stop around halfway up the Sea, 'either at a port on the Arabian side, like Jiddah, or on the Egyptian side at a port within reach of Aswan on the first cataract of the Nile'. From there cargoes would advance northward by Nile boats or camel. See Philip Curtin, *Cross-Cultural Trade in World History* (Cambridge, 1984), pp. 96–7.

52. Masters, *Origins of Western Economic Dominance*, p. 13; cf. James Grehan, *Everyday Life and Consumer Culture in 18th-Century Damascus* (Seattle and London, 2007).

53. Albeit that sovereignty over the seas in this context is a particularly difficult concept: see Molly Greene, 'The Ottomans in the Mediterranean', in Virginia Aksan and Daniel Goffman (eds), *The Early Modern Ottomans – Remapping the Empire* (Cambridge, 2007), pp. 104–17.

54. Goffman, *Izmir, passim*. Agricultural production shifted away from crops primarily for domestic consumption, such as grains, to those catering for an international market.

55. Ibid., p. 107.

56. See Chapters 2 and 7.

57. Thus even if, as Greene states, the character of the Mediterranean frontier evolved, generally speaking, from an offensive frontier from the mid-fourteenth to the end of the sixteenth centuries to a defensive one thereafter, the scope of Ottoman sovereignty over the Mediterranean's many outcrops of dry land reached its fullest extent only at this late stage in the history of Ottoman advance. See especially the essay by Molly Greene in Aksan and Goffman, *The Early Modern Ottomans* and her book, *A Shared World: Christians and Muslims in the Early Modern Mediterranean* (Princeton, 2002). Also, Ann Williams, 'Mediterranean Conflict', in Kunt and Woodhead, *Suleyman the Magnificent* pp. 39–55; Goffman, *Ottoman Empire and Early Modern Europe*, pp. 213–22. Recent scholarly work has drawn attention to the need for caution in eliding 'Ottoman' with 'Muslim' in this context. As the present work will go on to explore further, the Ottoman Empire (including the Mediterranean islands within it) always comfortably absorbed non-Muslim populations and there was a considerable degree of syncretic and two-way adaptation. Large swathes of the Empire's population remained non-Muslim and those of non-Muslim origin were very prominent amongst its elites (though much less so, of course, within its religious elite). But none of that should obscure the fact that the Ottoman dynasty was a Muslim one and their polity a self-consciously Islamic one.

58. Though caravans were on occasion successfully attacked, even on the *Hajj* route, which was 'harassed no fewer than nineteen times in the period 1674–1752, and was actually pillaged in 1671, 1691, 1711, 1740 and 1757'; in the aftermath of the last of these ambushes, 'thousands of pilgrims perished in the desert from thirst, exposure and exhaustion' (Grehan, *Everyday Life in Damascus*, p. 52). See also Suraiya Faroqhi, *Pilgrims and Sultans – The Hajj Under the Ottomans 1517–1683* (London, 1994). Such attacks would often spell disaster for traders, as the correspondence of English traders in Aleppo attests throughout the period.

59. Marcus, *Middle East on the Eve of Modernity*, p. 145; Watenpaugh, *Ottoman City, passim*.

60. Grehan, *Everyday Life in Damascus*, Chapter 2.

61. This paragraph draws extensively on Inalcik, *Economic and Social History*, ii, pp. 483–7.

62. Masters, *Origins of Western Economic Dominance*, pp. 115–16. The khan can still be seen there.

63. Grehan, *Everyday Life in Damascus*, Chapter 2.

64. Suraiya Faroqhi, 'Declines and revivals in textile production', in Suraiya Faroqhi (ed.), *The Cambridge History of Turkey*, vol. iii (Cambridge, 2008), p. 365.

65. That is, the *waqfs*. On them, see Suraiya Faroqhi, *Subjects of the Sultan – Culture and Daily Life in the Ottoman Empire* (London, 2000).

66. Masters, 'Aleppo', in Eldem et al., *Ottoman City*, p. 27. On this growth, see also Watenpaugh, *Ottoman City, passim*.

67. Ibid.

68. Perry, *View of the Levant*, p. 141.

69. Cited in Maclean, *Rise of Oriental Travel*, p. 84.

70. Lewes Roberts, *The Merchants Map of Commerce: wherein the universal manner and matter of trade is compendiously handled* (London, 1671), p. 134.

71. Maclean, *Rise of Oriental Travel*, p. 84.

72. Roberts, *Merchants Map of Commerce*, p. 134.

73. It used to be thought that the French were granted a set of capitulations as early as 1535, but these are now 'seen to be only the form of a treaty prepared and proposed by the French but never ratified': Susan Skilliter, *William Harborne and the Trade with Turkey, 1578–1582* (Oxford, 1977), p. 1. But the French and the Ottomans did at least conclude an entente in 1535.

74. Richard Hakluyt, *The Principal Navigations, Voyages, Traffiques And Discoveries of The English Nation*, vol. v (Kessler edn), p. 157. On the early history of English trade and diplomatic relations with the Ottoman Empire, Skilliter's *Harborne* cannot be surpassed and the present account is indebted to her exhaustive work. Most of the relevant primary sources are collected in volume v of the *Principal Navigations*. See also Arthur Horniker, 'William Harborne and the Beginning of Anglo-Turkish Diplomatic and Commercial Relations', in *The Journal of Modern History*, vol. 14, no. 3, (September 1942), pp. 289–316; Braudel, *Mediterranean*, i, pp. 612–13; Andrews, *Trade, Plunder and Settlement*, Chapter 4; Epstein, *Early History of the Levant Company*, Chapters 1 and 2; Lisa Jardine, *Worldly Goods – A New History of the Renaissance* (London, 1996), pp. 374–6. See also the dated but still useful work by Sir William Foster, *England's Quest of Eastern Trade* (London, 1933), Chapter 6. Nearly as broad in the context it places is the account in Dorothy Vaughan's *Europe and the Turk: A Pattern of Alliances* (Liverpool, 1954). On Harborne himself, see the very fine article by Christine Woodhead, 'Harborne, William (*c*.1542–1617), *ODNB*.
75. Andrews, *Trade, Plunder and Settlement*, p. 92.
76. Ralph Davis, *The Rise of English Shipping in the Seventeenth and Eighteenth Centuries* (London, 1972), p. 45.
77. Andrews, *Trade, Plunder and Settlement*, p. 88.
78. Braudel, *Mediterranean*, i, p. 615.
79. Davis, *Rise of English Shipping*, p. 5; cf. Edhem Eldhem, 'Capitulations and Western Trade', in Faroqhi, *Turkey*, iii, p. 290.
80. See Skilliter, *Harborne*, pp. 12–19. Skilliter implies at p. 6 that the hiatus was owed simply to the fact that Antwerp was, for a time, adequate to serve the needs of the English market.
81. Ephraim Lipson, *Economic History of England*, vol. ii (London, 1943), p. 336.
82. John Hale, *The Civilisation of Europe in the Renaissance* (London, 1993), p. 41; cf. Franklin L. Baumer, 'England, the Turk and the Common Corps of Christianity', *American Historical Review*, vol. 50, no. 1 (October 1944), pp. 26–48.
83. Eldhem, 'Capitulations', p. 288.
84. Richard Knolles, *The Turkish History . . . Written by Mr Knolles, and continu'd by . . . Sir P. Ricaut, to the peace at Carlowitz, in . . . 1699* (London, 1701), preface (unpaginated).
85. Brandon Beck, *From the Rising of the Sun: English Images of the Ottoman Empire to 1715* (New York, 1987), p. 2.
86. Paul Coles, *The Ottoman Impact on Europe* (London, 1968), p. 150.
87. Paul Rycaut, *The Present State of the Ottoman Empire. Containing the maxims of the Turkish politie, the most material points of the Mahometan Religion* (London, 1668), p. 217.
88. Hakluyt, *Principal Navigations*, i, pp. lxix–lxx.
89. Jardine, *Worldly Goods*, p. 374.
90. Chew, *Crescent and Rose*, p. 158.
91. Skilliter, *Harborne*, pp. xvii–xviii.
92. Ibid., pp. 49–75; p. 146.
93. See, generally, Walter Minchinton (ed.), *The Growth of English Overseas Trade in the Seventeenth and Eighteenth Centuries* (London, 1969).
94. e.g., the account in George Cawston and A.H. Keane, *The Early Chartered Companies* (London, 1896), Chapter vi.
95. Skilliter, *Harborne*, p. 84.
96. TNA SP 97/20, fo. 159.
97. Brenner, *Merchants and Revolution, passim*.
98. Chaudhuri, *Trading World of Asia*, pp. 6–7.

99. Skilliter, *Harborne*, p. 28.
100. Brenner, *Merchants and Revolution, passim.*
101. The letters patent are printed in Hakluyt, *Principal Navigations*, v, pp. 253–61. See also the 'Articles exhibited by Edward Osborn tutching ye trade into Turkquie', reproduced in Skilliter, *Harborne*, pp. 180–82.
102. Though they were also given the option of nominating up to another twelve members, while the Queen reserved to herself the right to appoint another two.
103. Alberto Tenenti, *Piracy and the Decline of Venice* (London, 1967), p. 145.
104. Theodore Rabb, *Enterprise & Empire: merchant and gentry investment in the expansion of England, 1575–1630* (Cambridge, MA, 1967), p. 48.
105. Skilliter, *Harborne*, p. 180.
106. Sonia P. Anderson, 'Osborne, Sir Edward (*c.*1530–1592)', *ODNB.*
107. Brenner, *Merchants and Revolution*, p. 17.
108. Imber, *Ottoman Empire*, pp. 57–8; see also Salih Ozbaran, 'Ottoman naval policy in the south', in Kunt Woodhead, *Suleyman the Magnificent*, pp. 55–71; Finkel, *Osman's Dream*, pp. 136–8.
109. Curtin, *Cross-Cultural Trade*, p. 140.
110. See Braudel, *Mediterranean*, i, pp. 543–70; F. C. Lane, 'The Mediterranean spice trade: further evidence of its revival in the sixteenth century', in B. Pullan (ed.), *Crisis and Change in the Venetian Economy in the 16th and 17th centuries* (London, 1968), pp. 47–58; C. R. Boxer, 'A note on Portuguese reactions to the revival of the Red Sea spice trade and the rise of Aceh, 1540–1600', *Journal of Southeast Asian History* X/3 (1969), pp. 415–28; Ralph Davis, *English Overseas Trade, 1500–1700* (London, 1973), p. 31.
111. Skilliter, *Harborne*, pp. 177–8.
112. Andrews, *Trade, Plunder and Settlement*, pp. 96–7.
113. See, for instance, TNA SP 97/18, fos 219–20; 242; 245–6; 302–3; 310; and a century later, TNA SP 97/53, fo. 5.
114. It is perhaps remarkable that early English attempts to gain direct access to the spice markets took place primarily through the Mediterranean and the Red Sea at all, rather than along the Cape route: see Chaudhuri, *Trading World of Asia*, p. 10.
115. John Keay, *The Honourable Company* (London, 1991), p. 11; Andrews, *Trade, Plunder and Settlement*, Chapter 12.
116. Foster, *England's Quest*, pp. 130–34.
117. Brenner, *Merchants and Revolution*, p. 78. It is worth pointing out that merchants in this era were anyway less specialised than they would generally become by the later eighteenth century: see Davis, *Rise of English Shipping*, p. 81.
118. Chaudhuri, *Trading World of Asia*, p. 26.
119. Inalcik, *Ottoman Empire*, p. 146.
120. See, inter alia, Jardine, *Worldly Goods, passim*; Neil McKendrick, John Brewer and J.H. Plumb, *The Birth of a Consumer Society: The Commercialisation of Eighteenth-century England* (London, 1982).
121. Wood, *Levant Company*, p. 17; Braudel, *Mediterranean*, i., p. 626.
122. Skilliter, *Harborne*, p. 198.
123. Epstein, *Early History of the Levant Company*, p. 19.
124. Skilliter, *Harborne*, pp. 183–4.
125. Wood, *Levant Company*, p. 74.
126. Masters, 'Aleppo', p. 26.

Chapter 2: Trading Places

1. Vinton Dearing, 'A Walk through London with John Gay and a Run with Daniel Defoe', in Plumb and Dearing, *Some Aspects of Eighteenth-Century England* (1970),

p. 35. On the Royal Exchange, see especially Ann Saunders, *The Royal Exchange* (London, 1991); Perry Gauci, *Emporium of the World: The Merchants of London 1660–1800* (London, 2007), ch.3; and anon., *Great Britain's Glory; or, A Brief Description of the present State, Splendor, and Magnificence of the Royal Exchange* (London, 1672). Compare also Linda Levy Peck, *Consuming Splendour* (Cambridge, 2005) on the New Exchange, at pp. 42–61.

2. Wren did not get to put his plan into action and the second exchange was the work of Edward Jerman (it too burnt down, in 1832, and the present building is the third on the site). In fact, the Exchange as an institution somewhat declined after the Great Fire and much business came to be done instead in the coffee houses springing up around it: see Davis, *Rise of English Shipping*, pp. 162–4.

3. Saunders, *Royal Exchange*, p. 19.

4. Ibid., p. 14.

5. On London as an emerging metropolis, see the various essays in F.J. Fisher, *London and the English Economy, 1500–1700* (London, 1990); A.L. Beier and Roger Finlay (eds), *London 1500–1700: The Making of the Metropolis* (London, 1985); and Anthony Wrigley, 'A simple model of London's changing importance in changing English society and economy, 1650–1750', *Past and Present*, vol. 37, no. 1 (1967). Also see, amongst others, Roy Porter, *London: A Social History* (London, 2000), chapter 6 and Liza Picard, *Restoration London*, (London, 1997). Placing these developments in a state-wide context, Charles Wilson, *England's Apprenticeship 1603–1763* (London, 1965), chapter 8. For the city in the early eighteenth century, see also David Hancock, *Citizens of the World – London Merchants and the Integration of the British Atlantic Community, 1735–1785* (Cambridge, 1995), pp. 86–8.

6. Cited in Minchinton, 'Introduction', in Minchinton, *Growth of English Overseas Trade*, p. vii.

7. Anon., *Great Britain's Glory* (unpaginated).

8. Saunders, *Royal Exchange*, p. 27.

9. Peck, *Consuming Splendour*, p. 45.

10. Thomas Brown, *Amusements serious and comical, calculated for the meridian of London* (1700), pp. 14–15.

11. Rabb, *Enterprise & Empire*, p. 51.

12. Matar, *Britain and Barbary*, p. 139.

13. His business included dealings in the Levant trade: see, for instance, *Cal. S.P. Venetian, 1626–28*, no. 465.

14. Susan Whyman, *Sociability and Power in Late-Stuart England: The Cultural Worlds of the Verneys 1660–1720* (Oxford, 1999), p. 38.

15. Ben Coates, *The Impact of the English Civil War on the Economy of London, 1642–50* (Aldershot, 2004). On 16 March 1660, Samuel Pepys wrote: 'Tonight I am told that yesterday, about 5 o'clock in the afternoon, one came with a ladder to the great Exchange and wiped with a brush the Inscription that was upon King Charles, and that there was a great bonfire made in the Exchange and people cried out "God bless King Charles the second!" ' Cited in Saunders, *Royal Exchange*, p. 17.

16. Though the consul was paid a lot more generously than the chaplain: in the Smyrna factory in the 1660s, two thousand dollars a year versus two hundred. Rycaut was among those to be rewarded with handsome bonuses by the Company: TNA SP 105/152, fo. 425.

17. *HMC Downshire*, vol i., p. 224. Though he went on: '. . . you must know that when these gentlemen have been some time with you, and find that matters there do not correspond with their expectations, they will then desire to return home at your expense and perhaps with various complaints against you'.

18. Fisher, *London*, p. 109.

19. Rycaut is the centrepiece of an excellent monograph by Anderson (cited above), on which the preceding two paragraphs draw. But on him, see also C.J. Heywood, 'Sir Paul Rycaut, A Seventeenth-Century Observer of the Ottoman State: Notes for a Study', in Ezel Kural Shaw and C.J. Heywood, *English and Continental Views of the Ottoman Empire 1500–1800* (1970); and Linda Darling, 'Ottoman Politics Through British Eyes: Paul Rycaut's The Present State of the Ottoman Empire', *Journal of World History*, vol. 5, 1994.

20. Richard Grassby, *The English gentleman in trade: the life and works of Sir Dudley North, 1641–1691* (Oxford, 1994), p. 19. Grassby's study is outstanding and reproduces North's economic works.

21. Whyman, *Sociability and Power*, p. 47.

22. Charles Owen, *The Danger of the Church and Kingdom from Foreigners* (1721), p. 13, cited in Gwylim Ambrose, 'English Traders at Aleppo', *The Economic History Review*, 3 (1931–1932), pp. 246–67, at p. 248.

23. Whyman, *Sociability and Power*, p. 43.

24. Ibid.

25. Frances and Margaret Verney, *Memoirs of the Verney Family During the Seventeenth Century* (London, 1892), vol. i, p. 369.

26. Compare the trouble that John Sanderson encountered with his apprentice: see pp. 24–31 of Foster, *Travels of John Sanderson*.

27. Christopher Brooks, 'Apprenticeship, Social Mobility and the Middling Sort, 1550–1800', in Jonathan Barry and Brooks, *The Middling Sort of People: Culture, Society and Politics in England, 1550–1800* (Basingstoke, 1994), p. 74.

28. TNA SP 110/23, fo. 64. A similar process would accompany attempts to gain places within trading houses: see, for instance, TNA SP 110/23, 14 December 1704.

29. *The Interest of England Considered in an Essay on Wool* (1694), p. 56, cited in Ambrose, 'English Traders', p. 249.

30. North, *Lives of the Norths*, ii, p. 299; Brenner, *Merchants and Revolution*, p. 70.

31. Davis, *Aleppo and Devonshire Square*, p. 65.

32. BL Add. MSS 32500, fo. 168.

33. Davis, *English Overseas Trade*, p. 9. On the 'commercial revolution', see Ralph Davis, *A Commercial Revolution: English Overseas Trade in the Seventeenth and Eighteenth Centuries* (London, 1967). Davis' revolution occurred in the later seventeenth century; see Brenner for an earlier dating, which the experience of the Levant Company in many ways supports. But these two readings can perhaps be squared by the further interpretation offered by Rabb in *Enterprise & Empire*: 'Although England could not be considered the leader of European commerce, industrial development, and overseas expansion for another half-century, by 1630 all the foundations for that position had been laid' (p. 2). See also David Ormrod, *The Rise of Commercial Empires: England and the Netherlands in the Age of Mercantilism, 1650–1770* (Cambridge, 2003).

34. Minchinton, *Growth of English Overseas Trade*, p. 10.

35. Davis, *Commercial Revolution, passim.*

36. Minchinton, *Growth of English Overseas Trade*, p. 2; cf. Andrews, *Trade, Plunder and Settlement*, p. 7.

37. TNA SP 110/23, fo. 112; TNA SP 110/33, fo. 3.

38. Davis, *Aleppo and Devonshire Square*, p. 75.

39. TNA SP 110/23, fo. 91.

40. Brenner, *Merchants and Revolution*, p. 4.

41. Ibid., p. 81.

42. Ibid., p. 82.

43. Epstein, *Early History of the Levant Company*, p. 68–9.

44. Ibid., pp. 69–71.

45. Rycaut, *History of the Turkish Empire*.
46. James Porter, *Observations on the Religion, Law, Government and Manners of the Turks* (1771), p. 372.
47. Anon., 'Observations on the Mutual Advantages of a Commercial Alliance with Turkey' 1791, p. 17.
48. Cited in Shaw and Heywood, *English and Continental Views*, p. 50.
49. Gary S. De Krey, 'Boddington, George (1646–1719)', *ODNB*.
50. Brenner, *Merchants and Revolution*, p. 43; based on the figures of A.N. Millard, 'The Import Trade of London, 1600–1640' (unpublished PhD thesis, London School of Economics, 1956).
51. Anon., *Great Britains Glory*, p. 17
52. Saunders, *Royal Exchange*, p. 16.
53. McKendrick, Brewer and Plumb, *Birth of a Consumer Society*, pp. 9–33; for the energetic debate which this immediately prompted see the references in Maxine Berg, *Luxury and Pleasure in Eighteenth-Century Britain* (London, 2005), at p. 9. For somewhat similar claims regarding the seventeenth century, though, see Joan Thirsk, *Economic Policy and Projects: The Development of a Consumer Society in Early Modern England* (Oxford, 1978).
54. Peck, *Consuming Splendour*.
55. Andrews, *Trade, Plunder and Settlement*, p. 4.
56. Dietz, 'Overseas trade and metropolitan growth' in Beier and Findlay, *London 1500–1700*.
57. Thirsk, *Economic Policy and Projects*, p. 8. Nuala Zahedieh, 'London and the Colonial Consumer in the late 17th Century', *Economic History Review*, 47:2 (1994); L. Weatherill, *Consumer Behaviour and Material Culture in Britain, 1660–1760* (1985).
58. Peck, *Consuming Splendour*.
59. TNA SP 105/48, fo. 254.
60. *Cal. S.P. Venetian, 1638*, no. 430.
61. Fisher, *London*, p. 193.
62. Tobias Venner, *Via recta ad vitam longam, or A plaine philosophical discourse of the nature, faculties, and effects, of all such things, as by way of nourishments, and dieteticall obseruations, make for the preseruation of health with their iust applications vnto euery age, constitution of bodie, and time of yeare* (1620), p. 126.
63. Thomas Tryon, *Wisdoms dictates, or, Aphorisms & rules, physical, moral, and divine, for preserving the health of the body, and the peace of the mind* (1691), p. 107.
64. Davis, *Aleppo and Devonshire Square*, p. 31.
65. Peck, *Consuming Splendour*, p. 85.
66. Brenner, *Merchants and Revolution*, pp. 25–6.
67. Ibid.
68. Ibid.
69. Thirsk, *Economic Policy and Projects*, p. 109.
70. Nuala Zahedieh 'Overseas Expansion and Trade in the Seventeenth Century', OHBE vol.i, p. 418.
71. Thomas Shadwell, *Bury Fair: A Comedy* (London, 1689), p. 17.
72. Davis, *Aleppo and Devonshire Square*, p. 136.
73. C.G.A. Clay, *Economic Expansion and Social Change: England 1500–1700*, vol. ii (Cambridge, 1984), pp. 149–150. See also Jonathan Israel, *Dutch Primacy in World Trade, 1585–1740* (Oxford, 1989), pp. 149–56.
74. Ambrose, 'English Traders', p. 248.
75. Israel, *Dutch Primacy*, p. 154.
76. Brenner, *Merchants and Revolution*, p. 31. Note, however, that Ralph Davis disagrees: see 'England and the Mediterranean 1570–1670' in F.J. Fisher (ed.), *Essays in the Economic and Social History of Tudor and Stuart England in Honour of*

R.H. Tawney (London, 1961). So too does the classic 'mercantilist' Thomas Mun: he wrote in 1621 that, 'Of all Europe, this nation drove the most profitable trade to Turkey by reason of the vast quantities of broadcloth, tin, etc. which we exported thither, enough to purchase all the wares we wanted in Turkey, whereas a balance in money is paid by the other nations trading thither.'

77. Anderson, *English Consul*, p. 158.
78. Grassby, *English Gentleman in Trade*, pp. 28–9.
79. Verney, *Memoirs of the Verney Family*, i, pp. 379–80.
80. North, *Lives of the Norths*, ii, pp. 3–7.
81. On apprenticeship, see Brooks, 'Apprenticeship'; Ilana Ben-Amos, *Adolescence and Youth in Early Modern England* (London and New Haven, 1994); Keith Wrightson, *Earthly Necessities: Economic Lives in Early Modern Britain* (London and New Haven, 2000). For a decidedly negative view, see Lawrence Stone, *Family, Sex and Marriage* (London, 1977), p. 102.
82. Stone, *Family, Sex and Marriage*, p. 102. Nathaniel Harley was bullied by his master until his brother 'discoursed him in a harsher style than perhaps he ever before heard either from my friends or me'.
83. Brooks, 'Apprenticeship', p. 74.
84. Davis, *Aleppo and Devonshire Square*, p. 66. In October 1661, Thomas Stanton, a merchant in Aleppo, had to appeal to the Ambassador: 'At that age when I might have been bound to a merchant . . . I was in arms for his Majesty, which prevented it.' Now, he was faced with the 'ruin of my employment' by those who insisted that he was not entitled to trade: *HMC Finch*, vol i, pp. 164–5. On routes of entry to the Company, see especially Brenner, *Merchants and Revolution*, pp. 69–74; Epstein, *Early History of the Levant Company*, pp. 104–8; Anderson, *English Consul*, pp. 69–74.
85. Lipson, *Economic History of England*, ii, p. 341.
86. *A Historical View of the Conduct and Proceedings of the Turky Company* (London, 1825).
87. That is, Sir William Hedges. Similarly, Sir Eliab Harvey wrote to John Covel: 'This afternoon I have got you chosen to go chaplain for Constantinople' (BM Add. MSS 22910, fo. 29). Appointments to the other posts in the Company's officialdom were no less nepotistic. The Earl of Winchilsea expressed to his cousin Sir John Finch the hope that 'by art and dextrous management this embassy might come to be entailed on our family' and he had some success, since Finch and Sir Daniel Harvey, another relative, both came to occupy the post: *HMC Finch*, vol i., p. 309.
88. Brenner, *Merchants and Revolution*, p. 72.
89. Davis, *Aleppo and Devonshire Square*, p. 64.
90. Neils Steensgaard, 'Consuls and Nations in the Levant from 1570 to 1650', *Scandinavian Economic History Review*, 15:1, (1967), pp. 13–55, at p. 50.
91. Wrightson, *Earthly Necessities*, p. 192.
92. Adam Smith, *The Wealth of Nations* (Washington DC, 1999), p. 844. 'The Turkey Company contribute to maintain an ambassador and two or three consuls', he went on, 'who, like other public ministers, ought to be maintained altogether by the state and the trade laid open to all his majesty's subjects'.
93. Though the Muscovy Company was a still earlier example of a joint-stock company. As for the Levant Company, there is evidence suggesting that it had ceased to be a joint-stock company by 1595: see the letters of John Sanderson referred to in Wood, *Levant Company*, at p. 22; and cf. the evidence from records of actual shipments from 1596 and subsequent years examined by T.S. Willan in 'Some Aspects of English Trade with the Levant in the Sixteenth Century', *English Historical Review*, vol. 70, no. 276, pp. 399–410. In a parliamentary debate on the position of the companies in 1604, it was mentioned that it had been a joint-stock until recently, but probably the change had taken place by the turn of the century:

Journals of House of Commons, i., p. 220; and see W.R. Scott, *The Constitution and Finance of English, Scottish and Irish Joint Stock Companies to 1720*, vol.ii (Cambridge, 1910), pp. 83–8.

94. Though the risk of the loss of ships was through shared ownership. There was a flourishing insurance industry in this era: see Davis, *Rise of English Shipping*.

95. See G.M. Trevelyan, *England under the Stuarts* (London, 2002), p. 45. For some interesting attempts to assess the early trading companies through the prism of contemporary economic theory, see Carlos and Nicholas, 'Theory and History: Seventeenth-Century Joint-Stock Chartered Trading Companies', *Journal of Economic History*, vol. 56, no. 4 (December 1996); Jones and Ville, 'Efficient Transactors or Rent-Seeking Monopolists? The Rationale for Early Chartered Trading Companies', ibid.; and for a recent neo-liberal interpretation of their place in the 'making of the modern world', see Niall Fergusson, *Empire – How Britain Made the Modern World* (London, 2003), pp. 20–21.

96. Sir James Porter, *The State of the Turkey Trade Considered* (London, 1771) p. 363.

97. *Cal. S.P. Venetian, 1603–1607*, no. 91. The company did manage to persuade the crown to contribute to presents for new sultans: see, for instance, *Cal. S.P. Domestic*, vol. xvii, no. 35; cf. *Cal. S.P. Domestic*, vol. clviii, no. 51.

98. Lipson, *Economic History of England*, vol. ii, p. 338.

99. Ambrose, 'English Traders', p. 248.

100. Richard Rapp, 'The Unmaking of the Mediterranean Trade Hegemony: international trade rivalry and the commercial revolution', *The Journal of Economic History*, vol. xxxv, no. 3, 1975. Also, Barry Supple, *Commercial Crisis and Change in England, 1600–1642* (Cambridge, 1964), pp. 159–62; Faroqhi, *Cambridge History of Turkey*, p. 299; Israel, *Dutch Primacy*, p. 154.

101. Brenner, *Merchants and Revolution*, pp. 61–74; Epstein, *Early History of the Levant Company*, Chapter 5; Wood, *Levant Company*, pp. 36–41.

102. Rabb, *Enterprise & Empire*, p. 46.

103. *Cal. S.P. Venetian, 1603–1607*, no. 109; Epstein, *Early History of the Levant Company*, p. 23.

104. *Cal. S.P. Venetian, 1603–1607*, no. 190.

105. Ibid., no. 91.

106. *Cal. S.P. Venetian, 1603–1607*, no. 306.

107. Ibid., no. 192.

108. Ibid.

109. Ibid., no. 427.

110. Ibid., no. 503; no. 510; no. 517; cf. *Cal. S.P. Venetian, 1607–1610*, no. 11; no. 323; no. 379.

111. *Cal. S.P. Domestic*, vol. cxix, October 27 1628; vol. cxlii, no. 28.

112. As argued by Brenner in *Merchants and Revolution, passim*.

113. 'House of Commons Journal Volume 1: 28 April 1621', *Journal of the House of Commons: volume 1: 1547–1629* (1802), pp. 595–6.

114. Ashton, 'Parliamentary Agitation for Free Trade in the Opening Years of the Reign of James I', *Past and Present* 38, 1 (1967), pp. 40–55.

115. Epstein, *Early History of the Levant Company*, p. 41.

116. *Cal. S.P. Domestic*, vol. x, November 16 1621.

117. Though this characterisation comes from the resolutely Marxist pen of Christopher Hill, in *The Century of Revolution* (London, 1980), pp. 31–2.

118. Frangakis-Syrett, *The Commerce of Smyrna in the Eighteenth Century, 1700–1820* (Athens, 1992), pp. 82–3.

119. The *Plymouth* was effectively on loan from the King: Winchilsea had to write apologetically for the delay in its return: TNA SP 97/17, fo. 175.

120. The Company agreed to fund the outward journey for a suite of up to thirty people: *Cal. S.P. Domestic*, vol. xvi, no. 29.
121. TNA SP 97/17, fo. 173.
122. Cited in Sonia P. Anderson, 'Finch, Heneage, third earl of Winchilsea (1627/8–1689)', *ODNB*.
123. *HMC Finch*, vol. i, p. 233. 'I have removed him from my steward's table to my owne, and use him more like a friend than a servant,' he added.
124. TNA SP 97/19, fo. 228; Abbott, *Under the Turk in Constantinople* (London, 1920), p. 287.
125. R.C. Anderson (ed.), *The Journals of Sir Thomas Allin, 1660–1678* (London, 1939), p. 1.
126. Ibid., pp. 1–6.
127. Ibid.
128. Brennan, *Travel Diary of Robert Bargrave*, p. 54.
129. BL Add. MSS 32500, fo. 184.
130. *HMC Portland*, vol. ii, p. 240.
131. Harley's forty-two days was 'quick': *HMC Portland*, vol. ii, p. 241.
132. North, *Lives of the Norths*, ii, p. 304.
133. Andrews, *Trade, Plunder and Settlement*, p. 9 (and also supplies the title of the second volume in N.A.M. Rodger's superb three-volume naval history of Britain).
134. Clay, *Economic Expansion and Social Change*, p. 217. Compare Walsingham's observation directed at Elizabeth I in 'A consideracion of the trade into Turkey' that the trade will 'sett a grett number of your grettest shippes a worke whereby your navie shalbe mainteyned' (see Skilliter, *Harborne*, pp. 28–30).
135. Kenneth R. Andrews, *Elizabethan Privateering: English Privateering During the Spanish War, 1585–1603* (Cambridge, 1964), p. 231.
136. TNA SP 110/22, fo. 17.
137. Ibid.
138. *Cal. S.P. Domestic*, vol. xcv, no. 22.
139. N.A.M. Rodger, *The Safeguard of the Sea: vol. 1, 660–1649* (London, 1997), p. 352.
140. Davis, *Rise of English Shipping*, ch.5.
141. Epstein, *Early History of the Levant Company*, p. 129.
142. Anderson, *English Consul*, p. 131.
143. TNA SP 105/149, fo. 293.
144. *An Historical View of the Conduct and Proceedings of the Turkey Company* (London, 1753), p. 9.
145. Ambrose, 'Levant Company', p. 50.
146. Davis, *Rise of English Shipping*, p. 45.
147. Molly Greene, 'Beyond the Northern Invasion: The Mediterranean in the Seventeenth Century', *Past and Present* 174, 1 (2002), pp. 42–71.
148. Cited in Rodger, *Safeguard of the Sea*, p. 205. Still, a diplomatic incident followed: see TNA SP 105/148, fo. 197.

Chapter 3: People of the Book

1. TNA SP 110/22, fo. 41.
2. Russell, *Natural History of Aleppo*, p. 133.
3. Cobbold MSS, Box 17.
4. John Verney to Ralph Verney, 20 June 1663 (Verney MSS).
5. *Cal. S.P. Domestic*, vol. lviii, p. 453.
6. BL Add. MSS 22910, fo. 51.
7. Parsons, *Travels*, p. 62.
8. Roberts, *Merchants Map of Commerce*, p. 108; Drummond, *Travels*, pp. 184–5.

9. Parsons, *Travels*, p. 61.
10. Maundrell, *Journey*, p. 198.
11. TNA SP 110/21, 30 May 1699.
12. BL Add. MSS 22910, fo. 44. For a catalogue of the books in the library in 1688, see TNA SP 105/145, fos 157–64; for Smyrna's in 1702, TNA SP 105/145, fos 301–4.
13. Ambrose, 'English Traders', p. 267.
14. Verney, *Memoirs of the Verney Family*, i, p. 382.
15. TNA SP/110/23, fo. 98.
16. TNA SP/110/23, fo. 108.
17. Foster, *Travels of John Sanderson*, p. 5.
18. TNA SP 110/21, 26 April 1699.
19. Verney, *Memoirs of the Verney Family*, i, p. 385.
20. Brennan, 'Introduction', in Brennan, *The Travel Diary of Robert Bargrave*, p. 34.
21. Ambrose, 'English Traders', p. 266.
22. Maundrell, *Journey*, p. 198.
23. Le Bruyn, *A Voyage to the Levant*, p. 240.
24. *HMC Portland*, vol. ii, p. 255. Finding ships large enough to carry them could present difficulties: see TNA SP 97/19, fo. 232.
25. Parsons, *Travels*, p. 63; *HMC Portland*, vol. ii, p. 244.
26. Teonge, *Diary*, p. 158.
27. Anderson, *English Consul*, p. 104.
28. Parsons, *Travels*, p. 63.
29. The Company refused to pay Consul Lannoy expense claims for his lavish entertainments, including a feast for the Dutch and French consuls: *Cal. S.P. Domestic*, vol. lxxi, p. 109. See also Teonge, *Diary*, pp. 149–53.
30. TNA SP 110/23, fo. 159; cf. TNA SP 110/33, fo. 9.
31. TNA SP 110/22, fo. 10.
32. TNA SP 110/23, fo. 151.
33. Joseph Pitton de Tournefort, *Relation d'un voyage au Levant* (Lyon, 1727), vol. ii, pp. 375 and 377, cited in Daniel Goffman, 'Izmir: from village to colonial port city', in Eldem et al., *Ottoman City*.
34. *HMC Finch*, vol i., pp. 330–31.
35. Nigel and Caroline Webb, *The Earl and His Butler in Constantinople* (London, 2009), p. 18.
36. TNA SP 110/23, fo. 58.
37. Russell, *Natural History of Aleppo*, pp. 12–13.
38. *Lowthorp's Abridgment of the Philosophical Transactions*, vol. iii, p. 605; *Observations in Turky; by Dr Brown*, n. 59 p. 1051 (1699?). Of course, disease was a far more common affliction in England in this era. Thus a letter to Dudley North shortly after his departure for the Ottoman Empire told of a 'sickly time', particularly smallpox: BL Add. MS 32500, fo. 9.
39. Le Bruyn, *A Voyage to the Levant*, p. 240.
40. Pococke, *Description of the East*, ii, p. 151.
41. Le Bruyn, *A Voyage to the Levant*, p. 241.
42. TNA SP 97/18, fo. 127.
43. TNA SP 110/22, fo. 3.
44. TNA SP 110/23, fo. 105.
45. TNA SP 110/23, fo. 108.
46. Neils Steensgaard, *The Asian Trade Revolution of the Seventeenth Century: The East India Companies and the Decline of the Caravan Trade* (Chicago, 1975), p. 48.
47. BL Add. MSS 22910, fo. 129.
48. TNA SP 110/23, fo. 107.
49. Russell, *Natural History of Aleppo*, p. 14.

50. *HMC Finch*, vol. ii, p. 60.
51. See, e.g., TNA SP 110/23, fos 164, 166.
52. TNA SP 105/156, fo. 153.
53. TNA SP 105/113, fo. 97.
54. BL Add. MS 34799, fo. 3, cited by Ambrose, 'Levant Company', p. 170.
55. TNA SP 97/18, fo. 326.
56. Nigel and Caroline Webb, *The Earl and His Butler in Constantinople* (London, 2009), p. 13.
57. Ibid., p. 14.
58. Ibid., p. 34.
59. TNA SP 110/23, fo. 141.
60. *HMC Portland*, vol. ii, p. 260.
61. See these instructions in TNA SP 105/145.
62. Though years before his death he incurred the wrath of the Company by stubbornly refusing to pay consulage, behaviour it called 'rude and uncivill': *Cal. S.P. Domestic*, vol. lix, p. 474.
63. Abbott, *Under the Turk*, p. 269.
64. TNA SP 105/109, fo. 265; TNA SP 105/145, fos 77–9.
65. North & Hampden to Jacob Turner & John Sayer, Galata, 16 February 1679.
66. TNA SP 110/33, fo. 13.
67. TNA SP 110/23, fo. 118.
68. TNA SP 110/23, fo. 154.
69. TNA SP 105/145, fos 134–7.
70. TNA SP 105/145.
71. Ambrose, 'Levant Company', p. 173.
72. See further Chapter 4. Thomas Vernon's marriage in Aleppo, for instance, caused him to have to protest his trustworthiness in desperate terms to principals: TNA SP110/33, fo. 30.
73. Thomas Fuller, *Historie of the Holy Warre* (Cambridge, 1647), p. 15.
74. Maclean, *Rise of Oriental Travel*, p. 96
75. Maundrell, *Journey*, p. 198.
76. Isaac Barrow, *Sermons preached upon Several Occasions* (London, 1679).
77. John Montagu, *A Voyage Performed by the Late Earl of Sandwich Round the Mediterranean in the Years 1738 and 1739* (London, 1799), p. 170.
78. Thomas Smith, *Remarks upon the manners, religion and government of the Turks . . . and a brief description of Constantinople* (London, 1678), cited in Shaw and Heywood, *English and Continental Views*, p. 18.
79. Lancelot Addison, *The Life and Death of Mahumed, the author of the Turkish religion, being an account of his tribe, parents, birth, name, education, marriages, filthiness of life, Alcoran, firs proselytes, wars, doctrine, miracles, advancement, etc.* (London, 1679), p. 126.
80. Humphrey Prideaux, *The True Nature of Imposture Fully Displayed in the Life of Mahomet; with a discourse annexed, for the Vindicating of Christianity from this Charge; Offered to the Consideration of the Deists of the present Age* (London, 1697), preface (unpaginated).
81. Barrow, *Sermons*.
82. *The Alcoran of Mahomet translated out of Arabick into French . . . newly Englished, for the satisfaction of all that desire to look into the Turkish vanities* (London, 1688), p. 12.
83. On which, Norman Daniel, *Islam and the West: The Making of an Image* (Edinburgh, 1960); R.W. Southern, *Western Views of Islam in the Middle Ages* (Cambridge, MA, 1962); R.A. Fletcher, *The Cross and Crescent: The Dramatic Story of the Earliest Encounters Between Christians and Muslims* (London, 2004).
84. Alastair Hamilton, *William Bedwell the Arabist, 1583–1632* (Leiden, 1985), p. 66.
85. Barrow, *Sermons*.

86. Prideaux, *True Nature of Imposture*, preface (unpaginated).
87. Fuller, *Historie of the Holy Warre*, p. 7.
88. Blount, *Voyage into the Levant*, p. 87.
89. Prideaux, *True Nature of Imposture*, p. 20.
90. Herbert, *Relation of Some Yeares Travaile*, p. 153.
91. Edward Brerewood, *Enquiries touching the Diversity of Languages and Religions, through the chief parts of the world* (London, 1674), p. 318.
92. Fuller, *Historie of the Holy Warre*, p. 7.
93. Herbert, *Relation of Some Yeares Travaile*, p. 154.
94. Beck, *From the Rising of the Sun*, p. 54.
95. Brerewood, *Enquiries*, p. 320.
96. Addison, *Life and Death of Mahumed*, p. 30.
97. Beck, *From the Rising of the Sun*, p. 57.
98. Ahmad Gunny, *Images of Islam in Eighteenth-century Writings* (London, 1996), p. 23.
99. Fuller, *Historie of the Holy Warre*, p. 8.
100. David Pailin, *Attitudes to Other Religions: Comparative Religion in Seventeenth and Eighteenth Century Britain* (Manchester, 1984), p. 103.
101. Prideaux, *True Nature of Imposture*, preface (unpaginated).
102. BL Add. MSS 10623, fo. 27.
103. Maundrell, *Journey*, p. 94.
104. Ibid., p. 198. On Islam's religious allure in this period see further Matar, *Britain and Islam*, passim.
105. Blount, *Voyage into the Levant*, pp. 112–13.
106. Kenneth Parker, *Early Modern Tales of Orient: A Critical Anthology* (London, 1999), p. 25.
107. John Covel, *Extracts from the Diaries of Dr John Covel, 1670–1679* (1893), p. 210.
108. Maundrell, *Journey*, p. 198.
109. William Gibson, 'Chiswell, Edmund (1671–1733)', *ODNB*.
110. The phrase is taken from the title of an excellent book on the early-modern Mediterranean: Molly Greene's *A Shared World: Christians and Muslims in the early modern Mediterranean* (Princeton, 2000).
111. Kafadar, *Between Two Worlds, passim*.
112. Bennison, 'Muslim Universalism and Western Globalisation', p. 77.
113. For attitudes to toleration in Europe in this period, see John Marshall's wonderful book, *John Locke, Toleration and Early Enlightenment Culture* (Cambridge, 2006).
114. Mark Goldie, 'The theory of religious intolerance in Restoration England', in Ole Grell et al. (eds), *From Persecution to Toleration: The Glorious Revolution and Religion in England* (Oxford, 1991).
115. Anita Desai (ed.), *The Turkish Embassy Letters of Lady Mary Wortley Montagu*, (London, 1994), p. 122.
116. North, *Lives of the Norths*, ii, p. 3.
117. Ibid., p. 32.
118. BL Add. MSS 32500, fo. 178.
119. Cobbold MSS, Box 17, reproduced in Grassby, *The English Gentleman*.
120. John Verney to Ralph Verney, Aleppo, Oct 22 1662 (Verney MSS). According to Alexander Russell, writing in the middle of the eighteenth century, 'of late years the far greater part' of Aleppo's English merchants had continued in their native dress, but 'it was formerly customary for all, or most of them, to wear the *Turkish* habit' (*Natural History of Aleppo*, p. 133).
121. Maclean, *Rise of Oriental Travel*, p. 84.
122. Robert Mantran, 'Foreign Merchants and the Minorities in Istanbul during the Sixteenth and Seventeenth Centuries', in B. Braude and B. Lewis (eds), *Christians and Jews in the Ottoman Empire*, (New York, 1982), p. 129.

123. Desai, *Letters of Lady Mary Wortley Montagu*, p. 111.
124. Ibid.
125. North, *Lives of the Norths*, ii, p. 34.
126. Goffman, *Ottoman Empire and Early Modern Europe*, p. 111.
127. Epstein, *Early History of the Levant Company*, pp. 54–5.
128. Fuller, *Historie of the Holy Warre*, p. 8. Among those who recognised the Ottomans' policy of tolerance was John Locke himself: see Nabil Matar, 'John Locke and the Turbanned Nations', *Journal of Islamic Studies*, 1991, 2(1), pp. 67–77.
129. Roy Porter, *Enlightenment – Britain and the Creation of the Modern World* (London, 2000), p. 21.
130. Maclean, *Looking East*, p. 68.
131. Russell, *Natural History of Aleppo*, pp. 66–7. See also Teonge, *Diary*, p. 94.
132. Ambrose, 'English Traders', p. 252.
133. Jacob Turner letters, 22 May 1687.
134. TNA SP 110/22, fo. 45.
135. TNA SP 110/21, 11 August 1699.
136. Cobbold MSS, Box 17.
137. TNA 110/22, fo. 181.
138. TNA SP 110/22, fo. 114.
139. TNA SP 110/22, fo. 126.
140. Curtin, *Cross-Cultural Trade*; Rudolph Matthee, *The Politics of Trade in Safavid Iran* (Cambridge, 1999), pp. 91 *et seq.*
141. TNA SP/110/23, fo. 151.
142. Nigel and Caroline Webb, *The Earl and His Butler*, p. 17.
143. Ibid., p. 17.
144. John Verney to Ralph Verney, 15 March 1665 (Verney MSS).
145. Mantran, 'Foreign Merchants', p. 134.
146. TNA SP 110/22, fo. 18.
147. TNA SP 110/22, fo. 32.
148. TNA SP 110/22, fo. 125.
149. Ibid.
150. North, *Lives of the Norths*, ii, p. 72.
151. Cited in Goffman, 'Izmir', p. 103.
152. Covel, *Diaries of John Covel*, p. 139.
153. Brennan (ed.), *The Travel Diary of Robert Bargrave*, pp. 99–100.
154. T. Simpson Evans, *The Life of Robert Frampton, Bishop of Gloucester, deprived as a non-juror, 1689* (London, 1876), pp. 51–2.
155. Edmund Chishull, *Travels in Turkey and Back to England* (1747), pp. 5–6.
156. BM Add. MSS 10623, fo. 1.
157. BM Add. MSS 10623, fos 2–3.

Chapter 4: Galata

1. John Freely, *Istanbul* (London, 1983), pp. 284–5.
2. Orhan Pamuk, *Istanbul: Memories of a City* (London, 2005), pp. 138–9; Julia Pardoe, *The city of the sultan; and domestic manners of the Turks* (London, 1837), p. 56; Mansel, *Constantinople*. The railway opened in the mid-1870s, making it the third oldest subway system in the world after London and New York's.
3. Desai, *Letters of Lady Mary Wortley Montagu*, p. 126.
4. When the sultan ceremoniously crossed the new bridge, he was openly called an 'infidel sultan': Virginia Aksan, *Ottoman Wars 1700–1870: An Empire Besieged* (Harlow, 2007), p. 366.
5. Pococke, *Description of the East*, ii, p. 134.

6. Anderson, *Journals of Sir Thomas Allin*, p. 15.
7. In addition to Allin's diary, an account of the voyage from Smyrna to Constantinople was penned, probably by Rycaut, and published in London in 1661, under the title *A narrative of the success of the voyage of the Rt. Hon. H. F. . . . his majesties Ambassadour Extraordinary to the . . . sultan Mamet Han, emperour of Turkey, from Smyrna to Constantinople; his arrival there, the manner of his entertainment and audience with the Grand Visier and Grand Seignior*. The same text appears in manuscript form at TNA SP 97/17, fo. 184. An almost identical account also features in Rycaut's *Memoirs*. See also the account of William Trumbull's audience in TNA SP 97/20, fo. 102.
8. Aaron Hill, *A full and just account of the present state of the Ottoman Empire in all its branches . . . faithfully related from a serious observation taken in many years travels thro' those countries* (London, 1710), p. 141.
9. Isobel Grundy, *Lady Mary Wortley Montagu – Comet of the Enlightenment* (Oxford, 1999), p. 152.
10. William Grelot, *A late voyage to Constantinople . . . Translated from the French by J. Philips* (London, 1683), pp. 57–8.
11. Rycaut, *History of the Turkish Empire*, p. 102.
12. *HMC Finch*, vol i, p. 96.
13. James Dallaway, *Constantinople Ancient and Modern, with excursions to the shores and islands of the Archipelago* (London, 1797), p. 124.
14. Pococke, *Description of the East*, ii, p. 134.
15. Mundy, *Travels of Peter Mundy*, p. 22.
16. Pococke, *Description of the East*, ii, p. 134.
17. Dallaway, *Constantinople Ancient and Modern*, p. 124. Under the stern rule of Kara Mustapha, however, the Ottomans would not allow churches destroyed in a fire to be rebuilt, as Winchilsea bitterly complained: *HMC Finch*, vol. i, p. 195.
18. *HMC Finch*, vol. ii, p. 155.
19. Desai, *Letters of Lady Mary Wortley Montagu*, p. 99; Montagu, *A Voyage*, p. 127.
20. A.C. Wood, 'The English Embassy at Constantinople, 1660–1762', *The English Historical Review*, vol. 40, no. 160 (October 1925), 533–61.
21. Fynes Moryson, *An Itinerary: containing ten yeeres travel through . . . twelve dominions*, i (Glasgow, 1907), p. 261. He notes that 'formerly the ambassadors of England were wont to dwell upon the sea shore in the plain'.
22. TNA SP 97/19, 25 May 1674.
23. Desai, *Letters of Lady Mary Wortley Montagu*, p. 126
24. Dallaway, *Constantinople Ancient and Modern*, p. 127.
25. Hill, *A full and just account*, p. 141.
26. Ibid., pp. 82–3.
27. Ibid., p. 107.
28. Brennan (ed.), *The Travel Diary of Robert Bargrave*, p. 87. This was during a bout of Ottoman–Venetian warfare over Crete.
29. Desai, *Letters of Lady Mary Wortley Montagu*, p. 127.
30. Ibid.
31. Dallaway, *Constantinople Ancient and Modern*, pp. 153–4.
32. Jardine, *Worldly Goods*, p. 72.
33. TNA SP 110/23, fo. 23.
34. North, *Lives of the Norths*, ii, p. 48.
35. Montagu, *A Voyage*, p. 124.
36. John Burbury, *A Relation of a Journey of . . . Lord Henry Howard from London to Vienna and thence to Constantinople Lord Howard* (London, 1671), p. 193.
37. Desai, *Letters of Lady Mary Wortley Montagu*, p. 130.
38. Lord Baltimore, *A Tour to the East in the Years 1763 and 1764* (Dublin, 1768), pp. 56–7.

39. Blount, *Voyage into the Levant*, p. 25.
40. George Sandys, *A relation of a journey begun An. Dom. 1610: four books containing a description of the Turkish Empire, etc.* (London, 1615), p. 29.
41. Burbury, *Relation of a Journey of . . . Lord Henry Howard*, pp. 193–4.
42. *HMC Finch*, vol. i, p. 247.
43. McKay, *Prince Eugene of Savoy* (London, 1977), p. 161; Nicholas Henderson, *Prince Eugen of Savoy* (London, 2002), pp. 224–5; William McNeill, *Europe's Steppe Frontier 1500–1800* (Chicago, 1964).
44. Desai, *Letters of Lady Mary Wortley Montagu*, p. 51.
45. Burbury, *Relation of a Journey of . . . Lord Henry Howard*, p. 210. For a useful and brief discussion of this history, see Bernard Lewis, 'The Ottoman Obsession', in Lewis, *Islam and the West* (New York, 1993), p. 75 *et seq*.
46. Rycaut, *History of the Turkish Empire*, p. 139.
47. Richard Knolles, *The General Historie of the Turkes from the first beginning of that Nation to the rising of the Othoman Familie . . . Together with the lives and conquests of the Othoman Kings and Emperours* (London, 1603), introduction (unpaginated).
48. Hill, *A full and just account*, p. 14.
49. Ibid., p. 3.
50. Ibid., pp. 3–4
51. Blount, *Voyage into the Levant*, p. 25.
52. Le Bruyn, *A Voyage to the Levant*, p. 49.
53. On this see, amongst other assertions of the new orthodoxy, Suraiya Faroqhi, 'Crisis and Change 1590–1699' in Inalcik, *Economic and Social History*, ii; Jane Hathaway, 'Problems of Periodisation in Ottoman History: The Fifteenth through the Eighteenth Centuries', *Turkish Studies Association Bulletin*, 20, 1996, pp. 25–31.
54. Bernard Lewis, 'Ottoman Observers of Ottoman Decline', *Islamic Studies*, 1 (1962), pp. 71–87 and, more recently, Caroline Finkel, 'The Treacherous Cleverness of Hindsight: Myths of Ottoman Decay', in Gerald MacLean (ed.), *Re-Orienting the Renaissance: Cultural exchanges with the East* (New York; Basingstoke, 2005); Holt, *Egypt and the Fertile Crescent*, p. 61.
55. K. Setton, *Western Hostility to Islam and Prophecies of Turkish Doom* (Philadelphia, 1992).
56. Haynes, *The Humanist as Traveller*, p. 76.
57. Fuller, *Historie of the Holy Warre*, pp. 284–5.
58. Inalcik, 'The Heyday and Decline of the Ottoman Empire', in P.M. Holt, Ann K.S. Lambton and Bernard Lewis, *The Cambridge History of Islam*, vol. 1A (Cambridge, 1971) p. 342.
59. Fuller, *Historie of the Holy Warre*, p. 284.
60. The literature on English views of the Ottoman Empire is vast, that on European views all the more so. It intersects, obviously, with literature on views of Islam already cited. But see also Beck, *From the Rising of the Sun*; Asli Cirakman, *From the 'Terror of the World' to the 'Sick Man of Europe': European Images of Ottoman Empire and Society from the Sixteenth Century to the Nineteenth* (New York; Oxford, 2002); Dunthorne, 'The Generous Turk', *The Historian*, 68 (2000); Shaw and Heywood, *English and Continental Views*; Christine Woodhead, 'The Present Terrour of the World? Contemporary views of the Ottoman Empire c.1600', *History*, 72 (1987), pp. 20–37. A particularly helpful guide through this morass is Rhoads Murphey's 'Bigots or Informed Observers? A Periodisation of Pre-colonial English and European Writing on the Middle East' in *Journal of the American Oriental Society*, 110/2 (1990), pp. 291–303.
61. Knolles, *The Turkish History . . . Written by Mr Knolles*, preface (unpaginated).
62. Brerewood, *Enquiries*, p. 316.
63. Beck, *From the Rising of the Sun*, p. 54.

64. Desai, *Letters of Lady Mary Wortley Montagu*, p. 52.
65. Hill, *A full and just account*, p. 4.
66. Ibid., p. 18
67. North, *Lives of the Norths*, ii, p. 48.
68. Rhoads Murphey, 'Merchants, Nations and Free-Agency', in Hamilton et al. (eds), *Friends and Rivals*, (Leiden: Boston, 2000) p. 34.
69. Goffman, *Britons in the Ottoman Empire*, pp. 115–16.
70. TNA SP 97/17, fos 153, 162–7; 179; Goffman, *Britons in the Ottoman Empire*; M.C. Fissel and Daniel Goffman, 'Viewing the scaffold from Istanbul: the Bendysh-Hyde affair, 1647–1651', *Albion*, 22:3 (1990), pp. 421–48.
71. *HMC Finch*, vol i., p. 357.
72. See, for example, TNA SP 105/109, fo. 211 recording the response of each member of the Smyrna factory to the oath. The Aleppo factory was more tractable: *Cal. S.P. Domestic*, vol. xxix, p. 492.
73. *HMC Downshire*, vol i., p. 289.
74. *Cal. S.P. Domestic*, vol. xvi, no. 29.
75. *Cal. S.P. Domestic*, vol. x, p. 195.
76. Murphey, 'Merchants and Free-Agency'.
77. *HMC Finch*, vol i., p. 418.
78. *HMC Finch*, vol. ii., p. 6.
79. Ibid., p. 71.
80. TNA SP 105/112, fo. 87.
81. *HMC Finch*, vol i, p. 398.
82. Grundy, *Lady Mary Wortley Montagu*, p. 256.
83. *Cal. S.P. Domestic*, vol. cxxxi, no. 74; *Cal. S.P. Venetian, 1621*, no. 671.
84. See, for instance, SP 105/115, 6 July 1704.
85. See, for instance, the difficulties already being caused in 1586 amongst John Sanderson's correspondence: Foster, *Travels of John Sanderson*, pp. 130–31.
86. Frangakis-Syrett, *Smyrna*, p. 90.
87. The Company insisted that this should not occur where individual traders were at fault: TNA SP 105/154, fo. 70.
88. TNA SP 110/23, fo. 124.
89. TNA SP 34/8, fos 36; 50; TNA SP 105/115, 23 May 1707.
90. TNA SP 110/23, fo. 133.
91. Sir John Finch went to the length of seeking a new clause in the capitulations to deal with this problem.
92. *Cal. S.P. Domestic, 1660–1661*, p. 59.
93. TNA SP/110/23, fo. 166.
94. TNA SP 97/19, fo. 200.
95. Wood, *Levant Company*, p. 102.
96. Davis, *Aleppo and Devonshire Square*, p. 139.
97. TNA SP 97/19, fo. 224.
98. *HMC Finch*, vol. ii, p. 79.

Chapter 5: Ambassadors

1. *HMC Downshire*, vol i., p. 224.
2. Ibid.
3. Goffman, *Britons in the Ottoman Empire*, p. 113; cf. TNA SP 97/20, fo. 102.
4. Hill, *A full and just account*, p. 141.
5. Godfrey Goodwin, *Topkapi Palace* (London, 1999), p. 37.
6. Ottaviano Bon, *The Sultan's Seraglio: An Intimate Portrait of Life at the Ottoman Court (from the seventeenth-century edition of John Withers)* (London, 1996).

7. Rycaut, *History of the Turkish Empire*, p. 104.
8. The real business of government, however, was done from the Porte (which, contrary to its common usage, in fact refers to the Grand Vizier's residence and not the sultan's).
9. *HMC Finch*, vol.ii, p. 85.
10. Rycaut, *History of the Turkish Empire*, p. 105.
11. Ibid.
12. TNA SP 97/17, fo. 151.
13. *HMC Finch*, vol. i., pp. 379; 382.
14. *HMC Finch*, vol. i., pp. 111; 145.
15. *HMC Finch*, vol. ii., pp. 154–5.
16. Elizabeth's commission to Harborne (1582): see Hakluyt, *Principal Navigations* (1904 ed.), v., p. 221.
17. Wood, 'English Embassy', p. 533.
18. With the exception of the North Africa fringes of that influence: see Chapter 7.
19. *HMC Finch*, vol. i., p. 119.
20. Ibid., p. 261.
21. TNA SP 97/17, fo. 150.
22. HMC Finch, vol i., p. 121
23. Matar, *Islam in Britain*, p. 13; Colley, *Captives*, Chapter 1.
24. TNA SP 97/17, fos 198, 210.
25. TNA SP97/20, fo. 167. This period of English-Ottoman diplomatic relations has been extensively explored by Colin Heywood. See 'An Undiplomatic Anglo-Dutch Dispute at the Porte', in Hamilton et al., *Friends and Rivals*; C.J. Heywood, 'English diplomatic relations with Turkey, 1689–1698', in William Hale and A.I. Bagis (eds), *Four Centuries of Turco-British Relations* (1984).
26. TNA SP 97/22, *passim*.
27. Grundy, *Lady Mary Wortley Montagu*, pp. 154–8.
28. See, for instance, the comment of Nathaniel Harley in 1693: 'I could wish there were put a full stop to trade and then we might hope to see a good conclusion of the war, without which farewell trade and everything else.' *HMC Portland*, vol. ii., p. 243.
29. *HMC Finch*, vol. ii, p. 148.
30. Ibid., p. 152.
31. TNA SP105/109, fo. 67.
32. *Cal. S.P. Venetian, 1626*, no. 466.
33. *HMC Finch*, vol. ii, p. 152.
34. *HMC Downshire*, vol i., p. 224.
35. Ibid., p. 223.
36. Ibid., p. 224.
37. *HMC Finch*, vol. i., p. 401.
38. Foster, *England's Quest*, p. 70.
39. Akdes Kurat (ed.), *The Despatches of Sir Robert Sutton* (London, 1953), p. 42; TNA SP 105/109, fo. 220.
40. TNA SP 97/22, fo. 43.
41. TNA SP 97/20, fo. 5.
42. That was certainly the Company's conclusion: see TNA SP 105/115, 6 July 1704.
43. TNA SP 97/20, fo. 20.
44. TNA SP 110/23 fo. 30.
45. Hill, *A full and just account*.
46. Matar, *Britain and Islam*, p. 4.
47. Moryson, *An Itinerary*.
48. Matar, *Britain and Islam*, p. 4.

49. Colley, *Captives* (though it is not necessarily appropriate to regard this as a manifestation of religious warfare between Muslim and Christian: see Matar, *Britain and Barbary*, Chapter 4).

50. Typical was that addressed to Thomas Glover in 1609 seeking one Peter Soper, 'captive in Constantinople', and a ransom for whose release had been deposited with the Company: TNA SP 105/110 fo. 42R.

51. Brennan, *The Travel Diary of Robert Bargrave*, pp. 108–9.

52. Although the word 'millet' was already in use by Ottoman officials in the seventeenth century, particular sects were referred to instead by the word *ta'ifi* (meaning 'group' or 'party'), whose government was ultimately supervised by the Muslim authorities: see Bruce Masters, *Christians and Jews in the Ottoman Arab World: the Roots of Sectarianism* (Cambridge, 2001), pp. 61–7.

53. On this topic, see Maurits H. Van den Boogert, *The Capitulations and the Ottoman Legal System* (Leiden, 2005); Eldem, 'Capitulations', pp. 283–336; Goffman, *Ottoman Empire and Early Modern Europe*, pp. 172–6; Inalcik, *Economic and Social History*, i, pp. 188–95. For a doctrinal perspective, Yohann Friedmann, *Tolerance and Coercion in Islam* (Cambridge, 2003); and for their evolution in practice, Masters, *Christians and Jews in the Ottoman Arab World*; Braude and Lewis, *Christians and Jews in the Ottoman Empire*.

54. Steensgaard, 'Consuls and Nations in the Levant', p. 17.

55. Eldem, 'Capitulations', p. 294.

56. Porter, *Observations*, p. 245.

57. Abbott, *Under the Turk*, pp. 26–32.

58. See Chapter 8.

59. Abbott, *Under the Turk*, p. 249.

60. *HMC Finch*, vol. ii, p. 72.

61. TNA SP 97/18, fo. 28.

62. TNA SP 105/145, fo. 79.

63. Wood, *Levant Company*, p. 16.

64. In this instance, part of the difficulty lay in the shakiness of the Ottoman state's own authority in North Africa, despite its nominal suzerainty throughout much of it. The limits to central state control in many parts of the Ottoman Empire, as well as its particular weakness in the Maghreb, would pose repeated challenges to the operations of the Levant Company in these regions: see Chapter 6.

65. Wood, *Levant Company*, p. 233, fn. 1.

66. TNA SP 97/20, fo. 5.

67. TNA SP 110/22, fo. 92.

68. Porter, *Observations*, pp. 238–40.

69. Masters, *Origins of Western Economic Dominance*, pp. 18–21.

70. Masters, 'Semi-autonomous forces in the Arab provinces' in Faroqhi, iii, p. 189.

71. Rycaut, *Memoirs*, p. 130

72. TNA SP 97/17, fo. 150.

73. TNA SP 105/145, fos. 73 *et seq.*

74. The Company sometimes acquiesced: see, for instance, TNA SP 105/152, fo. 205, where the General Court accepted reliance on the Cady's offices.

75. TNA SP 110/23, fo. 30.

76. North, *Lives of the Norths*, ii, p. 50.

77. TNA SP 97/21

78. Julian Hoppit, *A Land of Liberty? England 1689–1727* (Oxford, 2000), p. 100.

79. Sonia Anderson, 'The Anglo-Dutch "Smyrna Fleet" of 1693', in Hamilton et al., *Friends and Rivals*, pp. 95–6; N.A.M. Rodger, *The Command of the Ocean: A Naval History of Britain, 1649–1815* (London, 2004), pp. 152–4.

80. Anderson, 'Smyrna Fleet'.

81. Rodger, *Command of the Ocean*, p. 153; Hoppit, *Land of Liberty*, p. 100.
82. *HMC Portland*, vol. ii, p. 244.
83. Eldem, 'Capitulations', p. 292.
84. Braudel, *Mediterranean*, i, p. 640.
85. Ibid. As noted, this was to over-dramatise the extent of the transformation occurring by this time: see Greene, 'Beyond the Northern Invasion'.
86. Rawlinson, H.G., 'The Embassy of William Harborne to Constantinople, 1583–8', *Transactions of the Royal Historical Society*, iv. 5 (1922), pp. 1–27; Horniker, A.L., 'Anglo-French Rivalry in the Levant from 1583 to 1612', *The Journal of Modern History*, vol. 18, no. 4 (December 1946), pp. 289–305.
87. The English, along with the French and Venetians, played at a similar game when the Dutch tried to obtain capitulations in the early seventeenth century.
88. On the decline of Venetian trade in the region, see especially Rapp, 'Unmaking of the Mediterranean Trade Hegemony'; Pullan, *Crisis and Change*; and Suraiya Faroqhi, 'The Venetian Presence in the Ottoman Empire, 1600–30', in Huri Islamoglu-Inan (ed.), *The Ottoman Empire and the World Economy* (Cambridge, 1987).
89. Goffman, *Izmir*, pp. 64–5.
90. *Cal. S.P. Venetian, 1623–25*, no. 356.
91. Suraiya Faroqhi, *The Ottoman Empire and the World Around It* (London, 2006), pp. 140–42
92. Ibid.
93. Cited in Rapp, 'Unmaking of the Mediterranean Trade Hegemony', p. 510.
94. *Cal. S.P. Venetian, 1623–25*, no. 362.
95. *Cal. S.P. Venetian, 1619–1623*, no. 485.
96. Masters, *Origins of Western Economic Dominance*, p. 26.
97. Faroqhi, *Ottoman Empire and the World Around It*, pp. 145–6.
98. Greene, 'Beyond the Northern Invasion'.
99. Faroqhi, *Ottoman Empire and the World Around It*, p. 146.
100. Wood, *Levant Company*, p. 100.
101. Goffman, *Izmir*, Chapter 6.
102. Faroqhi, *Ottoman Empire and the World Around It*, p. 147.
103. Goffman, *Izmir*, p. 122.
104. Ibid., p. 123.
105. This account is based largely on Jonathan Israel, *Dutch Primacy*; idem, 'The Phases of the Dutch Straatvaart, 1590–1713: A Chapter in the Economic History of the Mediterranean', in Israel, *Empires and Entrepots. The Dutch, The Spanish Monarchy and the Jews, 1585–1713* (London, 1990), pp. 133–62; and Mehmet Bulut, *Ottoman-Dutch Economic Relations in the Early Modern Period* (Utrecht, 2000). The structure of the Dutch trade in Smyrna is dissected alongside that of the English in Elena Frangakis-Syrett, 'Commercial Practices and Competition in the Levant: The British and the Dutch in Eighteenth-Century Izmir', in Hamilton et al. *Friends and Rivals*, pp. 135–59.
106. Eldem, 'Capitulations', p. 292.
107. *Cal. S.P. Venetian, 1611–18*, no. 383.
108. Ibid., no. 534.
109. Israel, 'Trade, Politics and Strategy: The Anglo-Dutch Wars in the Levant (1647–1675)', in Hamilton et al., *Friends and Rivals*.
110. Israel, *Dutch Primacy*, p. 154.
111. TNA SP 97/17, fo. 173.
112. TNA SP 97/20, fo. 11.
113. Anderson, *English Consul*, p. 54.
114. Palmer to Jacob Turner on 12 August 1672. Cited in Joel Elin, 'The life and letters of Jacob Turner', unpublished PhD thesis, NY University (1975), p. 39.

115. Murphey in *Friends and Rivals*. Still, the pashas' correspondence makes plain that they did see themselves in competition with the other Frankish states and in an era of mercantilist assumptions the game was regarded as a zero-sum one.
116. Steensgaard, 'Consuls and Nations in the Levant', p. 22.
117. Ibid.

Chapter 6: Objects of Enquiry

1. G.A. Russell, 'The Impact of Philosophus Autodidacticus', in Russell (ed.), *The Arabick Interest of the Natural Philosophers in Seventeenth Century England*, (Leiden; New York, 1994) p. 232. See also C.R. Pastor, *The Idea of Robinson Crusoe* (Watford, 1930); Sami Hawi, *Islamic Naturalism and Mysticism: A Philosophic Study of Ibn Tufayl's Hayy Bin Yaqzan* (Leiden, 1974); Lawrence Conrad (ed.), *The World of Ibn Tufayl: Interdisciplinary Perspectives on Hayy ibn Yaqzan* (Leiden, 1996); Christopher Walker, *Islam and the West* (London, 2005), Chapter 7; G.J. Toomer, *Eastern Wisedome and Learning* (Oxford, 1996), pp. 218–23. See also the useful introduction and notes by Jim Colville in *Two Andalusian Philosophers* (London, 1999) and the introduction by A.S. Fulton to the 1929 edition of Simon Ockley's translation (London, 1929).
2. On this, see especially Rana Kabanni, *Imperial Fictions* (London, 1994); Martha Conant, *The Oriental Tale in England in the Eighteenth Century* (New York, 1908) and, more recently, Rosalind Ballaster, *Fabulous Orients: Fictions of the East in England, 1662–1785* (Oxford, 2005) and idem, *Fables of the East: Selected Tales 1662–1785* (Oxford 2005).
3. Porter, *Enlightenment*; cf. J.G.A. Pocock, *Barbarism and Religion* (Cambridge, 1999); Gertrude Himmelfarb, *The Roads to Modernity: The British, French and American Enlightenments* (New York, 2005).
4. James Tracy (ed.), *The Political Economy of Merchant Empires* (Cambridge, 1991), p. 217.
5. BL Add. MSS 22910, fo. 151.
6. James Buzard, 'The Grand Tour and After', in Peter Hulme and James Buzard (eds), *Cambridge Companion to Travel Writing* (Cambridge, 2002), p. 37.
7. Hamilton, *Bedwell the Arabist*, p. 88.
8. Toomer, *Eastern Wisedome*, p. 106.
9. D.F. Wright, 'Strachan, George (1592–1634)', *ODNB*.
10. P.M. Holt, 'The Study of Arabic Historians in Seventeenth Century England: The Background and the Work of Edward Pococke', *Bulletin of the School of Oriental and African Studies*, vol. 19, no. 3 (1957), pp. 444–55, especially at pp. 446–9.
11. Simpson Evans, *Life of Robert Frampton*.
12. Hamilton, *Bedwell the Arabist*, p. 94.
13. BL Add. MSS 22910, fo. 51.
14. Toomer, *Eastern Wisedome*, p. 106.
15. Leonard Twells, *The Lives of Dr. E. Pocock, by Dr. Twells . . . Mr Burdy* (London, 1816), p. 32.
16. Ibid., p. 69.
17. Ibid., p. 26.
18. Ibid.
19. Ibid., p. 30.
20. Ibid.
21. Ibid., pp. 64–5.
22. Cited in Toomer, *Eastern Wisedome*, p. 136.
23. Charles Burnett, 'The Introduction of Arabic Learning into British Schools', in C.E. Butterworth and B.A. Kessel (eds), *The Introduction of Arabic Philosophy into Europe* (Leiden, 1994).

24. A.J. Arberry, *Oriental Essays: Portraits of Seven Scholars* (London, 1960), p. 15.
25. Nabil Matar's trilogy has already been cited and various notable articles are also referred to below; Toomer's *Eastern Wisedome*. This chapter owes a heavy debt to the scholarship of both.
26. Conant, *Oriental Tale, passim.*
27. Matar, *Islam in Britain*, p. 189.
28. Mordechai Feingold, 'Decline and Fall: Arabic Science in Seventeenth-Century England', in F. Jamil Ragep and Sally P. Ragep with Steven Livesey (eds), *Tradition, Transmission and Transformation* (Leiden, 1996).
29. Toomer, *Eastern Wisedome*, p. 56.
30. Feingold, 'Decline and Fall'; for the broader intellectual context, see also Keith Thomas, *Religion and the Decline of Magic* (London, 1971).
31. Feingold, 'Decline and Fall', p. 442.
32. Thomas Baker, *Reflections Upon Learning Wherein is shewn the Insufficiency Thereof, in its several particulars. In order to evince the usefulness and necessity of revelation* (London, 1699), p. 220.
33. *The Alcoran of Mahomet / translated out of Arabique into French; by the Sieur Du Ryer, lord of Malezair, and resident for the King of France, at Alexandria; and newly Englished, for the satisfaction of all that desire to look into the Turkish vanities* (London, 1649). See further Matar, *Islam in Britain*, Chapter 3; 'Alexander Ross and the First English Translation of the Qur'an', in *The Muslim World*, 88 (1998): 81–92; Arberry, *Oriental Essays*, p. 14 *et seq.*
34. Alexander Ross, *Pansebeia: or a view of all religions in the world* (London, 1653); *House of Commons Journal*, 21 March 1649; see also entries for 19 March 1649 and 31 March 1649 and *C.S.P. Domestic 1649–50*, 59, 63, 70.
35. Toomer, *Eastern Wisedome*, p. 89
36. Arberry, *Oriental Essays*, p. 11.
37. A.J. Arberry, *British Orientalists* (London, 1933), p. 60.
38. 'Preface of the Editor', *An Account of South-West Barbary containing what is most remarkable in the territories of the King of Fez and Morocco . . . by Simon Ockley* (London, 1713).
39. Ibid.
40. *Four Treatises Concerning the Doctrine, Discipline and Worship of the Mahometans* (London, 1712), p. 5.
41. Compare the passage in Ockley's *History of the Saracens* at p. 301 of the first volume, criticising Byzantine historians for perpetuating fables about the Prophet Muhammad 'as if the Christian Religion was best serv'd by perverting of History'.
42. See the references in Pailin, *Attitudes to Other Religions*, at pp. 18; 46; 83.
43. Ibid., p. 99.
44. On Ockley, see the chapter dedicated to him in A.J. Arberry, *Oriental Essays. Portraits of Seven Scholars* (London, 1960); A.M. Kararah, 'Simon Ockley: his contribution to Arabic studies and influence on western thought' (Cambridge PhD thesis, 1955); the 'Memoir of Ockley' in Bohn's edition of *The History of the Saracens* (1847); the old article by S. Lane-Poole and present one by P.M. Holt in *ODNB*; Isaac Disraeli, *Calamities of Authors* (London, 1812), pp. 188–9.
45. *Sentences of Ali Son-in-Law of Mahomet . . . Translated from an Authentick Arabick Manuscript in the Bodleian Library at Oxford, by Simon Ockley, B.D.* (London, 1717), preface (unpaginated).
46. Stubbe, *Account of the Rise and Progress*. See also P.M. Holt, *A Seventeenth-Century Defender of Islam: Henry Stubbe and his Book* (London, 1972); J.A. Champion, *The Pillars of Priestcraft Shaken: the Church of England and its Enemies, 1660–1730* (Cambridge, 1992), pp. 120 *et seq.*
47. Stubbe, *Account of the Rise and Progress*, pp. 142–3; Holt, *Seventeenth-Century Defender of Islam*, pp. 19–20.

48. Stubbe, *Account of the Rise and Progress*, p. 143.
49. Ibid., pp. 150; 158–9.
50. Champion, *Pillars of Priestcraft*, pp. 108–10.
51. Henri de Boulainvilliers, *The Life of Mahomet. Translated from the French, etc.* (London, 1731).
52. Ibid.
53. See further John Marshall, *John Locke: Toleration and Early Enlightenment Culture* (Cambridge, 2006). Chapters 12 and 19 and Jonathan Israel, *Enlightenment Contested: Philosophy, Modernity and the Emancipation of Man 1670–1752* (Oxford, 2008), Chapter 24.
54. *The Koran, commonly called The Alcoran of Mohammed, translated into English immediately from the original Arabic; with explanatory notes, taken from the most approved commentators* (London, 1734), p. iii.
55. *ODNB* article by Arnoud Vrolijk. Frustratingly little is known about the man. See also P.M. Holt, 'The treatment of Arab history by Prideaux, Ockley and Sale', in B. Lewis and P.M. Holt (eds), *Historians of the Middle East* (London, 1962).
56. *The Koran* (Sale translation), p. iii; cf. Stubbe's assertion that 'it is manifest that the Mahometans did propagate their Empire, but not their Religion, by force of Arms' (*Account of the Rise and Progress*, p. 182).
57. *Reflections on Mohammedism and the conduct of Mohammed. Occasioned by a late learned translation and exposition of the Koran or Al Koran* (London, 1735), p. 3.
58. *A Defence of Mahomet (written in Arabick by Abdulla Mahumed Omar). A Paradox* (London, 1720), p. 179.
59. Peter Laslett, 'Introduction' to Locke, *Two Treatises of Government* (Cambridge, 1998), pp. 27–9.
60. Frantz, *The English Traveller*, p. 15. See also Buzard, 'Grand Tour'.
61. E.J. Finopoulos and W.B. Stanford (eds), *The Travels of Lord Charlemont in Greece and Turkey* (London, 1985). See also Cynthia O'Connor, *The Pleasing Hours: James Caulfield, First Earl of Charlemont 1728–99* (Cork, 1999).
62. Maclean, *Rise of Oriental Travel*, p. 118.
63. Blount, *Voyage into the Levant*, p. 1.
64. Blod., pp. 3–4.
65. Ibid.
66. Desai, *Letters of Lady Mary Wortley Montagu*, p. 104
67. Porter, *Observations*, p. 2.
68. Desai, *Letters of Lady Mary Wortley Montagu*, p. 133.
69. Ibid., p. 142.
70. Rycaut, *Present State of the Ottoman* Empire, preface.
71. Blount, *Voyage into the Levant*, p. 1.
72. Hill, *A full and just account*, p. 76.
73. Lewis, 'The Ottoman Obsession', p. 80.
74. Finopoulos and Stanford, *Travels of Lord Charlemont*, p. 197.
75. Blount, *Voyage into the Levant*, p. 1.
76. Ibid.
77. Desai, *Letters of Lady Mary Wortley Montagu*, p. 57.
78. Shaw and Heywood, *English and Continental Views*, p. 41.
79. Le Bruyn, *A Voyage to the Levant*, p. 54.
80. Bernard Lewis, *The Muslim Discovery of Europe* (London, 1982).
81. Sandwich, John Montagu, Earl of, *A voyage performed by the late Earl of Sandwich round the Mediterranean in the years 1738 and 1739* (London, 1799), p. 137.
82. Finopoulos and Stanford, *Travels of Lord Charlemont*, p. 168.
83. Porter, *Observations*, pp. 72–3.
84. Pococke, *Description of the East*, p. 133.

85. Chishull, *Travels*, p. 8.
86. Covel, *Extracts from the Diaries of Dr John Covel*, pp. 268–72.
87. Porter, *Enlightenment*, p. 101.
88. Desai, *Letters of Lady Mary Wortley Montagu*, pp. 53–4.
89. Ibid., pp. 61–2.
90. Finopoulos and Stanford, *Travels of Lord Charlemont*, pp. 176–7.

Chapter 7: Antique Lands

1. A point made in the discussion of the painting by Mark Crinson in *Empire Building – Orientalism and Victorian Architecture* (London, 1996), pp. 107–8. See also Katharine Sim, *David Roberts R.A.* (London, 1984), pp. 202–3.
2. Afaf Lutfi al-Sayyid Marsot, *Egypt in the Reign of Muhammad Ali* (Cambridge, 1984), p. 243.
3. Ibid., p. 246.
4. In 1841, Egypt ceased to be even nominally part of the Ottoman Empire. For a succinct account of Egyptian politics during this period, including the British role within them, see Khaled Fahmy, 'The Era of Muhammad Ali Pasha, 1805–1848', in M.W. Daly (ed.), *The Cambridge History of Egypt* (Cambridge, 1998), pp. 139–80.
5. Marsot, *Egypt in the Reign of Muhammad Ali*, p. 236.
6. Inalcik, 'When and how British cotton goods invaded the Levant markets', in Islamoglu-Inan, *Ottoman Empire and the World Economy*, p. 374.
7. Marsot suggests that Britain's economic interests directly motivated the military machinations of the 1840s, though the preferable view seems to be that these were primarily driven by concerns for the security of the Indian Empire: see Fahmy, 'The era of Muhammad Ali Pasha'.
8. Inalcik, 'When and how', p. 383.
9. John Sweetman, *The Oriental Obsession: Islamic Inspiration in British and American Art and Architecture 1500–1920* (Cambridge, 1988); Nicholas Tromans (ed.), *The Lure of the East: British Orientalist Painting* (London, 2008); Jocelyn Hackforth-Jones and Mary Roberts, *Edges of Empire: Orientalism and Visual Culture* (Oxford, 2005).
10. W.C. Brown, 'The Popularity of English Travel Books About the Near East, 1775–1825', *Publications of the Modern Language Association of America*, 53 (1938), pp. 827–36.
11. The phrase is Thackeray's.
12. I mean the term in the sense of the artistic/cultural 'movement', rather than in the sense defined by Edward Said's work of the same name, notwithstanding the overlap between the two.
13. Cook began enticing British tourists to Egypt in the 1860s: see Trevor Mostyn, *Egypt's Belle Epoque: Cairo 1869–1952* (London, 1989), Chapter 18.
14. There had already been two brief occupations on Egyptian soil nearer the beginning of the century: see further below.
15. Cited in Clarence Matterson, *English Trade in the Levant, 1693–1753* (unpublished Harvard University PhD thesis, 1936), p. 194.
16. Foster, *Travels of John Sanderson*, p. 131.
17. Ibid., p. 132.
18. TNA SP 110/33, fo. 15.
19. TNA SP 110/22, fo. 143.
20. *HMC Finch*, vol. ii, p. 141.
21. Hakluyt, *Principal Navigations*, v. (Kessinger edn), pp. 294–5.
22. The attempt was not, however, confined to these early years: see, e.g., TNA SP 97/34, fos 56–9.

23. William Lithgow, *Rare Adventures and Painefull Peregrinations* (1928), p. 242.
24. Wood, *Levant Company*, p. 78; cf. *Cal. S.P. Domestic*, vol. xliii, p. 117 and an earlier flurry of debate in London at TNA SP 105/149, fo. 327.
25. TNA SP 97/20, fo. 123.
26. The history of the attempts to establish a trade in Egypt are well covered in Wood, *Levant Company*. See pp. 32–5; 78–9; 124–5.
27. *HMC Downshire*, vol i., p. 292.
28. Masters, 'Semi-autonomous forces', p. 198.
29. Finkel, *Osman's Dream*, p. 169; see further Ann Williams, 'Mediterranean Conflict' in Kunt and Woodhead, *Suleyman the Magnificent*; Imber, *Ottoman Empire*, p. 44.
30. Matar, *Britain and Barbary*, Chapter 5.
31. Ibid., p. 136.
32. Rodger, *Command of the Ocean*, pp. 89–91.
33. The episode is recounted at length in Colley, *Captives*, Chapter 1. Also on Tangier, see Julian Corbett, *England in the Mediterranean* (London, 1904).
34. Robert Playfair, *The Scourge of Christendom: annals of British relations with Algiers prior to the French conquest* (1884), p. 46.
35. Anderson, *Journals of Sir Thomas Allin*, pp. 6–7.
36. TNA SP 97/17, fo. 159.
37. Rycaut, *History of the Turkish Empire*, p. 244. The Levant Company was sufficiently delighted to pay him a gratuity of 500 Guineas: TNA SP 105/154, fo. 2.
38. Grassby, *English Gentleman in Trade*, p. 58.
39. TNA SP 105/154, fo. 119. His appointment aroused some controversy: see TNA SP 105/154, fo. 121.
40. BL Add MS 32513.
41. On this, see especially Matthee, *The Politics of Trade in Safavid Iran*, Chapter 4.
42. Mathee, *Politics of Trade in Safavid Iran*, pp. 97–8.
43. The exploits of the Shirley brothers are recounted at length in Chew, *Crescent and Rose*.
44. *Cal. S.P. Domestic*, vol. ciii, p. 589.
45. For an account of the events surrounding the attack on Hormuz, see C.R. Boxer, 'Anglo-Portuguese Rivalry in the Persian Gulf', in E. Prestage (ed.), *Chapters in Anglo-Portuguese Relations* (Watford, 1935), pp. 46–129.
46. Eldem, 'Capitulations', p. 299.
47. Mathee, *Politics of Trade in Safavid Iran*, p. 160.
48. Ben Slot, 'At the Backdoor of the Levant', in Hamilton et al., *Friends and Rivals*, p. 118.
49. Mathee, *Politics of Trade in Safavid Iran*, p. 96.
50. Masters, *Origins of Western Economic Dominance*, p. 30.
51. *House of Commons Journals*, xii (1698), p. 436.
52. P.J. Marshall, 'The English in Asia', *OHBE*, vol i., pp. 278–9.
53. TNA SP 105/154, fo. 305.
54. *The Allegations of the Turky Company and others against the East-India Company, relating to the management of that trade, present to the . . . Privy Council . . . with the answer of the East-India Company thereunto, etc.* (London, 1681).
55. Cawston and Keane, *Early Chartered Companies*, p. 80.
56. Scott, *Joint Stock Companies*, p. 140.
57. Ralph Davis, 'English imports from the Middle East', in M.A. Cook (ed.), *Studies in the Economic History of the Middle East* (Oxford, 1970), pp. 198–9.
58. Chaudhuri, *Trading World of Asia*, p. 117. The principal source for Hedges' mission comes from his own pen: R. Barlow and H. Yule (eds), *The diary of William Hedges . . . during his agency in Bengal; as well as on his voyage out and return overland (1681–1687)*, 3 vols, Hakluyt Society (1887–9), pp. 74–5; 78.

59. Keay, *Honourable Company*, p. 154.
60. Chaudhuri, *Trading World of Asia*, p. 454.
61. Bayly, *Imperial Meridian*, Chapter 1. On relations with the Persian Empire, see Mathee, *Politics of Trade in Safavid Iran*.
62. Sir William Hunter (on whom see p. 241 below), cited in Keay, *Honourable Company*, p. 154.
63. Chaudhuri, *Trading World of Asia*, p. 119.
64. Scott, *Joint Stock Companies*, p. 143.
65. Steensgaard, *Asian Trade Revolution*.
66. Masters, *Origins of Western Economic Dominance*, at pp. 28–9.
67. This is also the view taken by Masters; but cf. Marcus, who in *Middle East on the Eve of Modernity* sees the major shift being apparent only in the nineteenth century. If these views conflict, however, the conflict is really just one of emphasis.
68. TNA SP 97/34, fo. 7 *et seq.*
69. TNA SP 34/30, fos 31B, 60B.
70. TNA SP 97/19, fo. 222.
71. Davis, *Aleppo and Devonshire Square*, p. 29.
72. Ambrose, 'Levant Company', p. 271.
73. Porter, *The State of the Turkey Trade Considered*, p. 361.
74. Edhem Eldem, *French Trade in Istanbul in the Eighteenth Century* (Leiden; Boston, 1999), pp. 113–47; Davis, *Aleppo and Devonshire Square*, pp. 189–206.
75. *The Turkey Merchants and their Trade Vindicated* (1720), cited in Davis, *Aleppo and Devonshire Square*, p. 32.
76. TNA SP 97/34, fo. 8.
77. TNA SP 105/145, fo. 305.
78. Eldem, *French Trade in Istanbul*, p. 42.
79. Ibid., p. 28.
80. William Eton, *A Survey of the Turkish Empire. In which are considered . . . Its government, history, . . . and population, etc.* (London, 1798), p. 472.
81. *The case of the governor and company of the merchants of England, trading into the Levant seas* (London, 1744).
82. Cited in Eldem, 'Capitulations', p. 321.
83. See Immanuel Wallerstein, *The Modern World System* (3 vols, 1974–88); and cf. Bernard Lewis, *What Went Wrong?* (London, 2002).
84. Marcus, *Middle East on the Eve of Modernity*, p. 150.
85. Inalcik, 'The Ottoman Economic Mind' in Cook, *Studies in the Economic History of the Middle East*.
86. Brennan, *The Travel Diary of Robert Bargrave*.
87. Anderson, *Journals of Sir Thomas Allin*, p. 14. Winchilsea claimed that when the *Plymouth* appeared off Constantinople, it 'affected the great Emperor himself with an apprehension and terror of his Majesties navy': *HMC Finch*, vol. i, p. 96.
88. Anderson, *English Consul*, p. 49.
89. TNA SP 97/20, fo. 75. The Company complained at commanders charging it extortionate sums for the pleasure of firing these salutes: *Cal. S.P. Domestic*, vol. lxvii, p. 22.
90. See TNA SP 97/20, fo. 75.
91. Goffman, 'Izmir', p. 94.
92. Frangakis-Syrett, *Smyrna*, p. 35.
93. Brennan, *The Travel Diary of Robert Bargrave*, p. 70.
94. Goffman, *Izmir, passim*.
95. Frangakis-Syrett, *Smyrna*, p. 26.
96. See Goffman, 'Izmir', pp. 105–10.
97. Masters, *Origins of Western Economic Dominance*, pp. 216–17.

98. R. Paris, *Histoire du Commerce de Marseille, V: Le Levant, 1660–1789*, pp. 505; 510–15; cited in Davis, *Aleppo and Devonshire Square*, pp. 28–9.
99. Frangakis-Syrett, *Smyrna*, p. 215.
100. Eldem, 'Capitulations', p. 315.
101. Frangakis-Syrett, *Smyrna*, p. 86.
102. Ibid., p. 218.
103. Eldem, 'Capitulations', p. 312.
104. Ibid., pp. 319–20.
105. TNA SP 97/34, fo. 11.

Chapter 8: The Last Pashas

1. On this Egyptian war, see Piers Mackesy, *British Victory in Egypt, 1801: The End of Napoleon's Conquest* (London, 1995); Piers Mackesy, *The War in the Mediterranean, 1803–1810* (London, 1957).
2. TNA SP 105/118, fo. 292.
3. On the Egyptian coffee trade, see Jane Hathaway, 'The Ottoman Empire and the Red Sea Coffee Trade', in Ebru Boyar and Kate Fleet (eds), *The Ottomans and Trade*, special edition of *Oriente Moderno* 25, 2006, pp. 161–71.
4. TNA SP 105/152, fos 406–7.
5. TNA SP105/118, fo. 291.
6. Nigel Leask, 'Bruce, James, of Kinnaird (1730–1794)', *ODNB*.
7. TNA SP 110/29, fo. 189.
8. Frangakis-Syrett, *Smyrna*, p. 32.
9. Ambrose, 'Levant Company', p. 219.
10. TNA SP 110/23, fo. 27.
11. Frangakis-Syrett, *Smyrna*, p. 32.
12. TNA SP 105/155, fo. 89.
13. TNA SP105/154, fo. 346.
14. Davis, *Aleppo and Devonshire Square*, p. 38.
15. Frangakis-Syrett, *Smyrna*, p. 32.
16. *HMC Downshire*, vol i., pp. 303; 335.
17. TNA SP 110/29, fo. 189.
18. TNA SP 105/333, fo. 15.
19. Shafik Ghorbal, *The Beginnings of the Egyptian Question and the Rise of Mehmet Ali* (London, 1928), p. 64.
20. Rosemarie Said Zahlan, 'George Baldwin: Soldier of Fortune?', in Paul and Janet Starkey (eds), *Travellers in Egypt* (1998), p. 26.
21. See Zahlan, 'George Baldwin'; James Mew, 'Baldwin, George (1744–1826)', rev. Deborah Manley, *ODNB*; Jasanoff, *Edge of Empire*, pp. 126–32; G. Baldwin, *Political Recollections Relative to Egypt* (London, 1801); G. Baldwin, *Narrative of Facts Relating to the Plunder of the English Merchants by the Arabs . . . in 1779* (London, 1780).
22. Baldwin, *Political Recollections*, p. 6.
23. Venomous correspondence passed between Baldwin and the ambassador in Constantinople: see TNA SP 97/53, fo. 25.
24. Russell, 'Later History', p. 120. Baldwin claims that Murray had earlier been supportive, however: *Political Recollections*, p. 5.
25. Baldwin, *Political Recollections*, p. 7.
26. Jasanoff, *Edge of Empire*, p. 119.
27. Ghorbal, *Beginnings*, p. 62.
28. Russell, 'Later History', p. 193.
29. Ghorbal, *Beginnings*, p. 62.

30. Russell, 'Later History', p. 195.
31. Michael Duffy, 'World-Wide War and British Expansion, 1793–1815', *OHBE*, vol. ii, pp. 196–7.
32. Inalcik, 'When and how', p. 377.
33. On Briggs, see Frederick Rodky, 'The Attempts of Briggs and Company to Guide British Policy in the Levant in the Interest of Mehemet Ali Pasha, 1821–41', *Journal of Modern History*, 5 (1933), 324–51.
34. Roger Owen, *The Middle East in the World Economy, 1800–1914* (London, 1981), p. 84.
35. Ibid., p. 85.
36. Crinson, *Empire Building*, p. 110.
37. Davis, *Aleppo and Devonshire Square*, p. 210.
38. Inalcik, 'When and how', p. 378.
39. Owen, *Middle East in the World Economy*, p. 85.
40. Ibid., p. 84.
41. Inalcik, 'When and how', p. 383.
42. *HMC Finch*, vol. ii, p. 76.
43. Anderson, *English Consul*, pp. 257–8.
44. Sandys, *Relation of a journey*, p. 17.
45. Ibid.
46. Andrew Wheatcroft, *The Ottomans: Dissolving Images* (London, 1995), p. 231; cf. James Porter, *Observations*, p. 81.
47. Pocock, *Barbarism and Religion*, ii, pp. 348–51.
48. Lithgow, *Painefull Peregrinations*, cited in Warner G. Rice, *Early English Travellers to Greece and the Levant* (1933), p. 223.
49. Baltimore, *Tour to the East*, pp. 60–61.
50. Ibid., pp. 75–6.
51. Dallaway, *Constantinople Ancient and Modern*, pp. 72–3.
52. Mostyn, *Egypt's Belle Epoque*, p. 127.
53. Roger Owen, *Lord Cromer: Victorian Imperialist, Edwardian Proconsul* (Oxford, 2004), pp. 90–91.
54. Wood, *Levant Company*, p. 190.
55. TNA SP 105/131, fos 14; 16–7; 18–20.
56. Cited in Ghorbal, *Beginnings*, p. 242.
57. 'Summary of Julian Corbett Prize Essay, 1965', *Journal of Historical Research*, vol. 40 issue 101, pp. 112–14, at 113.
58. Wood, 'English Embassy', p. 545.
59. *HMC Fortescue*, iv, pp. 359–60, cited in Wood, *Levant Company*, p. 183.
60. TNA SP105/109, fos 307; 309.
61. *A Collection for the Improvement of Husbandry and Trade*, no. 180, January 10, 1695–6, cited in Ambrose, 'Levant Company', p. 146.
62. *Proceedings of the Levant Company, respecting the surrender of their charters* (London, 1825), p. 3.
63. *Observations on the religion . . . of the Turks, to which is added the state of the Turkey trade*' (London, 1771), pp. 357–65.
64. Hancock, *Citizens of the World*, pp. 122–3.
65. Frangakis-Syrett, *Smyrna*, p. 86.
66. Ibid.
67. Russell, 'Later History', pp. 487–8.
68. Porter, *State of the Turkey Trade Considered*.
69. SP105/124, fo. 335; Russell, 'Later History', p. 294.
70. *Proceedings of the Levant Company*, pp. 5–6.
71. Ibid., p. 6.

72. Ibid., p. 11.
73. Ibid., p. 17.
74. Ibid.

Epilogue

1. Lawrence James, *Raj: The Making and Unmaking of British India* (London, 1997), pp. 316–17; Lady Betty Balfour, *The History of Lord Lytton's Indian Administration* (1899), pp. 106–33; Bernard Cohn, 'Representing Authority in Victorian India', in Eric Hobsbawm and Terence Ranger (eds), *The Invention of Tradition* (Cambridge, 1983); Mary Lutyens, *The Lyttons of India: Lord Lytton's Viceroyalty* (London, 1979), pp. 74–89; Sir Theodore Morison, *Imperial Rule in India* (1848), pp. 48–9.
2. In the Aligarh College, see especially David Lelyveld, *Aligarh's First Generation: Muslim Solidarity in British India* (Oxford, 1996) and M.S. Jain, *The Aligarh Movement: its origin and development, 1858–1906* (Agra, 1965).
3. Balfour, *Lord Lytton's Indian Administration*, p. 133.
4. Cawston and Keane, *Early Chartered Companies*, p. 89. For an excellent overview of this expansion, see F. Robinson, 'The British Empire and the Muslim World', in *OHBE*, vol. iv.
5. David Cannadine, *Ornamentalism: How the British Saw their Empire* (London, 2002), p. 5.
6. See especially Norman Daniel, *Islam, Europe and Empire* (Edinburgh, 1966) and, on India in particular, Thomas Metcalf, *Ideologies of the Raj* (Cambridge, 1994).
7. Sir William Wilson Hunter, *The Indian Musulmans: Are They Bound in Conscience to Rebel Against the Queen?* (2007). Sir Sayyed Ahmad Khan penned a trenchant response.
8. Peter Hardy, *The Muslims of British India* (London, 1972), p. 63.
9. The quotation is from the title of Jan Morris, *Pax Britannica: The Climax of an Empire* (London, 1979).
10. Gilbert Murray, *The Future of the British Empire in relation to the League of Nations* (1928), p. 12.
11. E.M. Forster, *A Passage to India* (London, 1989), p. 316.

$\mathscr{B}$ibliography

———— ❖ ————

Primary sources

Archival sources

Public Record Office
State Papers, series 97, 105 and 110

British Library
Add. MSS 10623, 19514, 19515, 22910, 32500, 32512, 32513, 32821, 33052, 34799, 38330, 38350
Verney MSS (microfilm copy of Claydon House MSS)
Calendar of State Papers, Domestic
Calendar of State Papers, Venetian
Historical Manuscripts Commission reports:
(i) Downshire MSS (1924)
(ii) A.G. Finch MSS (1913, 1922)
(iii) Duke of Portland MSS (1893–1931)

Suffolk Record Office
Cobbold MSS

Printed primary material

Addison, Lancelot, *The Life and Death of Mahumed, the author of the Turkish religion, being an account of his tribe, parents, birth, name, education, marriages, filthiness of life, Alcoran, firs proselytes, wars, doctrine, miracles, advancement, etc.* (London, 1679)
Alcoran of Mahomet translated out of Arabick into French . . . newly Englished, for the satisfaction of all that desire to look into the Turkish vanities (London, 1688)
Anderson, R.C. (ed.), *The Journals of Sir Thomas Allin, 1660–1678* (London, 1939)

The Alcoran of Mahomet / translated out of Arabique into French; by the Sieur Du Ryer, lord of Malezair, and resident for the King of France, at Alexandria; and newly Englished, for the satisfaction of all that desire to look into the Turkish vanities (London, 1649)

Anon., *A True and Strange discourse of the traveiles of two English pilgrimes: What admirable accidents befell them in their journey to Jerusalem, Gaza, Grand Cayro, Alexandria, and other places* (London, 1603)

Anon., *A narrative of the success of the voyage of the Rt. Hon. H. F. . . . his majesties Ambassadour Extraordinary to the . . . sultan Mamet Han, emperour of Turkey, from Smyrna to Constantinople; his arrival there, the manner of his entertainment and audience with the Grand Visier and Grand Seignior* (London, 1661)

Anon., *Great Britain's Glory; or, A Brief Description of the present State, Splendor, and Magnificence of the Royal Exchange* (London, 1672)

Anon., *The Allegations of the Turky Company and others against the East-India Company, relating to the management of that trade, present to the . . . Privy Council . . . with the answer of the East-India Company thereunto, etc.* (London, 1681)

Anon., *Observations in Turky; by Dr Brown* (1699?)

Anon., *The case of several merchants of the Levant Company complaining of the restraint of their trade* (London, 1718)

Anon., *A Defence of Mahomet (written in Arabick by Abdulla Mahumed Omar). A Paradox* (London, 1720)

Anon., *The Turkey Merchants and their Trade Vindicated* (London, 1720)

Anon., *Reflections on Mohammedism and the conduct of Mohammed. Occasioned by a late learned translation and exposition of the Koran or Al Koran* (London, 1735)

Anon., *The case of the governor and company of the merchants of England, trading into the Levant seas* (London, 1744)

Anon., *An Historical View of the Conduct and Proceedings of the Turkey Company* (London, 1753)

Anon., *Observations on the religion . . . of the Turks, to which is added the state of the Turkey trade* (London, 1771)

Anon., *A Historical View of the Conduct and Proceedings of the Turky Company* (London, 1825)

Anon., *Proceedings of the Levant Company respecting the surrender of their charters* (London, 1825)

Baker, Thomas, *Reflections Upon Learning Wherein is shewn the Insufficiency Thereof, in its several particulars. In order to evince the usefulness and necessity of revelation* (London, 1699)

Baldwin, G., *Narrative of facts relating to the plunder of the English merchants by the Arabs . . . in 1779* (London, 1780)

Baldwin, G., *Political recollections relative to Egypt* (London, 1801)

Barlow, R. and H. Yule (eds), *The diary of William Hedges . . . during his agency in Bengal, as well as on his Voyage out and return overland (1681–1687)*, 3 vols, Hakluyt Society, 74–5, 78 (London, 1887–9)

Barrow, Isaac, *Sermons preached upon Several Occasions* (London, 1679)

Blount, Henry, *A Voyage into the Levant. A brief relation of a journey, lately performed by H.B.* (London, 1636)

Bon, Ottaviano, *The Sultan's Seraglio: an intimate portrait of life at the Ottoman court* (from the seventeenth-century edition of John Withers) (London, 1996)

Boulainvilliers, Henri de, *The Life of Mahomet. Translated from the French, etc.* (London, 1731)

Brennan, Michael G. (ed.), *The Travel Diary of Robert Bargrave, Levant Merchant 1647–1656* (London, 1989)

Brerewood, Edward, *Enquiries touching the Diversity of Languages and Religions, through the chief parts of the world* (London, 1674)

Brown, Thomas, *Amusements serious and comical, calculated for the meridian of London* (London, 1700)

Bruyn, Kornelis, *A Voyage to the Levant, or, Travels in the principal parts of Asia Minor . . . done into English by W.J.* (London, 1702)

Burbury, John, *A Relation of a Journey of . . . Lord Henry Howard from London to Vienna and thence to Constantinople* (London, 1671)

Calvert, Frederick, Baron Baltimore, *A Tour to the East in the Years 1763 and 1764* (Dublin, 1768)

Chishull, Edmund, *Travels in Turkey and Back to England* (London, 1747)

Covel, John, *Extracts from the Diaries of Dr John Covel, 1870–1679* (London, 1893)

Dallaway, James, *Constantinople Ancient and Modern, with excursions to the shores and islands of the Archipelago* (London, 1797)

Desai, Anita (ed.), *The Turkish Embassy Letters of Lady Mary Wortley Montagu*, (London, 1994)

Drummond, Alexander, *Travels through different cities of Germany, Italy, Greece and several parts of Asia* (London, 1754)

Finopoulos, E.J. and W.B. Stanford (eds), *The Travels of Lord Charlemont in Greece and Turkey* (London, 1985)

Foster, Sir William (ed.), *The Travels of John Sanderson in the Levant, 1584–1602* (London, 1931)

Four Treatises Concerning the Doctrine, Discipline and Worship of the Mahometans (London, 1712)

Fuller, Thomas, *Historie of the Holy Warre* (Cambridge, 1647)

Gilbert, Vivient *The Romance of the Last Crusade: With Allenby to Jerusalem* (New York, 1923)

Grelot, William, *A late voyage to Constantinople . . . Translated from the French by J. Philips* (London, 1683)

Hakluyt, Richard, *The Principal Navigations, Voyages, Traffiques And Discoveries of The English Nation*, v (Kessinger ed., Montana, 2007)

Herbert, Sir Thomas, *A Relation of Some Yeares Travaile begunne Anno 1626 into Afrique and the greater Asia, especially the Territories of the Persian Monarchie, and some parts of the oriental Indies . . . of their religion, language, habit . . . and other matters concerning them* (London, 1634)

Hill, Aaron, *A full and just account of the present state of the Ottoman Empire in all its branches . . . faithfully related from a serious observation taken in many years travels thro' those countries* (London, 1710)

Knolles, Richard, *The General Historie of the Turkes from the first beginning of that Nation to the rising of the Othoman Familie . . . Together with the lives and conquests of the Othoman Kings and Emperours* (London, 1603)

Knolles, Richard, *The Turkish History . . . Written by Mr Knolles, and continu'd by . . . Sir P. Ricaut, to the peace at Carlowitz, in . . . 1699* (London, 1701)

The Koran, commonly called The Alcoran of Mohammed, translated into English immediately from the original Arabic; with explanatory notes, taken from the most approved commentators (London, 1734)

Kurat, Akdes (ed.), *The Despatches of Sir Robert Sutton* (London, 1953)

Larpent, Sir G., *Turkey, Its History and Progress* (London, 1854)

Lithgow, William, *Rare Adventures and Painefull Peregrinations* (London, 1928)

McCulloch, J.R., *Early English Tracts on Commerce* (London, 1952)

Maundrell, Henry, *A Journey from Aleppo to Jerusalem in 1697* (Beirut, 1963)

Montagu, John, *A Voyage Performed by the Late Earl of Sandwich Round the Mediterranean in the Years 1738 and 1739*, (London, 1799)

Moryson, Fynes, *An Itinerary: containing ten yeeres travel through . . . twelve dominions* (Glasgow, 1907)

Mundy, Peter, *The Travels of Peter Mundy in Europe and Asia, volume 1, 1608–1628* (Cambridge, 1907)

North, Roger, *Lives of the Norths*, vol. ii (London, 1826)

Ockley, Simon, *An Account of South-West Barbary containing what is most remarkable in the territories of the King of Fez and Morocco . . . by Simon Ockley* (London, 1713)

Ockley, Simon, *Sentences of Ali Son-in-Law of Mahomet . . . Translated from an Authentick Arabick Manuscript in the Bodleian Library at Oxford, by Simon Ockley, B.D.* (London, 1717)

Parish, Woodbine, 'Diary of a Journey with Sir Eyre Coote from Bussora to Aleppo in 1780', *Journal of the Royal Geographical Society of London*, Vol. 30 (London, 1860)

Parsons, Abraham, *Travels in Asia and Africa: including a voyage from Scanderoon to Aleppo . . . and a journey from Suez to Cairo and Rosetta in Egypt,* (London, 1808)

Perry, Charles, *A View of the Levant: particularly of Constantinople, Syria, Egypt and Greece* (London, 1743)

Pococke, Richard, *A Description of the East and some other countries*, vol ii, (London, 1743)

Porter, Sir James, *Observations on the Religion, Law, Government and Manners of the Turks* (London, 1771)

Porter, Sir James, *The State of the Turkey Trade Considered* (London, 1771)

Prideaux, Humphrey, *The True Nature of Imposture Fully Displayed in the Life of Mahomet; with a discourse annexed, for the Vindicating of Christianity from this Charge; Offered to the Consideration of the Deists of the present Age* (London, 1697)

Roberts, Lewes, *The Merchants Map of Commerce: wherein the universal manner and matter of trade is compendiously handled* (London, 1671)

Robson, Charles, *Newes from Aleppo* (London, 1628)

Ross, Alexander, *Pansebeia: or a view of all religions in the world* (London, 1653)

Royal Society, *Lowthorp's Abridgment of the Philosophical Transactions* (London, 1721)

Russell, Alexander, *The Natural History of Aleppo and parts adjacent* (London, 1756)

Rycaut, Paul, *The Present State of the Ottoman. Containing the maxims of the Turkish politie, the most material points of the Mahometan Religion* (London, 1668)

Rycaut, Paul, *The History of the Turkish Empire from the year 1623 to the year 1677* (London, 1680)

Sandys, George, *A relation of a journey begun An. Dom. 1610: four books containing a description of the Turkish Empire, etc.* (London, 1615)

Smith, Thomas, *Remarks upon the manners, religion and government of the Turks . . . and a brief description of Constantinople,* (London, 1678)

Stubbe, Henry, *Account of the Rise and Progress of Mahometanism, with a life of Mahomet and a vindication of him and his religion from the calumnies of the Christians . . . From a manuscript copied by Charles Hornby of Pipe Office, in 1705 'with some variations and additions.' Edited, with an introduction and appendix, by Hafiz Mahmud Khan Shairani* (London, 1911)

Teonge, Henry, The *Diary of H. Teonge, Chaplain on board his Majesty's ships Assistance, Bristol, and Royal Oak Anno 1675 to 1679 . . . With biographical and historical notes* (London, 1825)

Tryon, Thomas, *Wisdom's dictates, or, Aphorisms & rules, physical, moral, and divine, for preserving the health of the body, and the peace of the mind* (London, 1691)

Venner, Tobias, *Via recta ad vitam longam, or A plaine philosophical discourse of the nature, faculties, and effects, of all such things, as by way of nourishments, and dieteticall observations, make for the preseruation of health with their just applications unto every age, constitution of bodie, and time of yeare* (London, 1620)

William Eton, *A Survey of the Turkish Empire. In which are considered . . . its government, history, . . . and population, etc.* (London, 1798)

Secondary Sources

Abbott, G.F., *Under the Turk in Constantinople: A Record of John Finch's Embassy, 1674–1681* (London, 1920)

Abulafia, David (ed.), *The Mediterranean in History* (London, 2003)

Abun-Nasr, Jamil M., *A History of the Maghrib in the Islamic Period* (Cambridge, 1987)

Aksan, Virginia, *Ottoman Wars 1700–1870: an empire besieged* (Harlow, 2007)

Aksan, Virginia and Daniel Goffman (eds), *The Early Modern Ottomans – Remapping the Empire* (Cambridge, 2007)

Al-Sayyid Marsot, Afaf Lutfi, *Egypt in the reign of Muhammad Ali* (Cambridge, 1984)

Al-Sayyid Marsot, Afaf Lufti, *A History of Egypt* (Cambridge, 2007)

Ambrose, Gwylim, 'English Traders at Aleppo', *The Economic History Review*, 3 (1931–1932), pp. 246–67

Ambrose, Gwilym, 'The Levant Company, 1640–1753' (Oxford University B. Litt. Thesis, 1932)

Anderson, Sonia, *An English Consul in Turkey: Paul Rycaut at Smyrna, 1667–1678* (Oxford, 1989)

Andrews, Kenneth R., *Elizabethan Privateering: English privateering during the Spanish war, 1585–1603* (Cambridge, 1964)

Andrews, Kenneth, *Trade, Plunder and Settlement* (Cambridge, 1984)

Appleby, Joyce, *Economic Thought and Ideology in Seventeenth-Century England* (Princeton, NJ, 1978)

Arberry, A.J., *British Orientalists* (London, 1933)

Arberry, A.J., *Oriental Essays: Portraits of Seven Scholars* (London, 1960)

Armitage, David, *The Ideological Origins of the British Empire* (Cambridge, 2000)

Ashton, 'Parliamentary Agitation for Free Trade in the Opening Years of the Reign of James I', *Past and Present*, 38, 1 (1967), pp. 40–55

Ballaster, Ros, *Fabulous Orients: Fictions of the East in England 1662–1785* (Oxford, 2005)

Barr, James, *Setting the Desert on Fire* (London, 2006)

Bartels, Emily, *Spectacles of Strangeness: Imperialism, Alienation and Marlowe* (Philadelphia, 1993)

Baumer, Franklin L., 'England, the Turk and the Common Corps of Christianity', *American Historical Review*, 50, 1 (Oct., 1944), pp. 26–48

Bayly, C.A., *Imperial Meridian: The British Empire and the World 1780–1830* (London; New York, 1989)

Bayly, C.A., *Indian Society and the making of the British Empire* (Cambridge, 1998)

Bayly, C.A., *The Birth of the Modern World 1780–1914* (Oxford, 2004)

Beck, Brandon, *From the Rising of the Sun: English images of the Ottoman Empire to 1715* (New York, 1987)

Beier, A.L. and Roger Finlay (eds), *London 1500–1700: the making of the metropolis* (London, 1985)

Ben-Amos, Ilana, *Adolescence and Youth in Early Modern England* (London and New Haven, 1994)

Bennison, Amira, 'Muslim Universalism and Western Globalisation', in A.G. Hopkins (ed.), *Globalisation in History* (London, 2002)

Berg, Maxine, *Luxury and Pleasure in Eighteenth-Century Britain* (London, 2005)

Birchwood, Matthew, *Staging Islam in England* (Cambridge, 2007)

Black, J., *The British Abroad: the Grand Tour in the Eighteenth Century* (Stroud, 2003)

Boswell, James, *Life of Samuel Johnson* (Oxford, 1904)

Boxer, C.R., 'Anglo-Portuguese Rivalry in the Persian Gulf', in E. Prestage (ed.), *Chapters in Anglo-Portuguese Relations* (Watford, 1935)

Boxer, C. R., 'A note on Portuguese reactions to the revival of the Red Sea spice trade and the rise of Aceh, 1540–1600', *Journal of Southeast Asian History*, X, 3 (1969), pp. 415–28

Braude, Benjamin and Bernard Lewis (eds), *Christians and Jews in the Ottoman Empire: The Functioning of a Plural Society* (New York, 1982)

Braudel, Fernand, *The Mediterranean and the Mediterranean World in the Age of Philip II* (New York, 1992)

Braudel, Fernand, *The Perspective of the World: Civilisation & Capitalism 15th–18th Century Volume 3* (London, 2002)

Braudel, Fernand, *The Wheels of Commerce: Civilisation & Capitalism 15th–18th Century Volume 2* (London, 2002)

Brennan, Michael G., 'Introduction', in Brennan (ed.), *The Travel Diary of Robert Bargrave, Levant Merchant 1647–1656* (London, 1989)

Brenner, Robert, *Merchants and Revolution: commercial change, political conflict and London's overseas traders, 1550–1653* (London, 2003)

Brewer, John, *The Pleasures of the Imagination: English culture in the eighteenth century* (London, 1997)

Brooks, Christopher, 'Apprenticeship, Social Mobility and the Middling Sort, 1550–1800' in J. Barry and C. Brooks (eds), *The Middling Sort of People: Culture, Society and Politics in England, 1550–1800* (Basingstoke, 1994)

Brotton, Jerry, *The Renaissance Bazaar: from the Silk Road to Michelangelo* (Oxford, 2002)

Brown, W.C., 'The Popularity of English Travel Books About the Near East, 1775–1825', *Publications of the Modern Language Association of America*, 53 (1938)

Bruce Watson, I., 'Fortifications and the "Idea" of Force in Early English East India Company Relations with India', *Past and Present*, 88, 1 (1980), pp. 70–87

Brummett, Palmira, *Ottoman Seapower and Levantine Diplomacy in the Age of Discovery* (New York, 1994)

Bulut, Mehmet, *Ottoman-Dutch Economic Relations in the Early Modern Period* (Utrecht, 2000)

Burnett, Charles, 'The Introduction of Arabic Learning into British Schools', in C.E. Butterworth and B.A. Kessel (eds), *The Introduction of Arabic Philosophy into Europe* (Leiden, 1994).

Buzard, James, 'The Grand Tour and after', in Peter Hulme and James Buzard (eds), *Cambridge Companion to Travel Writing* (Cambridge, 2002)

Cannadine, David, *Ornamentalism: How the British Saw their Empire* (London, 2002)

Carlos and Nicholas, 'Theory and History: Seventeenth-Century Joint-Stock Chartered Trading Companies', *Journal of Economic History*, 56, 4 (Dec. 1996)

Cassirer, Ernst, *Philosophy of the Enlightenment* (Princeton, 1951)

Cawston, George and A.H. Keane, *The Early Chartered Companies* (London, 1896)

Champion, J.A., *The Pillars of Priestcraft Shaken: the Church of England and its enemies, 1660–1730* (Cambridge, 1992)

Chaudhuri, K.N., *The Trading World of Asia and the East India Company, 1660–1760* (Cambridge, 1978).

Chew, Samuel, *The Crescent and the Rose: Islam and England during the Renaissance* (New York, 1937)

Clark, J.C.D., *English Society, 1660–1832* (Cambridge, 2000)

Clay, C.G.A., *Economic Expansion and Social Change: England 1500–1700*, vol. 2, *Industry, Trade and Government* (Cambridge, 1984)

Clot, André *Suleiman the Magnificent* (London, 2005)

Coates, Ben, *The Impact of the English Civil War on the Economy of London, 1642–50* (Aldershot, 2004)

Cohen, Amnon, *Economic Life in Ottoman Jerusalem* (Cambridge, 2001)

Cohen, Mark R., *Under Crescent & Cross: The Jews in the Middle Ages* (Princeton, NJ, 1994)

Coles, Paul, *The Ottoman Impact on Europe* (London, 1968)

Colley, Linda, *Britons: Forging the Nation, 1707–1837* (London and New Haven, 1992)

Colley, Linda, *Captives: Britain, Empire and the World 1600–1850* (London, 2002)

Colville, Jim, 'Introduction', in Jim Colville (ed.), *Two Andalusian Philosophers* (London, 1999)

Conant, Martha, *The Oriental Tale in England in the Eighteenth Century* (New York, 1908)

Conrad, Lawrence (ed.), *The World of Ibn Tufayl: Interdisciplinary Perspectives on Hayy ibn Yaqzan* (Leiden, 1996)

Corbett, Julian, *England in the Mediterranean* (London, 1904)

Crinson, Mark, *Empire Building – Orientalism and Victorian Architecture* (London, 1996)

Curtin, Philip, *Cross-Cultural Trade in World History* (Cambridge, 1984)

Dalrymple, William, *White Mughals: love and betrayal in eighteenth-century India* (London, 2002)

Daly, M.W., *The Cambridge History of Egypt, Volume Two: Modern Egypt from 1517 to the end of the Twentieth Century* (Cambridge, 1998)

Daniel, Norman, *Islam and the West: the making of an image* (Edinburgh, 1960)

Daniel, Norman, *Islam, Europe and Empire* (Edinburgh, 1966)

Darling, Linda, 'Ottoman Politics Through British Eyes: Paul Rycaut's the Present State of the Ottoman Empire', *Journal of World History*, 5, 1994.

Darwin, John, *After Tamerlane: The Global History of Empire* (London, 2007)

Davis, Ralph, 'England and the Mediterranean 1570–1670', in F.J. Fisher (ed.), *Essays in the Economic and Social History of Tudor and Stuart England in Honour of R.H. Tawney* (London, 1961)

Davis, Ralph, *A Commercial Revolution: English overseas trade in the seventeenth and eighteenth centuries* (London, 1967).

Davis, Ralph, *Aleppo and Devonshire Square* (London, 1967)

Davis, Ralph, *The Rise of English Shipping in the Seventeenth and Eighteenth Centuries* (London, 1972)

Davis, Ralph, 'English imports from the Middle East', in M.A. Cook (ed.), *Studies in the Economic History of the Middle East* (Oxford, 1970)

Dearing, Vinton, 'A Walk through London with John Gay and a Run with Daniel Defoe', in J.H. Plumb and V.A. Dearing, *Some Aspects of Eighteenth-Century England* (1970)

Drayton, Richard, 'Knowledge and Empire', in *OHBE*, vol.ii

Duffy, Michael, 'World-Wide War and British Expansion, 1793–1815', OHBE, vol. ii.

Dunthorne, H., 'The Generous Turk', *The Historian*, 68 (2000)

Eldem, Edhem, Daniel Goffman and Bruce Masters (eds), *The Ottoman City between East and West – Aleppo, Izmir and Istanbul* (Cambridge, 1999)

Elin, Joel, 'A Seventeenth Century Levant Merchant: The Life and Letters of Jacob Turner' (PhD thesis, NY University, 1975)

Epstein, M., *The Early History of the Levant Company* (1908)

Esposito, John, *The Islamic Threat: Myth or Reality?* (Oxford, 1992)

Faroqhi, Suraiya, *Pilgrims and Sultans – the Hajj under the Ottomans 1517–1683* (London, 1994)

Faroqhi, Suraiya, *Subjects of the Sultan – Culture and daily life in the Ottoman Empire* (London, 2000)

Faroqhi, Suraiya, *The Ottoman Empire and the World Around It* (London, 2006)

Faroqhi, Suraiya, (ed.), *The Cambridge History of Turkey*, vol. iii (Cambridge, 2008)

Fedden, Robin, *English Travellers in the Near East* (London, 1958)

Feingold, Mordechai, 'Decline and Fall: Arabic Science in Seventeenth-Century England', in F. Jamil Ragep and Sally P. Ragep with Steven Livesey (eds), *Tradition, Transmission and Transformation* (Leiden, 1996)

Fergusson, Niall, *Empire – How Britain Made the Modern World* (London, 2003)

Finkel, Caroline, *Osman's Dream – The Story of the Ottoman Empire 1300–1923* (London, 2005)

Fisher, F.J., *London and the English Economy, 1500–1700* (London, 1990)

Fissel, M.C. and Daniel Goffman, 'Viewing the scaffold from Istanbul: the Bendysh-Hyde affair, 1647–1651', *Albion*, 22, 3 (1990), pp. 421–48

Fletcher, R.A., *The Cross and Crescent: the dramatic story of the earliest encounters between Christians and Muslims* (London, 2004)

Foster, Sir William, *England's Quest of Eastern Trade* (London, 1933)

Frangakis-Syrett, *The Commerce of Smyrna in the Eighteenth Century, 1700–1820* (Athens, 1992)

Frantz, R.W., *The English Traveller and the Movement of Ideas, 1660–1732* (Lincoln, Neb., 1934)

Freely, John, *Istanbul* (London, 1983)

Friedmann, Yohann, *Tolerance and Coercion in Islam* (Cambridge, 2003)

Fromkin, David, *A Peace to End All Peace* (London, 1989)

Fulton, A.S., 'Introduction', in *The History of Hayy ibn Yaqzan* (London, 1929)

Games, Alison, *The Web of Empire: English Cosmopolitans in an Age of Expansion 1560–1660* (Oxford, 2008)

Gauci, Perry, *Emporium of the Word: The Merchants of London 1660–1800* (London, 2007)

Gay, Peter, *The Enlightenment: an Interpretation: the rise of modern paganism* (London, 1995)

Ghorbal, Shafik, *The beginnings of the Egyptian question and the rise of Mehmet Ali* (London, 1928)

Goffman, Daniel, *Izmir and the Levantine World, 1550–1650* (Seattle and London, 1990)

Goffman, Daniel, *Britons in the Ottoman Empire, 1642–1660* (Seattle and London, 1998)

Goffman, Daniel, *The Ottoman Empire and Early Modern Europe* (Cambridge, 2002)

Goldie, Mark, 'The theory of religious intolerance in Restoration England,' in Ole Grell et al. (eds.), *From Persecution to Toleration: The Glorious Revolution and Religion in England* (Oxford, 1991)

Goodwin, Godfrey, *Topkapi Palace* (London, 1999)

Goodwin, Jason, *Lords of the Horizons: a history of the Ottoman Empire* (London, 1988)

Goody, Jack, *The East in the West* (Cambridge, 1996)

Grainger, John D., *The Battle for Palestine 1917* (Woodbridge, 2006)

Grassby, Richard, *The English Gentleman in Trade: the life and works of Sir Dudley North, 1641–1691* (Oxford, 1994)

Grassby, Richard, *Kinship and Capitalism: marriage, family and business in the English speaking world, 1580–1740* (New York and Cambridge, 2000)

Greene, Molly, 'Beyond the Northern Invasion: The Mediterranean in the Seventeenth Century' *Past and Present*, 174, 1 (2002), pp. 42–71

Greene, Molly, *A Shared World – Christians and Muslims in the Early Modern Mediterranean* (Princeton, N.J., 2002).

Grehan, James *Everyday Life and Consumer Culture in 18th Century Damascus* (Seattle and London, 2007)

Grundy, Isobel, *Lady Mary Wortley Montagu – Comet of the Enlightenment* (Oxford, 1999)

Gunny, Ahmad, *Images of Islam in Eighteenth-Century Writings* (London, 1996)

Hackforth-Jones, Jocelyn and Mary Roberts, *Edges of Empire: orientalism and visual culture* (Oxford, 2005)

Hale, John, *The Civilisation of Europe in the Renaissance* (London, 1993)

Hale, William and A.I. Bagis (eds), *Four Centuries of Turco-British Relations* (London, 1984)

Hamilton, Alastair, *William Bedwell the Arabist, 1583–1632* (Leiden, 1985)

Hamilton, Alistair, Alexander H. De Groot and Maurits H. van den Boogert (eds), *Friends and Rivals in the East* (Leiden and Boston, 2000)

Hampson, Norman, *The Enlightenment: An evaluation of its assumptions, attitudes and values* (London, 1980)

Hancock, David, *Citizens of the World – London merchants and the integration of the British Atlantic community, 1735–1785* (Cambridge, 1995)

Hathaway, Jane, 'Problems of Periodisation in Ottoman History: The Fifteenth through the Eighteenth Centuries', *Turkish Studies Association Bulletin* 20, 2, (1996), pp. 25–31

Hathaway, Jane, 'The Ottoman Empire and the Red Sea Coffee Trade', in Ebru Boyar and Kate Fleet (eds), *The Ottomans and Trade*, special edition of *Oriente Moderno*, 25 (2006), pp. 161–71

Hathaway, Jane, *The Arab Lands under Ottoman Rule, 1516–1800* (London, 2008)

Hawi, Sami, *Islamic Naturalism and Mysticism: A Philosophic Study of Ibn Tufayl's Hayy Bin Yaqzan* (Leiden, 1974)

Haynes, Jonathan, *The Humanist as Traveller: George Sandys' 'Relation of a Journey Begun An.Dom.1610'* (London, 1986)

Hazard, Paul, *The European Mind: the critical years 1680–1715* (New York, 1990)

Henderson, Nicholas, *Prince Eugen of Savoy* (London, 2002)

Heywood, C. J., 'Sir Paul Rycaut, A Seventeenth-Century Observer of the Ottoman State: Notes for a Study,' in Ezel Kural Shaw and C. J. Heywood, *English and Continental Views of the Ottoman Empire 1500–1800* (Los Angeles, 1970)

Hill, Christopher, *The World Turned Upside Down* (London, 1975)

Hill, Christopher, *The Century of Revolution* (London, 1980)

Himmelfarb, Gertrude, *The Roads to Modernity: The British, French and American Enlightenments* (New York, 2005)

Hobson, John M., *The Eastern Origins of Western Civilisation* (Cambridge, 2004)

Hodgson, Marshall, *The Venture of Islam* (Chicago, 1974)

Holland, Robert, 'The British Empire and the Great War, 1914–1918', in Judith M. Brown and Wm. Roger Louis (eds), *OHBE, vol. iv*

Holt, P.M., 'The Study of Arabic Historians in Seventeenth Century England: The Background and the Work of Edward Pococke', *Bulletin of the School of Oriental and African Studies*, 19, 3 (1957), pp. 444–55

Holt, P.M., 'The treatment of Arab history by Prideaux, Ockley and Sale', in B. Lewis and P.M. Holt (eds), *Historians of the Middle East* (London, 1962)

Holt, P.M., *Egypt and the Fertile Crescent, 1516–1922* (London, 1966)

Holt, P.M., *A Seventeenth-Century Defender of Islam: Henry Stubbe and his book* (London, 1972)

Hoppit, Julian, *A Land of Liberty? England 1689–1727* (Oxford, 2000)

Horniker, Arthur, 'William Harborne and the Beginning of Anglo-Turkish Diplomatic and Commercial Relations', in *Journal of Modern History*, 14, 3 (Sept. 1942), pp. 289–316

Horniker, A.L. 'Anglo-French Rivalry in the Levant from 1583 to 1612', *The Journal of Modern History*, 18, 4 (Dec. 1946), pp. 289–305

Hourani, Albert, *Europe and the Middle East* (London, 1980)

Hourani, Albert, *Arabic Thought in the Liberal Age* (Cambridge, 1983)

Hourani, Albert, *Islam in European Thought* (Cambridge, 1991)

Howell, David, 'Introduction', in Henry Maundrell, *A Journey from Aleppo to Jerusalem in 1697* (Beirut, 1963)

Huntington, Samuel, *The Clash of Civilizations and the Remaking of World Order* (Washington, D.C., 1992)

Iliffe, John, *Africans: The History of a Continent* (Cambridge, 1995)

Imber, Colin, *The Ottoman Empire, 1300–1650* (London, 2002)

Inalcik, Halil, 'The Heyday and Decline of the Ottoman Empire', in P.M. Holt, Ann K.S. Lambton and Bernard Lewis, *The Cambridge History of Islam*, Volume 1A (Cambridge, 1970)

Inalcik, Halil, *The Ottoman Empire – The Classical Age 1300–1600* (London, 1973)

Inalcik, Halil and Donald Quataert, *An Economic and Social History of the Ottoman Empire* (Cambridge, 1994)

Irwin, Robert, *For Lust of Knowing: the orientalists and their enemies* (London, 2006).

Islamoglu-Inan, Huri (ed.), *The Ottoman Empire and the World Economy* (Cambridge, 1987)

Israel, Jonathan, *European Jewry in the Age of Mercantilism, 1550–1750* (Oxford, 1985)

Israel, Jonathan, *Dutch Primacy in World Trade, 1585–1740* (Oxford, 1989)

Israel, Jonathan, 'The Phases of the Dutch Straatvaart, 1590–1713: A Chapter in the Economic History of the Mediterranean', in Jonathan Israel (ed.), *Empires and Entrepots. The Dutch, The Spanish Monarchy and the Jews, 1585–1713* (London, 1990), pp. 133–62

Israel, Jonathan, *The Dutch Republic: its rise, greatness and fall* (Oxford, 1995)

Israel, Jonathan, *Radical Enlightenment: philosophy and the making of modernity* (Oxford, 2001)

Israel, Jonathan, *Enlightenment Contested: philosophy, modernity and the emancipation of man, 1670–1752* (Oxford, 2006)

Itzkowitz, Norman, *Ottoman Empire and Islamic Tradition* (Chicago, 1972)

Jacob, J.R., *Henry Stubbe: Radical Protestantism and the Early Enlightenment* (Cambridge, 1983)

Jardine, Lisa, *Worldly Goods – A New History of the Renaissance* (London, 1996)

Jardine, Lisa, *Going Dutch: How England Plundered Holland's Glory* (London, 2008)

Jardine, Lisa, with Jerry Brotton, *Global Interests: Renaissance Art between East and West* (London, 2000)

Jasanoff, Maya, *Edge of Empire: Lives, Culture and Conquest in the East* (London, 2005)

Jones, S.R.H., and Simon Ville, 'Efficient Transactors or Rent-Seeking Monopolists? The Rationale for Early Chartered Trading Companies', *Journal of Economic History*, 56 (1996), pp. 898–915

Kabanni, Rana, *Imperial Fictions* (London, 1994)

Kafadar, Cemal, *Between Two Worlds: The Construction of the Ottoman State* (Berkeley and Los Angeles, 1995)

Kararah, A.M., 'Simon Ockley: his contribution to Arabic studies and influence on western thought' (Cambridge University, PhD thesis, 1955)

Keay, John, *The Honourable Company: A History of the English East India Company* (London, 1991)

Khoury, Dina Rizk, *State and Provincial Society in the Ottoman World: Mosul, 1540–1834* (Cambridge, 2002)

Kiernan, V.G., *The Lords of Human Kind* (London, 1988)

Kunt, Metin and Christine Woodhead (eds), *Suleyman the Magnificent and his Age* (London, 1995)

Lane, F C 'The Mediterranean spice trade: further evidence of its revival in the sixteenth century', in B. Pullan (ed.), *Crisis and Change in the Venetian Economy in the 16th and 17th Centuries* (London 1968), pp. 47–58

Langford, Paul, *A Polite and Commercial People: England, 1727–1783* (Oxford, 1989)

Laslett, Peter, 'Introduction' in Peter Laslett (ed.), *Two Treatises of Government* (Cambridge, 1998)

Letwin, William, *The Origins of Scientific Economics: English Economic Thought 1660–1776* (London, 1963)

Lewis, Bernard, 'Ottoman Observers of Ottoman Decline', *Islamic Studies* 1 (1962), pp. 71–87

Lewis, Bernard, *Istanbul and the Civilisation of the Ottoman Empire* (Norman, OK 1963)

Lewis, Bernard, *The Muslim Discovery of Europe* (London, 1982)

Lewis, Bernard, *The Jews of Islam* (Princeton, NJ, 1984)

Lewis, Bernard, *Islam and the West* (New York, 1993)

Lewis, Bernard, *What Went Wrong?: The Clash between Islam and Modernity in the Middle East* (London, 2002)

Lipson, Ephraim, *Economic History of England* (London, 1943)

Lloyd, T.O., *The British Empire 1558–1995* (Oxford, 2003)

Lowry, Heath W., *The Nature of the Early Ottoman State* (Albany, 2003)

Macfie, A.L., *Orientalism* (London, 2002)

McKay, *Prince Eugene of Savoy* (London, 1977)

McKendrick, Neil, John Brewer and J.H. Plumb, *The Birth of a Consumer Society: the commercialisation of eighteenth-century England* (London, 1982)

Mackenzie, John, *Orientalism: History, Theory and the Arts* (Manchester, 1995)

Mackesy, Piers, *The War in the Mediterranean, 1803–1810* (London, 1957)

Mackesy, Piers, *British Victory in Egypt, 1801: The End of Napoleon's Conquest* (London, 1995)

Maclean, Gerald, *The Rise of Oriental Travel: English Visitors to the Ottoman Empire, 1580–1720* (London, 2006)

Maclean, Gerald, *Looking East: English Writing and the Ottoman Empire before 1800* (London, 2007)

Maclean, Gerald (ed.), *Re-Orienting the Renaissance: cultural exchanges with the East* (New York, Basingstoke, 2005)

McNeill, William, *Europe's Steppe Frontier 1500–1800* (Chicago, 1964)

Mansel, Philip, *Constantinople: City of the World's Desire* (London, 1995)

Marcus, Abraham, *The Middle East on the Eve of Modernity – Aleppo in the Eighteenth Century* (New York, 1989)

Marshall, John, *John Locke: Toleration and Early Enlightenment Culture* (Cambridge, 2006)

Marshall, P.J., 'The English in Asia', in *OHBE*, vol. 1(Oxford, 1998)

Marshall, P.J., *Bengal – the British Bridgehead* (Cambridge, 2006)

Marshall, P.J. and Glyndwr Williams, *The Great Map of Mankind: British Perceptions of the World in the Age of Enlightenment* (London, 1982)

Massey, W.T., *How Jerusalem Was Won* (London, 1919)

Masters, Bruce, *The Origins of Western Economic Dominance in the Middle East – Mercantilism and the Islamic Economy in Aleppo, 1600–1750* (New York, 1988)

Masters, Bruce, *Christians and Jews in the Ottoman Arab World: the roots of sectarianism* (Cambridge, 2001)

Matar, Nabil, 'Alexander Ross and the First English Translation of the Qur'an', in *The Muslim World*, 88 (1998), pp. 81–92

Matar, Nabil, *Islam in Britain, 1558–1685* (Cambridge, 1998)

Matar, Nabil, 'John Locke and the Turbanned Nations', *Journal of Islamic Studies*, 2, 1 (1991), pp. 67–77

Matar, Nabil, *Turks, Moors and Englishmen* (New York, 1999)

Matar, Nabil, *Britain and Barbary* (Gainesville, 2005)

Matterson, Clarence, 'English Trade in the Levant, 1693–1753' (unpublished Harvard University PhD thesis, 1936)

Matthee, Rudolf, *The Politics of Trade in Safavid Iran* (Cambridge, 1999)

Melman, Billie, *Women's Orients: English Women and the Middle East* (Basingstoke, 1992)

Metcalf, Thomas, *Ideologies of the Raj* (Cambridge, 1994)

Minchinton, Walter (ed.), *The Growth of English Overseas Trade in the Seventeenth and Eighteenth Centuries* (London, 1969)

Montgomery-Watt, W., *Muslim-Christian Encounters* (London and New York, 1991)

Mostyn, Trevor, *Egypt's Belle Epoque: Cairo 1869–1952* (London, 1989)

Murphey, Rhoads, 'Bigots or Informed Observers? A Periodisation of Pre-colonial English and European Writing on the Middle East' in *Journal of the American Oriental Society*, 110, 2 (1990), pp. 291–303

Nasir, S.J., *The Arabs and the English* (London, 1976)

O'Connor, Cynthia, *The Pleasing Hours: James Caulfield, First Earl of Charlemont 1728–99* (Cork, 1999)

Ogborn, Miles, *Global Lives: Britain and the World 1550–1800* (Cambridge, 2008)

Ormrod, David, *The Rise of Commercial Empires: England and the Netherlands in the age of mercantilism, 1650–1770* (Cambridge, 2003)

Ottaviano Bon, *The Sultan's Seraglio: an intimate portrait of life at the Ottoman court (from the seventeenth-century edition of John Withers)* (London, 1996)

Outram, Dorinda, *The Enlightenment* (Cambridge, 1995)

Owen, Roger, *The Middle East in the World Economy, 1800–1914* (London, 1981)

Owen, Roger, *Lord Cromer: Victorian imperialiast, Edwardian proconsul* (Oxford, 2004)

Pailin, David, *Attitudes to Other Religions: comparative religion in seventeenth and eighteenth century Britain* (Manchester, 1984)

Pamuk, Orhan, *Istanbul: Memories of a City* (London, 2005)

Pardoe, Julia, *The city of the sultan; and domestic manners of the Turks* (London, 1837)

Parker, Kenneth, *Early Modern Tales of Orient: a critical anthology* (London, 1999)

Parry, J.H., *The Age of Reconnaissance* (London, 1973)

Pastor, C.R., *The Idea of Robinson Crusoe* (Watford, 1930)

Pearson, J.B., *A Biographical Sketch of the Chaplains to the Levant Company, maintained at Constantinople, Aleppo and Smyrna, 1611–1706* (Cambridge, 1883)

Peck, Linda Levy, *Consuming Splendour* (Cambridge, 2005)

Picard, Liza, *Restoration London* (London, 1997)

Playfair, Robert, *The Scourge of Christendom: annals of British relations with Algiers prior to the French conquest* (London, 1884)

Pocock, J.G.A., *Barbarism and Religion* (4 vols) (Cambridge 1999–)

Porter, Roy, *Enlightenment – Britain and the Creation of the Modern World* (London, 2000)

Porter, Roy, *London: A Social History* (London, 2000)

Porter Smith, Byron, *Islam in English Literature* (Beirut, 1939)

Pullan, Brian (ed.), *Crisis and Change in the Venetian Economy* (London, 1968)

Quataert, Donald, *The Ottoman Empire, 1700–1922* (2nd ed.) (Cambridge, 2005)

Rabb, Theodore, *Enterprise & Empire: merchant and gentry investment in the expansion of England, 1575–1630* (Cambridge, MA, 1967)

Rapp, Richard, 'The Unmaking of the Mediterranean Trade Hegemony: international trade rivalry and the commercial revolution', *The Journal of Economic History*, xxxv, 3, 1975

Rawlinson, H.G. 'The embassy of William Harborne to Constantinople, 1583–8', *Transactions of the Royal Historical Society*, iv, 5 (1922), pp. 1–27

Robinson, Francis, 'The British Empire and the Muslim World', in *OHBE*, vol. iv

Rodger, N.A.M., *The Safeguard of the Sea: A Naval History of Britain, 600–1649* (London, 1997)

Rodger, N.A.M., *The Command of the Ocean: A Naval History of Britain, 1649–1815* (London, 2004)

Rodinson, M, *Europe and the Mystique of Islam* (Seattle, 1987)

Rodky, Frederick, 'The Attempts of Briggs and Company to Guide British Policy in the Levant in the Interest of Mehemet Ali Pasha, 1821–41', *Journal of Modern History*, 5 (1993), pp. 324–51

Russell, G.A., *The Arabick Interest of the Natural Philosophers in Seventeenth Century England* (Leiden, New York, 1994)

Russell, Ina, 'The Later History of the Levant Company, 1753–1825' (Manchester University unpublished PhD thesis, 1935)

Said, Edward, *Orientalism* (London, 1980)

Saunders, Ann *The Royal Exchange* (London, 1991)

Scammell, G.V., *The First Imperial Age: European Overseas Expansion c.1400–1715* (London, 1989)

Schama, Simon, *The Embarrassment of Riches: an interpretation of Dutch culture in the golden age* (London, 1987)

Schwab, Raymond, *The Oriental Renaissance: Europe's rediscovery of India and the East, 1680–1880* (New York, 1984)

Schwoebel, Robert, *The Shadow of the Crescent: The Renaissance Image of the Turk* (Nieuwkoop, 1967)

Scott, W.R., *The Constitution and Finance of English, Scottish and Irish Joint Stock Companies to 1720* (Cambridge, 1910)

Searight, S., *Britain in the Middle East* (London, 1969)

Setton, K., *Western Hostility to Islam and Prophecies of Turkish Doom* (Philadelphia, American Philosophical Society (Philadelphia, 1992)

Shaw, Ezel Kural and C.J. Heywood, *English and Continental Views of the Ottoman Empire, 1500–1800* (Los Angeles, 1972)

Shaw, Stanford J., *History of the Ottoman Empire and Modern Turkey* (Cambridge, 1976)

Sim, Katharine, *David Roberts R.A.* (London, 1984)

Simpson Evans, T., *The Life of Robert Frampton, Bishop of Gloucester, deprived as a non-juror, 1689* (London, 1876)

Skilliter, Susan, *William Harborne and the Trade with Turkey, 1578–1582* (Oxford, 1977)

Southern, R.W., *Western Views of Islam in the Middle Ages* (Cambridge, Mass., 1962)

Steensgaard, Neils, 'Consuls and Nations in the Levant from 1570 to 1650', *Scandinavian Economic History Review*, 15, 1 (1967), pp. 13–55

Steensgaard, Neils, *The Asian Trade Revolution of the Seventeenth Century: The East India companies and the decline of the caravan trade* (Chicago, 1975)

Stern, Philip, 'Politics and Ideology in the Early East India Company-State: The Case of St Helena, 1673–1709', *Journal of Imperial and Commonwealth History*, 35, 1 (March 2007), pp. 1–23

Stern, Philip, ' "A Politie of Civill & Military Power": Political Thought and the Late Seventeenth-Century Foundations of the East India Company-State', *Journal of British Studies*, 47, 2 (April, 2008), pp. 253–83

Stone, Lawrence, *Family, Sex and Marriage* (London, 1977)

Supple, Barry, *Commercial Crisis and Change in England, 1600–1642* (Cambridge, 1964)

Sweet, R, *Antiquaries: the discovery of the past in eighteenth century Britain* (London, 2004)

Sweetman, John, *The Oriental Obsession: Islamic inspiration in British and American art and architecture 1500–1920* (Cambridge, 1988)

Tenenti, Alberto, *Piracy and the Decline of Venice* (London, 1967)

Thirsk, Joan, *Economic Policy and Projects: The Development of a Consumer Society in Early Modern England* (Oxford, 1978)

Thomas, Keith, *Religion and the Decline of Magic* (London, 1971)

Thomas, Lowell with Kenneth Brown Collings, *With Allenby in the Holy Land* (1938)

Tidrick, Kathryn, *Heart Beguiling Araby* (Cambridge, 1981)

Tinniswood, Adrian, *The Verneys: a true story of love, war and madness in seventeenth-century England* (London, 2007)

Toomer, G.J., *Eastern Wisedome and Learning* (Oxford, 1996)

Tracy, James D., *The Rise of Merchant Empires: Long-Distance Trade in the Early Modern World 1350–1750* (Cambridge, 1990)

Travers, Robert, *Ideology and Empire in Eighteenth Century India: the British in Bengal* (Cambridge, 2007)

Trevelyan, G.M., *England under the Stuarts* (London, 2002 edition)

Trevor-Roper, H, *From Counter-Reformation to Glorious Revolution* (London, 1992)

Tromans, Nicholas (ed.), *The Lure of the East: British Orientalist Painting* (London, 2008)

Turner, Jack, *Spice: The History of a Temptation* (London, 2004)

Turner, K., 'From Classical to Imperial: Changing Views of Turkey in the Eighteenth Century', in Stephen Clark (ed.), *Travel Writing and Empire: Postcolonial Theory in Transit* (London, 1999)

Van den Boogert, Maurits H., *The Capitulations and the Ottoman Legal System* (Leiden, 2005)

Vaughan, Dorothy, *Europe and the Turk: A Pattern of Alliances* (Liverpool, 1954)

Verney, Frances and Margaret, *Memoirs of the Verney Family During the Seventeenth Century* (London, 1892)

Vitkus, Daniel, *Turning Turk: English Theater and the Multicultural Mediterranean, 1570–1630* (New York, 2003)

Wahrman, Dror, *The Making of the Modern Self: Identity and Culture in Eighteenth-Century England* (New Haven and London, 2004)

Walker, Christopher, *Islam and the West* (London, 2005)

Wallerstein, Imanuel, *The Modern World System*, 3 vols (New York, 1974–88)

Watenpaugh, Heghnar, *The Image of an Ottoman City: imperial architecture and urban experience in Aleppo in the 16th and 17th centuries* (Boston, MA, 2004).

Weatherill, L., *Consumer Behaviour and Material Culture in Britain, 1660–1760* (London, 1985)

Webb, Nigel and Caroline, *The Earl and His Butler in Constantinople* (London, 2009)

Wheatcroft, A., *Infidels: the conflict between Christendom and Islam, 638–2002* (London, 2003)

Wheatcroft, Andrew, *The Ottomans: Dissolving Images* (London, 1995)

Wheeler, Roxan, *Complexion of Race* (Philadelphia, 2000)

Whyman, Susan, *Sociability and Power in late-Stuart England: The Cultural Worlds of the Verneys 1660–1720* (Oxford, 1999)

Willan, T.S., 'Some Aspects of English Trade with the Levant in the Sixteenth Century', *English Historical Review*, 70, 276, pp. 399–410

Wilson, Charles *England's Apprenticeship 1603–1763* (London, 1984)

Wittek, Paul, *The Rise of the Ottoman Empire* (London, 1938)

Wood, A.C., 'The English Embassy at Constantinople, 1660–1762', *English Historical Review*, 40, 160 (Oct. 1925)

Wood, A.C., *A History of the Levant Company* (London, 1935)

Woodhead, Christine, 'The Present Terrour of the World? Contemporary views of the Ottoman Empire c.1600', *History*, 72 (1987), pp. 20–37

Woolrych, Austin, *Britain in Revolution* (Oxford, 2004)

Wormald, Jenny (ed.), *The Seventeenth Century* (Oxford, 2008)

Wrightson, Keith, *Earthly Necessities: economic lives in early modern Britain* (London and New Haven, 2000)

Wrightson, Keith, *English Society 1580–1680* (London, 2003)

Wrigley, Anthony, 'A simple model of London's changing importance in changing English society and economy, 1650–1750', *Past and Present*, 37 (1967)

Yapp, M.E., 'Europe in the Turkish mirror', *Past and Present*, 137, 1 (1992), pp. 134–55

Yardley, Michael, *Backing into the Limelight* (London, 1985)

Zahedieh, N., 'London and the Colonial Consumer in the late 17th Century', *Economic History Review*, 47, 2 (1994), pp. 239–61

Zahlan, Rosemarie Said, 'George Baldwin: Soldier of Fortune?', in Paul Starkey and Janet Starkey (eds), *Travellers in Egypt* (London, 1998)

Index

Cooper, Ashley, third Earl of
    Shaftesbury 178
corsairs *see* pirates
cotton trade 97, 192, 205, 208, 210, 223–4,
    273(n6)
    Dutch 157
    Smyrna 214
    British exports to Egypt 223–4, 229,
        235–6
    and British trade embargo 223
Covel, John 100, 108, 182
    writings 163
Crete 26, 29, 38, 55, 155
Crow, Sir Sackville 123
currant trade 26, 37, 43, 55–6, 129
    and Levant Company 62, 63
Curzon, Robert 21
Cyprus 26, 30, 31, 42–3, 97, 157

Dallam, Thomas 141
Damascus, appointment of consul 29
Defoe, Daniel 56–7, 116, 162–3
deism 175, 186
Digby, Sir Kenelm 71
dragomen 101(&n), 140
    at audience with Grand Vizier 133, 134
    in Harvey dispute 142
Dryden, John, on London 46
Dundas, Henry 222
Dutch ambassador and peace treaty of
    Karlowitz 138
Dutch trade
    in competition with Levant Company
        40, 156–9
    first trade with Indies 40, 41
    traders in Galata 107
    traders' treatment by Grand Vizier 134
    Smyrna 158–9, 269(n105)
    conflict with English 159
    Amboyna massacre 160
    see also ships, Dutch

East India Company 38, 41, 60, 206–7,
    219, 220, 246(n6)
    and Levant Company xii, 3, 41, 194,
        202–6, 218, 274(n54)
    as offshoot of Levant Company 4, 41
    re-export of goods to Levant 41
    importance in City of London 53
    ships 70
    Amboyna massacre 160
    silk trade 205–6
    London headquarters 219
Egypt
    British interest 12, 193, 195, 223
    and Ottoman Empire 24, 198, 273(n4)

viceroy 191–2, *192*
Napoleonic invasion, effects on 193,
    214, 220, 221–2, 222, 229, 232
Levant Company's attitude to 195–6,
    196–7, 198, 217–18
humiliation of traders 196
spice trade 197
trade with Britain 197–8, 223–4,
    274(n26)
French occupation, end of 216–17
under British rule 216–17
British military encampment outside
    Alexandria *217*
dangers to English traders 217, 221
British consuls appointed 223
Baedeker on 229
see also Alexandria; Cairo; Suez
Elgin, Lord 232
Elizabeth I, Queen of England
    grant of charter to Turkey
        merchants 4, 36
    and the French 31
    expulsion from Catholic Church 32
    communication with the sultan 33–4
    on Levant Company's monopoly 61;
    revocation of Company's charter 62, 63
    appointment of ambassador to
        Constantinople 68, 135
    instructions to Harborne 136
    and Ottoman trade 259(n135)
England
    as Protestant country 35
    birth of consumerism 54–5
English trade with the Orient 252(n74)
    see also Levant Company;
        Ottoman Empire
Enlightenment 12, 13, 162
    and perception of the Ottoman world
        12, 162, 163, 182, 225–6, 228
    and Maundrell 20
    and markets 95
    and *Hayy ibn Yaqzan* 162
    and Islam 168, 175, 176
ethnic diversity, in Ottoman Empire 93
Eton, William 234
European trade with Middle East 13, 210
Europeans, attitudes towards Orient
    13–14, 160, 227, 242
Evelyn, John 68
Eyre, Sir John 126

factors, Levant Company xii, 3–4, 10–11,
    122, 195–6, 208, 243–4
    characteristics 5
    cultural and literary pursuits 5, 75
    writings 5–6